The Philosophy of Higher Education

Providing a comprehensive introduction to the philosophy of higher education this book, steps nimbly through the field, leading it into new areas and advancing an imaginative ecological realism.

Each chapter takes the form of a short essay, tackling a particular topic such as values, knowledge, teaching, critical thinking and social justice. It also examines key issues including academic freedom, the digital university and the Anthropocene, and draws on classic as well as contemporary texts in the field.

Composed of five parts, the book travels on a compelling journey:

- Part one identifies foundations of the field, distinguishing between the ideas of university and higher education,
- Part two examines key concepts, including research, culture, academic freedom and reason,
- Part three focuses on higher education as a set of educational practices and being a student,
- Part four is concerned with the university as an institution and includes the matters of leadership and the spirit of the university,
- Part five turns to the university in the world, and argues for an ecological perspective.

Written in a lively and accessible style, and ideal for anyone coming to the field for the first time but also of interest to experienced scholars, this book offers sightings of new possibilities for higher education and the university.

Ronald Barnett is Emeritus Professor of Higher Education, University College London Institute of Education, UK.

The Philosophy of Higher Education

A Critical Introduction

Ronald Barnett

LONDON AND NEW YORK

First published 2022
by Routledge
2 Park Square, Milton Park, Abingdon, Oxon OX14 4RN

and by Routledge
605 Third Avenue, New York, NY 10158

Routledge is an imprint of the Taylor & Francis Group, an informa business

© 2022 Ronald Barnett

The right of Ronald Barnett to be identified as author of this work has been asserted by him in accordance with sections 77 and 78 of the Copyright, Designs and Patents Act 1988.

All rights reserved. No part of this book may be reprinted or reproduced or utilised in any form or by any electronic, mechanical, or other means, now known or hereafter invented, including photocopying and recording, or in any information storage or retrieval system, without permission in writing from the publishers.

Trademark notice: Product or corporate names may be trademarks or registered trademarks, and are used only for identification and explanation without intent to infringe.

Revised edition: January 2022

British Library Cataloguing-in-Publication Data
A catalogue record for this book is available from the British Library

Library of Congress Cataloging-in-Publication Data
Names: Barnett, Ronald, 1947– author.
Title: The philosophy of higher education: a critical introduction / Ronald Barnett.
Description: Abingdon, Oxon; New York, NY: Routledge, 2022. |
Includes bibliographical references and index.
Identifiers: LCCN 2021013771 (print) | LCCN 2021013772 (ebook) |
ISBN 9780367563936 (hardback) | ISBN 9780367610289 (paperback) |
ISBN 9781003102939 (ebook)
Subjects: LCSH: Education, Higher—Philosophy.
Classification: LCC LB2322.2 .B367 2022 (print) | LCC LB2322.2 (ebook) |
DDC 378.001—dc23
LC record available at https://lccn.loc.gov/2021013771
LC ebook record available at https://lccn.loc.gov/2021013772

ISBN: 978-0-367-56393-6 (hbk)
ISBN: 978-0-367-61028-9 (pbk)
ISBN: 978-1-003-10293-9 (ebk)

DOI: 10.4324/9781003102939

Typeset in Sabon LT Std
by codeMantra

For Søren
  - In friendship and gratitude

From Arthur Schopenhauer (1788–1860):
 '... as the world is in one aspect entirely idea, so in another it is entirely will.'
 (*The World as Will and Idea*, 1997: 5)

 'Thinking has to be kindled ...'
 ('On Thinking for Yourself', *Essays,* 2004: 91)

From Friedrich Nietzsche (1844–1900):
 '... there is nothing more harmful than liberal institutions ... they undermine the will to power...'
 '... our universities are, against their will, the actual forcing-houses for this kind of spiritual instinct atrophy.'
 (*Twilight of the Idols*, 2003: 103, 73)

 'I tell you: one must have chaos in one, to give birth to a dancing star .... You still have chaos in you.'
 (*Thus Spoke Zarathustra*, 1969: 46)

Contents

Acknowledgements ix

Introduction: the case for this book 1

PART I
Foundations 13

1 The philosophy of higher education: realist, critical, practical and imaginative 15
2 Higher education and university: conflicts on the three planes 26
3 Values and higher education, and ethical evolution 37
4 Knowledge and truth: matters of interest 48

PART II
Key concepts 61

5 Research: towards an ecological transdisciplinarity 63
6 Culture: sighting a culture of constructive argument (CCA) 74
7 Academic freedom – and academic responsibility 85
8 Thought and reason – and their dilemmas 96

PART III
Teaching, learning and the student 107

9 Teaching: a provocative matter 109
10 Curriculum: making it explicit 120
11 Being a student: a committed uncertainty 131
12 Critical thinking: the three crazy escalators 142

PART IV
The university as an institution — 153

13 The place of the university — 155

14 The spirit of the university — 166

15 Academic leadership and management – and keeping clear water between them — 177

16 Time, space and the digital university — 188

PART V
Higher education and the world — 199

17 Higher education and the university: two very public matters — 201

18 The lure of engagement: traps for the unwary — 212

19 Social justice – and onwards to *ecological* justice — 223

20 Beyond the Anthropocene — 234

Envoi: a constitution for universities on Earth — 245

Bibliography — 247
Index — 277

Acknowledgements

My warm thanks go, in the first place, to colleagues who kindly read the manuscript of this book and offered me their thoughts on it, namely Martin Gough, Tony Harland, Jill Jameson, Kelly Mathews, Wes Shumar and Sharon Stein. I have gained much from their suggestions and feeling the encouragement flowing my way from each of them. I also thank the anonymous reviewers of the proposal I originally submitted for this book for their very helpful comments and their provocative suggestions: I fear, though, I have not been able to do justice to them all.

In tackling the venture of this book, with its being quite wide-ranging, I have also been much fortified by conversations over recent years with many intellectual friends who have included Denise Batchelor, Eva Bendix, Søren Bengtsen, John Cowan, Gloria Dall'Alba, Nuraan Davids, Martin Davies, Keri Facer, Eric-Jean Garcia, Paul Gibbs, Beena Giridharan, Sinclair Goodlad, Carolina Guzmán-Valenzuela, Jill Jameson, Petar Jandric, Lorraine Ling, Peter Ling, Ingrid Lunt, Bruce Macfarlane, Rajani Naidoo, Jon Nixon, Rikke Nørgård, Michael Peters, Richard Pring, Michael Reiss, Sharon Rider, Tone Dyrdal Solbrekke, Sharon Stein, Paul Temple and Yusef Waghid. And I remember particular colleagues from whom I learnt much in so many ways, and who are no longer with us, including Richard Aldrich, Roy Bhaskar, Gunther Kress, Tony Lambert, Paul Ramsden, David Watson and Gareth Williams.

I would like to record my appreciation of the encouragement that I have received from Sarah Hyde, Editor, Routledge Education, Taylor and Francis, who has given this whole venture much support all the way from the outset, and without whom this book would not have appeared.

Lastly, I thank Routledge publishers for permission to draw on two earlier diagrams of mine, Figure 2.1 (the three planes) and Figure 20.1 (ecosystems of the university).

Introduction
The case for this book

Beginnings

For over thirty years, the philosophy of higher education has been evolving, but there is no single book that offers an overview of the field. Here, I attempt to do just that, and I try also to accomplish a number of other goals. As well as identifying many of its key issues, I try to show something of the value and significance of the philosophy of higher education. I believe that anyone who is interested in higher education will be helped by engaging with large matters that do not normally come into public view and that philosophical considerations can even pave a way to practical principles. Moreover, urgency attaches to this matter, not only of providing some clarity on complex matters but also of opening spaces for *possibilities* in front of the university in the twenty-first century.

The book has been written with a number of audiences especially in mind:

- Academic developers, in the support they give to new higher education lecturers and in playing their part in widening the very notion of academic development in their institutions;
- PhD students in the field so that they can form a *synoptic* understanding of the field and see where their own topic fits in;
- Senior leaders and managers who sense that their pressing challenges are throwing up matters – institutional, national and international – that might merit philosophical consideration (e.g. over academic freedom *and* in their university's engagements with the wider world);
- Advanced students in professional doctorates and Master's courses who want to dip into the field and gain some insight into a philosophical approach and angles;
- New scholars in higher education studies, in forming a sense of lines of inquiry and gaining a handle on some of the literatures;
- Academics in general – across all disciplines – who just might wish to gain reflective insight into their daily tasks in teaching, in their relationships with their students and in their research and scholarly and outreach activities; and

DOI: 10.4324/9781003102939-1

- Professional staff who work alongside academic faculty – in all manner of offices and units in universities – and who wish to place their own work in a wider context.

For all these audiences (and there is much overlap between them, as individuals wear multiple hats simultaneously), this book offers a ready resource in moving into the field, and it brings together a wealth of material not available in a single place.

In writing this book, I have also borne in mind experienced scholars in the field, for I am taking the opportunity to bang the drum not just for the philosophy of higher education as such but also for a particular conception as to how the field might develop.

The very field of the philosophy of higher education

Offerings in the philosophy of higher education can be identified from the 1970s onwards (Niblett, 1974; Brubacher, 1977). However, the philosophy of higher education began to take off in the 1990s, perhaps especially with the publication of my own (1990) book, *The Idea of Higher Education*. That book deliberately projected the phrase – 'the philosophy of higher education' – and made a pitch for it. Since then, the field has mushroomed, with work being undertaken by scholars and advanced students all around the world. As a result, the field is now populated with plots and sub-plots, and, as testimony to its buoyancy, the past few years have seen the formation of a learned society (the *Philosophy and Theory of Higher Education Society* – PaTHES), the establishment of an international Journal (*Philosophy and Theory in Higher Education*), and two book series from major publishers (Springer's on *Debating Higher Education: Philosophical Perspectives* and Routledge's on *World Issues in the Philosophy and Theory of Higher Education*).

Major other resources have appeared, including the 1,300-page two-volume work on the idea of the university (Barnett and Peters, 2018; Peters and Barnett, 2018), volume one containing extracts from many of the key texts of the past two hundred years; and a number of compendia have also appeared (e.g. Gibbs and Barnett, 2014; Karlsohn, 2016; Higgs and Waghid, 2017; Bengtsen and Barnett, 2018; Stoller and Kramer, 2018; Gibbs, et al., 2019; Barnett and Fulford, 2020). Over the past thirty years, too, the field has matured, with literatures forming and from ever-widening perspectives, and with scholars gaining reputations for their work on discrete topics.

Within the covers of this book, I reconnoitre the field, now vibrant and disparate, and, in places, I stretch it out. I hope that the book's table of contents alone helps to mark out the breadth of the ground before us. At a glance, it includes foundational matters (of knowledge, culture, academic freedom and so on); higher education as a set of educational practices, especially those of teaching and learning and the matter of being a student; the university as an institution; and relationships between higher education and the wider society and, indeed, the whole world.

However, as well as going into these particular matters, I do two other things. *First*, I conduct these inquiries against a temporal horizon (Amsler and Facer, 2017). The philosophy of higher education has to have a sense of history, but it would be failing if it did not incorporate a forward-looking perspective. This is not to specify a future; it is to identify some of the challenges and responsibilities facing higher education, and it is to discern concepts and ideas that open spaces in which futures can adequately be glimpsed.

Second, I show a way through, not only a direction of travel but also resources with which we might equip ourselves. I advance *a particular conception* of the philosophy of higher education. The stance adopted here is that work in the field should contain *seven elements*, that it be conceptual, social, realist, critical, ecological, imaginative and practical (and more or less *in that order*). We should be critical of what we see but also imaginative as to the future, and our philosophical efforts should contain some sense of the way higher education is in the world *and* that it has *possibilities*. A shorthand might be a *critico-imaginative and ecological realism*.

This book tries, therefore, both to convey a fair sense of the philosophy of higher education – its range of topics – *and* to offer a lead as to how to conduct work in the field. In other words, as well as providing a sketch of *the* philosophy of higher education, I also nail my colours to the mast of *a* philosophy of higher education. It is a geography *and* a particular journey. It is also a topology and a geology. I identify surface features and their undulations and I burrow down, to gain a sense of the large forces at work that cause universities and higher education to be changing, both as institutions and as embodiments of ideas about them. Institution and ideas: *both* are in motion and each affects the other.

Crisis – what crisis?

Over the years, books on higher education have played upon the theme of crisis, among the first of which – in the United Kingdom – was *The Crisis in the University* by (Sir) Walter Moberly, published as far back as 1949. Reiterations of that ilk followed (Scott, 1984; Reeves, 1988; Bahti, 1992): permanent crisis seems to be the situation. Others have deployed even starker language, as did the Canadian Bill Readings in his justly acclaimed (1997) book, *The University in Ruins*, and, more recently still, we have been told that universities are 'at war' (Doherty, 2015). I have deliberately eschewed such forlorn terminology in my own books. It is, after all, easy to demonstrate profound difficulties facing universities and higher education, and it is bad news that captures the headlines. It is much more difficult to identify practical principles that are feasible and *glimpse any potential* that lies deep in universities and higher education.

Higher education *is* facing difficulties: that is evident. Indeed, that first book of mine – *The Idea of Higher Education* – identified a *double undermining* of higher education, it being confronted with a loss of faith in the idea of objective knowledge *and* an evaporation of the university's institutional autonomy and that reading would now have to be intensified. Nevertheless, that higher education is in crisis has always seemed to me to be an exaggeration. Yes, universities and higher education worldwide have been under the severest challenges and in *some* nations *can* fairly be said to be in crisis. But their being able to withstand dictatorships, wars, economic crashes, institutional malaise, upheavals in knowledge production and the arrival of the digital revolution suggests that talk of a general crisis of the university has been overblown – until *now*.

As I write this, a crisis *has* cast a shadow across the world. The reader might think I have in mind the virus that has befallen human life. That *is* there, and is having grave effects, including on higher education – not least on the students' experience and on the durability of some universities. But that shadow lies inside the even darker shadow cast by the crisis of the natural environment. The one crisis sits within the other, *both* being symptomatic of the interconnectedness of the world *and* of humanity's imprint upon it. In this sense, <u>*both*</u> *crises are ecological crises*. In saying this, I have in mind not only that the entities in the world are connected with each other; the rhinos, glaciers, pangolins and bats are contiguous with humanity. More than that, humanity's understandings of the world – formal and informal – can cause, do cause, could cause and *should* cause the world to be different.

A squid in turbulent waters

What might we draw, then, from these two crises, so far as the philosophy of higher education is concerned? The first is a multiple point, that the field should contain *breadth* and *depth*, and *interconnectivity* and a *temporal* aspect. Higher education and the university have to be set in the widest possible context, in time and in space. We have to have a sense of time past, present and to come and – as Latour (2016) has so aptly put it – *in* the Earth. We have to open the way for possibilities for higher education and universities; for what it might be to be educated in the twenty-first century; and for what might it be for the university to play its full part in the world. Given the turbulences in which the university and higher education find themselves, addressing this set of challenges is no small venture: it is to open the way to the *possibility of* <u>*intentional*</u> *possibilities*.

My view is that the philosophy of higher education has to be an Earthly philosophy and a philosophy of life (Barnett and Bengtsen, 2020). By Earth here, I mean this total planet with all that is in it and beyond it; a sense of the Earth as a microscopic object in the universe (whether or not Earth is the only planet supporting human life). And by 'life' I mean all of life, organic and inorganic, and human institutions *and* thought. It is in this context that the philosophy of higher education has to be given *ecological bearings*. This is not to trumpet the claims just of the natural environment – although that *is* important for, as it is said, 'who speaks for the (melting) glaciers?' – but it is to situate human being in and on the whole Earth, with all of the entities and interconnections that it exhibits, *including the thought and actions of humanity itself*.

One philosophical approach that has found its way into thinking about higher education is that promulgated by the European continental philosophers, Gilles Deleuze and Felix Guattari, both separately and in their joint writings (Guattari, 2000; Deleuze, 2006; Deleuze and Guattari, 2007). A favoured metaphor of theirs is that of the rhizome which spreads out, in ways that cannot be forecast, and with no definite pattern. This metaphor is intended to be liberating. No longer do we need to search for the essence of concepts or to concern ourselves with *definite* structures; matters are more open than that. The problem is that this depiction of the world, for all of its provocations, is inadequate. Not only the rhizome but so much of their other imagery is too stable.

Deleuze and Guattari speak of multiple plateaus, of surfaces that are 'smooth' and 'striated' and of 'assemblages'. In each of these metaphors, there is variation, and a sense of possibilities. After all, like the pieces of a jig-saw puzzle, the components of an assemblage can be disengaged from each other and moved elsewhere (Delanda, 2013). And we may think that this imagery depicts the university of the twenty-first century very well. A single university is located in many spaces, and is indubitably an assemblage with its inchoate entities, which can be unplugged from each other. Not uncommonly, a research centre in a university is lured – doubtless by an attractive offer – to a rival university; or a programme of studies, taught on a face-to-face basis, changes its format and becomes an online offering. But that imagery of rhizomes, plateaus and assemblages is just *too static*. It downplays the turbulence of the world (natural and ideological), and it lacks a proper sense of the interplay between, say, a university and its wider environment, which are continually in *vibrant motion*.

We need a lively imagery for higher education and the university, not only of fluids and liquids but also of tempestuous flows that run against each other. We may even speak of dams waiting to burst, and of locks, with the occasional boats confined by the lockkeeper (as academics and students are incarcerated by *some* states). There is a dynamic in these waters, both local and global. *The university is like a squid*, with a hard shell but able to transport itself across the world and with some rapidity (Barnett, 2011: 111). It can probe the smallest and the largest entities, and with some finesse. The individual student is treated with respect, *and* the university can take on powerful states.

On this reading, higher education is a matter of the student's venturing forward, but with no certainty as to what might be encountered. Research is another kind of venturing, its increasing pace generating its own hazards among the currents at play. Let the metaphor of the rhizome not tempt us, then, and let us instead embrace a much more dynamic imagery of excited and perpetual motion, and one suggestive of great turmoil and yet of some kind of direction, even if wayward at times. The philosophy of higher education has to be a case study in the philosophy of motion (Nial, 2018, 2019) *and* in the philosophy of life.

Utopias? No and yes!

Higher education has long been provided in institutions known as universities (or the term's counterpart in other languages). The story is complicated. Although the modern university can trace its origins to the European Middle Ages, much more ancient forms of higher learning were in operation across the Middle East (especially in Egypt) and Far Eastern lands (in India, China and Persia). As we proceed well into the twenty-first century, there are around *twenty-five thousand* universities across the world, exhibiting much variety. Within the formal national systems of higher education are to be found both public and private institutions and both those where its members (faculty and students) spend much time on campus and those where most activities are conducted at a distance. Furthermore, quite recently, we have witnessed cooperative and 'open' universities springing up (Wright and Shore, 2019: 18–21), outside the state structures of higher education.

Inevitably, therefore, the two concepts of university and of higher education, and their contiguous concepts – knowledge, academic freedom, teaching, research, culture, learning and student and the rest – are all in motion. Like butterflies, they are not easily caught, and if they were caught they would be diminished. For concepts always exceed their presences in the world: 'objects do not go into their concepts without leaving a remainder' (Adorno, 2014: 5). There is always unrealised potential in our important concepts, and, especially since the world is in motion, that potential is always open to new imaginings. It is the task, therefore, of the philosophy of higher education to be vigilant about key concepts, to be on the lookout for shortcomings in their realisation and to be alert to possibilities for *new* concepts. The philosophy of higher education cannot rest with being a matter of conceptual geography or conceptual genealogy. It has to take the form of conceptual *construction*, being both imaginative and creative, and even utopian (Barnett, 2013).

Some seem to think that one should be utopian *tout court*; that is to say, utopian without conditions. I disagree and, elsewhere, I have urged that the identification of *feasible* utopias should be a goal of the philosophy of higher education and that higher education utopias should be subjected to a tribunal of 'conditions of adequacy' (Barnett, 2018a). Some consider that this is unduly limited and that utopian thinking should not be hemmed in by considerations of what is feasible. There are three responses.

What, firstly, is the alternative: to be concerned with the *non*-feasible? Where is the sense in *that*, in utopias that are non-feasible? This would be self-indulgence in a situation in which time is not on our side. Second, to lose oneself in the non-feasible is to lose contact with the world – with the *Real* of the world – and therein lies intellectual *inauthenticity*. If the philosophy of higher education is to have integrity, there has to be *some* degree of contact with, and realisability in, the world. Third, it is much *more* difficult to discern utopias that are feasible than to imagine non-feasible utopias. This calls for an alertness to the way the world *is* (difficult though that discernment is) *and* the world of *ideas*. This is an uncomfortable situation in which to be – hopping repeatedly between the way the world is and the ways in which it might be (cf. Niblett, 1974; Derrida, 1992) – but there is no alternative if the philosophy of higher education is to possess practical value.

The character of this book

A book of this kind could begin from contemporary problems and issues, or it could take as its launch-pad the works of luminaries who have dwelt on higher education and the university in their writings. I favour the first option, identifying problems that need to be addressed, but I go further. We need an approach that does justice to the three conditions of the university and higher education that I have intimated, their: (i) being both real *and* imaginative projects; (ii) being in motion; and (iii) playing out on different levels. These conditions suggest *a dynamic field* spread across tilted and interactive planes (a schema that I elaborate in chapter 2 and exemplify in many of the following chapters). This will enable us to do justice to the incessant motion, the interconnections between the elements and their conflicts, and the practical and conceptual challenges before us.

Philosophy deals principally with concepts (cf. Deleuze and Guattari, 2013: 2–34), and it has become a commonplace to say that, of any concept x, it is contested. Of course! But the more interesting questions remain: where lies the conceptual contest? Which are the warring parties? How do we account for both the emergence of a concept and for the rival camps with their own ideologies and agendas? What room for manoeuvre is there in realising the unmet *potential* within the key concepts? 'Learning', 'teaching', being a 'student', 'academic freedom' and even what it is to be a 'university' or to offer 'higher education' is each controversial, and it is worthwhile to eke out an interpretation or two, but what are the prospects of bringing *alternative* imaginaries into effect?

We are obliged, therefore, to deal with the interplay between key concepts, their problem spaces, and their possible exemplification. 'A concept requires a junction of problems where it combines with other existing concepts.' This is not to seek coherence, or harmony, or conflict resolution; usually, *none is available*: 'There is no reason why concepts should cohere ... everything holds together only along diverging lines' (Deleuze and Guattari, 2013: 18, 23).

I interweave concepts at two levels. At the first level, each chapter has its panoply of concepts, near and far. There is a constellation of concepts which are in sight through much of this book, and I have mentioned several. They include those of motion, ecology, supercomplexity, interconnectivity, (*not* truth but) truthfulness, becoming, freedom, reason, possibility, will, imagination, ontology, wellbeing, vitality, spirit and life. At a second level, in interweaving such large concepts and glimpsing something of their interconnections, I try to inject *air and space* for multiple possibilities. Nothing specifically is ruled in; but this is not a situation of anything goes, since ideas that do not advance the wellbeing of the university, higher education and the Earth are excommunicated. There is much potential in this constellation of concepts (just identified). I hint at, rather than state, that potential, so as to leave matters open for imaginative thought and action in the wide variety of contexts of universities and higher education.

My speaking of 'potential' indicates that the philosophy of higher education has a right to work for a better future, but not brazenly, insistently, assuredly or pushingly but, rather, tentatively, carefully, restrainedly and diligently. However, ethical matters lie not just in higher education and the university but even in writing about such intricate sets of practices. It is easy enough – and it is the intellectual's stock-in-trade – to make the simple complex; it is much more demanding to make the complex (appear) simple.

The style of the chapters

Each chapter takes the form of a short essay – with an argument addressed to the topic in question – and I am conscious that many readers will want to delve into those chapters that connect with their immediate interests. I would just add the following points. First, higher education and universities generate a very large set of *interconnected* issues. One cannot properly understand learning or research or academic freedom without setting these matters in their conceptual and institutional hinterland. Any tendency to isolate matters, so that one becomes a specialist in matters relating just to teaching and learning or only to technical issues of knowledge and truth or to societal matters of public goods, and the public good, should be resisted, for one is liable to end up with a partial view of an issue. In every case, one should try to stand back and see an issue and its surroundings *synoptically*.

My aim, in each chapter, is several. I sketch the territory in question and some of its main venturings in relevant literatures, both past and present; the underlying forces at work; the lines of demarcation; the conflicts and even wars (in ideas) that are simmering; large horizons; and possibilities (both conceptual and practical). There will inevitably, for some readers, be gaps in the inventory; some will even think that vital matters are missing. 'Please state your silences'; 'Where are you *not* going?' it will be asked. Logically, given the itinerary of any journey, there is an infinite number of sights that one could have visited and resources that could equip one for the journey. I would ask only that it be acknowledged that an overloading of the suitcase will make for a sluggish journey.

Imaginative examples are supplied to illustrate the argument as it proceeds. This is not for the sake of supplying a practical gloss but for two reasons, *pull* and *push*. My argumentation is *pulled* by the way the world is and its problems. Especially in a practical field such as higher education, scholarly inquiry has to be in part a social philosophy. But, and more importantly, a social philosophy – again such as that of the philosophy of higher education – has to furnish examples, often fictional but realisable, if it is to gain traction. A philosophy of higher education has to *push* its exemplifications before it. It has to be a dance between the universality that lies in concepts and particular possibilities (Badiou, in Badiou and Žižek, 2009). A realist philosophy – of the kind advanced here – has to live in the *Real* of the world: it has to generate empirical warrant. Exemplification is vital.

In several of the chapters, I also do some justice to a schema of three planes that I advocate, a schema that depicts the university as existing both independently *of* perceptions of it, and *in* ideas of it (formally, the university as Real and as Idea). On occasions, too, I take the opportunity to revisit earlier ideas of mine, but I nuance them as one must; after all (as Heraclitus was alleged to have observed (Kahn, 1987:53)), one can never step into the same waters twice. As befits the vein of interconnectedness, which runs through this text, some themes simmer, and there are contiguities between the essays here. I have provided cross-references (especially in the index) but sparingly.

Although young, the field – of the philosophy of higher education – has a growing vitality with shoots on shoots appearing, a vitality that is opening opportunities for further work. On occasions, I observe gaps in our understandings, and I venture into some of those gaps, and perhaps others may follow, so as to draw the philosophy of higher education into new territories.

A word, if I may, on my references. For the most part, my references are indications as to where can be found other texts that are contiguous with my argument at its various points and indicate further reading possibilities. In itself, a citation here says nothing as to whether that text supports or departs from the position I am taking. Sometimes, I take up the cudgels and engage directly with a text, but I do so in order to clarify my own position. After all, 'philosophy is not a dialogue' (Žižek, in Badiou and Žižek, 2009: 50). It is the making, as Badiou puts it, of decisions, and I try to lay out issues, indicate where decisions have to be made and then make them. Philosophy has to have a certain amount of courage.

I have also tried to tread the thin line between an analytical and philosophical robustness *and* an accessibility for the wide and many audiences I mentioned earlier. To that end, I have eschewed endnotes to chapters and restrained the references and the length of the bibliography. I have striven for accessibility, even if I do not always quite achieve it.

Perhaps I might add a note about the literary style. I try to avoid technical terms (and explain them where I do use them), but I deliberately exploit the English language as it is within my compass. This is a book about higher education, under which umbrella all life should be found in some way. It follows that the language, the words, should be proportionately wide, but what of clarity? Notwithstanding certain philosophers' contrary views on the matter, I believe clarity to be critically important. However, clarity has to take its place alongside other writerly virtues of honesty and acuity and of finding and inventing words and neologisms that seem adequate to ideas as they unfold. I am trying to find a mode of expression that has a personal integrity and yet does justice to the wide and challenging matters before us, that is compressed within the limited space available, and that just may resonate with the wide range of audiences I have in mind.

It should be admitted that an enterprise such as this can be undertaken only with a fairly large degree of hubris. That a single person might have the temerity not only to survey a whole field but also to take up a position on each topic is surely a sign of over-weaning self-belief: some treading-on-toes is inevitable, I fear. My hope is that a unitary text of this kind may have value in doing some justice to the interconnectivity of the field. There may be advantage in a single narrative.

The book's structure

There are five parts, each consisting of four chapters.

Part one provides *foundations* for the whole book. *Chapter 1* provides an overview of the field, *chapter 2* emphasises differences between the concepts of university and higher education (which are often conflated) and sets out my fundamental schema of three planes, *chapter 3* examines the ethics of the field and *chapter 4* grapples with issues of knowledge and truth.

Part two examines *key concepts*, research and scholarship (*chapter 5*), culture – of and beyond the university (*chapter 6*), academic freedom – for both teachers and students (*chapter 7*), and thought and reason (*chapter 8*).

Part three focuses on higher education as a set of *educational practices*, namely teaching (*chapter 9*), curriculum (*chapter 10*), learning and being a student (*chapter 11*), and critical thinking (*chapter 12*).

Part four is concerned with the university as an *institution*, being concerned with the place of the university (*chapter 13*), the spirit of the university (*chapter 14*), academic leadership and management, which I sharply distinguish (*chapter 15*), and time, space and the digital university (*chapter 16*).

Part five turns to the university and *the world*, looking at public aspects of higher education and the university (*chapter 17*), matters of engagement and responsibility (*chapter 18*), social and epistemic justice (*chapter 19*), and higher education in those suggested new layerings of the Earth, the Anthropocene and the Ecocene (*chapter 20*).

I conclude with a note proposing that we urgently need a constitution for the university and higher education, with all that that implies for the philosophy of higher education (which I hope to pursue on another occasion).

Like some credit-based programmes of study, this journey can be entered at any point and proceed in many directions. I would just suggest that, early on, the reader might have a go at the first two chapters, for they offer a framework and even some bearings for the whole voyage.

Part I
Foundations

1 The philosophy of higher education

Realist, critical, practical and imaginative

> 'Life activates thought, and thought in turn affirms life.'
> Gilles Deleuze (2012: 66), *Pure Immanence: Essays on a Life*

Introduction

The philosophy of higher education is a very broad field of study. In principle, the whole world can come into view in the university: that is part of the meaning that the term '*uni*versity' has acquired, that nothing can be ruled out of its inquiries whether in its educational practices or its research and scholarly activities. Everything in the universe is potentially a matter for examination: the philosophy of higher education is universal in its scope. Nevertheless, there are some central questions in the field, such as 'what might count as a higher education?'; 'how is the idea of the university to be understood?'; 'what does academic freedom *mean*?'; and 'what is it to *be* a student in higher education'?

Systematic reflection in the field was begun by Germanic philosophers in the early nineteenth century (Peters and Barnett, 2018). They were concerned with the idea of the university, but they treated the topic in a very broad way, being concerned with what it was to develop as a student, which fields of study were important and their relationships, issues such as the nature of mind and reason, and the relationship between the university and the state. Subsequently, in England in the mid-nineteenth century, John Henry Newman (1976) gave some of these issues a somewhat different treatment, being much more focused on the student, who he looked to gain a 'philosophical outlook' in a liberal education.

Those ideas have stood up remarkably well, but they served previous ages, and the philosophy of higher education has now to be put onto an entirely different footing. But what foundations might help in deriving an adequate philosophy of higher education for the twenty-first century?

DOI: 10.4324/9781003102939-3

A tale of two – or three – cities

With the coming of mass higher education in the mid-twentieth century, philosophical work tended to focus on matters to do with teaching, learning and students. More recently still, as pleas have arisen for higher education to be more responsive to society, so philosophical work has widened to include matters of social justice, the relationship between the university and society, and the public goods of higher education. But this is all very recent, and it is worthwhile reminding ourselves as to the path that higher education has taken.

Crudely, we can say that, since its medieval incarnation, the story of higher education is *a tale of two cities*, of academe and of work. For the first eight hundred years or so, the two cities got along very well with each other, but, since the Industrial Revolution, tension has multiplied, with the city of work coming to expect more and more from the city of academe. In turn, the philosophy of higher education has to give at least a nod in the direction of the philosophy of skill and expertise (Fridland and Pavese, 2021).

However, now another city is forming, which we might term simply 'life'. It is not just that in its disciplinary inquiries the university peers into life in all forms (from nanoparticles to the life of the universe), or even that the humanities and the social sciences are directly concerned with human life, but that life beyond the university and higher education is knocking at the door, so to speak. The university and higher education are being asked to speak not only about life, but *for* life and *from* life (Barnett and Bengtsen, 2020). The questions – 'Who speaks for the rhinos?,' 'For the glaciers?,' 'For indigenous peoples?' – press themselves forward.

Given these observations, it is evident that philosophical work in and around higher education cannot seriously be undertaken without placing higher education in its institutional, societal and worldly settings. For example, the idea of academic freedom has to have a character in the twenty-first century different from its interpretation in the nineteenth or twentieth centuries.

Concepts and society have their own autonomy, but they take in each other's washing to a large extent, with each gaining energy from the other. More broadly still, large concepts such as 'cognitive capitalism', 'cognitive justice', and debates over the (de)coloniality of universities and the digital revolution prompt searching questions about knowledge, mind, education and the responsibilities of universities both here-and-now and as they unfold.

It follows that the field of the philosophy of higher education has to be understood and practised as a *species of social philosophy*. It follows, too, that the relationship between the field and social theory has to be porous: it has to allow for a 'transgression of boundaries' (Laclau, 1999: xiii; Adorno, 2019). The field is bound to be concerned about *universities as a set of social institutions* and which are interconnected with other social institutions, and the field has also to have an interest in higher education as a complex of social practices (Schatzki, 2002, 2008) and not only those of teaching and research and those associated with being a student but also the myriad of other practices within the ambit of higher education. The field has also to allow, too, for universities having a worldwide span, for they are *cognitive exporters, importers* and *sharers* on an international scale.

The emergence of the field

When the philosophy of higher education started to take off in the 1990s, eyebrows were raised and questions asked: 'What was special about higher education?' 'How did the philosophy of higher education differ from the (much-longer-established) philosophy of education?' The very phrase – 'the philosophy of higher education' – seemed portentous to some, pretending to a substance that it did not possess (White, 1997). In fact, it is a relatively easy matter to deal with those questions, for higher education possesses a number of features that distinguish it from education more generally. Here are ten such features:

First, higher education has a definite source in the Europe of the Middle Ages (although existing well before that in many lands) and a trajectory that has spilled out across the world. This trajectory has witnessed a dominant institutional form – the university – and, for over two hundred years, what it is to be a university has spawned a large, and often philosophical, literature. *Second*, even now, higher education is undertaken only by a portion, albeit an expanding portion, of a people, its students attending (more or less) voluntarily. This gives rise to philosophical and ethical issues about the right to higher education, and fairness and justice, even cross-nationally. *Third*, it is largely a site in which adults congregate. The educational relationship has to grapple with the maturity of students, who may even be older and more experienced than their teachers.

Fourth, higher education is closely associated with research and scholarship, such that even most of the universities that are mainly teaching-oriented would still acknowledge the significance of research. Conceptual questions arise, therefore, as to the relationship between research and teaching. *Fifth*, universities are massive institutions consuming huge resources, perhaps hundreds of millions of dollars or their equivalent annually (or more), and may have tens of thousands of members of staff and students (or even more): not infrequently, a university is the largest employer in a town, and towns vie to be a 'university town'. Nice issues emerge over the place of the university.

Sixth, universities are bound up with knowledge and truth. There is a rawness about these relationships, since matters of knowledge and truth are matters for inquiry *within* universities. Questions arise, therefore, over the university as an *epistemological space*.

Seventh, students are characteristically in an in-between state, enjoying 'the gift of the interval' (Oakeshott, 1989: 101). They usually have a social freedom that allows them to participate in political and social movements, such that they often take on an oppositional stance (and may even contribute to political transformation, as happened in Chile in 2012–2013, where a radical student movement helped in ushering in a new government). *Eighth*, their size, complexity and power have given rise to major issues of the relationship between universities and the state. The concepts of academic freedom and institutional autonomy are testimony to the challenges – conceptual and political – in that relationship.

Ninth, universities are not just major players in the digital revolution but have been active in its development and are part of *global* communications networks. *Tenth*, they play a *direct* part in the production of 'cognitive capital' (Boutang, 2011) around the world.

These ten features mark out higher education as a particular segment of education that both *warrants* and *deserves* philosophical attention. Higher education *warrants* philosophical attention because of its sheer scale and global presence. There are now around twenty-five thousand universities and about two hundred million students, one-tenth of which are international students. Collectively, academics across the world are now producing annually upwards of two-and-a-half million papers in the academic literature (Marginson, 2020). It is also striking that even low-income countries, where schooling has to command much effort and resource, are fast developing their higher education systems. And higher education also *deserves* philosophical attention. The set of characteristics just identified indicate that the university – with higher education – stands in its own economic, social and cultural spaces, with responsibilities to, and possibilities in, a nation, a region and indeed the whole world.

Critique and imagination

The work of philosophy lies in concepts, but three riders should be added. First, having a care for concepts brings a concern for conceptual clarity. Clarity is not always possible, but it can help to lessen confusion; otherwise, there are tendencies to slide over complex matters without disentangling issues. This has been understood as an under-labourer view of philosophy (Locke, 1968/1690: 58), a rather disparaging term, implying a subservience to the main venture of design and action, but clarifying our thinking can open ways of looking at matters. For example, in the next chapter, I suggest that the concepts of higher education and university should be distinguished from each other. Both are important, but nothing is gained by collapsing them or, worse still, confusing them.

Having a concern for concepts may be felt to be a conservative intellectual endeavour, liable to leave things as they are, but there is no reason why this should be the case. Being clearer about concepts can open the way to critical judgements. Once we are clearer about the conditions that might attach to the idea of higher education, we can ask of any higher education programme of studies or any institution of higher education – 'But is it really higher education?' Our concepts, therefore, can serve as *critical standards* by which we can appraise institutions and their practices (Magee, 1978).

The German philosopher and critical theorist, Theodor Adorno (2014: 5), spoke of there being an unrealised potential in our key concepts: 'objects do not go into our concepts without leaving a remainder.' Reality *never* fulfils the promise of our concepts. The concepts both of higher education and university harbour huge scope that is never fully realised in the world. Moreover, society can suppress the potential in our concepts (another key element in Adorno's philosophy). The philosophical quest, therefore, lies in the dual task of excavating the potential that lies within concepts *and* an analysis of their shortfall in the world. In this way, conceptual analysis has (i) to import the non-conceptual (Adorno, 2008: 70, 68) and (ii) to be an inherently *critical* task.

Moreover, being clearer about our key concepts more readily enables us to pose searching questions. For example, we can begin to ask seriously, and *distinguish*, the questions: 'What is the connection between higher education and democracy?' and 'What is the connection between *universities* and democracy?'

Philosophy is also a discerning of *new* concepts. This idea marks it out as an *imaginative* enterprise, and such an enterprise exhibits different models (Murphy, Peters and Marginson, 2010). If we think of the university with its global span, its never-quiet digital activity, its cross-national reach, its involvement in producing new knowledge, its often tense relationships with the state (and awkward questions over institutional autonomy) and the ways in which culture wars are played out on campuses (resulting in disputes over academic freedom), and if we put all of that in the context of a fraught and even a bespoiled world (natural and human), then questions of responsibility are bound to arise. Just what might be the responsibilities of universities – and their academics and students – in the twenty-first century? Such a question calls for a *global* imagination.

It may be said that this is not a philosophical question, but that would be wrong, not least because we have here a large concept – 'responsibility' – that prompts philosophical consideration. Just what is it to speak of a 'responsibility'? Is it even legitimate to speak of a university having responsibilities? (I believe it is.) Are there considerations that might hold across *all* disciplines? Might educational practices be widened to reflect matters of value, of responsibilities towards the whole Earth and all peoples?

I suggest, then, that key among the tasks of the philosophy of higher education are the following five: *first*, to identify and interrogate key concepts in the field; *second*, to chart any shortfalls that those concepts are exhibiting in the world (shortfalls that may signify ideological elements at work but which signify also philosophy's limitations; Althusser, 2017: 177–179); *third*, to open a space in which practical principles might be discerned for higher education; *fourth*, to suggest new possibilities for higher education; and *fifth*, to propose new concepts to help in realising any such possibilities.

Head in the clouds and feet on the ground

Philosophers of higher education should live in two domains, two worlds even (cf. Niblett, 1974). They should live in the world of concepts – that rather austere world of sheer thought and reason – and they should live in the world of institutions of higher education and their social practices, but also beyond in the whole world. This is not so much a case of hopping from one domain to the other but rather – to use another metaphor – of riding both horses at once. Actually, this metaphor works rather well, for the circus rider is typically aboard one horse while keeping the other going alongside. Just so here. The primary domain is that of concepts – of knowledge, academic freedom, truth, culture, university and higher education itself and so forth – but one keeps the social practices of universities and the pedagogical practices of higher education alongside, as it were, *and* maintains an eye on the wider world. Each exerts influence on the other: *ideas and the world* – separate but joined.

This is a *realist* conception of the philosophy of higher education. Realism has of late come back into the philosophical fold, and several variants are suddenly available for the cognoscenti (Harman, 2009, 2018; Gratton, 2014; Ferraris, 2015; Delanda and Harman, 2017). The essential idea is that there is a real world independent of our thoughts – *although never fully fathomable* – and this is so with higher education. Higher education is not just a matter of our concepts or our constructions of it. Rather, it is also now a massive global enterprise, or, more accurately, set of enterprises: it has a location in the *Real* of the world. It straddles the world, exerting huge influence, economically, socially, epistemologically and culturally, and it colours our concepts. Any serious philosophy of higher education has to concern itself with these social facts and ride that horse alongside.

A form of realism that is especially helpful is that of the philosophy of critical realism established by Roy Bhaskar (2011b: 180–192). A feature of Bhaskar's realism is that it is especially sensitive to the entities of the world not only being in motion but also possessing powers. In other recent realisms, there is a tendency (particular in Harman) to depict the entities in the world as all on a level. We receive highly democratic realisms ('flat ontologies') from some of those new realisms, but power and hierarchy are ontologically important and, therefore, are not to be neglected in the philosophy of higher education.

Bhaskar's philosophy is actually a succession of philosophies, evolving through a number of distinct stages (2010b), and it contains a number of insights helpful here. The world is layered, and, in this layering, Bhaskar distinguished between the empirical, the actual and the real. These categories emerged from his philosophy of science (2008a), and, even though he extended his philosophy to the social world (2015), still the categories require a little improvisation for our purposes.

There are aspects of higher education, more or less immediately before us, that are susceptible of *empirical* observation and analysis. Patterns can be discerned, say in flows of students, in the numbers of research papers produced on a cross-national basis, in the streams of institutional income from various sources and so forth. Topics are being added continuously. For example, matters of coloniality, identity and higher education as a supplier of public goods have emerged. That said, there are bound to be features of higher education that have not yet been discerned and perhaps have not even been recognised as worthy of study. Such aspects are *actual*, not yet subject to empirical inquiry. They are present and *exert influence* in the world, even though they have not been recognised.

Beyond these two domains – empirical and actual – lies the domain of the *Real*. Over recent decades, concepts such as globalisation, knowledge economy, cognitive capitalism, neoliberalism and the digital age have emerged. One cannot go into a university and witness any of these features of higher education as such. Certainly, one can identify happenings that seem to exemplify some of these concepts, but they have a degree of ineffability attaching to them. 'Globalisation' never could adequately be cashed out; it is a term that stands for a complex of phenomena beyond human observation and yet points to forces that are profoundly influential in the whole world. To use another term in Bhaskar's (2008a) armoury, they constitute 'generative mechanisms', which produce in their wake further phenomena. For example, the presence of global university rankings hint at deep-seated and yet powerful forces within the knowledge economy.

Such large terms are an expression of our ignorance: their meanings can never be finally exhausted, nor their influences ever completely laid bare; but, still, they exert considerable influence. Sometimes, too, powerful states deliberately seek to hide their activities, not least in the cyber world. It follows that any serious philosophy of higher education has to be sensitive to large forces, moving globally, and yet largely hidden from view.

The potential that lies within concepts can often suggest itself in the detection of *absences* – yet another of Bhaskar's key ideas (Bhaskar, 2008b). Absences are systemic. Across the world, the humanities are being discouraged and even deliberately excluded: their absence may prompt thinking about their value, and perhaps new possibilities *and* responsibilities can be identified for them. But as well as being structural, absences may lie in the *conceptual* landscape. For example, higher education has been witness to a slide from 'knowledge' to 'skills' in the public debate. In the process, the notions of 'critical thinking' and 'critique' fade from view but even less noticed is the near-absence of 'understanding'. This absence is not happenstance but has to be explained in the way that higher education has been incorporated into the economy and state apparatuses. After all, understanding indicates the presence of a thoughtful and independent mind, and this presence will be worrying to some.

Absences, therefore, are structural, real and deep-seated and indicative of differential power. The philosophy of higher education, then, has to be alert to there being shifting conceptual sands and conceptual – and even ideological – *distortions* at work, and the absences that ensue in their wake.

This conception of the philosophy of higher education might be captured in this aphorism: *head in the clouds but feet on the ground*. There would be a will here to soar above the fray of this immediate world, so as to glimpse new possibilities for higher education and new forms at that. But there would also be a determination to keep one's feet on the ground, especially given what I have just said about being sensitive to the large forces at play (and possibly malign at that). This is at once a social, a realist, a critical, a practical and an imaginative sense of the philosophy of higher education.

Testing ideas of higher education

But on what basis might imaginative concepts be encouraged? In the history of humanity, the imagination has given rise to highly pernicious ideologies. The imagination cannot be assumed to produce worthwhile ideas. Indeed, many lament that higher education embodies pernicious ideas that promote an unbridled entrepreneurialism, the student being tacitly understood as a kind of customer (prompted by an excessive marketisation of higher education), the university lying 'in ruins' with any connection with culture having been lost (Readings, 1997), and – across the world – an overbearing 'Global North' exerting a 'postcolonial' set of attitudes over the 'Global South'.

Whatever the validity of these suggestions, what is plain is that what are needed for the twenty-first century are not just new concepts but *good* concepts. What then is to count as a good concept? Good concepts need to have their feet on the ground and yet reach into the starry firmament in imagining *worthwhile* possibilities. In fact, there are many new ideas and even experiments now in play in higher education; for example, in cooperative higher education, in reaching out to indigenous communities, in ideas of the public good, in sustainability and in pedagogies and curriculum design. We need, however, to be able exercise judgement in each case, and here are *five 'criteria of adequacy'* (Barnett, 2013: 126–128) of any proposed idea of higher education:

(i) *Range*: does any idea being suggested lend itself to conceptual and/or theoretical exposition? Can it have practical or policy implications? Can it be cashed out across educational and research practices of the university?
(ii) *Depth*: is the idea sensitive to the deep structures of higher education (to the kind of subterranean forces of the kind noted earlier)? Can it accommodate both the raw experience *and* the poetry of higher education?

(iii) *Feasibility*: can the idea be realised in the best-of-possible worlds? Does it lend itself to being taken up by imaginative institutional leaders, with practical projects being envisaged and put into action?
(iv) *Ethics*: does the idea have an ethical component? Is it prompted or buttressed by a definite value background? Is it guided by considerations of wellbeing in relation both to the human world *and* the natural world?
(v) *Emergence*: does the idea possess qualities of emergence, such that it can legitimately take on a new form in the context of unforeseen exigencies?

Together, these conditions set the bar high for any proposed concept in the field of higher education; perhaps too high. Surely, it may be said, it is better to let a thousand conceptual flowers grow: we need more ideas and so let them have a hearing and see to what extent they flourish. Battering new ideas of the university and higher education with such a set of standards could extinguish some good ideas before they have a chance to flower, but these responses are misplaced. In the process of being tested against these (five) criteria, any idea or concept coming forward will either *justifiably* wither away or will be fortified.

For a better world

Part of the pitch here has been that the philosophy of higher education cannot but concern itself with the world. In the first place, concepts do not spring from the ether or lie on neutral ground but are often already present in public or political debate. They have a tendency to be ideologically loaded.

Part of the task, therefore, is to subject key concepts to forensic analysis. For example, it is often suggested that it is a responsibility of universities to provide the economy with the kinds of skills that are needed. But what concepts of skills and need are at work here? Perhaps 'skills' are not problematic after all: we do want our doctors, architects, social workers, engineers and our teachers to be skilful. What *is* important is the relationship between the matter of skill and what it is to be human within a considerate society.

The philosophy of higher education, then, *has* to concern itself with the world, both to understand how and why it is that the conceptual landscape is as it is and, then, to begin to discern new vistas, new worlds even, within which new concepts can plausibly be lived out. In short, the philosophy of higher education achieves its fulfilment when it is part of a project to bring into being a better world.

Talk of wanting to usher in a better world is likely to generate two *opposed* responses, of overreach and underreach. First, there will be those for whom such talk is a sign of the philosophy of higher education *overreaching* itself: the field should content itself in being not much more than a technical examination of concepts. To think otherwise would turn the field into a questionable value-laden and *normative* project. Such a rejoinder, however, is pusillanimous and is liable to end up as an apologia for the *status quo*. It fails to recognise that our concepts and ideas of higher education are already ideologically loaded, and heavily impregnated with societal and state interests; and so higher education runs the danger of being co-opted into *uncritically* serving those interests.

For example, when placed in a geopolitical context, perhaps the concept of research may be adjudged to have served to advance the interests of the Global North. The question then arises as to whether new concepts of research might be encouraged that do justice to knowledges across regions of the world, indigenous communities, feminist perspectives and professional life (in processual and practical knowledges) and so forth. An idea of research as *ecological transdisciplinarity* can then open (chapter 5).

The second response would be to suggest that situating the philosophy of higher education against a horizon of a better world is actually liable to *sell the field short*. What is required – it may be suggested – is a return to the university's origins in faith, religion and theology. Those of this persuasion often remind us of Newman's wish to give a special place to theology in the curriculum, and, recently, there have been efforts to inject a theological perspective both into a contemporary idea of the university (Astley et al., 2004; Heap, 2017) and in developing a framework for the field itself (Hauerwas, 2007; Higton, 2013).

Resources are readily to hand, too, to install intellectual foundations for such a theologically sensitive project, in critical realism (Shipway, 2011; Hartwig and Morgan, 2014; Wright, 2014) and in left-leaning critical theory, notably Žižek (2001, 2003), Eagleton (2007, 2009), Sloterdijk (2009) and Habermas (2010a, 2010b). In a sentence, we have here the makings of an intriguing project – for another day – which is unlikely substantively to dislodge the field (of the philosophy of higher education) but which, a là Habermas, can provide conceptual resources to tilt the field towards 'a philosophy of and for universal self-realisation' and *transcendence* (Bhaskar, 2002b, 2010a: ix; Singh, Bhaskar, and Hartwig, 2020: 64ff.).

The philosophy of higher education, therefore, has, as one of its tasks that of seeking concepts and ideas that can play their part in bringing about a better world. Of course, there will be conflict over what is to count as a better world and universities as institutions, and higher education as a pedagogical space, are sites where such arguments can be worked through. Conflict over values and ends has to be part of a university and of realising the potential of higher education (Maxwell, 2012).

Some universities are moving in this direction: for instance, many are addressing the United Nations' Sustainable Development Goals and forging imaginative efforts to see where their resources can be used in that endeavour. Philosophy can help here, for example, in addressing the very concepts of development and sustainability. What is meant by 'development', not least against a global horizon? Perhaps higher education and universities should help to bring about an *improved* world rather than simply sustain it.

Conclusions

The philosophy of higher education has to be a total philosophy, being concerned with life in its fullest extent. An adequate philosophy of higher education should reflect life, embody life, exhibit life, express life, advance life. If it does not do these things, it will be an impoverished philosophy. And 'life' here has to mean all of life, human and nonhuman, animal and vegetable, and the whole cosmos. The philosopher of higher education should be – in Bertrand Russell's (1967) self-description – a citizen of the universe.

However, the philosophy of higher education should be alert to its becoming jejune, living in a purely conceptual or abstract realm. The motto should be 'head in the cloud but feet on the ground'. The field has to concern itself with practical issues, including the nature of universities, state-university relationships, communication (not least in an Internet age), pedagogical and curricula changes, being a student, academic leadership and many other matters. It has to have a bird's eye view of global developments, the broad pattern of higher education across countries of the world, and the shifts in the main ideologies of the age. It has to be, therefore, a social *and* realist philosophy but one which is critical, practical and imaginative, and which works at local, national and the global levels.

If the university is to live out its possibilities in the fraught world of the twenty-first century, it has too to have *spirit*. But then, teasing out the nature of this spirit, and how it might be sustained – and not least in its educational practices – are also part of the tasks of the philosophy of higher education.

2 Higher education and university

Conflicts on the three planes

Introduction

The terms 'higher education' and 'universities' have become largely synonymous, and there is much casual movement in their use, but it was not always so. Whereas the word 'university' (and its variants across languages) is of medieval origin – and *much* earlier incarnations of universities were to be seen across the Orient – the phrase 'higher education' is a newcomer, arising in the twentieth century (with the dawn of mass higher education).

Although an association is often made between universities and research, in fact only a tiny proportion of the world's universities are research intensive (perhaps 2%), *teaching* being by far the dominant activity. Also, universities are places where students study at a 'high' level. There is, therefore, a natural affinity between 'higher education' and 'universities' and the two terms – 'universities' and 'higher education' – have become interchangeable.

Here, I want to address head-on this matter of the *conceptual* relationship between 'higher education' and 'university'. I shall argue that far from being interchangeable, we should keep clear water between the two concepts. In doing so, spaces open not only for our understanding of the two concepts but also for their practical and policy possibilities. And I shall depict the spaces and the movements of these concepts by means of a *dynamic schema of three-planes*, which will serve us in our inquiries throughout this book.

The politics of terminology

Research into higher education began systematically in the 1960s and, for understandable reasons, the research programmes that developed had a primary interest in students and their experience and learning approaches, teaching methods, matters of curricula and student assessment. Interest in doctoral and postgraduate work has also developed apace, especially in the twenty-first century. Ever since the emergence of mass higher education, therefore, there has been a strong research interest in *educational processes and practices*.

Alongside this interest in educational processes, other strands of research have emerged, concerned with management issues, comparative analyses

DOI: 10.4324/9781003102939-4

across systems, matters of identity (of students, faculty and administrators) and considerations of cross-national flows and internationalisation. Strikingly in all of this work, whether in the streams concerned with educational processes or those connected with systems aspects, the term 'higher education' is the dominant umbrella term. Several major journals include the phrase 'higher education' in their titles. Certainly, the term 'universities' may be seen in the titles of empirical papers, in relation to policy matters, global rankings and the public goods provided by universities, but mention of universities is still *comparatively* limited.

Over the past thirty years, the field of the *philosophy and theory of higher education* has formed (chapter 1). Here, too, we can see a parallel tendency to give preferential treatment to educational processes, the idea of the university being less in evidence. This is striking since philosophical work in the field *started* with the idea of the university. From the early nineteenth century, works on 'the idea of the university' appeared in a steady stream for over one hundred and fifty years. For a long time, the idea of the university was a distinctly *philosophical* idea, built around interests in knowledge, reason, mind, freedom, spirit and culture (Peters and Barnett, 2018). However, that line of work on the idea of the university – the early 1800s to mid-1900s – has become rather neglected in scholarly work on higher education.

I, myself, may have unintentionally contributed to this situation. The title of my first book, *The Idea of Higher Education* (1990), was chosen, *first*, to launch the philosophy of higher education as a field of study. *Second*, the title was chosen as a riposte to books over the previous thirty years or so on the philosophy of education, with compulsory schooling as their horizon. My book's title had the *academic-political intention* of indicating that higher education deserved philosophical attention in its own right. *Third*, that title – *The Idea of Higher Education* – was chosen against the long history of books on the idea of the *university*. I was sensitive to the fact that universities formed only part of higher education (then, across the world, there were several systems of higher education in which universities constituted only a part). *However*, an *unintended* upshot of that book's title may have been to deepen neglect of the idea of the university.

The very idea of higher education

In the English language, the term 'higher education' has a number of meanings, referring to an entire national system, to institutions that form such a system, to educational processes that warrant the name of higher education, and to the global enterprise (of higher education). We speak naturally of students in 'higher education', of institutions of higher education, of higher education systems and of the funding of higher education. 'Higher education' has become the term of art in this area, but the term has become unduly elastic.

However, there is a specifically educational meaning of the term. Here, we may pose the question: 'What is "higher" about higher education?' To speak of 'higher education' is to imply that educational processes have to fulfil criteria (even if vague) so as to warrant the appellation 'higher education'. The adjective 'higher' gains traction from a sense of an educational experience in which a student develops a capacity to hover over whatever one encounters – including *one's own work* – and to critique it. Hence, the centrality of the idea of critical thinking (chapter 12) within the idea of *higher* education.

On this reading, 'higher education' becomes an inherently *conditional* concept, harbouring values and implying conditions of a genuinely higher education. Admittedly, such a suggestion can elicit a fear of smuggling in an apologia for an education that sustains elites. Nevertheless, in the English language, we see two separate clusters of usages of the term 'higher education': on the one hand, a reference to a *system* of higher education, and, on the other hand, an interest in the *educational processes* that can properly be termed '*higher* education'.

The idea of the idea of university

'University', too, has two lines of interpretation. On the one hand, the university is a particular social institution, there being some twenty-five thousand universities in the world. Universities, therefore, possess a material aspect with a strong physical presence. Very often, they are huge enterprises, with upwards of twenty thousand members of students and staff of many kinds and may be the largest organisation in a region (UNAM in Mexico City and the University of Buenos Aires both have student populations of over two hundred thousand). Across the world, universities exhibit many forms – private and public; face-to-face and at-a-distance; research intensive and teaching intensive; and are in national systems that are steeply stratified or have relatively little differentiation between their universities.

Alongside this institutional sense of 'university', there is a second interpretation, namely the university as an idea. While, as an institution, the university has the origins of its modern incarnation in Europe in the Middle Ages (and well before that, in Egypt, India, China and Persia), the university as an idea is of relatively recent origin.

It was only at the end of the eighteenth century that systematic reflection on the idea of the university took off, in the hands of German philosophers. Since there, over the past two hundred years, there has been a steady, if intermittent literature on the matter, with several strands of writing, in Germany, England, France, Scandinavia and the USA. More recently, scholarly inquiry has examined the idea of the university from Latin American (Diaz Villa, 2012; Guzmán-Valenzuela and Bernasconi, 2018), African (Assié-Lumumba, 2018; Metz, 2018) and Chinese (Li and Eryong, 2020) viewpoints.

This is an idea *always* in motion. Of late, a pessimistic strand has appeared, with many declaring that there is a 'crisis in the university', that it is 'in ruins' and even wonder as to its 'death' (Wright and Shore, 2019): 'It may well be asked whether after two centuries anything at all remains of the idea of the university' (Wittrock, 1993: 346). However, the idea of *the idea of* the university refuses to die (Rothblatt, 1997). Recently, efforts have been made to develop positive and even utopian ideas of the university (Barnett, 2018a). Some both lament a lost sense of the university *and* yet are hopeful as to the future (Nybom, 2018).

Comparing the concepts of higher education and university

We have, then, *institutional* differences between 'higher education' and 'university' (higher education is the major function of universities, but the university does much else besides), and we have a *conceptual* distinction between them. *So far as the concept of higher education is concerned*, the distinction allows us to inquire into what it is to be a higher education student. For example, the matter arises as to whether there is a conceptual relationship between research and higher education: in saying that a student is taking a course of study in higher education, is it implied that their educational experience bears a connection with research? Important policy decisions turn on our thinking on the matter.

And *so far as the concept of the university is concerned*, the distinction allows us to inquire into the conditions as to what it is to *be* a university (Barnett, 2011). Are there particular forms of institutional autonomy that a university as such should enjoy? Does the idea of a 'teaching university' or even the idea of a 'technological university' make sense? In many countries, there *are* criteria that need to be met, and perhaps they could benefit from some philosophical consideration.

Critical questions

The concepts each of higher education and of university possesses a critical edge. As indicated, with the concept of higher education, we can pose the question of a programme of studies: 'does it really amount to a higher education?' In a parallel way, we can ask of a university: 'Is it living up to the promise of the idea of university?' In either case, the implication is that the educational process *or* the institution is *falling short* of conditions to be satisfied in order for higher education or a university to live up to those titles.

Some say that considerations of this kind are passé. It is felt, among those of a postmodern persuasion, that to think that there might be conditions that can be attached to 'higher education' and 'university' is to form them into 'grand narratives', which we were long ago urged to eradicate (Lyotard, 1984). But that attack undermined itself since, taken seriously, philosophy was then deprived of a critical edge: there would have been nothing that counted *as* higher education or the university. This must have manna to dictators and authoritarian regimes if they ever came across this thinking, for they then had licence to manipulate universities howsoever they wished, and some have been doing just that.

The philosophers had only themselves to blame, for they had deprived themselves of tools of philosophical engagement. For example, in reflecting on the university, philosophy might bring into view the idea of *responsibility* (Derrida, 1992), but it had no way of identifying any particular responsibility that the university might possess. Indeed, far from conditions attaching to the university, it was 'without condition' (Derrida, 2001a). We should, I suggest, resist such emptiness and attempt to fill in the opening gaps, despite the ensuing difficulties. Thankfully, a post-post-modern era is now with us (Peters, 2011a), where large questions have become permissible once more.

A constellation of concepts

I have been indicating that 'higher education' possesses two strands of public meaning. On the one hand, the term 'higher' is used as an adjective: in the English language, it possesses the sense of a '*higher*-education system', specifying one part of a national system of education. And when we speak of students in higher education, we are referring to students within that segment of an education *system*. On the other hand, as noted, 'higher education' can refer to the *educational processes* that typify higher education. This is a more internal meaning. Here arise interests in the teaching and assessment practices, the experiences that students enjoy and the educational situations into which they are placed and the hopes entertained for their futures. This latter meaning of 'higher education' comes into play in matters of national audit and evaluation, where there would be concerns as to whether programmes of study are of the requisite quality. And on such judgements might lie national allocations of monies to individual institutions.

Here, a third meaning of higher education is implicit where it possesses a *legislative* and *judgemental* character. And this meaning has a philosophical aspect, since judgement is called for as to what counts *as* higher education. Some require that the idea of higher education be taken as pointing to educational processes that have a tight relationship with research; others propose a connection between 'higher education' and scholarship OR enquiry (Rowland, 2000); and still others suggest – as I have just intimated – that the concept of higher education derives its force through its being bound up with critical thinking (Barnett, 1990); but these are only some of the options on view.

Let us now turn again to the concept of 'university'. Characteristically, universities as institutions possess incredible complexity of a kind that is not fully understood. A large multi-faculty university may possess many hundreds of courses, tens of thousands of students and typically hundreds if not thousands academic staff and as many staff in managerial, administrative and support roles, with a budget – say – of some hundreds of millions of dollars or euros, and will be active locally, nationally and globally. These institutions have such an extraordinary range of functions that Clark Kerr (1995) spoke of 'the multiversity', but that term understates the situation. There is a complexity here that is dynamic and replete with conflict, across its epistemic cultures, value structures and worldly encounters.

Even though universities are investing effort in putting their research and teaching onto digital platforms and are distributed spatially and geographically (Meusburger et al., 2018), still they have a materiality and hardness about them. They are 'hyperobjects', to use a term from the realist philosopher Timothy Morton (2013). They possess a significant presence in the world independently of thought about them. Furthermore, universities are hybrids, being both closed and open systems. They are always evolving, and unforeseeably so: they possess qualities of *emergence*. As complex entities in the world (Beckett and Hager, 2018), they are always in motion and possess an indeterminacy in the global university space.

Universities are 'real' in this formal sense. Not only do they have a presence that is independent of human perceptions of them, but they also exert effects on human life and society; for example, in shaping would-be student preferences in seeking admission, in their economic presence in a region, in international communication, and the sheer movement of academic bodies around the globe, both academics and students. But they also exert powers at *ever-deeper* levels, in developing a world of 'cognitive capitalism' (Boutang, 2011) and in enhancing the *reflexive* capacities of society. Universities both solidify the dominant economic world order *and* provide resources for critically reflecting on that very world they are helping to cement. Universities provide a nice example of the *ontological stratification* to which Roy Bhaskar (2008a) pointed in his *Critical Realism*.

Ideas of the university

Many universities have been a product of ideas either of individuals or of groups. In the UK, several of the mediaeval colleges of the universities of Oxford and of Cambridge were established to fulfil specific aims in the minds of their founders. Centuries later, University College London was founded – the 'godless college of Gower Street' (Taylor, 1968), as it was then called – by a group of utilitarians, who had a pragmatic mission in mind for the College (Young, 1992). Later still, the UK's Open University was set up as a kind of people's university, its teaching provided largely on a distance-learning basis and deliberately intended to widen access to higher education. In parallel, the 'new polytechnics' were formed, inspired by ideas of being 'comprehensive' (Robinson, 1968). In the USA, many universities have been established or reformed as a result of particular ideas. One thinks of Robert Hutchins (1936) at Chicago in the 1930s or Clark Kerr (2001) in the 1960s in reforming the University of California system.

There are four points here. First, universities are large institutions which exert significant effects on peoples across society. They have a robustness in the world, which comes about because – to use a modish term – universities are somewhat inchoate *assemblages* (DeLanda, 2013) of departments, functions, legal powers and accountabilities, and networks and technologies, and these take on a collective presence such that we can speak of a university possessing its own 'corporate agency' (to steal from List and Pettit, 2011).

Second, ideas help to shape universities. Many universities have long formed their own 'mission statement' (Engwall, 2020) – which have been the subject of empirical research – but they can only be properly interrogated through the particular ideas that they contain. On the other hand, we may speak, in a transcendent vein, of 'the mission of the university' (Ortega y Gasset, 1946), looking to see reflected in every university a *universal* vision of its possibilities. Ortega looked to universities to impart 'the vital system of ideas' that energised culture. Whatever we may feel about such large conceptions, they can help to shape a *cultural imagination* of the university. Universities owe much to ideas *and* yet have a presence independent of those ideas.

Third, universities have their being simultaneously in *the worlds of the real and of ideas*. Each person who is connected with a university will have their own ideas at least of that particular university and probably of what it means to be a university.

Fourth, these two domains – the university as institution and as idea(s) – *interact*. A single town may possess two universities, and it will be hazily understood that the two universities differ (not least by the taxi drivers), in the students whom they recruit and in their place in the world. In that town, individuals' ideas will shape their stance towards each university (perhaps, in one case, sensing a forbidding remoteness). Ideas about what it is to be a university are held, therefore, in a culture – in an 'imaginary' (Taylor, 2007) – which will also influence a particular university's development.

Critiquing the university

In establishing his philosophy of Critical Realism, Roy Bhaskar (2008a, 2008b) was at pains to emphasise the 'real' aspect of the world and entities within it. There was an 'ontological' substrate to the world that philosophers (such as Hume and Heidegger) and social theorists (especially the constructivists) were overlooking. This ontological dimension was hugely significant in that it had causal powers and acted as a set of 'generative mechanisms' on the world, including human life. As he turned to consider the social world, Bhaskar came to allow for a particular notion of critique. The real dimension could be evaluated for its impairments, or 'absences', and so critique had the task of helping to 'absent absences'. Later, Bhaskar turned to consider what a fully realised world could be, and he developed the idea of a meta-reality towards which the world might turn.

This philosophy of Bhaskar's reminds us that a higher education system is not exhausted by its immediate presences. Even rigorous empirical research will not exhaust it for there are hidden layers that lie beyond sight. Terms such as 'globalisation', 'neoliberalism', 'the knowledge economy', 'cognitive capitalism' and even 'epistemic violence' serve as indications of our ignorance, hinting of huge but largely invisible forces at work. To speak of realism does not mean that matters are self-evident (Ferraris, 2015).

Second, despite any sense of a tsunami of forces, there are always possibilities, and this is where well-founded critiques can play a part. Those critiques can be imbued with values that can help to realise a new kind of higher education, and they invite considerations as to what it might be to be a university in the twenty-first century and beyond (after all, many of today's students will be alive in the twenty-second century). What, for example, are the absences to be confronted so as to promote students' *lifelong* development?

Here, Bhaskar could have gone further in acknowledging the role of the imagination. Philosophy can furnish us with imaginative ideas and concepts (a role valiantly played by Bhaskar himself). We noted in the last chapter that Theodor Adorno (a co-founder of the 1930s school of Critical Theory) was fond of observing that the world does not exhaust our concepts. Characteristically, our concepts contain unrealised potential, often suppressed by the world, and it is in this glimpsing of unrecognised potential that the idea of emancipation can come into play (Bhaskar, 2002a). The concept of higher education *can* be linked to possibilities of human beings, of society as a learning space and of democracy and fairness, but, in practice, matters go awry. So part of the philosopher's task is to discern gaps, opened by our concepts, between the way the world is *and* ways it might be.

The Žižekian option

Slavoj Žižek's philosophy is helpful here, especially his (2009) book on *The Parallax View*. Identifying gaps between the way the university is and the way it might, or should be, and so identify a 'noncoincidence of [the university] with itself' (30) is *not* to open the way to any neat resolution of the matter. On the contrary, it is ultimately to reveal the university for what it is, a place of perpetual conflict, of tension, of antimony. It is NOT a matter of it being a place of instrumentalism *or* concern for persons in themselves; *not* of extracting value from the world *or* enhancing the world; *not* of neglecting otherness *or* of affirming otherness; and *not* of facts *or* wonder. It is all of these things at once, and irrevocably so.

Žižek offers the idea of a 'parallax gap', of 'two closely linked perspectives between which no neutral ground is possible' (4). This is the precisely the nature of the university but actually, it is a raft of such parallax gaps (plural); a set of antinomies that can never be 'sublated … into a higher synthesis'

(4). Increasingly, to draw on another of Žižek's ideas, the university is like a number of Moebius strips, each of which present 'two sides of the same phenomenon which … can never meet' and yet which encircle each other (4).

In imagining the university anew, we should not delude ourselves that we are going to supplant the university with a purer version. Rather, we have 'to accept the Real in all its idiocy' (348), and we see this repeatedly in the university. Work goes on in a single university's faculty of engineering – and may even involve students – both in finding ways of more efficiently extracting fossil fuels from the Earth or of designing a dam that will displace a peoples or of inventing forms of surveillance *and* of producing prosthetics for disabled athletes or savagely reducing car pollution or shoring up the leaning tower of Pisa.

Possibilities for the salvation of the university can never produce a 'higher synthesis': to the contrary, its differences 'are posited as such' (299). To be a university now is to be an institution of irremediable conflict-in-motion. By all means let us strive for a better future for the university, but let us 'do it with an inner distance, without full attachment' (281).

Three planes of the university

Let us now build upon these observations about the nature of the university in the twenty-first century. The university is in total motion: it lives in the here-and-now *and* in the future; it is composed of intersecting systems *and* peoples' ideas; and it exhibits irredeemable conflict. It can be understood as having its *being* on three planes (Barnett, 2016) (Figure 2.1).

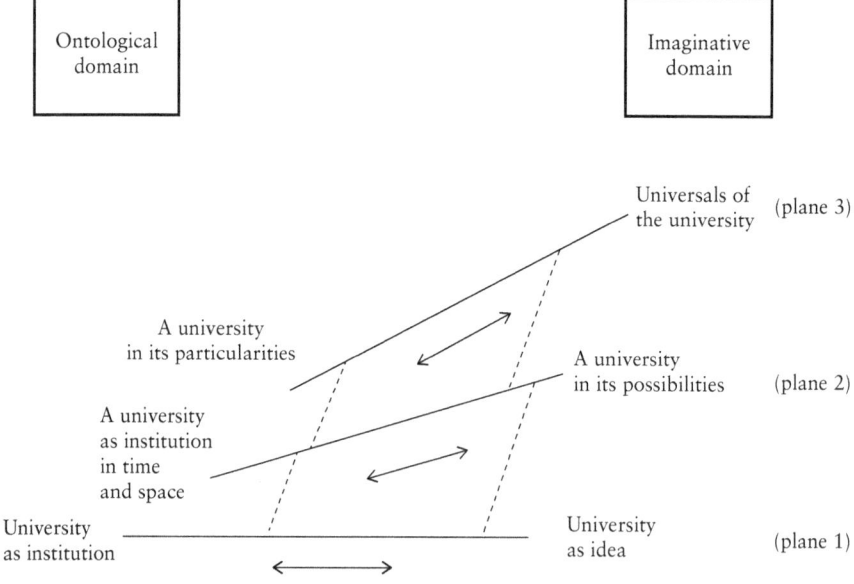

Figure 2.1 Three planes of the university and their interconnections across its ontological and imaginative domains.

Plane one is that of the university both as *institution* and as *idea*: institution and idea are *not* on different planes; there is no hierarchy between them. *Plane two* is a university in its time and space, its past and present, *and* its future possibilities as they might be imagined. *Plane three* is that of the *particulars* of a university – the near-infinite entities that make up a university, with its students, its departments, its programmes of study, its technologies, its resources, its fabric – and the *universals* of the university, the large concepts (always unfolding) through which we understand an institution as a university.

There are *six* things to note about this depiction of the university. *First*, the left-hand side deals with the real character of the university, as it is in the Real of the world (even though obscure to a significant degree), and the right-hand side deals with the speculative, the conceptual and the imaginative aspects. More formally speaking, the left-hand side addresses the *ontological* character of the university, whereas the right-hand side addresses its *ideational* character. *Second*, the trajectories on the right-hand side become steeper as they take on increasingly imaginative and even metaphysical insights, as they open into the ultimate, and most desirable, realm. *Third*, the planes do not meet on the left-hand side for the planes are separate aspects of the university's being. The university lives simultaneously and uneasily on all three planes.

Fourth, this depiction runs together talk of 'the university' (a generic category) and '*a* university'. This is deliberate: a single university is a university in virtue of its association with certain large ideas of being a university (disputable though those ideas will be). *Fifth*, the *poles* of each plane interact: on plane one, ideas of the university and the university as an institution affect each other. On plane two, what a university is in its time and its space affects its possibilities in the world and those possibilities affect the gathering of its particulars. On plane three, the particulars of a university only take on meaning in the context of what it is to be a university – its universals – but the universals of what it is to be a university are forever unfolding in the wake of the changing particulars.

Sixth, the planes themselves interact, and crazily so, without pattern. There are *multiplicities* (Deleuze and Guattari, 2007) here. Ideas, institutions, the university in its historical and present settings, imaginings, universal concepts and the possibilities for a single university and for universities more generally all vie together and in *continuous motion*. To draw on the vitalist philosopher, Henri Bergson, this is a 'dynamic schema' (quoted in Lefebvre and Schott, 2020: 6).

This schema may seem to be an overly complex way of understanding the university. In fact, it is no more than a *reconstruction of common understandings of the university*. One passes a university by rail or road. There it is before us, in its materiality, but it is understood that this is not the extent of the university. It has a history, it embodies sets of values which assuredly conflict with each other, it has its networks and resources, and it has expanding possibilities. It is a 'university' in its keeping company with a generally held set of ideas as to what counts as a university, and it has responsibilities to the world.

What is more, *both* sides of the three-planar schema are witnessing huge turbulence. The left-hand side, the institutional fabric of universities and higher education, is all the time widening, as the wider world calls for more and more from its universities and from the students as they go into the world AND the right-hand side, the ideational side is now exploding, as new ideas of the university multiply around the world (Barnett, 2013).

I have been drawing extensively on Roy Bhaskar's philosophy of critical realism, but I have intimated that it needs some adaptation for our purposes. I suggest that the three-planar schema that I have just introduced possesses five strengths when placed alongside Bhaskar's work: first, it plays up the role of the *imagination*; second, it emphasises that *all is in motion*; third, there is a dynamic *within* each plane; fourth, there is *interaction* – a two-way interaction – between the world of *ideas* and the *real* of the world (of higher education); fifth, there is unresolvable conflict both among the ideas of the university circulating on the three planes *and*, more especially, between those ideas and the way the university is in the world (the forces it is subjected to and the ideologies that it serves). *All five elements are crucial for the philosophy of higher education.*

Conclusions

The concepts of 'higher education' and 'university' are central to the philosophy of higher education. They overlap, and significantly so: a 'university' is an institution that offers higher education, and usually (though not always) programmes of higher education are provided by universities. However, it is important to keep clear water between the two concepts: treating them as synonymous is liable to neglect their potential. Each concept – 'higher education', 'university' – serves as a critical standard to which we may subject educational processes (to see to what extent they justifiably count as 'higher education') and individual institutions (to see if they can justify the appellation of 'university'). These are not narrow exercises but acquire value in identifying the *possibilities* in each case.

The world never fully exemplifies the potential of large concepts such as 'higher education' and 'university': there is always an unmet gap. Moreover, the *whole world is in motion*, and so instantiations of 'higher education' and 'university' continue to unfold. This is a region marked by conflict that can never be overcome, *among* ideas and *between* ideas and the university as it is in the world. The philosophical imagination is called for so as to discern unmet possibilities in existing concepts, to critique the ways matters stand and to help in shaping new forms of higher education and university. These philosophical tasks continue evermore to stretch out before us: discerning and addressing tensions between the ideational and the real of higher education, and in opening air for the imagination, can never be exhausted.

3 Values and higher education, and ethical evolution

Introduction

The matter of values in higher education is seemingly intractable. The sceptic may wonder whether it can make sense *even to try* to alight on any set of values to be associated with higher education. Isn't such talk liable to smuggle in question-begging agendas? On the one hand, the university is an extremely complex institution, and is in motion in an even more complex world, and so will legitimately exhibit many values, some of which will conflict. On the other hand, higher education is a space that should allow for debate *about* values, and it would be presumptuous either to rule out or rule in any set of values in advance of that debate.

Moreover, the idea that the university might be aligned to *any* set of values not uncommonly gives rise to some squeamishness, especially as to whether universities should explicitly declare themselves in favour of a particular value position in regard to *specific* issues (around ethnicity, gender, free speech, and so forth). And yet, so some suggest, there are values that are intrinsic to basic educational practices and should be common across academic life.

On the one hand, then, the university should be a *value-free* zone; on the other hand, the university is necessarily a value-*laden* institution. The university – and its educational practices of 'higher education' – cannot *but* swim amid values. Moreover, the university is held in a *value situation*, in which it is viewed through values in the wider society, where the dominant value perspective is to understand institutions in virtue of their value in the economy: this is the university's real value situation that it cannot evade.

It seems impossible, therefore, to say anything of substance – about values and the university – that can elicit a consensus. The idea of *the ethical university* seems rather like that of an ethical foreign policy: it would be nice to have (sometime). This, I shall try to show, is an entirely legitimate position, but it is unduly pessimistic.

DOI: 10.4324/9781003102939-5

A justifiable reticence?

On what basis might a university accept or reject a large monetary gift? (Basken, 2019). Might a curriculum be such that it is likely to confront students, say, from some ethnic or other backgrounds, with difficult value issues? Can a group of researchers set up a project that is manifestly in favour of a value position? Might a university commit itself to a certain set of values (for example, in committing itself to the United Nations' Sustainable Development Goals)? These are typical of the value-laden issues in higher education.

A particular matter lurks: are there values that are indisputably *inherent* in the university and its educational processes OR are such values simply *emergent* in exigencies (say a change in a university rector or in the impending presence of a controversial visiting speaker)? In a world of uncertainty, can a university simply adopt whichever value set it wishes in relation to different events, or is there an injunction on it to abide by a certain value frame? (Gibbs et al., 2019). Contingency or universality? (Butler et al., 2000): that is the question.

Efforts *are* made, both collectively across universities and by individual universities and academic institutions, to spell out sets of values with which they wish to be identified – of which the (recently updated) *Magna Charta Universitatum* of a number of European universities is a striking example. However, the meta-value issues remain largely unaddressed. Doubtless, there is reluctance to do so because of their apparent intractability. There is, though, another explanation for this reticence. Over the past half century or so, universities have been caught up in the emergence of the knowledge economy. Knowledge counts, but it is knowledge no longer oriented towards reason and truth as such but knowledge that has a pay-off in the world: 'anything goes if it pays' (Berman, 1995: 111).

Given such reflections, it is customary to speak of a world of 'performativity', a term promoted by the French philosopher, Lyotard (1984). What matters is the performance of the student, the institution or, indeed, a whole system of higher education (Macfarlane, 2020). This is a sense of higher education encouraged by instrumental reason: knowledge is valued as a means to ends. In *this* milieu, the ends are limited (concerned with 'impact', financial return and institutional positioning) and simply taken as read. Issues of values as such – it is intuited – need not arise at all, for the dominant value framework for higher education is already set. *It is a value framework devoid of the very mention of values*. Indeed, talk of values may be actively forbidden in the weekly Rector's management team meetings.

However, universities have *not* become value-free environments. Many proclaim their values in value statements, which they place in their corporate strategies and websites, but, rather than signing up to any set of values that might be felt to characterise the university as such, they attempt to strike out for a value set of their own, not least to demonstrate their distinctiveness in a competitive academic market. Still, by and large, universities have become places where matters of values are rather marginal to the activities of the day. Debate over values, whether in a senior management team or a course team, just gets in the way of making decisions and moving the immediate business onwards. As a result, universities and their programmes of study fall into a mess of values, being an amalgam of the *value interests* in the circuits, internal and external, in which they move.

The 'of-courseness' problem – and the idea of a value background

Notwithstanding their elusiveness, it could be suggested that there resides within universities a pool of universal values that sustains them. Universities have an inner value background or set of 'imaginaries', as the Canadian philosopher, Charles Taylor (2007), might put it. However, there is no reason to assume that the value background of the mediaeval university and that of the twenty-first century university coincide. After all, the mediaeval university was a small affair on the fringe of a largely illiterate society, and now it is a major institution, attracting perhaps around half of the young people of society. And whereas its centre of gravity turned on a bookish culture (the books being chained in libraries) separate from the world, now the centre of gravity is the Internet and interactions *with* the world. Given such an evolution, it would be surprising if the value background of universities did not evolve.

In particular, it can fairly be suggested that the past two hundred years have witnessed a value-frame widening from a largely *internal* set of values – around interests in the development of students as human beings ('*Bildung*' and 'liberal education') and in human reason and collective understanding – to embrace *external* interests of the wider society (especially the economy) and an emphasis on individuals (Stiegler, 2015). In most countries, the advance of 'cognitive capitalism' (Boutang, 2011) secretes its values into the university, but other value frameworks jostle for attention, perhaps service to the nation or to a profession. More recently still, some universities are heeding voices that they should have concerns for ecological matters, for the dispossessed, for formerly colonised countries and for black, Asian and minority ethnic (BAME) communities. Values of social, epistemic and ecological justice flow into the university, and so it becomes a jostling of internal and external values.

Higher education, then, is a site of a *value contest*. It is a hothouse not just of the 'plurality' but also of the 'incompatibility' of values, which Isaiah Berlin often explored (Berlin, 1998) and which prompt questions about their possible 'cross-pollination', not least across ethnic and religious traditions (Sahin, 2019). However, there are strong value frameworks that are often imbibed unreflectively: *of course*, a value of higher education lies in its fostering economically valuable skills; *of course*, its value lies in its enhancing an 'innovative' society; *of course*, its value lies in its promoting social justice; *of course*, universities should be 'producing' students who are going to be more or less immediately employable.

A problem with these mantras of the university is that they act as a conservative force. In their 'of-courseness', they go unexamined. Behind *all* 'of-courseness' sits an assumption that universities are of value in addressing the problems of the world. This is a movement of *value incorporation*.

Four difficulties arise. *First*, this 'of-courseness' tacitly accepts that the value of the university lies in serving the needs of its society *as presented by society*. *Second*, it assumes that the evolution of the value background of universities has come to an end. The value background *as it is now* is assumed to represent the endpoint of the university's *value evolution*. *Third*, the value backgrounds of universities differ. The value background of a large and multidisciplinary research-intensive university will not be identical to the value position of a new university that sees itself educating students from ethnic or 'first-generation' backgrounds. Higher education is a site of *value difference*.

Fourth, the 'of-courseness' stance implies that the values that ground universities are unidirectional, always giving clear ethical instructions. To the contrary, it is evident that there is normally some *optionality* in determining both a university's value basis and the actions that might follow. Universities are – more or less – *moral* agents. Typically, they have *some* space in which to move: they can choose to move in some pools of ethical considerations rather than others; and, indeed, they are all the time faced with ethical dilemmas, caught in tensions between ethical principles (academic freedom *and* social justice).

There is a more specifically philosophical problem. Are there any values *especially* associated with what it is to be a university? Given that there are some twenty-five thousand universities in the world, and that the term 'university' has come to stand for a wide variety of educational institutions, some might say that there can be no universal set of values grounding universities. But *this cannot be right*. However they might be in the world, universities are intimately associated with knowledge, truth, reason and critical dialogue, and these interests secrete enduring – if hazy – values. This value background includes concerns for truth-telling, reasonableness, criticality, epistemic honesty, integrity, disinterestedness, appropriateness and respect for others (in truth-oriented conversations). And it is on the basis of there being just such a value background that we can identify epistemic misconduct (Gallant, 2011), and develop a concern with academic integrity (Robinson, 2019), and even raise the possibility of a 'global academic ethics' (Heuser and Drake, 2011).

This is not to say that this is simply *the* form of life that characterises universities. It *is* that but, as Ernest Gellner was fond of observing, the 'form-of-life' thesis (introduced by Ludwig Wittgenstein [1978]) solves nothing. Questions arise along the lines of '*Why* give high marks to knowledge, truth, reason and critical dialogue?' 'To what extent is such a form of life compatible with other values – such as efficiency, competitiveness and contribution to a society's economy and innovative potential?' And 'Might the older value set be *compatible with, and expand to embrace*, new value sets – for instance, around wellbeing, cooperation, worldviews of indigenous communities, and the natural world and sustainability?' Do these newer concerns reside in a separate ethical constellation and/or are there *natural affinities* between them and the university as a space of thought and inquiry?

The value background of the university is not given, therefore, but is always in motion (Macfarlane, 2020). Vigilance is required because universities may be moving into a space that is injurious to its inherent callings. A corollary is that *possibilities* for *a new and justifiable* value base – say, of care as such (Dall'Alba, 2012) – will be neglected.

The poetry of moral goods

Recently, a debate has emerged over the 'public goods' provided by universities (chapter 18), and it is timely for a parallel debate about the 'moral goods'. Public goods and moral goods differ. Public goods are goods that can be widely enjoyed but still retain their value. In principle, knowledge is precisely of this kind. In contrast, moral goods are both more internal *and* collective. How are we to be both in ourselves and in relation to each other and who or what is to come into the reckoning? If the world – and even planet Earth – can be said to possess inherent value, then there is a claim upon the university's relationships with all that is in the world, including Nature. In principle, therefore, the moral goods of the university are very extensive, and there are two philosophical approaches.

There is the virtue approach, which we shall come to shortly, and there is the *near-poetic approach* of the kind exemplified separately by Gaston Bachelard and Henri Lefebvre. Neither philosopher wrote about higher education – or even education so far as I know – but each brought a forensic sensitivity to matters of space, and place, and time.

For anyone seriously interested in the rhythms of life, 'nothing is immobile', Lefebvre wrote. If the 'rhythmanalyst', as Lefebvre (2004) called such a person, 'considers a stone, a wall, a trunk, [he or she] understands their slowness, their interminable rhythm … An apparently immobile object, the forest, moves in multiple ways' (20). This 'rhythmanalyst calls on all [his or her] senses. [He or she] thinks with [his or her] body … in lived temporality' and is acutely sensitive to the micro details of his/her surroundings; to the 'odours of the morning and evening, of hours, of sunlight or darkness, of rain, or fine weather' (21).

Rhythms beget values. The university is beset with busyness, freneticism, haste, urgency, constant action, fast work, pressing deadlines and incessant and near-instantaneous flows of data and of quick decision-making. In speed lies power (Virilio, 2005). A contrasting set of values is contained in quietness, contemplation, carefulness, crafting, inwardness, thought and solitude.

The widespread movement in favour of 'slow' activities that celebrates attentiveness and carefulness may be in vain, but it is understandable.

Suppose, too, we consider the university to be a house: we might then share with Bachelard (1994) that 'the house shelters day-dreaming, the house protects the dreamer, the house allows one to dream in peace' (6). 'The house is a large cradle' (7). It is – or can be – a 'dwelling-place in our lives' (5) with its 'cellar and garret, nooks and corridors'. This kind of close attention to the detail of living in the spaces of higher education helps us to attend to universities as 'the sites of our intimate lives'. This is not to romanticise higher education; rather, it is to open questions about the *ethical character of the spaces of academic life*.

If an academic has become silent, feeling oppressed and yet unable to speak about it, how has that come about? Was it the email attachment, the (lack of) office space, the last (possibly punitive) assessment, the soulless instruction from an administrative office, the dismissive rudeness from a senior professor, the cold rejection to a submitted paper, the belittling rejoinder in a seminar or even a fear of brutality on the part of the state when in the streets outside? All of these are distinctive rhythms and spaces and moments, sometimes alone, sometimes with others, sometimes in a familiar room, sometimes in another place. This is, for Bachelard, a 'concrete metaphysics' and a 'metaphysics of consciousness'. However, given that the higher education and the world are now so intertwined, it is not clear that there is any secure and neutral space where such a metaphysics could concretely be explored: no longer does the academic house afford 'the privilege of its values within' (7).

So how to capture the 'values within' of the university and higher education? Are there particular sounds, interactions, pleasures, delights and satisfactions still to be found within? The students are to be seen collaborating, the paper is ready to be submitted after many months' work, the smile in the seminar room signals a mutuality, the giving-way to a counterpoint takes a conversation forward, a moment of elation reflects that something has happened in the laboratory or in the analysis of the data (perhaps a new pattern or entity has been discovered), and the end-of-week celebration in the department marks a colleague's new book. There is rhythm here, timeliness, empathy, consideration and deep communication; 'deep' because these acts travel on the surface of a deep mutuality of values, experiences and hopes. This life calls one forward, and envelops one, even if, at times, it hurts.

There are *moral goods enfolded in this form of life*, and *necessarily so* if it is to be sustained. But those goods – of forbearance, of understanding, of mutuality, of releasement, of a reaching-out, of collectivity – can only be understood as founded on a shared belief in a life of struggles to understand the world in its multitudinous aspects, and of a truthfulness allied to integrity. By and large, *this very strange life* calls for its members – students and staff – to say what they mean and to mean what they say, to hold themselves up to perpetual scrutiny to onerous standards in their disciplinary and professional communities and to *listen* to the world. Individuals and epistemic groups carry this life forward, but it is a life, an epistemology, ultimately 'without a knowing subject', (as Popper (1975) put it); a life of otherness, in which the world, *and* the standards inherent in trying to understand the world, stand beyond oneself.

This poetic philosophy of higher education, in which moral goods are felt in its collective inner life, has its counterpart in a more conventional approach within analytic philosophy and social theory that focuses on academic life as sets of social practices (Schatzki et al., 2001). I have mentioned Charles Taylor who has drawn attention to horizons of values that serve as a living background in the life of communities. This communitarian philosophy has also been developed by Alisdair MacIntyre, not least in relation to universities.

Academic virtues

For MacIntyre (1985: 191–195), universities sustain practices that possess internal goods with their own 'standards of excellence'. In turn, virtues are acquired human qualities 'the possession of which tends to enable us to achieve those goods which are internal to practices'. Universities are institutions concerned with external goods, but they also sustain practices with their internal goods. There is, thus, a complex relationship between universities, goods (both internal and external), practices and virtues.

This virtue approach has been influential of late, being taken up especially by Jon Nixon (2008), in relation especially to universities as institutions; Bruce Macfarlane (2004, 2007, 2009), in relation to many university practices; and George Allen (2017), in relation to following the rules of the academy. All three scholars have sought to tease out virtues characteristic of universities. Associated with this approach are efforts to tease out the 'epistemic virtues' embedded in epistemic practices (Brady and Pritchard, 2003).

However, this whole way of construing a university as an institution either in possession of, or in want of, moral goods, has its limits since the university qua institution swims in a *multiplicity* of value positions, with their conflicting means of measurement, timeframes and timbres. Is it to be by means of performance indicators or their contribution to peace on Earth by which universities are to be judged? Is it to be a lifetime's earnings or the student's lifelong well-being by which the student experience is to be measured? Is it to be an interest in a quest for innovation in the economy or is it to be a concern for the natural environment?

It is unclear as to the stance that the university should adopt in such a value maelstrom. Is it to be a kind of *value umpire*, seeing fair play between competing interests, and to attempt a position of value neutrality? Or is it to be a kind of *value entrepreneur*, seizing the main chance, and alighting on whichever values fit the immediate exigencies? The university, after all (so we are told), has to live 'in the real world'.

Life values, university values

For Nicholas Maxwell, the university has lost its way over the past three hundred years, having misinterpreted what it is to reason. Instead of seeing matters in the round, the university has broken up problems into discrete segments and has tackled each small problem one by one. What is needed, Maxwell (1984, 2014) argues, is a new idea of the university, a university of *wisdom*, that – in the first place – perpetually asks, 'What is of value in life?' In other words, the matter of value has continually to be placed on the higher education table. And here, Maxwell – a philosopher of science – sees a role for the humanities and the social sciences in orchestrating such a debate. And it would be under the umbrella of such a debate that universities could (then) tackle their more discrete inquiries. MacIntyre himself seems to be of a similar mind in remarking that

> The contemporary research university is ... by and large a place in which certain questions go unasked or rather, if they are asked, it is only by individuals and in settings such that as few as possible hear them being asked.
> (2011: 174)

There is, though, a problem in that this approach to values in education can lead to a *debating-society conception* of the university. This would be tantamount to a continuation of the disputations of the mediaeval universities, and it sets up two pathologies. It invites the suspicion that the debate is interminable. Furthermore, it is assumed that the debate is to be governed by the university: its speakers and topics, the manner of their inquiries and the participants are all to be determined by the academy itself. It is a learned society conception of the university. It will be rejoined that no such closure is intended but, then, there is an onus to say something as to how voices and interests from beyond the academy are to be drawn in.

What is needed is an unflinching effort to identify values that are characteristic of the university, and not in mediaeval times but in the twenty-first century (and well beyond). Two paths have opened: to search for values characteristic of practices within the university *and* to look for values reflected in the university's relationships with the wider world.

It is probable that the two lists will turn out to contain *conflicting* values – conflicts not just between internal and external values but on both sides of this big ditch. For example, a concern for truth may conflict with sensitivity to persons *within* the university (conflict of *internal* values), while universities-for-the-global-economy may conflict with universities-for-peace-in-the-world (conflict of values in the university's relationship with the *external* world). Still, ethical pluralism notwithstanding (Berlin, 1979), let us deal directly with these challenges.

For a shot at the first list (values internal to the university), let us note that the university is a social institution concerned to encourage its members in making claims within well-founded inquiry. It is a *claiming culture*, but the claims – whether in a first-year undergraduate essay or an academic paper or a statement in a consultancy report or even in a university's corporate plan – have to be publicly cashable. (And so we are increasingly seeing lists of references even in consultancy reports emanating from universities and in universities' corporate plans.)

There is at work here a culture of reason and truthfulness. Both elements are crucial and they interact, with reason and truthfulness gaining from each other. False beliefs (say, about supposed differences between different groups of people) can affect one's reasoning in socially catastrophic ways, and having a suitably wide approach to the development of critical reason can help one's grasp of truth (Buchanan, 2015).

If high value is to be accorded to reason, evidence, truthfulness, steady argumentation, carefulness and critique, a *foundational set of values* has to be present. These include the values of (i) freedom to utter (in any medium); (ii) respect for persons in a dialogue oriented towards truth; (iii) disinterestedness, in speaking and revealing the truth as it is perceived; and (iv) authenticity, such that – normally – one says what one means and means what one says. Unless this *bedrock of values* is in place, and sustained in the practices of universities, that higher set of values of reason, truthfulness, steady argumentation, carefulness and critique will flounder. And just that fourfold bedrock of values (enumerated above) is in jeopardy all over the world.

There is, therefore, a *hierarchy of values* in being a university. Of course, each of these foundational values is open to questioning: for example, to what extent is freedom to utter to be respected? This freedom does not normally allow the undergraduate to heckle the professor giving a lecture to the first-year students, but it does permit the student to pose a critical question to the professor about the latter's position.

The university as a moral agent

Let us turn to the other side of the big ditch, of values inherent in the exchanges between the university and the wider society. The university has to be considered as a moral agent, having *powers* to act in morally defensible ways. However, there is dispute over the breadth of this agency. Some would confine it to *sharing with the world* the epistemically internal considerations of truth-telling, rigour, respect for persons, fairness and so forth. Others look to widen the university's ethical space to include awareness of an unequal and oppressed world and of social injustice, and a recognition of the other, including Nature. There is here a presumption that the university should be injecting a value substrate *into* the world.

However, if the university is to be associated with the idea of moral goods, then it must be its own moral agent having both autonomy and capacities to shape the moral goods that are *its*. But an implication must be that the university should have the space to provide society with moral goods that were *neither requested nor expected* by the wider society

What is at issue here is not exactly 'the moral foundations' of universities (Miller, 2012, chapter 8) or 'the moral bases of academic practice' and the virtues within universities (Nixon, 2008), important as those issues are. Rather, what is at issue are the following matters: 'What legitimacy attaches to virtues possessed by the university being – as it were – transferred into the wider world?' And more disconcertedly, 'Is it not presumptuous for the university to see itself as having something of moral worth for the wider world?'

These are matters of social and political significance, at both the national and global levels. Tensions easily arise. In a world of 'fake news', 'post-truth' and populism, does the university possess legitimacy in deliberately providing a value stream into the world of freedom of inquiry, disinterestedness, a care for truthfulness and so forth? There are the makings here of a tension not uncommonly to be found between a society and its universities.

Suppose that a university is minded to orchestrate its activities around the United Nations' Sustainable Development Goals and suppose that to do so might run *counter* to the espoused national interest: on what basis might it be suggested that that university has the moral right to act in that way? In a divided world, an attempt to strike *any* ethical position on the part of the university is liable to create some antipathy towards the academic world. A state of hubris beckons, in which the university comes to believe in the universal worth of its moral goods. Nevertheless, with the world falling short of its possibilities, the university has a responsibility to play its part in mitigating those impairments.

Conclusion: a state of ethical evolution

Trying to locate an ethical base for the university produces an uncomfortable ride. If we recall the three-planar schema of the previous chapter, we can understand the reasons for this discomfort. Those three planes pointed up the turbulence and indeterminacy of the university. The university is in motion within, and in interplay with, a world that is itself in motion. Moreover, the university has its being on sloping planes which, dynamically, link the university's being in the world and in the realm of ideas. Given these interrelationships, it is inevitable that the university is a site of multiple and clashing value systems. The university is a site of *value turbulence*.

However, the university is not without a value anchoring. It possesses internal values – of truthfulness, reasoned argument, tolerance, respect and carefulness – that have value in the wider world, and increasingly so. This is not to suggest that the university should seek to impose any such values on the wider world. On the contrary, there can be *no ethical trickle-down*, not least because moral conflicts are playing out *within* the university. Epistemic virtues supply but one set of considerations within the university's ethical pot, and those values are all the time widening *legitimately but in tension with each other*.

All the university can do, therefore, is to be clear that being a university harbours a certain set of values, that it will encounter value conflicts, that it needs to be ethically vigilant and that values can *legitimately* widen. Its moral goods are always going to be a mix. The values of a university can be shared with the wider world but only with a degree of modesty, so that *its value set is open to new values that are in sympathy with its central values*. Yes, the university needs to be on its guard for ethical corruption, but it also needs to be alert to legitimate ways of *widening* its ethical base (to live with and for new strangers in *both* the human and natural worlds). The university has always to be in a state of ethical *evolution*.

4 Knowledge and truth

Matters of interest

> Our knowledge forms an enormous system. And only within this system has a particular bit the value we give it.
>
> (Ludwig Wittgenstein, *On Certainty*, 2003/1969, para 410)

Introduction

Knowledge and truth should be at the heart of any philosophy of higher education, but they are not given sufficient attention. This should concern us on several fronts. Universities and their practices may be caught in narrow or outdated or even ideological conceptions of knowledge and truth. Universities may block new forms of knowledge, resisting them as not really counting as knowledge. One thinks, for example, of the struggles faced by engineering, sociology, the professions allied to medicine, education and art and design as well as the performing arts in being recognised as worthy of study in universities. Perhaps indigenous knowledge and feminist knowledge, which are knocking at the door, are part of this pattern of exclusion and ultimate acceptance.

In holding out for what they may consider to be bone fide claimants to know, universities may be repudiating conceptions of knowledge that could open possibilities for understanding the world. Perhaps a new world – a digital age, a fluid age, an ecological age – needs entirely new kinds of knowledge. Perhaps the traditional disciplines, as homes for propositional knowledge, should be displaced from their pedestal and more practical, processual or embodied forms of knowledge be accorded legitimacy. Or perhaps the highest marks should be given to *combinations* of forms of knowledge – transdisciplinary knowledge indeed – that are more adequate in helping our understandings of the world (Gibbs, 2017). At least, these matters should be on the table. And then could come into play the idea of epistemic justice which is all the time widening (Kidd et al., 2017).

The twenty-first century has brought two further sets of challenges to university knowledge. First, a 'post-truth' age has emerged, and with it the belief that 'we have had enough of experts'. Implicitly, these ideas suggest an emperor's clothes situation, namely that the knowledge safeguarded by the university is not all that is claimed for it. Its disinterestedness, purity and solidity rest on weak foundations and are even spurious. Academic knowledge is either unduly partial or self-serving or both.

The other great challenge facing knowledge and the university is that not only does it harbour undisclosed interests but that those interests are *injurious*. If it is the case that humanity has wreaked terrible onslaughts on its total environment – the Earth and much that it contains, and its heavenly atmospheres – it may be that, in part, this is because its sense of what it is to know harbours a will to power (to steal from Nietzsche [1968]). Not only is the very work of the scientist in the laboratory one of control (of the immediate and causal conditions of a situation) but at a deeper level still, science – so it may be felt – harbours an inner will to control humanity's total environment. And this consideration transcends even the Earth as planetary explorations get under way, and concerns arise about the colonisation of Earth's neighbours. In short, so it is suggested, the environmental crisis has emerged partly as a result of epistemologies, endorsed by universities, that seek knowledge in the hope of controlling and even exploiting the wider world (a point made especially in feminist thought (Plumwood, 2002; Code, 2006)).

Knowledge and human interests, and border controls

Across the world, universities have been giving priority to the STEM disciplines (science, technology, engineering and mathematics). Increasingly, governments are not just reluctant to invest public funds into the humanities but act so as to discourage their take-up. (China focuses its higher education policy framework almost entirely on STEM subjects.) It is hardly surprising if it comes to be assumed that it is mathematically oriented disciplines that are of most worth. In turn, a 'crisis of the humanities' (Plumb, 1964) has been apparent in universities for more than half a century.

In the 1960s, in the United Kingdom, C. P. Snow (1978) captured this great divide, in depicting science and the humanities as 'the two cultures' and, while both he and others modified that position to recognise a wider range of disciplines (Kagan, 2009), still it prompts a fundamental question for the university. Are different forms of knowledge so fundamentally different that they constitute 'epistemic cultures' (Knorr Cetina, 1999), signifying quite separate forms of life and holds on the world? Is knowledge in the university, then, to be construed as a matter of *competing cognitive interests*? Admittedly, this is not a new situation: over two hundred years ago, Kant (1992) observed a 'conflict of the faculties' although, not surprisingly, philosophy was given a special and even legislative position in the university's epistemological hierarchy.

There are three issues here, those of (i) dominant academic epistemologies, (ii) demarcation (and priority) and (iii) unification.

(i) **The dominant position**

The dominant Western epistemology harbours a sense of a separateness of humankind and the world: *there* is the world and *here* is knowledge about it. In Richard Rorty's famous (1980) evocation, it is as if in trying to know the world, we hold a mirror up to nature. However, in seeking to understand this situation, we may be liable to think that we cannot get beyond this 'correlation' between our perceptions of the world and the world itself (Meillassoux, 2014) and so on; we can never really know the world as such. For indigenous and Eastern cultures, understanding the world is quite different since humanity is embedded *in* the world (van Wyk and Higgs, 2012). Knowing becomes an awareness of a world that *includes* oneself, one's community and the world. One doesn't just know *about* the world (held to be separate from one's knowing efforts); rather, one knows the world *directly*.

For the most part, universities favour the *apartness* stance; not entirely, by any means. There are profound differences across the disciplines and professional fields, especially between the natural sciences and related technological domains on the one hand, and the humanities and the performing arts on the other hand. But the *dominant* epistemology posits a world separate from the knower, and it is the student's or researcher's task to reveal the world as it is. Low marks are given to those who smuggle in their own personal perspective; or, at least, this was the case until recently.

Now, there is dispute on the matter, at least in the social sciences. There, many consider that objectivity is impossible and that the researcher or student should not only start off by (i) declaring their own starting point (their 'positionality') but (ii) should be aware of how their own framing of a situation might colour their interpretations and so (iii) should strive to let the data speak for themselves. The motivation is understandable, but data *never* speak for themselves. Wanting to avoid the trap of scientism, these empathic researchers end up in the paradoxical position of being unduly scientific and objectivist.

A radical critique of this way of construing knowledge – as a relation between the knower and the known – has developed within feminist epistemology in which the knower is seen as part of the world and so knowing, the world and ethics are seen as entangled. In this 'ethico-onto-epistemology' (Geerts and Carstens, 2019), understanding arises not from outside the world but 'from within and as part of it' (Barad, 2007).

This matter raises profound issues of the role of the university. Is its knowledge to be an attempt to reveal the world as it is or is its knowledge a means by which universities act to *interpret* the world or even – whisper it softly – a basis on which to take up a position and to *act* in the world and so deliberately *change* the world?

(ii) **Axes of demarcation**

There are two sets of considerations here, which constitute *axes of demarcation*. One axis is our knowledge of the natural world *and* of the human world. The other axis is direct access to the world *and* frameworks through which data (or experience or impressions) are *interpreted*. Placed upon each other, the two axes produce four options (Figure 4.1):

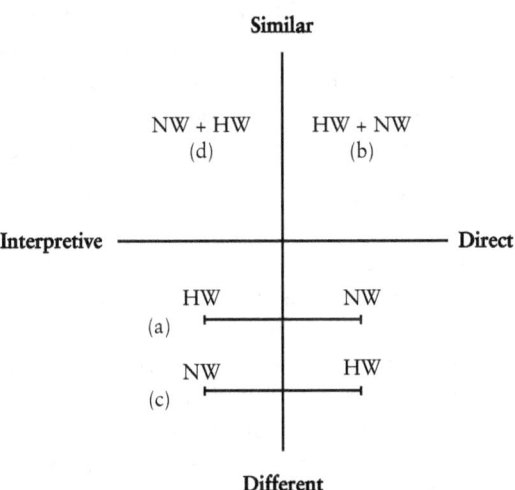

Figure 4.1 Axes of demarcation: conceptions of our knowledge of the natural world (NW) and human world (HW).

(a) Knowledges that deal with the natural world and those that deal with the human world *differ*. Those that deal with the natural world have the task of revealing the world, their having direct access to it. This is knowledge that is unadorned, devoid of any unnecessary interpretation. This position is scientism. On the other hand, knowledges that deal with human world have a licence, and even a responsibility, to *interpret* the world (Gadamer, 1985; Margolis and Rockmore, 2000).

(b) Knowledges that deal with the natural world and those that deal with the human world are *not* fundamentally different: *both* have the task and the responsibility to reveal the world as it is, without any undue framework invented by human minds getting in the way. In the social sciences, this approach took the name of positivism (Adorno et al., 1977).

(c) Knowledge of the natural world and knowledges of the human world differ, but, as compared with (a), the difference is reversed. Here, it is considered that scientists, in interpreting the world, have to bring complex and arcane theoretical frameworks to bear in interpreting the data with which they are confronted. Their frameworks are theory-laden (Kuhn, 1970). So far as our understanding of the human world is concerned, however, we have direct – and empathic – access to it (human investigators seeking to understand other humans). Moreover, there is a serious risk here of imposing our predispositions upon the phenomena we are investigating. This would amount to a pollution of the data, and so every attempt must be made to allow the data to speak for themselves. *Verstehen* calls!

(d) Knowledges that deal with the natural world and those that deal with the human world are no different, but, in comparison with (b), the relationship with the world turns around. In *neither* case is it possible to see the world without some kind of framework coming into play. In both kinds of knowledge – of the natural world and of the human world – frameworks are necessary in order to produce knowledge.

Are these matters of interest just to the knowledge police who patrol the epistemological borders of higher education? They are surely of the highest significance, for they concern the character of humanity's attempts to know the world. If science is felt to offer a window directly into the world, such a stance is liable to put up the shutters if it be suggested that scientists have access to the world only through frameworks, their accounts being always 'theory-laden'. What credibility attaches then to their frameworks, not least when they appear in public to buttress political decisions?

In universities, these matters take on significance in relation to professional education (Schön, 1987). For example, what is the primary kind of knowledge that is needed in the nursing and related professions? Is it propositional knowledge that treats the world as separate and enables operational activities that require instrumental techniques, or is it 'knowledge-in-action' or is it interpretative knowledge where human communication, empathy and understanding between the nurse and the patient are required? Are patients human beings or are they mere assemblages of molecules and anatomical structures? Is professional knowledge not *embodied* in professionals' being and their professional processes? (Eraut, 1994; Dall'Alba and Sandberg, 2020; Loftus and Kinsella, 2022).

Many believe that nursing studies (and comparable 'caring' professions) have become dominated by science-oriented understandings of knowledge and that empathic, sensuous understandings of the world have been placed in jeopardy. Lecturers in nursing studies who wish to develop a research profile are obliged to author papers in journals that favour quantitative surveys and statistical techniques and where qualitative work faces difficulties in securing publication. Legitimised knowledge in medicine is of a technicised and mathematicised kind, in which the patient (singular) tends to vanish and patients (plural) are reduced to points in big data sets in health systems. Importantly, this pattern has been challenged over recent decades, such that the humanities, the performing arts, the idea of wellbeing. and a humanising of medicine have found their way into the profession.

All this has profound implications for higher education policy, not least as it plays out on the global stage. Publications, journals, search engines, audit procedures and funding arrangements come to be attuned to science-based forms of knowledge, and, in the process, humanities are skewed in that direction or are marginalised as feeble forms. A sense of the human condition is shunted into a marshalling yard of elements in the natural world. The humanities come to be dismissed as not providing real knowledge, if not actually repressed in the formation of national knowledge policies.

(iii) **Unity – or, rather, *re*unification**

A sense emerges, then, that what counts as knowledge is a matter not just for philosophers or educationalists but is a matter of large political and social significance. *All* epistemologies are social epistemologies. Sometimes, falls in the numbers of students taking the humanities or the closure of a university humanities department or an outspokenness by ministers of higher education are observed (as they ask out loud why public monies should be spent on the humanities), but rarely are dots joined, and effort made, to inquire into the epistemologies at work.

Considerations along these lines are apt to bring a sense that this is just the way the world is. The twenty-first century has brought a diffuse sense that the epistemologies dominant in the Global North (which now has to include China) are deficient. There is a justified view that climate change, the degradation of the total environment and the manipulation of human beings are *pari passu* with the development of modernity and its narrow range of epistemologies. But other elements are also evident, including a new reverence for Nature (Moog and Stones, 2009; Feyerabend, 2016), a growing concern for *care* not only towards human beings but also the plant and animal worlds (Noddings, 2003), an interest in feminist epistemology (Longino, 1996; Tuana, 2017) and a significance attaching to emotional and spiritual wellbeing. 'Clashes of knowledge' (Khine, 2008; Meusburger et al., 2008) simmer within universities, and across science, cultures and religions.

Against this background, attention turns to indigenous cultures and epistemic coloniality (Quijano, 2000; Grosfoguel, 2007), not just as a matter of epistemic injustice but of epistemic *self-interest*, it being sensed that these modes of understanding may help those who see themselves as 'moderns' in facing challenges of Earthly life (Latour, 1993). Nice questions arise as to ways of 'grafting indigenous ways of knowing onto non-indigenous ways of being' (Ahenakew, 2016). In prospect is a knowledge ecology that brings together, in some ways, the epistemologies of the Global North and Global South (cf. Guzmán-Valenzuela and Gómez, 2019), but 'It remains to be seen whether [Western] "epistemologies" [will] fail us in ... build[ing] effective affinities' (Haraway, 2016b).

These concerns are fuelling a rethinking of university epistemologies. Alongside a sense that knowledge is worthwhile in providing for extracting benefit from the external world has emerged a sense that knowledge should help us to live *together with* the external world and to *be* in it. Warmer epistemologies, with concerns for wellbeing and 'the needs of strangers' (Ignatieff, 1994), are finding places of their own alongside the icy knowledges of science and its distancing of the world. Against an inner belief that the knower and the world are separate has arisen an interest in knowledges that *unite* the knower and the world.

Here, we alight on the fundamental matter of the relationship between facts and values. Alongside the assumption that facts and values inhabit quite different epistemological spaces have developed efforts at *reconciliation*. Some even seek to motivate forms of knowledge – 'ecology', 'feminist studies', 'inclusion studies', decoloniality, 'transdisciplinarity' – that wear their values on their sleeves. Now it is commonly accepted that knowledge and action in the world may helpfully proceed in tandem, with feedback loops between them. And so has emerged – over the past fifty years or more – professional knowledge, knowledge for the caring professions and knowledge with a processual and immediately aesthetic character, all of which are *value-laden*. Facts and values; data and interpretation; theory and practice; the world and the knower: the borders are coming down.

What we are witnessing, therefore, is a subtle set of *epistemological wars*. Can the terms 'need' or 'should' or even 'must' appear in the pages of a doctorate dissertation? Should the first-person voice be injected? The purists would outlaw such textual devices as polluting accounts of the world, whereas the evangelicals assume that right – and history – is on their side. The underlying matter is whether or not the warring parties can ultimately live together and can be reconciled, or whether one or other party has to be declared victor and one or more parties entirely vanquished. The signs are unclear.

Interior design

Does knowledge have a purpose? Is it a force to manipulate and control the world? Is it a means of understanding the world or of engaging with the world? It is evident that epistemologies are *worldly* through and through. Even debates that, prima facie, seem to be internal to epistemology and likely to be only of interest to paid-up members of the philosophy clan turn out to be of large educational import. Here are two.

First, the 'KK' (*knowledge-of-knowledge*) issue. If I know X, must it be that I also *know* that I know X? If I simply know X – without knowing that I know X – what does my knowing amount to? Perhaps I am ventriloquising X, having heard it elsewhere. Perhaps I am subject to an ideology, not critically evaluating my own knowledge claims. It is a crucial part of any serious knowing, *especially in higher education*, that I am able to reflect on my knowing and so be sure as to the extent of my understanding. I might see that my knowledge is of a meagre kind and liable to fall apart at the first challenge. We encounter this when individuals come into the teaching profession and, having felt that their knowledge was secure (perhaps they have even achieved a doctorate *en route*), then find that their grasp of matters is rather flimsy. On the other hand, I might realise that, in my tacit knowledge, I know more than I knew I knew (Polanyi, 1978; Marcus, 1997).

This knowledge-of-knowledge criterion as a *necessary* condition of knowledge has institutional and educational import. If it is granted that knowledge has to contain this reflexive element, then that must weigh upon disciplines in higher education. To warrant their entry into universities, disciplines should have the resources to reflect upon *themselves*; hence, in part, the need for a discipline-specific research base. The jury is out on the extent to which disciplines possess these reflexive resources. Some consider that science lacks such powers and that this is where the humanities score; others demur, observing that scientists not infrequently write books reflecting on science in the world, whereas the humanities seem more reluctant to self-reflect. Whatever the truth of the matter, it is a pedagogical challenge of the first order that teaching in higher education constructs the subjects being taught so as to incorporate self-reflexive elements. This is an epistemological and a curriculum matter before it is a psychological matter.

A second issue is that of JTB. For some time, in analytical philosophy, it was accepted almost as a dogma that knowledge lay in 'justified true belief' (Nagel, 2014). It is not enough that I believe that x, but that, in order to count as knowledge, my belief must be true, and it must be justified as true. These three elements – belief, truth and justification – were commonly accepted as conditions of knowledge. However, that agreement was shattered by an academic note by Edmund Gettier (1963), who provided examples in which the three conditions could be satisfied but where we would be reluctant to accord the accolade 'knowledge'. There may be occasions where a person (p) justifiably believes that x, and x is true, but it turns out that x is true not for the reasons that p believes, but for some other quite spurious reason. All three conditions – belief, truth and justification – are present but their co-presence does not amount to knowledge.

We may note – *en passant* – that not only was Gettier's note just that, a single three-page note and was said to be the only thing he wrote, but it was highly influential (spawning 'Gettier cases', as scholars argued the toss in the journals). So much for producing material in great volumes, as is required in so many academic audit systems of the world. More importantly, the argument indicates that knowledge rests on a social *surround* that envelopes belief. Knowledge has to be believed by some people, but it needs also to be encased in a body of beliefs that possess durability. Knowledge takes on an *institutional* character and comes to possess an independence of human mind.

But independence, durability and a cognate cluster of affirmed beliefs still do not count as knowledge, for why should astrology or witchcraft not be admitted into the university? Ultimately, epistemological entrants into the university have to possess legitimacy, but on what basis? (Gellner, 1974). There are *no* indisputable criteria. *All* legitimations are questionable. Should Marxism, psychoanalysis, chiropractic or complementary medicine be included? Media studies? Performing arts? The knowledges of nomadic or indigenous communities? What are to be the bases for inclusion and exclusion? *Any such judgement is inherently controversial*, with worked-through legitimations being seldom on offer. The formal case – for inclusion *or* exclusion – is usually thin to put it mildly.

Truth: a matter of argument

What, art thou mad? art thou mad? Is not the truth the truth?
Shakespeare, *Henry IV Pt 1*, Act 2, Sc IV

Even though it be felt to be an 'institution of truth' (Hannah Arendt, quoted in Rider, 2018), the university muddles along, hardly giving thought to the matter of truth. Against the background of a 'post-truth' age, in which claims to truth have their place in a 'power game' (Fuller, 2018), this is a grave omission.

There are different readings of the idea of 'post-truth'. The term could refer to a situation in which it suits certain interests to *manipulate* public understandings of matters and to rest those beliefs even on falsehoods. *Second*, the voicing of 'post-truth' could point to a situation where individuals come to believe that the idea of truth no longer has serious application. 'Truth' is seen as an outdated 'meta-narrative' that gets in the way of comprehending the world. *Third*, the term 'post-truth' could refer to a situation in which competing framings of the world are proliferating. Epistemic plurality is giving rise to incommensurable truths, with little – if any – guidance on hand by which demarcations between truth and non-truth can be provided. In *this* sense, 'post-truth' could be heralding an openness to *new* ways of understanding the world.

So far, the philosophy of higher education has had little to say about these matters. Perhaps there is some justification for this neglect, since the standard accounts of truth seem to be inadequate for comprehending truth in the vicinity of the university. There are three standard accounts – truth as correspondence, as coherence and as pragmatic stances in the world (but there are others besides (Wrenn, 2015)). Truth as correspondence posits a relationship in which accounts mirror, or 'correspond', to the world; truth as coherence looks for coherence among claims about the world; and truth as pragmatism sees truth as a vehicle for judging the practical consequences of a claim in the world. Whatever their merits, all three accounts are inadequate in getting to grips with truth in the university.

A further idea of truth has been advanced by Jürgen Habermas, that of truth-as-consensus. This idea sprang out of Habermas' search for a rational basis of human communication. In his theory of communicative action, he proposed that human interaction contains a joint search for consensus among participants in a speech situation. Even if this is true – and it is highly controversial – it should be ruled *out* for universities and higher education. The university is a peculiar human institution not only for the handling of dispute but – much less recognised – for the *generation* of dispute. (This was embodied in the mediaeval universities in their disputations.) *Higher* education is an educational process in which students come to handle dispute. This is why student essays frequently take the form of x says this and y says this other, the student showing a capacity to attend to arguments *and* to live with differing viewpoints. So truth-as-consensus will not do for higher education.

What is needed here is an idea of *truth-as-argument*. Without such an idea of truth, we cannot be in the company of a university. But then truth has to be understood as residing in interactive processes and in – to use Bernard Williams' (2002) term – a spirit of 'truthfulness'. Truth is not an endpoint to be reached, where disputes and issues are finally settled, and accounts rendered, with some being declared bankrupt. Rather, it is a guiding light which always goes on ahead of us. In the process, we may even widen our sense as to what or who might be worthy co-travellers on the journey. We might even seek to argue for and from the glaciers and the rhinos, and so reflect an idea of truthfulness as *speaking-for-the-other*.

Criteria of truth jostle with each other, therefore. There are two ways of looking at this situation, the single ditch or the double ditch. Through much of his writings, Ernest Gellner (1969) pointed to the 'big ditch', by which he had in mind that between objective knowledge and relativism. On the one hand, a sense that there is available a set of techniques and instruments that produce objective truths about the world (not that, favouring Kant, Gellner felt that unalloyed truth could ever be obtained); on the other hand, a sense that no such techniques are available and all our so-called truths are theory-laden, are subtle carriers of hidden frameworks and are bound to bear the imprint of our social and psychological selves. Gellner was at pains to find a way through the quandary. We have to go forward carefully (the ratchet won't allow slipping back), and without hubris, given the difficulties of attaining truth about the world.

In Jürgen Habermas' early idea of 'knowledge-constitutive interests' (1978), there are *two* big ditches, with three forms of knowledge, each having its own embedded structure of interests, namely (i) technical-instrumental knowledge with an interest in control; (ii) hermeneutic knowledge, with an interest in meaning, interpretation and human understanding; and (iii) critical

58 *Foundations*

knowledge, with an interest in emancipation. These interests bequeath their own truth criteria, and so claims can be interrogated for the extent to which they enable control of the world, understandings of being human and enabling a freeing from hidden ideologies. But then, we may ask, do we not *also* need truth criteria to cope with contemplative knowledges (pure mathematics, algebra, logic, philosophy and possibly branches of cosmology, computer science and complexity studies), with explicitly performative knowledges (kinaesthetic, aesthetic, performing arts) and with processual and interactive knowledges (of those characteristic of the caring professions)?

It seems both that we cannot do without the category of truth in higher education *and* that it is impossible to say anything definitive about it. Should we, therefore, just keep our heads below the parapet and put the matter of truth to one side? It has always mattered but, in the current age, even more so: 'the truth of our beliefs is worth caring about' (Wrenn, 2015: 180). The university has become a recipient of global mistrust, and it is partly through a *suitable* idea of truth that the university will find its legitimation.

My own suggestion – floated earlier – is that of the idea of *truth-as-collective-argument*. But the idea would have to be filled out, for the kind of argument that is to be tolerated in the university is argument that gives way, that hears the other out without pulling down the shutters arbitrarily and does not *unduly* tread on toes (but a little toe-treading would be quite permissible). It would be a conception of truth-as-argument-that-opens, rather than as-argument-that-closes. It would be a conception of truth as embodied in the 'sharing of a form of life' (Vattimo, 2011: xxxi) that is held to be valuable.

Conclusions

Two hundred years ago, the founders of the modern university gave knowledge and truth attention, but, since then, these matters have been given a wide berth in thinking about higher education. It is time to re-attend to these two concepts, for their neglect has helped fuel fires that are being fanned in the direction of the university. Lacking any sure sense as to how knowledge and truth can be cashed out provides succour to those who see the university as bound by ideologies, as harbouring dubious interests, as promulgating mere opinions or as unable to escape charges of 'epistemic injustice', relativism or partiality.

Higher education is not in a good place to address such charges, and it senses its weaknesses on these matters. But there is one straw in the wind. Its very reluctance to face these matters have led it to be quite open epistemologically. The past half century or so has witnessed a steady flow of new epistemologies finding their way into the university – aesthetic, performative, processual, caring, digital, computational, multimodal, feminist and indigenous – all with their tacit understandings of truth. So there are epistemological riches to hand. The university is *already* home to an ecology of knowledges (cf. de Sousa Santos: 2016). Do we have to arbitrate between these forms of knowledge? We do not. To the contrary. The only condition is that claims to know must be willing to subject themselves to encounters from all points of view in an open and argumentative *institutionalised transdisciplinarity* (Baptista and Rojas-Castro, 2020) and never seek to vanquish (or 'cancel') other contenders. Generous knowledge openings and truth-as-argument might even help to lead to a better planet.

Part II
Key concepts

5 Research

Towards an ecological transdisciplinarity

Introduction

Extraordinarily, the concept of research rarely appears as a point of discussion within the philosophy of higher education. The justification for its absence could run as follows. Research is simply a name given to a diffuse set of practices in the university and although research might be linked to a number of concepts that have philosophical interest – knowledge, truth, autonomy, academic freedom and even spirit – in itself, it possesses no weight as a concept, and so it is rightly neglected. But this neglect is a large mistake.

Universities are characteristically understood in virtue of their involvement with research. In the English-speaking world, the terminology has emerged of 'research-led' or 'research-intensive' universities or even simply 'research universities' (Rhoten and Calhoun, 2011; Benson et al., 2017). World rankings give such high weightings to research that, in order to be well-placed in them, research has to have a highly significant presence in a university. Research, indeed, has come to constitute much of what is meant by the term 'university'. The term 'world-class' university is question-begging (Rider, 2020), but it has become influential, and it presumes an intimate connection with research.

Prima facie, this is extraordinary: of the twenty-five thousand or so universities in the world, it is perhaps in less than 2% of them that research takes up much of their efforts, and yet there is considerable overlap between what it means to be a university and the presence of research.

The idea of research cannot, therefore, be evaded in the philosophy of higher education, and once we put on our philosophical hats, a number of questions arise. What might count *as* research? Is it *necessarily* the case that a university should engage in research? Need there be *any* relationship between research and teaching? Nowadays, such questions have policy, evaluation and worldly implications.

The very idea of research

Although the term 'research' has been in circulation for hundreds of years, it was only in the eighteenth century that it began to acquire a general usage, when individuals possessed of liberty, wealth and education began to undertake their own amateur but often systematic inquiries. These amateur inquiries could be literary or cultural, but they were often early scientific investigations, in geology, natural history, chemistry or biology. 'Research' was a good term for it implied delving into entities or matters that were to hand and were usually part of life. Sometimes the findings, such as they were, were published in pamphlets.

Subsequently, the term *research* entered universities, gradually taking on a systematic presence through the nineteenth century. The impetus for this movement came from German philosophers of the late eighteenth and early nineteenth century, in developing ideas of the university (Östling, 2018: 29–35). For them, it was essential that the university was to be understood as a special space of intellectual freedom and where teaching and research were *conjoined*. Those ideas, together with the complex concept of *Bildung*, were picked up by the Prussian administrator, Wilhelm von Humboldt, in setting up the University of Berlin in 1810, so fuelling 'the research imperative' (Tenorth, quoted in Östling, ibid, 44).

Those German philosophers were idealists, seeing reason as a motor of human history and development and research as integral to its development (Ringer, 1990: 102–113). In that German conception, it was understood that research was quickly becoming specialised, but there was nevertheless a firm understanding that research should provide 'access to the whole of knowledge and the opportunity of exchange with all sorts of specialists' (Jaspers, 1965: 57). Crucially, it was fuelled by spirit, a supra-personal movement, without which inquiry was 'meaningless' (ibid, 103). Research had its value in opening to an interconnected universe of knowledge and so imparting a 'philosophical point of view' (ibid, 60).

This sketch raises a question: does the character of modern research dampen or enlarge its spirit? It may be increasingly voluminous – the research journals and their papers rise exponentially – but it lacks an element of collective *integration* and of reason feeding on reason. The forward movement anticipated by those German philosophers two hundred years ago may actually be dissipating, not least in contemporary audit environments leading to a risk-averse 'normalization' of research (Blake et al., 1998) and so leading to a fall in academic creativity (Murphy, 2018).

What is evident in this schematic history is that the idea of research has undergone continuing evolution and is *continuing to evolve*. As the twenty-first century passes, it can surely be ventured that, in using the term 'research', many have in mind systematic processes of inquiry in the natural sciences, usually in laboratories or other controlled situations, often requiring expensive and sometimes physically very large instrumentation, and involving collaboration across a large team (and perhaps across cross-national sets of teams). Papers – especially in the sciences – characteristically follow a tightly prescribed structure and are heavily mathematical, and the territory is digitally loaded. The majority of research papers (China now being the largest producer) have multiple authors, and, authorship of single papers may run to over one thousand names, a phenomenon of 'hyper-authorship', which is skewing evaluation of the 'impact' of research (O'Malley, 2019a).

Of course, not all research is of this ilk. The social sciences, for example, provide qualitative research. I would wager, however, that the *generally held* conception of research even there is that it is empirical, involving rigorous fieldwork with sophisticated methodologies, and is increasingly data-driven, dependent on digital processing. The structure of their papers typically follows that of the natural sciences. The humanities, too, are moving in this direction. The emerging idea of research would be likely to include, too, the presumption that that research is dependent upon external funding and so is 'income bearing'.

There is much empirical speculation in these last paragraphs. Still, I would draw four inferences. First, a *dominant imaginary* has arisen in which *bona fide* research is mathematically based, constitutes an inquiry into the external world, receives funding, is conducted in teams and leads to publications in refereed journals (with processes of peer review), relies on digital processing, deploys technical languages and obeys a standard pattern in the format of journal papers. These characteristics are associated with an ever-finer proliferation and differentiation of epistemic communities, with self-enclosed tendencies.

Second, this understanding is in motion, and with a certain impulse, due to large global movements in the production of knowledge and in academic publishing (which is itself dominated by a few corporations). Note that that phrase – 'the production of knowledge' – would have made no sense even in the 1950s. It has its place amid systematic, organised and large-scale processes of inquiry. Now, knowledge is to be *produced*, whereas once it would have been *revealed*. The modes of knowledge production are themselves all the time undergoing change, not least as a 'Mode 2' knowledge emerges, at once 'contextualised', operationally oriented and 'transgressive' (Gibbons et al., 1994; Nowotny et al., 2001) and preferably with both an immediate use and an exchange value.

Third, the dominant interests give high marks to science. It is costly and is closely associated with economic development; hence, the phrase 'the knowledge economy' is now being succeeded by 'cognitive capitalism' (Boutang, 2001). The short-term financial return on science-related research outstrips that of research in other areas, and so, despite its costs, huge resources are ploughed into science, technology, engineering and mathematics research. In turn, the acronym 'STEM' is commonly recognised across the world and some systems of higher education – especially that of China – are focused on STEM disciplines.

The problems of the humanities

Fourth, the humanities have a hard time. It is not even obvious that the humanities are felt to be a form of research. At one time, the term 'scholarship' was much used, but that term is becoming archaic as the practices that it designated have experienced a 'demise' (Rolfe, 2013: 17–19) and, so too, the notion of being a scholar. 'Scholastic reason' plays in its own 'field' (Bourdieu, 2000b), but few are interested in it. Scholarship, after all, rarely generates much of a financial return or has obvious *impact* in the wider world; certainly, not sufficient for a 'paper trail' that charts a clear link between scholarly endeavours and a specific change in the world. Scholarship may change utterly the way we think about ourselves, but thought cannot be seen, and so its significance can be easily downplayed.

There is, though, a separate feature of work not only in the humanities but also in the social sciences. Academic inquiry with a human orientation normally has a *locale*. It is a story of this tribe, or that social class, or this nation, or that ethnic group, or this gender or that historical period or a certain culture; whereas STEM research is couched in the (more or less) universal language of mathematics, work in the humanities is often conducted in local or national languages. The story of the women of cotton-mills in northern England in the nineteenth century (Morgan, 1992) gains a fascination precisely in virtue of its *specificity*. One can almost see the individual women as they labour in the routinised rhythms of the factories. An 'intersectionality' is heavily present here, as social class, gender, economic geography, physical geography, technologies and labour relations conspire together to produce a picture of a group of poorly paid women. But this very specificity renders that kind of research as having a lesser value (in many minds) than a scientific account of the natural world.

Science is quite different, its claims being assumed to be universal. Understand one molecule and one understands all such molecules. The social sciences find themselves in a liminal situation, being judged by the universality of science while sharing the particularity of the humanities. This is why doctorate students, having pursued qualitative studies, are subject to awkward questions near the end of their oral examinations about the transferability – or, usually, the *non*-transferability – of the central findings of their dissertations. And this context-specificity of the human sciences adds to the disregard in which they are often held.

The point of these reflections is not to wring one's hands yet again over the crisis in the humanities, which has actually faced it for nearly a century. Rather, it is to offer an *explanation* of this crisis and so account for the emergence of a sense that research and natural science are *coterminous*.

There are yet other explanations of the fate of the humanities. With their arcane languages and notations, the sciences attract an aura of specialness. Their opaqueness (to many) produces at once a respect and a distance. The humanities were once special, but, as Gellner (1964: 72) in effect put it, 'we are all clerks now.' Literacy abounds in society, whereas once it was rare. The immediacy of the humanities marks them out as familiar and – as in the adage – familiarity is liable to breed contempt. In an educated society, one can acquire languages; read the classics; go to libraries, museums and galleries;

and – provided one has the necessary funds – gain access to much of so-called high culture. Given a little effort, one can engage with the humanities, whereas a serious engagement with the natural sciences is out of the question. If research is understood as a delving into unknown worlds, then the humanities are going to come off badly, for they are assumed to be reflecting just on the here-and-now.

Furthermore, there is meaning in human affairs that is lacking in the natural world. Concepts such as trust, empathy, making promises and intention have no equivalent in the physical sciences. The 'double hermeneutic' element in the humanities – where the inquirer not only seeks an understanding of meanings but has her own meanings in understanding those meanings – is, for many, part of the intrigue of the humanities. However, for the sceptics, it becomes a symbol of the dubious character of the knowledge that they impart. Furthermore, rocks, wave patterns, quarks, black holes and stochastic patterns cannot speak back in quite the way that a human being – even a fictional character – may speak.

Another striking difference is evident in the matter of values. The sciences pretend to be value-free (while harbouring large value-laden interests). In contrast, the humanities wear their values on their sleeves, being not at all coy about their values. Indeed, they proudly proclaim them. This advocacy is understandable, for the humanities are under siege and feel a need to trumpet their values, sensing that they have few friends at court. They can be forgiven if they sometimes exaggerate their significance. After all, they sense – rightly – that they lack both economic power and cultural power (Bourdieu, 1990: 48).

The humanities have two kinds of values. They insist on their own epistemic values, the values that are inherent in working seriously in the humanities – of scrupulousness, care, sensitivity to language, criticality, integrity and so on. But they are also prone to declare their interests in wider societal values, of equity, of 'otherness', of hospitality to strangers, of a welcoming of difference and of citizenship and justice. They proclaim that they are essential to democracy (Nussbaum, 2010, but compare Small, 2013), to a re-composition of humanity (Braidotti, 2016) and even to 'everyday life' (Levenson, 2017), and, being so important, they require complete 'immunity' from whatever society might seek from them (Derrida, 2001a).

Whatever the merits of these special pleadings, the humanities open windows directly into human life. Whereas the laboratory is a cameo of an exercise of power and control over the environment, the humanities have a task that is both more modest and much larger. It is more modest because they wish merely to provide a pathway into a deeper understanding of what it is to be human. Normally, there is present no element of control. But their task is much larger for the humanities possess a depth that the sciences must lack. They allow humankind to share new meanings with humankind and so open directly *possibilities for humankind*. The humanities open glimpses into 'being-possible' (Heidegger, 1998).

Given a science-dominated sense of research, the humanities can do nothing right. Their inquiries are saturated with a conventional language (particularly a national language), and recognisable terminology, they wear their values on their sleeves, they focus their attention on particulars and tell us meaningful stories about those particulars (and so are non-universalisable) and they offer no powers of control over the world. *On every count, the humanities come up short*. They are clearly not candidates for the title of 'research'. No wonder that, from Beijing to Canberra, and from London to Washington, they come in for a hard time from the local Minister for Higher Education. Their work just does not count as research.

Recapitulation and development

To recap, the concept of research is in motion. It slid into the university in the early nineteenth century and continues to undergo change. In summing up the present state of play, we can do worse than recall a phrase already encountered, that of 'cognitive capitalism' (Boutang, 2011). Research has fallen prey to a global capitalism that is characterised by cognitions of various kinds, and, indeed, through its own 'academic capitalism' (Slaughter and Rhoades, 2009; Münch, 2020), research directly advances this new capitalism.

We have witnessed, therefore, the emergence of a 'global research culture', possessive of certain characteristics. It is a culture, however, that is subject to continuing change. Since Boutang advanced the idea of 'cognitive capitalism', the digital age has galloped onwards; a development that has given rise to the additional phrase 'algorithmic capitalism' (Peters, 2011b). We have here not only a supra-capitalist world (gaining rents from data) but also a fourth industrial revolution (4IR). The Internet of Things, surveillance cameras, self-monitoring devices, driverless cars, robots and so on are readily apparent. This seemingly irrevocable march of the digital world is one reason for some to speak of a 'post-human' world (Herbrachter, 2013). It is a world that, on some readings at least, is supplanting *human being* as such, as the analogue human is overtaken by digital processors, and presages the bio-digital manipulation of human beings.

At one level, research is tilted to reflect these digital developments, and we see this right across the disciplines, including the professional fields and the humanities, and it is splaying out into a *worldly* interdisciplinarity. Mediaeval bones were uncovered in the heart of England – as the result of work of local historians – and were subsequently determined to be the bones of the malevolent King, Richard III. The academic inquiry (mostly in the University of Leicester) involved bone anatomy, radio-carbon dating and DNA-sequencing, topographical analysis (pinpointing not just where on the battlefield the King was killed but the angle at which the fatal blow was struck), textual analysis of documents and social history. The bones were displayed in the local city of Leicester, with interested people forming an almighty queue, and subsequently the bones were interred in the city's cathedral amid much pomp and pageantry, and doubtless the ringing of tills in the locality.

It is evident, then, that the concept of research is continuously in motion, the latest incarnations of the concept shifting in the direction of digital processors. *Bona fide* research is expected to generate great data banks, but now, too, in order really to win its spurs, it is assumed that research should spill over into the economy, which is increasingly a digital economy. The digital – we can now use the term as a noun – claws at research to claim it as its own. And in this enveloping of the digital, speed becomes power (Virilio, 2005), a pattern that is affecting the legitimation of knowledge claims. The two-year wait for publication in 'world-leading' journals is giving way to swifter means of publication.

But this intermingling of research, the digital and the economy, is only a sub-sub-story here, the sub-story being that, as with all concepts, the concept of research is dynamic and is always on the move. However, there is a larger story still.

Two hundred years ago, research was understood to consist of a rooting around in texts, but texts are no longer to be *seen* as such in digitally based academic inquiry. Even scholars in the humanities are less prone to possess a personal library of books. BC (before computers), one might have difficulty in entering the room of an academic in the humanities, with books and papers strewn across the floor, as well as looming at one, from floor to ceiling (if not also on shelving built within the space of the room itself). Now, that experience is passé as the digital makes available an inexhaustible cornucopia of texts. With a laptop, Chaucer's modern-day clerk can continue her learning – and her teaching – wherever she may be.

Scholarly considerations

A contemporary Internet notice of a conference is entitled '*Cambridge: City of Scholars, City of Refuge (1933-1945)*'. That title conjoins mention of 'scholars' with a period of war and turbulence in the mid-twentieth century, and there is nothing especially strange in that. On the contrary, conjoining a university in fenland England with the suggestion that it was *then* a city of scholars – and a refuge for scholars at that – is immediately understandable. However, today, much more likely would be the title 'Cambridge: City of *Research*'.

There are major fault-lines here. Some believe that, in order to justify the title 'university', research should be heavily present, and, on this view, 'teaching university' is an oxymoron. Others deny that, not least since that only a tiny fraction of the world's universities are research-intensive. The way to pass through the eye of this needle lies, it is suggested, in the idea of scholarship. Scholarship denotes a love of texts, and a close, careful and critical reading of them. It conjures a capacity to see beyond a situation and have at one's fingertips a battery of conceptual, theoretical and, indeed, empirical resources to bring to bear (Rhode, 2006). Such a scholarship is associated with a calling higher even than research, namely that of wisdom.

That idea of scholarship has given way to 'research'. Academics would much rather term themselves as a 'researcher' than a 'scholar', the term 'scholar' now having become archaic. The scholar is felt to dwell in the past, whereas 'research' at least holds out the hope of something new being uncovered; perhaps a genomic sequence or a planetary body or the solution to a longstanding mathematical problem or a cure for a particular cancer. Efforts may be made to retain the idea of scholarship with terms such as 'scholarly enquiry' (cf. Rowland, 2006) or even 'scholarly research', but they fail to catch on. It is empirical research that counts, and so we see such neologisms as 'pedagogical research', arising especially out of idea of the scholarship of teaching and learning inspired by Boyer (1990).

There is now talk of 'slow scholarship', 'slow' being understood not so much in terms of pace but more in terms of attentiveness, carefulness, diligence, deliberation and thoughtfulness (Leibowitz and Bozalek, 2018). This is very curious, that it needs to be suggested that scholarliness should be accompanied by these qualities, for that is what is – or, at least, was – meant by 'scholarship'. That there is a need to pump up such virtues shows just how much scholarship – insofar as there remains a place for it – is now subject to the machinery of efficiency, sheer performance and output that dominates academic work across the globe. Fast scholarship has become a fact rather than the oxymoron that it deserves to be seen as.

Some meanings are more meaningful than others

The deep story here is *not* of a simple revolution; of the concept of research having one interpretation and giving way rather swiftly to another interpretation. Concepts are not typically like that for they swirl in constellations, their orbits intersecting, as the modes of life that they represent also intersect, and as they form new connections with the world.

Here, we have to make two further moves. First, the term 'research' has witnessed several offshoots. 'Research' is held to be synonymous with science, with projects that attract income to a university, with laboratory work, texts composed of arcane symbols, systematic efforts to produce new knowledge across all disciplines, large-scale and visible activities (as in 'science parks'), academic inquiry that can be measured in some way (where there might be 'metrics') and academic projects that have manifest 'impact'. But the concept of research is also widening, to embrace ensembles with practical, ecological, feminist and interdisciplinary leanings, and even human states – such as wellbeing – attract attention.

The concept of research, then, is being stretched this way and that, as a child might pull out a piece of plasticine in different directions. It possesses a dominant set of interpretations, but multiple interpretations co-develop, with research being understood – and practised – quite differently across intellectual fields. The scholar of Bach's music conducts her research not only in musty collections in and around German churches and not only in raiding Internet archives, but also in her efforts in performing the music on an early music instrument or in imaginatively deploying musical software.

However, and second, the concept of research moves on a sloping discursive landscape with some interpretations carrying more force than others. In its dominant interpretation, as noted, 'research' is understood to be associated with the natural sciences, mathematics, highly controlled spaces (affording 'replicability'), big data and large group activity. This movement is backed by large interests that straddle politics, industry (and particular industries at that), the military, and communications and technology. The idea of research changes to reflect these concentrations of cognitive power such that science, research and knowledge form a tight nexus (Rouse, 1987). As a bearer, therefore, of large and often undisclosed and collective interests, we are entitled to consider, when we hear talk of 'research', that we are in the presence of an ideology. Paul Feyerabend said as much over a generation ago (1978), and that story has been compounded ever since.

Lessons from a global crisis

As this is being written, the world is in the grip of a pandemic, the Coronavirus – Covid-19. It is a virus that implicates virology, biology, medicine, the human body, statistics, engineering, health policy and organisation, transnational relations, culture, zoology, agricultural practices, food distribution, human rights, animal rights, the state and its relationships with the polity, societal communication, responses to aloneness (as well as impending death), wellbeing, the matter of community, being a professional, the role of public intellectuals, decision-making (at personal, family, organisational, national and world levels), matters of citizenship and fairness *and many other matters*. In short, the virus is testimony to the interconnectedness of the world and is a wonderful example of the assemblages and networks to which Latour (2007) and DeLanda (2013) have directed our attention and it is testimony, too, to the idea of trajectory, with which Latour has been developing his whole philosophy of networks (Latour et al., 2011: 48). In sight is a maze of vibrant networks.

There are a number of features of this maze. *No one point of entry can claim to be the main entrance* (Latour et al., 2011). There are innumerable entrances, and each may claim our attention. Moreover, there are *four classes of entities* in this maze – the physical world, the human world, the animal world and the world of ideas and concepts – and *each of these worlds has causal effects on the others*. It appears that ideas within cultures about food have been influential not only in encouraging animal–human transmission but also that those practices have been encouraged by global food supply chains that have disrupted local agricultural and food hygiene practices. The resulting disease has in turn formed geographical patterns of human transmission, especially by air travel. In turn, scientists have worked – with varying degrees of global cooperation – to unravel the structure of the virus, and health and social care, and political systems respond in their different ways. In turn, human rights, citizenship, the public good and personal responsibility provoke public debate.

All these entities, and others, are interwoven. It is not only that parts of the natural and human worlds collide but that, unwittingly, ideas themselves (in cultural traditions, in the lifeworld) contribute to the behaviour of the virus. And ideas in turn – in medical science and the social sciences – can *alter* the flow of the virus. To put it more formally, the worlds of the real and of ideas interact, with flows going in both directions (recall our diagram, Figure 2.1, page 34). Academic inquiry can intentionally be turned upon – and have 'impact' on – the *real*.

Indeed, *all* of the matters just identified are objects of academic enquiry, of medicine, statisticians, virologists, biochemists, engineers, food distribution analysts, political scientists, modellers, sociologists, psychologists, geographers, historians and philosophers. It is evident that no satisfactory understanding of the virus can be attained within a single discipline. Moreover, the disciplines themselves are *actors*, with their pronouncements having causal effects on the very situation that they are trying to understand, a situation that compounds the epistemological complexity in question.

This is *doubly* a complex *ecological situation*. At one level, it is a matter of and for the *knowledge ecology*: what are its constituents? What are and what could be their interconnections? Is something awry in the way in which this knowledge ecology is working? Where is it impaired? But this situation is ecological in an even larger sense.

We have here a *general ecological situation* with its interconnected entities of research, and knowledge, and their interactions with the world. It is complex for there are multiple *open* ecosystems of the physical world, the animal world, the human world, social institutions, and thought about the world, both informally in the general public and formally, across academic fields of many kinds. The complexities are multiple and real. Research endeavours can affect the world, in human biology, behaviour and social and psychological dimensions, *whether these effects are intended or not*. There are qualities of emergence here. Situation X prompts situation Y, but situation Y cannot be foretold. The elements and their interactions are too complicated for that. Connectivity, complexity, motion, indeterminacy and emergence are fundamental aspects of the world (cf. Maccarini, 2014), and, so too, are our sensations of the world (Harman, 2018: 159), and it is a world in which the university both has its being and seeks to understand and to act.

Conclusions

The modern concept of research is only two hundred years old and is continually in motion. Two movements are evident, and they are in tension with each other. On the one hand, the concept of research has been colonised by the physical sciences and their cognate fields (collectively known as STEM) and is narrowing further in being strongly associated with the digital revolution, databanks, and surveillance technologies and with the growth of biopower. Logics of algorithmic and information capitalism are at play. BUT, alongside this cognitive ideology, research is acquiring new forms as disciplines, activities and interests intermingle in *cognitive-practical complexes*.

The hope must be that this latter movement, and with it the concept of research, will continue to widen. If the natural world and the human world are interconnected (as various crises reveal), it follows that efforts to comprehend the world have also to be *re*-connected. All the disciplines have to be understood as contributing to a single endeavour, that of speaking for and even *from* the world (Bengtsen, 2014: 187). In their different ways, the humanities, the social sciences, the physical sciences and the professional fields should be speaking from the glaciers and the rhinos, and for the voiceless, the dispossessed and the vulnerable.

It follows that the idea of research has to be understood as working at three levels of: (i) individual disciplines and fields; (ii) their pooling their resources in open-ended ways and so possessing qualities of cognitive-practical emergence; and (iii) working under the aegis of the *transdisciplinary value of concern for the world*, a shorthand for which would be *ecological transdisciplinarity* (cf. Nicolescu, 2014, 2016). Unless research is understood and reconfigured in this way, it will fall short of its responsibilities and its possibilities.

6 Culture

Sighting a culture of constructive argument (CCA)

Introduction

'"Culture" is said to be one of the two or three most complex words in the English language.' So Terry Eagleton opens his (2000) book on *The Idea of Culture*. If that is the case – and it surely *is* the case – how much more problematic must it be to place the idea of culture in the company of higher education and universities. Are we to dwell on culture *within* higher education and universities *or* is the key matter one of how universities connect with culture in the wider world? Or is the main issue that of *educational processes* as cultural activities as against the university as a cultural *institution*? And having regard to educational processes, do some disciplines offer a connection with culture more markedly than others?

I shall say something about all these matters, but I would just offer this preliminary observation. To my knowledge, no major work has *ever* been published with a title such as *Culture and the University*, and, while there have been some sorties on *some* aspects of this matter (Becher, 1989; Sporn, 1996; Becher and Trowler, 2001; Valimaa and Ylijoki, 2008), it has not been tackled systematically. If that is right, the university has been somewhat non-reflexive about its own cultural self.

The Eagleton–Scruton debate

A good starting point for our inquiry is what might be termed the Eagleton-Scruton debate. Terry Eagleton, as we have already noted, is a leading cultural analyst, for whom culture is present in many forms simultaneously, each of which deserves critical scrutiny, of the postmodernists no less than the marketers. Roger Scruton was an unashamedly conservative (English) philosopher, who spent much effort in arguing for culture; culture with a capital C, as it were. For Scruton, culture was the embodiment of all that is enduring and is among the best contributions that humanity has made to life on this planet; indeed, it has played a very large part in forming humanity, in constituting what it is to be human.

Scruton's (2016) perspective is not uncritical; to the contrary, it is thoroughly critical, in allowing for judgements as to what is truly to count as

DOI: 10.4324/9781003102939-9

culture in its best forms – 'high culture' (149) – albeit as judged by a few. So the difference between Eagleton and Scruton lies not in one being critical and the other not, but in the *purposes* to which that critical capacity is directed. Whereas Scruton is wanting to conserve and legitimise *elite* culture – albeit giving it a role in uniting peoples 'as living here and now' (80) – Eagleton is more interested in understanding the changes to culture, especially the ways it splays out and buttresses a marketised society while still providing spaces for other cultural formations. Indeed, Eagleton ends his book (2000: 129) with no less than a fourfold division of culture: culture as civility, identity, commercialism and radical protest.

The one (Scruton) appears to be normative while the other (Eagleton) is self-evidently analytical. However, the approaches of both Eagleton and Scruton are *both* analytical *and* normative. Eagleton's normativity is more implicit, but it opens issues about the role that culture *could* be providing in society. In short, both Eagleton and Scruton are at once critical, normative and analytical, so the fundamental difference between them cannot lie in those three moments.

On what, then, does this disagreement between Eagleton and Scruton turn? I suggest that the difference is *temporal*. As remarked, Scruton was a self-proclaimed conservative philosopher, wishing to preserve that which is best in *past* human endeavour. On the other hand, while much of Eagleton's scholarship has historical components, one senses a restless drive to help the world to move *forward*. His extraordinary analytical powers – whether in looking at religions, fiction, theories, historical episodes and even his sympathy for Christianity – have been deployed to identify possibilities for societal development. The distinction here, then, lies in approaching culture to *conserve* what is felt to be the best of enduring traditions and looking to culture to find *new* spaces in and for the world.

Robbins or Readings – who was right?

These features – the *normative/analytical* distinction and the *temporal* perspective – can be seen in two influential conceptions of the relationship between culture and higher education.

In the United Kingdom in the 1960s, a major policy report identified four aims of higher education, one of which was 'the transmission of a *common culture*' (Robbins, 1963: 7 [RB's emphasis]). A generation later, in a justly acclaimed book, Bill Readings (1997) considered that the link between universities and culture had been severed. We have here, therefore, both a sense that a common culture can and *should* constitute a central aim of higher education, *and* a view that an unbridgeable gulf has opened between universities and culture. How might we explain this profound difference of view? Is it that the world moved on, with large transformations having profoundly affected the relationship between universities and culture? Or is it that these two views represent a great polarity in understanding culture?

Robbins was representative of the prestigious parts of higher education in the UK and had led a national commission inquiring into UK higher education at the very moment of its transition – in Martin Trow's (1970) terminology – from elite to mass higher education (which many countries were then undergoing). His call for higher education to be seen as the transmission of a common culture was surely intended to do two things. First, one aim was to play up the role of higher education as a unifying institution in society, not least at a time of a growing liberalism and multiculturalism, and cultural and social experimentation. Second, it was to ensure that higher education, on the eve of its eruption into a mass system, might sustain a unity of purpose across the whole higher education system (which then in the UK included a large polytechnic and vocationally oriented college sector).

The intention here, therefore, was *normative*. Robbins (and his Committee, despite the social exclusivity of its members) must have felt that, in what was already a multi-cultural and multi-ethnic society, higher education had a particularly important function in helping to furnish and to 'transmit' something of a common culture. Robbins' *temporal frame* was of the moment *and* the future. The Robbins Report – for all of its length and numerous researches reflected in twenty-plus appendices – was a manifesto for a *future* unitary culture.

The university: a culture-free zone

Readings' position was quite different, being more *analytical*. For Readings, the idea of a tight connection between universities and culture was just one of three large ideas of the modern university, they being 'the Kantian concept of reason, the Humboldtian idea of culture, and now, the techno-bureaucratic notion of excellence' (14). Our interest here lies in that second idea, the Humboldtian idea of culture. Wilhelm von Humboldt was the founder of the University of Berlin in 1810 (Wyatt, 1994; Östling, 2018), and Kant, who died in 1804, did not live to see its founding. In that sense, therefore, we can say that the Humboldtian idea of culture succeeded the Kantian concept of reason, but we may also observe that the two ideas overlapped both in time and conceptually. It follows that the modern idea of the university – the bureaucratic, corporate, economic and informatically driven idea of the university of the late twentieth century and early twenty-first century – has had two intertwined strands in its foundations, namely reason *and* culture.

For Readings, the relationship between culture and the university had a double articulation. In one articulation, culture is a matter of national identity, and this was to be developed through reason. Even in the late eighteenth and early nineteenth centuries, the separate disciplines were beginning to be formed, so leading to much defending of epistemic turf and, in Kant's famous formulation, to '*The Conflict of the Faculties*' (still with us, although with philosophy deposed from its self-proclaimed superiority). However, in

Germanic philosophy, all knowledges were part of *Wissenschaft* (Ringer, 1990), and so, despite the hierarchy, there was a unity in inquiry.

In the other articulation, culture was a matter of 'the cultivation of character – *Bildung*' (64). In universities, this character was to be developed through 'the synthesis of teaching and research' (65). This joint presence of teaching and research was pivotal since it was through this co-presence that 'the University produces not servants but subjects.' And, for Readings, this 'is the point of [a] pedagogy of *Bildung*, which teaches knowledge acquisition as a *process* rather than … as a product' (67). In this process – as Humboldt (2018) put it himself – universities conceive of science and scholarship as 'inexhaustible tasks', their students being 'engaged in an unceasing process of inquiry' (cited in Peters and Barnett, 2018: 47).

In both of its articulations – forging a national identity through reason *and* the cultivating the individual student's character – this University of Culture has been extinguished. The university has become *a culture-free zone*. In university websites, one looks in vain to see mention of universities seeing themselves as having cultural responsibilities, in either of the two senses of the Humboldtian university (the cultivation either of national identity or of personal character). Indeed, the very juxtaposition of 'university' and 'culture' tends to produce a nervousness, unless placed in a particular context, such as the study of culture (in anthropology or cultural studies), a university's interactions with cultural institutions or in recognising the many cultures of its students. The issue remains, therefore, as to whether that juxtaposition – 'culture' and 'university' – can make sense in the twenty-first century.

Fault-line

A fault-line is emerging here: (i) 'culture' and 'higher education' reside in separate conceptual waters and to overlap them is to commit a category mistake, OR (ii) higher education is separate from but has *an irradicable connection with* culture.

The separateness thesis: Higher education is a largely technical matter of acquiring knowledge and skills. Culture is not a matter for universities (except as an object of study, in anthropology, aesthetics and cultural studies). Teachers have to focus on learning outcomes and should not concern themselves with culture. Furthermore, the conduct of universities lies in the management of technical matters – finance, external contracts, administrative systems and so on. Justifiably, mention of 'culture' has no place in university websites.

The connectedness thesis: Higher education cannot but be concerned with culture for it is a cultural process. Both the Germanic idea of *Bildung* – and its Scandinavian cognates – and the English idea of liberal education (expressed by Newman, 1873; Arnold, 1932; Eliot, 1948; Leavis, 1943, 1969; and Oakeshott, 1989, among others) invoked culture, both internally (in the educational process) and externally (in what the graduate takes into society).

Culture permeates higher education: an education in the arts or science *is* a cultural process.

Moreover, it is argued, and with justification, that culture is evermore present, higher education across much of the world having become subject to 'the politics of corporate culture' (Giroux, 2001), a culture that has found its way – via the ideology of neoliberalism (Giannakakis, 2019) – even into the heart of higher education. 'Entrepreneurialism' and 'innovation' become explicit features of the curriculum, but, more insidiously, students are encouraged to see themselves as consumers of an education in which they can express their wants and their consumer rights. Higher education, as an educational process, has become a site of 'cultural pedagogy' (McClaren, 1995).

On *both* sides of this divide – culture and the university as separate *and* as integral (and whether benign *or* injurious) – lies a crucial distinction: *on the one hand*, culture in the wider society and the university's responsibility towards that wider culture, and, *on the other hand*, culture understood as a cultivation, *within* the university, of a student's character. The distinctiveness of these two paths has not often been acknowledged, still less their co-presence and their relationships.

The assumptions implicit in the first set of ideas – that it made sense to speak of a common culture in a modern pluralist society *and* that there lay a responsibility upon higher education to advance it – have disappeared and many will think 'and justifiably so'. Modernity is pluralist, and, if universities have a responsibility towards the wider culture of society, it is to reflect and even to celebrate its *many* cultures, whether of a racial, ethnic, gender, religious, indigenous, epistemic or other origin. If culture is to have a place in higher education, then it has to be that of multi-culture or even some kind of inter-culture or trans-culture.

To use a metaphor, the common culture branch of the university and culture has fallen off, lying in the forest and quite dead, but many other shoots are springing up around it. A university with students from many nations is happy to be a space for multi-ethnic and multi-religious events, celebrating and exhibiting cuisines, music and rituals of many cultures. Universities with indigenous communities on their doorstep are becoming active in reaching out to them, sensitive to their cultural traditions. Far from the university being a site of a common culture, now it is proudly a site of *many* cultures (even if it shrinks from the term 'culture' as such).

Cultivating the student's character

And what of that other path, in construing the relationship between higher education and culture as the cultivation of the individual student's character? Actually, that path goes in two directions, one that links the cultivation of character to 'virtues', felt to derive from the student going deeply into a discipline or field, and a much less trodden line in intimating that the university as such is a cultural site.

The virtues approach takes its cue especially from Alisdair MacIntyre, the central idea being that there are worthwhile human qualities – or virtues – that are inherent to the practices of higher education; they are 'internal goods'. Moreover, it is the task of universities to orchestrate themselves such that they promote human virtues among all their students.

This line of inquiry sets up several issues. For example, which are the virtues that are *especially* to be prized and, then, on which grounds? Are the virtues – whichever they are – to be developed primarily through the *content* of the student's programme (and so a matter of curriculum) or are they primarily to be elicited in the *educational process* (and so a matter of pedagogy), and not only between the teacher and the student but also between the students themselves? In principle, can the virtues be developed in any programme of study or are they more easily developed within *certain* disciplines? (Do quantum mechanics, civil engineering, ancient history, management studies, modern languages, legal studies, and sports science offer equal opportunities for such virtues to be acquired?)

Here arises a major issue in the cultivation of virtues. Are they more enhanced in programmes of study *or* in the life of the university at large? Just as Gorky spoke of his experience of life as *his* universities, so it may be more the university as an *institution* that is responsible for advancing the student's virtuous character. However, a nuanced situation surely confronts us. *Some* virtues emerge naturally from an exposure to the disciplines – for example, truthfulness, inquisitiveness and criticality – and so form '*epistemic virtues*' (Brady and Pritchard, 2003). *Other* virtues, of conviviality, tolerance and openness, derive much more from being in a large educational organisation for some years, in the presence of others (often from many countries) and being granted a significant degree of distance from the world (in Oakeshott's [1989] memorable phrase, 'the gift of the interval').

The jury has yet to adjudicate these two matters, those of (i) disentangling the respective cultural contributions in being a student in a programme of study in higher education *and* in being a member of the complex institution that is the university and (ii) the differences *between* the disciplines in their contribution to the cultural formation of students. (In fact, the jury has barely begun to consider either case.)

On the latter issue, it is surely apparent that disciplines *do* vary in the pattern of virtues that they are prone to uphold *and* that there are more possibilities for some virtues – say, of diligence, fortitude, courage, persistence, carefulness and so on – being acquired across *all* of the disciplines than is often acknowledged. Many who write from *within* the humanities seem to believe that the humanities are uniquely placed in furthering all the virtues, but that argument cannot hold water. Furthermore, the *pedagogical relationship is surely more influential than the curriculum* in promoting the student's virtues, and, so again, cultural resources are to be found in all disciplines.

However, institutions of higher education also possess considerable *cultural powers* in their own right. As large organisations, often with students from all over the world and many open events, debates and activities – especially those that possess a culture of openness, interaction and critical debate – universities can do much to help students in their taking on virtues, irrespective of – and, all too often, in spite of – the often rather closed experiences within their study programmes. Particular virtues emerging from universities as *institutions* are those of tolerance, openness, adventurousness, resourcefulness, resilience, hospitality and friendliness. (This is not to claim that these virtues are universally cultivated by universities.) The student who remarks to her parents at the graduation ceremony that 'being here has changed my life' may be acknowledging that it was the university as such – *much* more than her programme of study – that helped in her becoming a person in her own right.

Another branch here is that of '*Bildung*' (which, for Readings, formed a main plank of the University of Culture). It is often observed that the idea of *Bildung* is notoriously difficult, difficulties that are compounded when in the context of higher education. In it are to be found the student becoming an autonomous subject, the formation of the student's character and the student coming into a proper relationship with the state, becoming a citizen, emancipation and acquiring a free mind of reason (Ringer, 1990). With so many elements jostling, it was inevitable that, from its inception in the early nineteenth-century Germany, there have been differences of view as to which elements are to be seen as primary. Moreover, the concept continues to undergo evolution, it being always reinterpreted for its age (Løvlie and Standish, 2003). Not yet an empty signifier, *Bildung* can be put to multiple uses.

All this raises a further matter on which we should alight, namely the relationship between *Bildung* and liberal education. John Henry Newman's mid-nineteenth-century work, *The Idea of a University*, has received much praise as the most eloquent expression of liberal education. For Newman, not only was the university a place both of liberal education and of culture but the two tasks were one and the same. Newman had had the discipline of investing himself in prodigious and arduous amounts of study – as well as being a theologian, writer and poet, he was a dedicated scholar, pushing himself, even as a student, to undergo upwards of ten hours of serious reading each day (Faber, 1954) – and this ascetic way of life was reflected in his educational thinking about the university. The university (Newman, 1976) was to be a place for the 'cultivation of mind' through 'work of discipline and habit' so as to acquire 'a philosophical outlook'. This was a liberal education in the sense that knowledge was 'its own end'. However, the idea of liberal education possesses its own ambiguities – as to whether the implied freedom is one of personal autonomy in the pedagogical *process* or a matter of an autonomous mind emerging from exposure to reason-based forms of *knowledge*.

In sum then, the ideas both of *Bildung* and liberal education are susceptible to multiple interpretations. *Bildung* has its place amid social traditions and service to the state and, therefore, is attuned to culture in the wider society, whereas liberal education is more interested in the education of the individual and of the cultivation of his or her mind. But both are seized of the student not only being free but becoming a subject through their own efforts. *Bildung*, it might be said, is the richer concept of the two, since it harbours the dual senses of culture, not only the cultivation of a rational mind but also the culture of the wider society. But these can only be suggestions since the relationship between *Bildung* and liberal education, especially in the context of higher education, has yet seriously to be investigated.

Retrospect, development and prospect

To recap, from the late eighteenth to the first half of the twentieth century, it was considered that higher education had an important connection with culture; *directly*, by enabling students to be encultured through the development of their reasoning powers within the disciplines; and *indirectly*, with universities reflecting and enhancing the culture of the wider society. The critical reasoning of students as graduates would spill over into society and so enable *society* to go on becoming ever more imbued with the spirit of critical reason.

On this understanding, the university possessed two cultural functions – the cultivation of students' minds and enhancing culture in the wider world – and these two functions were organically interconnected as species of the continuing project of Enlightenment. Through the university's cultural functioning, society would be helped in becoming a growing place of autonomous reason. The connecting tissue between these two ideas – culture in higher education and the advancement of culture in the wider society – lay in a largely unspoken assumption that students would emerge from the university as *cultural citizens*, able to handle themselves as persons sensitive to others in a globalised world (Nussbaum, 2010, 2018).

This set of ideas was born out of a society that was more or less held together by a set of broadly held worldviews, *and* in which universities recruited from a narrow social class base, already possessed of 'cultural capital' (Bourdieu and Passeron, 1990). Under such conditions, it made some kind of sense – as we saw – for a major national report to urge that higher education had, as a principal aim, that of the transmission of a common culture. Students were to be the recipients of *and* the flagbearers for that common culture. But even then, the very idea of culture, and certainly that of a common culture, was becoming an object of suspicion. And this severing of culture and the university was explicitly noted, with regret, by Readings, the university – as a 'post-historical' institution – having become a culture-free zone.

This tension between the modern university and culture has long roots. It was a long-running theme in the writings of the polymath Ernest Gellner that the Enlightenment, with its emphasis on reason, in effect eschewed culture, and doubly so. Descartes' famous cry, '*Cogito ergo sum*' – 'I think, therefore I am' – was a claim that, with reason on her or his side, the educated person had no need of resources other than pure reason (Gellner, 1992). Far from seeing reason as constitutive of culture, it placed reason and culture in different domains, and reason was felt to be all-powerful while culture was wanting.

Subsequently, this philosophical perspective was reinforced socially. 'The two cultures' debate of the 1960s and 1970s emphasised that reason came not in 57 varieties but in just two, of science and the humanities (Snow, 1978). The humanities had long assumed that they were the bearers of cognitive culture, but it was all a bit desperate. Rearguard actions have been and still are being fought, but, *on the terms in which that battle is being fought*, it was bound to end in tears. Whatever the efforts of the humanists have been – with their spokespersons in quite different camps (the cultural elitism of Leavis [1979], the cultural ambiguities of Derrida [2001] and the cultural citizenship of Nussbaum [2010]) – as a matter of fact, it is science that has triumphed. Moreover, increasingly it is the *particular* clustering of sciences that afford bio and informatic power that have emerged as fuelling the dominant culture. When we are told that 'we listen to the science,' it is *particular* sciences and particular scientists that are being heard. The pendulum has swung: *now* to be educated is to understand the dance of the molecules and electrons and their digital manipulation.

Culturally, therefore, the world has moved on since the 1960s so rendering talk of *Bildung* and liberal education obsolete, and the philosophy of higher education *should* leave these two ideas behind. The idea of a universal idea of culture – of the kind that propped up both of those concepts – is problematic, for society has long been *multi*-cultural, with all manner of groupings, often in tension with each other. In turn, 'culture' gives rise to sensitivities over exclusion, multiculturalism, culture wars and even colonisation *and* coloniality.

There *is* overlap between higher education and culture, but it is now a matter for sociology, focusing internally on the epistemic cultures across the disciplines (Becher and Trowler, 2001; Kreber, 2009), externally, in the 'cultural capital' that universities offer to the wider world (Bourdieu, 2000b), and on the 'culture complex' (Bennett, 2013) that has grown up between the cultural disciplines of the academy and the cultural apparatuses of the wider society, or, even more widely, as the universities in the Global North are felt to impose their cognitive cultures upon the Global South. Crudely, as a proposition in social theory, we can say that the university is a site of *five spaces of culture*: communicative, cognitive, material, expressive and practical (Barnett, 2018c). However, there seems to be no ground on which a *conceptual* relationship between the university and culture can be defended, but such a judgement would be premature.

A culture of constructive argument (CCA)

In his (1979) book, *The Future of Intellectuals and the Rise of the New Class*, Alvin Gouldner observed the emergence of a 'new class' composed of both critical intellectuals *and* a technical intelligentsia. 'Both are committed to CCD', that is to a culture of critical discourse. Surely, Gouldner was mistaken: whereas the critical intellectuals *are* signed up to a culture of critical discourse and societal reflexivity, it is doubtful that the technical intelligentsia have even any *wish* to be such signatories.

However, the idea of a culture of critical discourse prompts the idea that there just might be a common discursive culture in universities. We can term this – as an opening gambit – a culture of *rational* discourse. Cues for this idea can be dredged from the work of Jürgen Habermas and could be said to be constituted by conditions of equal participation (the student can critique the professor), of truthfulness (there being a critical dialogue between the participants) and of sincerity (for the most part, participants can be relied upon to mean what they say). At its root, this form of life relies on – to steal from Habermas (1984: 24) – 'the force of the better argument'.

There is deep within universities – and as we may term it for our next move – a *culture of constructive argument* (CCA). The idea of argument is crucial here. At its heart lies neither – as Habermas has been wont to suggest – a collective drive towards consensus (which may or may not transpire) – nor even the giving and taking of reasons, *necessary* though that is (chapter 4). What is central is the production of *further* reasons or even *counter*-reasons. These further or counter-reasons are put up not for mere enjoyment or to offend but to press the debate or inquiry forward, even if they shatter the possibility of consensus.

Such a culture of constructive argument calls for a societal space to be accorded both to universities as institutions *and* to the pedagogical relationship in programmes of study. There are, therefore, implications both for overbearing states and for any who would prevent argument from ever getting going whoever they may be.

Conclusions

Readings was doubly wrong. Neither the university as an institution *nor* higher education as a set of educational processes is devoid of culture. To the contrary, in a pluralist world, in an institution of many disciplines, socioeconomic classes and ethnicities, and management styles, the university is a place of cultures (and many more than just 'six cultures'; Berquist and Pawlak, 2008). Moreover, it has manifold connections with the wider world and so projects different forms of cultural capital into the world. The university and higher education cannot but be spaces of cultures, and, indeed, five such spaces were identified here.

The question is whether anything approaching culture with a capital C can be detected. Is there a unifying idea of culture that can hold across both the educational process that constitutes higher education and the university as a major sociocultural institution, *and* that ought to be held out for and defended if necessary? I have suggested that there is and that it can be located in a *culture of constructive argument*.

This idea has a number of merits. A culture of constructive argument (CCA) could serve as a meta-culture under which cultures (plural) can play out in the university: assenting to the rules of the CCA would be a condition of entry. *This* idea of culture could be evident in educational processes across disciplines and professional fields; it could do justice to the cultivation of the student (enabling the student to become his or herself as a person); and it could crystallise the cultural value of the university in enhancing the public domain as a space of democratic argument. In a world of increasing surveillance – in which certain ideas and positions are prevented from being heard – a culture of constructive argument in higher education may be a necessary condition even for the survival of the world itself.

7 Academic freedom – and academic responsibility

> Our task is ... to give a new definition to academic freedom.
> Hans-Georg Gadamer (2018/1992: 130), *'The Idea of the University, Yesterday, Today, Tomorrow'*

Introduction

The matter of academic freedom has been in play for over two hundred years, and it remains vibrant. Indeed, of late, it has become as lively a topic as ever, not least following reports of attacks on members of universities (O'Malley, 2019b), and a number of major scholarly volumes have appeared (Bowen et al., 2014; Berubé and Ruth, 2015; Bilgrami and Cole, 2015). The matter has been taken up in the law courts (Wright, 2007), been a topic of large cross-national empirical research (Karran et al., 2017), served as the basis of cross-national declarations (Global Forum, 2019; Bonn Declaration, 2020) and been the subject of an influential statement issued in 2014 by the University of Chicago.

In its turbulent history, the idea of academic freedom has had three incarnations (which we shall come to). Nevertheless, some questions seem to be perennial. Does the idea of academic freedom still have value? Is it an absolute idea or is it relative to contexts? *Who* might be said to have a right to academic freedom? Do students have this right? Does the idea of academic freedom play differently as between teaching and research? Might a *visitor* to a university speaker justifiably claim a right to academic freedom? Does academic freedom bring any *duties*? On all of these matters there is dispute.

Before getting going, I would just observe that the concept of academic freedom presents a nice cameo of the plot of this book, namely, that the philosophy of higher education has to be not only a social philosophy but also to be realist. We cannot sensibly propose meanings for our concepts *in abstracto*. So too for academic freedom, the concept having application in historical and societal contexts. After all, it has to do duty for Argentina in the 1920s (at the time of the promulgation of the Cordoba protocol on

DOI: 10.4324/9781003102939-10

autonomy; Aguiar Pereira, 2019) and for the separate settings, say, of the USA, South Africa and China in the twenty-first century.

However, a critical realist perspective, drawing on Bhaskar's ideas of a stratified ontology (which we encountered earlier), would not rest here – for then we would be looking at just the 'empirical' level of reality. Ultimately, if we are to ground academic freedom, we should be seeking ways in which it can connect with deeper ontological levels, for example, in aiding the circulation of ideas in a polity and in its capacity to affect the way the world *is*, and so be a 'generative mechanism' in and for the world. But we are getting ahead of ourselves.

Beginnings

The concept of academic freedom was implicit in the European university in the Middle Ages: both King and Pope sought to provide the university with significant elements of autonomy. However, it was only with the systematisation of the nation-state in early-twentieth-century Europe that the idea of academic freedom came to be formalised. It was no coincidence that its first codification took place in Germany alongside the formulation of the idea of the university, for the two went hand in hand. The Germanic idea of the university (chapter 6) essentially contained two elements: those of reason and of enculturation. Through participating in a reasoning process, professors were called upon to exercise public *judgement* (Fuller, 2009). In turn, they would be autonomous subjects and so would help to promote a society imbued with the spirit of universal reason. Autonomy and freedom were, therefore, built into the early modern idea of the university and of higher education.

Broadly, since the Second World War, universities have been enfolded into the wider society, not least with the emergence of the Internet. In this interconnected age, academic freedom has become an ambiguous notion. Individuals and institutions are simultaneously both more free and more hemmed in. On the one hand, a climate of entrepreneurialism, open access and independence in learning suggests freedom and openness; but, on the other hand, surveillance techniques, the evaluative state (Neave, 1998) and even state heavy-handedness (Doherty, 2015) with possible dismissal and even incarceration (or worse still) are indications that academic freedom is at risk.

The late-twentieth-century position on academic freedom came to possess three elements. *First*, a distinction was made between academic freedom and academic autonomy (although not always observed; Russell, 1993). Academic freedom was a right that owed to individual members of the academic community, while academic autonomy was felt to be a condition of the university as such. There are two sets of claims here. In order to fulfil their functions and responsibilities, (i) academics need academic freedom and so (ii) universities need to have a significant degree of autonomy, especially from the state.

Second, academic freedom was understood to be a freedom enjoyed by members of the academic community. However, the concept of academic freedom has rarely been spelt out and (so some believe) 'an authoritative definition of academic freedom does not exist' (Stølen and Gornitzka, 2019), but we should not shrink from that implied challenge. Here, therefore, is a stipulative definition to help us: *academic freedom is properly enjoyed by academics in academic settings in the pursuit of academic activities that attach to their field of study*.

That definition may seem innocuous, but it has no less than four problematic elements: who is to count as an 'academic'? What is to count as an 'academic setting'? What is to count as an 'academic activity'? What is to count as 'their field of study'? However, despite its openness, it also has bite. On this definition, a professor of nanotechnology enjoys *no* academic freedom in relation to the field of feminist literature. Any serious concept of academic freedom must specify freedoms, but it thereby constitutes *limitations* on freedom. In short, 'one is free to speak within one's expertise, but not beyond it' (Fuller, 2009: 175), and, in this second stage of the concept, as Fuller notes, we see a more limited conception compared to its first stage, the early Germanic idea.

Third, academic freedom implicates students. Originally, in the Germanic conception, academic freedom was extended beyond academics' right to teach as they wished ('Lerhfreiheit') to include students' right to learn ('Lerhnfreiheit'; Searle, 1972: 170–175; Fuller, 2009). This provision made sense given that higher education then recruited a tiny number of students such that the professors and students shared a similar social and intellectual 'habitus' (Bourdieu, 2000b). Students were not only permitted but were expected to proffer their own, freely formed, ideas. Heidegger (2004) reflected this sense of freedom being accorded to students with his urging that the professor's task was 'to let learn'.

Each of these three planks of academic freedom is problematic. First, it is difficult to maintain a tight conceptual distinction between institutional autonomy and academic freedom. Institutional autonomy is a *necessary* condition of academic freedom, but it is not a sufficient condition. Universities have responsibilities in ensuring a measure of academic freedom (Bowen et al., 2014) but, in practice, they too often remain silent where academic freedom is being threatened by others *or* even restrict it themselves (whether knowingly or unwittingly).

Institutional autonomy is *also* important in its own right, not least since universities and higher education collectively constitute a major institution through which society can reflect upon itself. Gordon Redding speaks of higher education 'as a major part of a society's brain' (2019: 25). To continue the analogy, I would prefer to speak of it being a major part of a society's *mind*. By having autonomous universities in their midst, the interstices of a complex society may be probed and held up as a mirror, so enabling society to learn about itself (Habermas, 1987a). University autonomy is an instrument for society to possess reflexive capacities and calls for at least a little 'distance from the State' (cf. Carlin, 2016: 168).

88 Key concepts

However, valuable as this institutional autonomy is, it is always in peril, and not only in illiberal regimes: after all, 'capitalism has need not of autonomy but of conformism' (Cornelius Castoriadis, quoted in Baruchello, 2013: 109). It follows that academic institutions need to possess autonomies so that they can contribute in their own way to the wider higher education ecosystem (chapter 20). Admittedly, there is a paradox here (Butler, 2018: 158), namely that governments should protect their universities from those same governments: the governments should restrain themselves. For some hundreds of years, this extraordinary situation has been with us, but it is far from clear that it will be maintained.

Academic freedom – horns of a dilemma

Let us move to the second plank of academic freedom, the idea itself. I suggested earlier, as a way of getting our exploration underway, that academic freedom may be understood to be a set of freedoms *properly enjoyed by academics in academic settings in the pursuit of academic activities that attach to their field of study*. We observed that this definition contains a boundedness, such that academic freedom can be properly exercised only within one's recognised field of study. The professor of nanotechnology cannot claim rights to academic freedom in the field of feminist literature.

But consider the case of the professor of nanotechnology who, in her *spare time*, becomes an expert in feminist literature. She does not hold a university position in feminist literature but has nevertheless developed a considerable expertise in the field. On occasions, she may attend conferences or other events in feminist literature and may even have been invited to contribute to a major journal in the field. Such 'academic moonlighting' may be unusual and may be 'viewed with suspicion' by those in the field being visited, but it happens (Reisz, 2018). So would this be an activity where academic freedom can come into play?

We have here – picking up the key terms of our definition – an academic, an academic setting (more than one, actually) and an academic activity, but is it an example of the academic's 'own field of study'? The response might be something like this: 'This is a trivial case. All we need do is to allow that an academic can gain a serious level of competence in any field of study and she or he would then merit the right to academic freedom.' That our professor of nanotechnology is not employed and does not receive a salary in virtue of her efforts in feminist literature is neither here nor there. She has an international expertise in feminist literature and has the right to claim academic freedom should the issue arise.

However, consider the case of the amateur astronomer, who spends much time with his telescopes looking at the starry sky, and one day sees an object hitherto unnoticed and, drawing it to the attention of the academic community, finds that he has made an original discovery. Suppose that this discovery is published in an academic journal, perhaps in collaboration with a member of the astronomy department in a university. Here we have an academic activity, and our citizen astronomer demonstrably has expertise but is not on the payroll of an institution of higher education. Does this case differ from our professor of nanotechnology who moonlights in feminist literature? Both could be said to be *instances of unpaid amateurism*, but it is not clear whether *both* could be said to enjoy academic freedom.

The point of these two examples is to indicate how difficult it is to provide *any* workable definition of academic freedom. *One is caught on the horns of a dilemma*: either one frames academic freedom so broadly that it offers no way of demarcating situations deserving of academic freedom or one draws it in so tightly that it can do little work in the intertwined character of higher education in the twenty-first century.

That very term 'situations' is problematic, for it includes both settings and persons. *So far as settings are concerned*, does it include the academic expressing a point of view on national or social media? An academic acting as a whistle-blower alleging some malpractice in a university's administration (for instance, drawing attention to a neglect of international students in one's university (Maslen, 2020))? A public event held on a campus and of an intellectual nature, but not conducted under the auspices of the university? The situation in which academic staff provide academic services to an external company and receives a fee?

So far as persons are concerned, does it include members of a university's professional staff or academics in management positions (any of whom might wish to speak out on university activities that they find problematic)? Visitors to a university, who are engaging in academic events, and who may have been invited by members of the university? A student on a clinical practice, aggrieved at practices she observes in a hospital, and who wishes to speak out on the matter? The legitimacy of the context is *always* open to dispute.

Academic freedom and civic freedom

A way of cutting through these difficulties is to say that *none* of these examples counts as a matter of academic freedom. Academic freedom has slid into a third stage where the idea is being called up to defend an *unduly wide range* of activities and situations. Academic freedom has become so elastic that it has lost its force and its conceptual substance. Much better to return it to its previous stage and to limit academic freedom to the right of academics to teach and to research in *strictly confined* academic situations. The matter of students and their academic freedoms is a moot issue. All the other cases just identified fall under the *civic* freedom of 'free speech', namely the right of citizens to say and to inquire into whatever they wish, provided there is no injury to others. This is a more limited freedom than academic freedom (cf. Searle, 1972: 175–178), but so be it.

However, while this division – between academic freedom and civic freedom – can carry us part way, it won't entirely meet the bill. Take the case of a visitor to a university, having been invited to participate in a public event, who is 'no-platformed' by, say, a group of students determined not to allow the invited speaker the platform to air their known position on a controversial topic (say, abortion). This is not obviously a situation in which the speaker can claim the right to academic freedom, but the matter is far from straightforward.

Suppose that the speaker has attested expertise in the field (acquired in whatever discipline). In that case, the speaker, having been invited to the event to speak on the basis of her or his point of view could justifiably claim that her or his academic freedom was being impaired. However, *this* claim produces a curious outcome. Suppose now that, alongside our academic is another speaker, who is *not* an academic but speaks from a well-informed position and has something equally controversial to say. Only her or his civic freedom was available as a bulwark against being no-platformed. In the same event, therefore, and on the same platform, academic freedom would come into play for one invited speaker but not for the other.

This situation would not do the academic community any good. Far better to see the whole event as falling entirely under the umbrella of civic rights, such that all the speakers are seen as equal participants, having equal rights to be heard as citizens and not in virtue of their possession – or not – of an academic status. But note that an implication of this gambit is that the university has no particular responsibility to safeguard the event as a matter of academic freedom. It may have a responsibility towards public order, but that is a separate matter.

The condition of the university

I have just opened the way to my position, which is that many apparent instances of academic freedom should be construed as matters of civic freedoms, and these are weaker and even more controversial than academic freedoms. However, the matter does not end there, for now arises the issue of the university as an institution.

The very term 'university' implies a space of open debate. Ever since its mediaeval inception, that debate has been cross-national and between universities, a feature much extended with the Internet age, with its interactive – and potentially intrusive – powers. However, the university has also extended its role as a site that encourages and even celebrates structured debate and debate not only on arcane matters within disciplines but on large matters in the public sphere. Many universities host a bewildering array of public events, including small-scale seminars, webinars and conferences, on key topics of the day. This is a recent contribution of the university to the formation of a twenty-first-century public sphere,' to which academics and members of the public happily co-contribute'. The use of the Internet in such open events compounds the difficulties of operationalising any idea of academic freedom, not least since geopolitics may be involved.

Much has been made of Derrida's (2001) idea of the university without condition. Empirically, the idea was always problematic. Since its Medieval days, the university has been subject to social and political conditions, which connects us again to Bhaskar's philosophy. In keeping with his critical realism, Bhaskar (2011a: 75–76) distinguishes (i) gaining one's freedom by forming an understanding of the constraints acting on one so as to adopt a 'practice of liberation'; (ii) emancipation as acting in one's real interests and having the powers to do so; and (iii) a stronger sense of liberation, that of 'the transformation of unneeded, unwanted and oppressive ... sources of determination'. Questions arise, therefore, as to the understanding that universities possess of the undue limitations on their powers and their dispositions to struggle continuously to effect some level of emancipation from those constraints.

So the idea of the university without condition is not only *ontologically* problematic but it is also *conceptually* problematic. A fundamental condition of the university is that it be a centre for debate; and debate that fulfils sub-conditions of turn-taking, respect for differing views, provision for participants to have their say, a spirit of truthfulness, a will to speak (even if difficult at times), a baseline of sincerity (even if the devil's advocate may creep in at times) and a degree of systematicity (even if the debate moves in a dog-leg pattern). That this *panoply of conditions* of being a university is in jeopardy in many countries is important. The idea of academic freedom cannot sensibly point to a university without condition: 'academic freedom is a conditioned freedom and ... it cannot rightly be thought or exercised without those conditions' (Butler, 2015: 293). Moreover, as part of any autonomy that it enjoys, the university has responsibilities in *upholding* these conditions of academic freedom.

There are two further difficulties. First, the basic idea is that of the university adopting the role of a neutral umpire. Qua institution, it takes no sides but allows the debate – or even the dispute – to take place. But what if the line of argument of one of the speakers runs against values that underlie such a sense of the university? Suppose there are suspicions that a speaker will turn out to be an apologist for an egregious instance of state oppression or will be profoundly disrespectful of a social group. This is the classic liberal's dilemma, for two fundamental values clash, *both* of which are integral to the idea of the university – those of free speech and of respect for persons. Does our university allow the academic the academic freedom to voice their (possibly racist) views *or* does it concur with the no-platformers?

This is a genuine dilemma in that it shows that *both principles cannot always be upheld simultaneously*. Some will say that academic freedom trumps civil liberty: the apologist for racism (or, say, Nazism) should be allowed a hearing and those who wish to critique that position should also be allowed to have their day. Others will say the reverse; the racist or the Nazi apologist should not be permitted 'the air of oxygen'. Invoking social justice, the demand of the speaker to be heard would be *refused*. Moreover, our refusenik may plead that the matter of academic freedom can seriously be invoked only in a particular context (notwithstanding the problems of the idea of context – see earlier in this chapter and pp. 231–32 below). Perhaps, in South Africa, say, concerns with racism and a determination *not* to allow universities to act as a space for the promulgation of racist beliefs or policies should command greater weight than a concern for academic freedom.

Accordingly, there is often *no* space available to the university to act as a neutral umpire. To provide a space for the enunciation of racist ideas *is* unequivocally problematic, however a university acts. One stance is as follows: 'let the racist have his day but then subject those views to critique'. Let it not be assumed, *a priori*, that the racist cannot be satisfactorily rebutted in an open space of debate. This is the John Stuart Mill (1969/1859) position: in principle, a society is strengthened through its capacities for providing spaces for alternative points of view to be held. And the university is the primary institution in society for opposed views to be brought against each in measured debate.

Mill's view (ibid: 142–146) contains a sophistication rarely acknowledged. For Mill, it would be important not just that the apologist for the Apartheid regime should be heard but that the critique of the apologist's position should be heard, and that one has a right to hear the *critic's* position and his/her critique. (I myself attended just such a debate on the Apartheid regime at that time, and I can still recall some of the critic's actual words in rebutting the apologist's position.) Allowing such a debate on a university campus can be especially *educative* and to forbid such a debate constitutes an infringement of participants' *right to learn*. Academic freedom is important not just for the speaker and for the listener but for the collective good.

Do students have a right to academic freedom?

For Heidegger (2004), the stance of the teacher towards his or her students should be, as noted, to 'let learn'. This is in keeping with the view inherited from the early nineteenth-century thought in Germany that there was no distinction in the pedagogical status of professor and student: pedagogically, *both* were in a state of ignorance. Epistemologically, it was true that the professor was ahead of the student, and it was the professor's duty to remain ahead of the student. But, in the pedagogical relationship, both came together in a quasi-public space of always questioning. The pedagogical space was one of joint inquiry.

It was on the basis of this high-blown conception of teaching and learning that just as professors had the right to teach as they wished (Lerhfreiheit) so students had the right to learn as they wished (Lerhnfreiheit). Students were free to decide whether or not to attend their lectures or to submit themselves for examination. This idea that students should enjoy academic freedom made social and cultural sense in a situation in which a tiny fraction of young people became university students. Under such conditions, it could be assumed that both teacher and taught were in possession of a common fund of cultural and epistemic capital, which could serve as the basis of a joint educational situation, and that the students would take advantage of any academic freedoms extended to them. However, amid 'mass higher education', no such assumptions can be made.

Now, students are placed in tightly regulated programmes of study, with stated 'learning outcomes'. In such circumstances, students have often to be *encouraged* to seize the positive freedoms that are extended to them (Macfarlane, 2017). Admittedly, this is not always the case. Student movements in favour of anti-colonialism, women's rights, political reform, and even curriculum reform (to press for the end of 'white' curricula, or for a wider economics syllabus that is less implicitly endorsing of neoliberalism), have been seen across the world.

However, instrumentalism in society is spawning instrumentalism within the university, not least among students (on whom are often levied high levels of fee). Under market conditions, tensions may result from the *differential* application of academic freedom to the teacher on the one hand and the students on the other hand (Finn, 2020). If students are caught up in state regulatory systems or their own desire to acquire instrumentally valuable skills – and so are *forgoing* their academic freedoms – then there is a responsibility upon those who teach them to encourage those students to take on the *burdens* of academic freedom. A price of student being granted freedom is that they exercise it and even venture to transgress epistemic and pedagogical boundaries (hooks, 1994).

The power of academic freedom

Academic freedom confers not just special privileges but also discomforting responsibilities. The 'duty of truth' may even call for one to 'speak out [even] when the consequences may be unfavourable to oneself' (Gibbs, 2019: 40). Other callings include not only sincerity, care, scrupulousness and having courage but also judgement about the boundaries of one's own responsibilities. Do academics, in making utterances in public or in the classroom, have a responsibility to take into consideration the stance of their university? Or the position of the government? Should one 'speak truth to power', whatever the cost even to the students? We are here in the presence of *competing responsibilities*.

Power is liable to be nervous and may even fear the academic voice (Bilgrami and Cole, 2015). The voice of power will speak of risk to 'the security of the nation' and even from within the university of 'reputational risk'. The expression of academic freedom, therefore, is always relational, taking on form within contexts – whether pedagogical, intellectual, institutional, epistemic, social or cultural. There are always trade-offs.

Both academic freedom and institutional autonomy become important precisely at the point where they are in jeopardy; where universities become 'counter-majoritarian' institutions (Ignatieff, 2018). Even for the university to explore academic freedom will be anxiety-provoking to some. But to shrink from doing so would be to abandon the responsibilities that attach jointly to institutional autonomy and to academic freedom.

There are, then, two options for the idea of academic freedom. The first is to suggest that, in the twenty-first century, the idea is now empty or hopelessly overloaded (*which amount to the same thing*) and that it can bear no conceptual weight. It has become an empty signifier and can do no serious work. The other option is to suggest that the term has *discursive* power. It can be drawn upon as a means of reminding those in positions of power – professors, managers, governments – that they have a duty of care towards higher education, whether students or the university and so provide spaces in society for the academic voice.

These two options are not incompatible. Even though 'academic freedom' has become a near-empty concept, with so many interests and ideas overloading it and pulling this way and that, still it possesses discursive power. Those in power – both beyond and *within* the academy – can become more than a little defensive and their nervousness compounded by the suggestion that they are limiting academic freedom. 'We have had too much of experts' may quickly and surprisingly give way to 'We shall listen to the experts.'

Conclusions: academic responsibility and worldly responsibility

The concept of academic freedom has gone through three stages: first, the Germanic concept of the nineteenth century gave the professors a licence to be public mandarins, demonstrating their capacities for reason on the matters of the day (Ringer, 1990). This was bound to end as academic inquiry was professionalised, but then a second stage unfolded in the twentieth century, in which academics were granted a space to pronounce within the limits of their disciplinary expertise. In turn, this too was bound to fade as the university and the wider society swam in each other's waters, and the boundaries were lost. Here, in this third stage – now unfolding – it is not at all clear that the concept of academic freedom has any locus.

With the university and the world intermingling, the academic space that academic freedom implied is fast being lost. Paradoxically, now, all manner of situations and events are claimed to raise matters of academic freedom but in an interconnected and indeterminate world, there can be no end to the disputes that arise, and the potential for situations where the cry of 'academic freedom' might be heard is now limitless. Difficulties arise in research, in teaching and in the university's engaging with the wider society. It is no longer clear as to where or how to locate academic freedom.

Where now? We are on a cusp. There are manifest infringements on the academic estate, even if these are conducted 'in the national – or the public – interest'. And the academic estate cannot be sure that it has sufficient friends at court to speak for it. However, the very interconnectivity that has led to this amorphous situation into which academic freedom has fallen paradoxically opens a new possibility. The space may be opening and the time close by for the academic estate to play its part in doing justice to that interconnectivity of the world and to do so publicly.

Worldly responsibilities are opening as the academic community is obliged to think through its place in an unpredictable, fluid and divided world, and, surprisingly, it may be a world looking for a calm, disinterested and yet authoritative voice to aid public understandings. This would amount to a new and fourth stage of academic freedom: it would conjoin stages one and two, but now placed into the turbulent and challenged world of stage three. The idea of academic freedom is continually on the move, and there just may be a new and positive stage for it near at hand.

8 Thought and reason – and their dilemmas

> ... true dissidence today is perhaps simply what it has always been: *thought*.
> (Julia Kristeva, 1977, quoted in Arndt and Mika, 2018: 47)

Introduction

In identifying key matters in the philosophy of higher education, it would be easy to duck the matters of thought and reason. They might be felt to be too abstract to warrant inclusion. In this chapter, though, I aim to show that the two concepts are foundational. Unless we accord space to them, any view of the philosophy of higher education will be deficient.

In modern philosophy, there has been much attention paid to the matter of reason, especially in work with an educational orientation. These include work by David Bakhurst (2011), Harvey Siegel (1990, 1997) and Stephen Toulmin (2001). Mainstream philosophy has seen major works in and around reason, notably Derek Parfitt's *Reasons and Persons*, Robert Brandom's (1998) *Making it Explicit*, and John McDowell's (2002) *Mind and World*. Much less consideration has been given to the matter of thought as such. *Thought and Action* by Stuart Hampshire (1970) – a book rather neglected in the philosophy of education – stands out here. Bakhurst's book is of particular interest here since it brings both reason and thought together and has an explicit interest in education. Part of my pitch here will be that the ideas of reason and thought are intertwined and, in understanding higher education, we should give both concepts a fair wind and *together*. We should, though, also come at them in a critical spirit for they do not possess the unassailability that their advocates sometimes pretend.

Preliminary considerations

Surely, it may be felt, higher education is a set of educational processes that enables students to reason and to think. It is – in any discipline – a phase of education that turns especially on thought and reason. By extension, too, universities must be understood as institutions that constitute spaces to encourage thought and reason, and such elements are to be found, *par excellence*, in academics' research and scholarly activities.

Moreover, it would *reasonably* be anticipated that thought and reason characterise the decision-making processes of universities, and on two grounds. First, thought and reason are part of the DNA of universities, part of their value structure, and so are part of what it is to *be* a university; second, as complex organisations, presumably, any university (and its leaders and senior managers) would wish to conduct its activities and form its policies and decisions on rational bases and be seen to be thoughtful in those processes.

Thought and reason are connected, then, but they differ. Of the two concepts, thought is prior. Reason is a vehicle for the channelling of thought: it 'puts a check on thinking' (Heidegger, 1996: 45). Such channelling of thought is desirable – so it might be felt – because thought can be unduly emotional, culturally loaded, ideological and even *ir*rational. As it might be said, thought can even get out of hand and reason has to keep it in check. Reason disciplines thought. Thought is indicative of the presence of a mind at work, while reason is a *particular* mode of thought. Furthermore, thought is more internal than reason; reason is a collective and, indeed, public process. The two matters interweave, therefore, and both are important in higher education and the university.

Thought is elemental in the university: the university even stands for thought. There can be no unthinking university, if it is to be worthy of the title of 'university' (Bengtsen and Barnett, 2018; Waghid and Davids, 2020). But what might be meant in saying that a university thinks? Or that it thinks about higher education? (Gibbs and Barnett, 2014). Thought is always thinking within frameworks. It follows that, if it is to escape its confines, thought has to be 'dissident'; it has to stand outside in some sense (Arndt and Mika, 2018).

Reason has been a legacy of the Enlightenment: through reason, humanity was both to achieve emancipation from superstition and develop life on this planet in a morally superior way. Some continue in this lineage; for example, Robert Brandom (1998: 5) depicts 'us as reasonable beings ... subject to the peculiar force of the better reason'. However, reason has also come in for a battering, it being seen as a dampening of people's possibilities, especially in reason's severing of 'sensuous' interconnections with self, community and nature (Abram, 1997).

The interplay between reason and passion was a running issue through much of Nietzsche's writing: on the one hand, the cool, contemplative Apollonian spirit and, on the other hand, the wildness and the intoxication of the Dionysus will (Nietzsche, 2008). For the Frankfurt School of critical theorists of the 1930s and 1940s, reason, as developed in the West, 'secreted malicious tendencies of domination and had opened the way to Auschwitz' (Adorno and Horkheimer, 1989). Subsequently, Foucault (1991) saw a biopower within the disciplines, which were aptly named, for – in their organised use – they exerted discipline over populations. Over decades, Maxwell (1984, 2014) has depicted the processes of academic inquiry as profoundly non-rational, not least in its tendencies to split up large matters and fragment them into discrete inquiries. And the ecologists see in reason an anthropocentricism, such that the ecologies of the Earth are neglected, leading to worldly crises (Code, 2006; Mickey, 2016). The dominant mode of reason is depicted as mere Western reason, assuming its superiority, strangely cut off from the world, and delegitimising the thinking of African, Asian and Latin American cultures.

So we have two quite different philosophies of reason: on the one hand, reason emancipates, frees from superstition and provides the wherewithal for control over a wayward world *and* oneself. Reason is a *standard* of legitimate thought. On the other hand, reason unduly limits and even corrupts the mind, the body and humanity's relationships with the whole Earth. Reason instrumentalises *both* human beings and the Earth. *This is a profound schism that higher education has yet to address*, not least because, on *either* side of the chasm, 'the principle of reason' is a matter of being, 'a statement of beings', indeed (Heidegger, 1996: 44–46).

Immediate implications

I have just touched upon the matters of control and discipline, but this is not, necessarily, to cast a pall over proceedings. The student's essay may bear the signs of much effort and the points made in it may be plentiful; too plentiful in a way. In the middle of a paragraph, sentence (a) may make perfect sense and its following sentence (b) may also make perfect sense: unfortunately sentences (a) and (b) just do not hang together. It may be that they jar, or even conflict, or that there is no thread that comfortably joins them together. The narrative has faltered, let down by a faulty reasoning process. *Both* reason and thought are wanting: the thought processes were pressed *insufficiently* by the reasoning, which was left incomplete. Thought sometimes needs to be tamed by reason.

This does not imply that students should take courses in logic. It is simply to observe that a significant part of higher education lies in the evocation of disciplined thought, evident especially in the student's powers of, and *propensity* to, reason. This is not to down-value other modes of thought, still less to suggest that icy reason trumps all other kinds of thought, or to insist that it must be entirely in the mind for, especially in higher education – with so much of it constituting forms of professional education – practical and embodied reason (Ullman-Margalit, 2000) has a large part to play. Instead, it is to suggest that, in the educational processes that constitute higher education and in research and scholarship, reason matters.

However, some consider that reason is a particularly Western and even injurious mode of thought and that universities and higher education have become machines for energising this mode of thought. Critical voices come thick and fast. As intimated, it is suggested that Western reason is actually *irrational*, or is the voice of colonisers, or is the bearer of a masculine approach to the world, or is a direct cause of the ecological crises in front of the world. What counts as reason is not neutral, either in its selection, its location or its effects: 'the principle of reason is not simply reason' (Derrida, 2004: 135). Even if what counts as reason has its virtues, still there are disbenefits to be notched up on the ledger.

A space for reason*ing*

The university could be said to be 'a space of reasons', an idea pressed by David Bakhurst (2011). In order to be intelligible and to count as a reason, a reason has to be connected to other reasons; hence a space of reasons. This is a metaphor, and so it can have various meanings. Bakhurst distinguishes three ways in which the metaphor can be understood: '(1) to demarcate a specific mode of intelligibility; (2) to describe the site of giving and asking for reasons; (3) to express the idea of reality as a normative space'. Bakhurst observes that 'it is the second ... use ... that is most likely to be viewed as a fertile notion among educational theorists and practitioners because it suggests a framework for modelling educational interaction and its settings' (115), but Bakhurst is not enamoured with this view.

Bakhurst's preference for 'a specific mode of intelligibility' implies that reason is a *unitary* mode of intelligibility. There are two problems here. It is better to see the humanities and related forms of inquiry as offering a mode of intelligibility that is distinct from that of science; but, and moreover, the university is home to *many* modes of inquiry. The science-humanities classification is totally inadequate here. Where would archaeology fall? What of ecological studies? Or the performing arts? Or the understanding of indigenous cultures? And, if the idea of emotional intelligence can carry weight, perhaps we should allow for *reasoning through the emotions* (Karlsohn, 2018). In higher education, there are a multitude of 'modes of intelligibility', and they are increasing. As Bakhurst observes, there are 'implications for educational policy', not least in the context of a jostling for resources.

The other problem with the idea of a space of reasons is that it can unwittingly invite undue attention being paid to 'the nature of our rational powers', as Bakhurst puts it. To speak of the space of reasons does not mean that it is only reason that matters, crucial though that is, especially in universities. 'The force of the better argument' (Habermas, 1984: 25) is favoured by conditions that go beyond the mere giving and taking of reasons. Tone, graciousness, empathy, listening, carefulness and reticence (and other qualities not immediately rational) have to find their way into the space of reasons.

What of the third aspect of 'the space of reasons' to which Bakhurst points, that of 'reality as a normative space'? This is a highly ambiguous phrase. It could mean that the space of inquiry into 'reality' is fuelled by values or by a conflict between values. It could mean that inquiry has a latent orientation towards a future of some kind for the world. And it could remind us that reality is a large space, in which resides values and which invite our attention.

As the twenty-first century moves on, many are wanting to draw on the theme of ecology, especially to deploy it for the interconnectivity that it connotes. Whether we recognise it or not, *we are all ecologists now*. This sense of ecology views 'reality as a normative space' in which can be found *all three senses* just identified. Ecological inquiries are motivated by a belief in the interconnectedness of all things; they are energised by a wish to see even greater interconnectedness; and they consider that the world, understood ecologically, is not value-free but is both value-laden *and* value-depleted, and they consider that inquiry can help to restore ecological equilibrium – or 'sustainability' – to the world. Some go even further and wish to see all disciplines, especially science, being animated by the 'precautionary principle' (Høyer, 2012: 178). Reason has a stickiness, attaching itself to value-laden projects.

Considerations such as these suggest that *the idea of the university as a space of reasons needs some refinement*. There is no one space of reasons but several such spaces; and those spaces are all the time widening, even if some are closing. Classifications of academic knowledge reveal hundreds if not thousands of fields of inquiry, with their own conglomerations of topics and concerns and their own reasoning and argumentative processes. Moreover, there are increasing crossovers and dissolutions of boundaries so that reasoning processes are becoming more and more localised. Many groups are evolving assemblages of concepts, theories, embodiments, practical interests and policy attunements. The communities involved are not just 'epistemic communities' (Haas, 2016) but are – as we may term them – *epistemic-civic* communities, with their own reasoning processes.

These epistemic-civic communities are always in motion. For example, the hard sciences and the medical sciences have found that conventional processes of producing papers in academic journals are inadequate in keeping pace with the fast research of global science, as it relies more on digital processes and immediate interactions. We may assume that face-to-face conferencing will recede, to be replaced more by videoconferencing and the like. Or, for another example, imagine students in sports science working on projects in which they engage with local sports teams in the latter's quest for improved fitness, with all the human, emotional, kinaesthetic, technical and ethical considerations that are involved. There are complexes of practical reasoning in play here (Bourdieu, 2000a; Ullman-Margalit, 2000).

Let us, therefore, abandon the idea of the university as a single space of reasons: reasons neither form a unity nor inhabit a single space. Instead, we should opt for the idea of the university as a space of reason*ing*. This move – 'reasoning' rather than 'reason' – has several benefits. It focuses attention on the *spaces* of reasoning. Reasons have their substance in multiple and radically different processes of reasoning – practical, cognitive, embodied, interactive, processual and so forth. Reason*ing* is active, collective, *inter*-active, dynamic, always in motion. It is not thingified, as the term 'reason' implies.

The pedagogical processes of higher education have the challenge of bringing students into spaces of reasoning so as to encourage their own thought processes, their own powers of reasoning in the company of others (who may hold quite different and yet still reasoned positions) and their own complexes of body-and-mind. The idea of a space of reason*ing* also opens to *a-rational elements that are essential to inquiry*.

The idea of a space of reasoning allows for depth and height. Reasoning can peer into the deep societal forces that are distorting reason itself and can, with imagination, ascend to glimpse alternative modes of thought, of care, or consideration for invisible communities, or that afford 'recognition' (Honneth, 2005). This would be deploying reason to recover thought that has been 'left alone' (McArthur, 2018). Tellingly, in that text, McArthur recounts the story of economics having fallen into just this malady: much reason but rather little thought, a situation that groups of students across the world have sought to right.

The right to think

It could be judged that the right to think is being accorded to fewer people. The manipulation of societal thought processes by the mass media, digital surveillance, the inclination of governments to make decisions on behalf of a nation's peoples, the domination of social media by private corporations – all these are suggestive of boundaries of thought being drawn in. It may be felt that at least universities remain a place to think. And higher education is precisely that part of the educational system where students are trained to think, whatever their fields of study. There are two responses to this hopeful line.

First, the right to think is increasingly being denied *even to universities*. Universities are accepted as a fund of expertise and economic innovation but *also* warily seen as places of dissent, critique, partiality and even protest and revolt. As a result, the right to speak is accorded more to the representatives of just some disciplines, depending on the needs of the moment. If academics appear alongside government spokespeople, it is academics from certain disciplines. Some governments will deny academics a hearing, even to the point of imprisoning them. Academics' *and students'* thinking and reasoning publicly can bring them into confrontation with the authorities, such that they are portrayed as being hostile to good order and even as prejudicial to a nation's security. Some disciplines – characteristically the humanities and social theory – do not come onto the political radar, except as a hostile force to be marginalised. At best, they retain a voice but heed is not paid to it. The right to speak is being rationed across the higher education sector.

In this milieu, *self-censorship* is surreptitiously present. The writer or speaker may be so intent on communicating that she or he takes the part of the other (the reader or listener) and anticipates their responses and lessens what is said. It may be present in an over-inclination to observe the rules of the thought police of a discipline, particularly as embodied in journal editors,

102 *Key concepts*

so as to minimise the possibility of rejection. It may be present in the student wanting to secure a good examination grade, who assumes that the examiners have preferred lines of reasoning. It may be present in the running of a university, where the senior managers desist from saying or writing anything that might displease the authorities. And it may be present in the wider society, where students and academics shrink from speaking out for fear of raising the ire of the state.

We may label these respectively as communicative, epistemic, pedagogic, institutional and state forms of self-censorship. Variously, they contain elements of empathy, control, authenticity and timidity, and they possess positive and entirely negative moments, even in the same act. Thought in the university is never without conditions.

The thoughtless university

A second line of consideration is more disturbing still. It is that the academy *itself* restricts the right to think, and in many ways. It incorporates an instrumentalism into its own practices ('How can this paper be written such that it has the greatest impact?'); its power structures can subjugate certain kinds of voice (on the basis of gender or ethnicity or region); and it accords more discursive room to disciplines that are societally and economically dominant. Groups spring up, fiercely defending their own turf, with their favoured concepts, value orientations and luminaries (who have to appear in the bibliographies). Amid ever-tighter audit systems, academic work becomes risk-averse, and a culture of playing-it-safe emerges. Unsurprisingly, academics-turned-whistle-blowers, who critique their universities, are unlikely to be thanked for their pains. So, in many ways, the academic community silences itself. And, in the end, the university forgets its duty to think and to care about thought, so much so that it hardly knows what thought is: 'In universities especially, the danger is … very great that we misunderstand what we hear of thinking' (Heidegger, 2004: 15).

A recent commentary of this ilk is that of the French philosopher Bernard Stiegler. Stiegler (2015) was concerned with the irrationality that he saw was concerned with the irrationality that he saw as built into the world, particularly in the domination exerted by its economic order. 'Reason cannot avoid engendering the temptation of irrationality' (17), and 'stupidity' is one form of this irrationality (others being a collective 'madness', 'ignorance', 'vulgarity' and 'fantasy'). Stiegler had a particular interest in universities, where 'knowledge cannot be separated from stupidity' (33). This point offers hope for, while what counts as knowledge can be deformed into ignorance, so too it offers possibilities of greater understanding. Teachers and professors not only 'have a right' but 'a sovereign duty', indeed 'an exceptional responsibility', in their concerns for reason and truth. However, this task has been undermined by limitations accompanying knowledge in a digital age, with its 'exteriorization of the mental functions of perception and imagination' (159).

In this milieu, the desire for impact and public projection, sheer pace and an oversupply of data run together. It is easier to pack one's bibliographies with hundreds of items rather than give them the thought they deserve. The university runs the risk of being complicit in these movements. Let us not use (Stiegler's term) 'stupidity' but rather that of 'thoughtlessness'. However, there remain spaces for thought in the university, not least because knowledge inquiry sponsors thought. There remains a potential for *thoughtfulness* in universities.

Stiegler is right in calling for a 'radical transformation of the university' (155), but his solution – in avoiding the factional interests that lie behind knowledge policies – will be controversial: 'ideally, the knowledge that can be taught at university ... is universalizable ...' (163). This idea of universalisable knowledge is problematic, and I pick it up below.

The virtues of thought

Thought is difficult, and it requires virtues of courage, carefulness, reticence, forbearance, perseverance, steadfastness, vigilance and discipline. Through thought, one may see things anew: thought pushes itself into the world. From quantum mechanics to literature, disciplines possess the power of destabilising taken-for-granted ways of understanding. Thought, therefore, is 'a dangerous exercise' (Deleuze and Guattari, 2013: 41). It is hardly surprising that dictators are wary of universities, for thought yearns for freedom, both for itself and for others. It is against a horizon of these considerations that one should place Michael Ignatieff's call (in a BBC interview) for 'free universities'. One cannot be told what to think.

Thought requires space, both internal and external. Academic freedom is a condition of *internal* space; institutional autonomy is a condition of *external* space. The British conservative political philosopher, Michael Oakeshott, spoke (1989: 127) of the university as 'the gift of the interval'. Oakeshott was succeeded by Kenneth Minogue (1973) for whom, again, the university was situated in its own space separate from society. To think that the university might concern itself with the ills – literally – of the world was to commit the crime of 'Monism', in which there was no break between the hallowed thought of the university and the rudimentary and often mistaken thought of the world. But this general position – of university and world *separateness* – is now untenable.

Is it possible, then, to have one's cake and eat it? Is it reasonable both to seek the university as a space for thought, free of an undue press of the claims of the world, and yet also to have a concern *for* the world? This may be the most fundamental question before higher education.

The answer has to be that *there is no easy answer* available. Thought is always conditioned, and it cannot be entirely free of the world; it is part of the furniture of the world. The universities, and its teachers and its researchers and scholars, have all the time to be hopping unsteadily from a sense of

104 Key concepts

independence to a sense of entrapment *and vice versa*. But this is not to let the parties off the hook. Governments, national audit agencies and senior management teams should be trying to grant as much space to universities and their pedagogical and intellectual practices as is practicable, and teachers and researchers should have an eye on the world, even as they try to strike out on their own. This is not a comfortable situation in which to be, but it is how matters stand.

The universality of reason

Is reason universal? By and large, the philosophers consider that it is, and the sociologists consider that it is not. This is a matter of great moment for universities, accused as they are of coloniality (or 'post-colonialism') and of imposing epistemologies of the Global North onto the Global South (de Sousa Santos). The critics come armed with talk of 'epistemic injustice', 'epistemicide' or 'epistemic violence'. However, the critiques are usually pitched at a high level of abstraction, being rarely cashed out with practical examples. What, for example, could such terms mean either for research in medicine or for the education of medical students? A pandemic is a global phenomenon, and research into it is worldwide (and includes research conducted in the 'Global South'). To what extent are students in universities to be inducted into the medical practices of indigenous communities? Vaccines, produced partly through the efforts of universities in the Global North, will be deployed in every country to inoculate all peoples, even if unevenly. Perhaps there are pointers here to a possible 'knowledge ecology' (de Sousa Santos, 2016) and with reciprocal benefits.

For example, the relationship of Asian, African and indigenous cultures to nature generally differs from those of scientific and technological cultures. In the former, divisions between the knower and the known are porous, traditional communities not possessing the sharp boundary between the knower and nature that tends to characterise science-dominated cultures (cf. Horton, 1973), and this latter separation has been a contributory cause of the global ecological crisis. The presumed universality of the thought processes of the West has produced a universal crisis (Plumwood, 2002).

It has also been observed that curricula in the universities of the Western world are dominated by approaches from and examples in the West. End 'white curricula' emerged as a plea. What was not always clear was whether this concerned just curricula in the humanities and social sciences. Was it also to apply to quantum mechanics? Is the problem of epistemic justice discipline-specific or does it *uniformly* transcend discipline boundaries?

As suggested, there is a big ditch between philosophy and sociology here. Ever since Kant, philosophers have followed the path of universality. And given its name, it can plausibly be suggested that an institution called 'university' might have some connection with the theme (of universality). A contemporary voice, declaring boldly – and often – in favour of the very idea of universality, is that of Slavoj Žižek (1997: 103–125). Žižek's position contains sophistications within sophistications. He takes his cue from Hegel and engages with the 'negativity' inherent in universality. Its inner message, and one that higher education is perhaps now heeding, is that it tears one away from one's roots and identity, even if it supplies another identity. The universality of the academic world is, in other words, alien, and a repudiation of organic community. Universality is but an abstract space, devoid of meaning; *except that*, as Žižek observes, it supplies its *own* meanings.

There remains a fundamental issue: is 'universality' an umbrella notion under which competing claimants for universality vie with each other (neoliberalism and the public sphere; logic and emotion; empiricism and sheer reason; Western reason and community-based reason) OR is it a space of alternative universalities? If it is the first, then there is a quasi-political struggle to be held, as to whether one or another universality is to seize the high ground. If the second, then we just have to live uneasily with multiple senses as to what is universal.

This is the conundrum at the heart of a fascinating dialogue between Judith Butler, Ernesto Laclau and Žižek (2000). Žižek opts for the former reading; Butler for the second. Here, Butler has the edge, so far as the university is concerned. The university cannot evade the concept of universality, but it has to do so in a nuanced fashion. Not only does it have to concern itself with particularities, to attend to particular voices, regions and traditions, but that plea also becomes a universal. And so the university has to be a space of universal thought, but that very idea is filled in increasingly with rival senses as to what is to count as universality, including the insistence on particularities, on context and on tradition.

Conclusions

The philosophy of higher education *has* to accord space to the concepts of thought and reason, not least because the university is bound up with thought and reason. Indeed, the university has become an institutional site of battles *over* thought and reason. The university has come to view itself as a neutral space for thought and reason, but it has been put in the dock for being partial, not just for harbouring, but actually favouring, injurious forms of thought. Reason itself has been accused of being irrational, working within over-restricted frameworks and a form of tyranny (the barbs coming from both the right *and* the left).

These dilemmas play out in *three seas*, of disciplines and their educational practices, the university in its collective actions, and the university in engaging with the world (cf. Barnett, 2018b). In each case, thought only becomes thought when it can think about itself; when the disciplines and students can think about their own thinking and practices; when the university can think about its decision-making and collective formation of ideas; and when the university can think about the ways it engages with the world. At each level, there are problems of curtailment of thought or lopsided reasoning processes, as the powers of disciplines, institutions and the state exert themselves, and as the digital world distorts thought (and not only through its logarithms).

And so both the university as an institution and higher education as a form of human development are caught in a fork. In allying themselves to thought and reason, they run the risk of being partial, ideological and even impositional – all that they would shun as self-descriptions; on the other hand, the university and higher education cannot allow themselves to be allied to thoughtlessness or irrationality. But there are grounds for hope: 'We find ourselves in a kind of historical breathing space ... it is once again possible to give serious attention to thought, thanks to current material conditions' (Adorno, 2008: 57–58). This, of course, is far from easy. Universities, and their educational processes, will, I fear, have to live with the inevitable discomfort; striving to find some kind of universality and impartial reason but knowing that these ideas will always be battlegrounds and spaces of unease.

Part III

Teaching, learning and the student

9 Teaching

A provocative matter

Introduction

From the mid-twentieth century, teaching in higher education came to play second fiddle to research. Nations invested heavily in research believing that that policy would increase national productivity. Money and status flowed to research, and better terms of employment and higher salaries were enjoyed by those who were 'research active'. It then became apparent that teaching was being neglected and so attention turned in that direction. Governments set up teaching audits, teaching professionalism in higher education became an issue, national and international organisations and academic associations were formed, movements took off (such as the Scholarship of Teaching and Learning) and academic journals were established focusing on teaching in higher education.

It might have been thought that here was a springboard for philosophical work on the matter of teaching in higher education. Is teaching in higher education to be understood as different from teaching in schools or adult education? How might the relationship between teaching and research be construed? Does the idea of the 'teaching university' carry water?

There was some work along these lines even in the 1960s (Philips Griffiths, 1965), but the matter of *teaching* in higher education has largely taken a philosophical backseat. *Learning* has become the focus, both in policy debates and the literature. Universities' Teaching and Learning Strategies quietly became '*Learning* and Teaching Strategies', and a discourse of 'learnification' emerged (Biesta, 2016: 124–127). It is the student's *learning* that matters, together with 'the student experience' and levels of 'student satisfaction'. And this has point, given that students are often asked to contribute substantially towards their course fees.

Teaching in higher education became a kind of afterthought, coming into play only to enable learning to transpire. Teachers have become near-invisible, having been much displaced by curriculum managers and designers, digital experts, learning developers, student mentors and so forth. Any serious understanding of teaching in higher education has, therefore, to be developed against this complex but real background.

The problem of teaching in higher education

As implied, the first task of many universities and their academic staff was that of conducting research and then 'disseminating' or 'transmitting' it to their students. Associated with this sense of the relationship between research and teaching was the bucket theory of mind (Popper, 1975): the mind was an empty vessel, the task of the university teacher being that of filling that it with the fruits of research. The major university teaching space, the lecture theatre, with its serried rows of fixed seats, embodied these axioms about research, teaching and learning. Recently, as the notions of 'lecture' and even 'teaching' have given rise to some diffidence, lecture theatres have been redesigned to allow for interaction (between the lecturer and students *and* among the students). Simultaneously, the ideas of 'learning spaces' (Boddington and Boys, 2011; Bligh, 2014), the 'flipped classroom' (Al-Samarraie et al., 2020) and digital learning have emerged. So the idea that teaching is an adjunct to research has receded, but it is now stranded awkwardly between research and learning.

A key issue is the responsibility of the teacher. Many consider that university teachers have two responsibilities – to their discipline *and* to the students. It is surely on account of this double orientation of university teaching that it is *both* an 'attempt word' and a 'success word' (Passmore, 1980: 20). Good university teachers heed the calls both of their scholarly field (and *attempts* to convey something of the world that it perceives) and of their students (whose learning they *succeed* in bringing on). Some even say that the discipline and the student are two kinds of love (Elton, 2000; Rowland, 2006).

However, is the teacher's love *greater* towards the discipline *or* the student? Perhaps, especially in higher education, the teacher should be – *in the first place* – an authority in her discipline, and it is on this basis that her authority as a teacher rests. If research is to be 'transmitted', it must have both logical and temporal priority. *But* some think that her professionalism derives from her understanding of teaching in a more general sense *and* of what it is to be a student in today's higher education. In contemplating teaching in higher education, research has a part to play, but we should keep clear water between the two. Teaching is a set of practices with its own inherent value and demands (Biesta, 2017, 2019; cf. Schatzki, 2012).

How, then, should teaching in higher education be construed? If higher education is an educational process in which students come into their own space, and form their own *interpretations* and *judgements* (Nixon, 2012a), the concept of teaching *does* become problematic. Teaching might even get in the way of the student's own *becoming* (Mills, 1994): at best, it seems to point to an educational relationship in which the teacher gradually recedes so as to allow the students to form their own personal independence.

But what of disciplines where there are life issues at stake, say medicine, engineering, architecture or the law? Doesn't 'teaching' have a fairly straightforward set of meanings there – to impart contemporary knowledge and to inculcate pertinent skills? A *higher* education, however, calls for a more subtle sense of teaching. It calls for encouragement so that the student is able, *ultimately*, to go it alone and to be able to be critically to reflect on her or his own thinking, actions and values as an autonomous person (chapter 12). The very term '*higher* education' calls for a reflexive set of capabilities.

Epistemology or ontology?

Given the considerations just sketched, many feel that teaching in higher education is wrongly construed as an *epistemological matter*; of the teacher having command of a discipline, and enabling the student to form a goodly connection with a body of knowledge. Instead, teaching in higher education is much better construed primarily as an *ontological matter*, of so setting up the pedagogical situation that eventually students take off on their own and move into a different place, each becoming a new *being* in the world. Gradually, they not just come into their own understandings and interpretations about matters (Nixon, 2012a) but come also to *be* in a different relationship to the world, whether as geologists in the field, as trainee doctors in clinical settings, as would-be lawyers in moots and as dancers in the performing arts.

It follows that all manner of issues arise in those higher education programmes that are oriented towards practices in the wider world (Higgs et al., 2012), for here are entwined practices upon practices (the educational practices of higher education and the practices specific to particular professions in society and their workplaces). Concepts of practice, praxis, pedagogic design, (inter)-professionality and personhood come into play and in bewildering relationships. There is an especially *dense and layered complexity* here.

Significant is it, too, that knowledge is *embodied*, especially in the professional areas but more generally too. To really know x, one has to live it: 'The world is not what I think but what I live through' (Merleau-Ponty, 1994: xvi–xvii; Nørgård and Aaen, 2019; Dall'Alba and Sandberg, 2020). The whole body comes into play, not separately from mind but as an expression *of* mind (cf. Ryle, 1968). Teaching in higher education, therefore, is an ontological matter even more than it is an epistemological matter.

It follows that the teacher's task is not to teach, in any ordinary sense of teaching. It is to set up educational situations so that students acquire the energies to go on by themselves and become their own agents. It is to engender a forward motion in their students for *lifelong* learning. Teaching in higher education is to encourage in the student a process of *perpetual becoming*. All this is to see teaching in higher education as *a dispositional process*; to look to students ultimately as *willing themselves* forward and taking on powers of their own. To put the point straightforwardly, the teacher's task is to *in*-spire the students.

If the university teacher accomplishes this, their work is done. Their students have the resources of the university available to them in the library, the other students, the Internet and their networks and can take off by themselves. They come to be *intellectual entrepreneurs* (Shumar and Robinson, 2018), able to maximise their learning opportunities, to take risks and to emerge with their own *learning capital* (as it might be termed), on which they can build through their lives. They would be equipped, indeed, to develop their own *learning ecologies* in their local and global communities (Barnett and Jackson, 2020).

It is crucial, then, that knowledge retains a centrality in higher education but that it needs to be in the service of the educational processes. Over the past half century or so, an interest in knowledge has been displaced by an interest in skills, leading one leading commentator to urge that that knowledge should be brought 'back in' (Young, 2008). Of course, it should never have been excommunicated in the first place, but it can only achieve its educational value in higher education if it is kept in check, and the students given space to develop their own understandings, placings and assimilations of the material that they encounter and to make something of it in their own schemas.

For some, the image of emerging from the cave into enlightenment is beguiling, but the metaphor misleads, for total enlightenment (or emancipation) is not on the cards. Rather, it is a case of *never-ending darkness* coupled with occasional shafts of light, and it becomes a task of teaching to help students cope with that perplexing situation. A 'dark education' beckons (Saari, referenced in Lysgaard et al., 2019: 115).

Some consider that, if students are to acquire a self-fuelled will to learn, they should be allowed to learn, and many draw upon Heidegger's (2004) idea of 'letting learn'. This assumes that students already possess the dispositions of *self-orchestrated* learning, but this is naïve. There is much empirical evidence that testifies to student anxiety: this has long been the case (Zweig, 1963), but, now, non-completion (or attrition) rates are on the rise, and students are committing suicide and in increasing numbers. Letting learn, accordingly, is a necessary but *cannot be a sufficient* way of conceiving of teaching in higher education.

Picking up an idea of Jacques Rancière (1991), much play has been made of the idea of 'the ignorant schoolteacher' (Derycke, 2011; Pelletier, 2012; Biesta, 2017: 68–72). It may be initially attractive, conjuring a sense of democratic co-creation, but it holds traps for the unwary. Especially in higher education, teachers should be authorities in what they say and do, arising from their *own* thinking and reasoning. It is *not* that higher education teachers should be researchers but rather that they be deep *scholars* of their field of study. They should be *scholar-teachers*.

Disciplines or fields matter (Kreber, 2009). It is in them and through them that students acquire and deepen their dispositions for learning through *life*. It is an astonishing but largely unnoticed feature of higher education, as it has developed over the past two hundred years or so, that – by chance – a higher education, at its best, provides a means by which dispositions for life can be sedimented. Since this feature has not been studied closely, it is even less clear as to the range of dispositions that are characteristically developed by different programmes of study and their *overlap* across disciplines. Which are the dispositions typically advanced by a programme, say, in geology as compared with modern languages or business studies or in the performing arts? We do not know. (I take up this matter again in later chapters.)

Teaching as ontology: three tasks

Three tasks face the teacher who is concerned to promote the student as a person with *agentic dispositions* in a challenging world: affirmation, support and energising. The task of *affirmation* is a response to the student's state of anxiety. In mass higher education, the student's anxiety is a contingent matter, but *student anxiety is also part of the meaning of higher education* since higher education is precisely a process in which one is *dis*placed.

That old idea of education as initiation (Peters, 1970: 54) captured something of this sense of the student coming to stand in a new place in the world. And this would be so whether we have in mind performative fields – whether in the arts or applied sciences – or the purer fields – whether in the humanities or the notational fields. There is an unsettlement here, a letting go of ways of relating to the world and moving to a *place of no-place*, of continuous strangeness; and this is likely to be a dislocating process, which calls for *teaching-as-affirmation*.

Teaching in higher education is also a matter of *support*. This is a response to the student's *possible* state of being. The student *could* so come into a state of anxiety that it becomes unbearable. The student's anxiety overpowers him, and he think of leaving the course or worse. And amid mass higher education, students may not have ready access to their professors or tutors. It is part of the teaching task to be alert to a possibly raised level of anxiety and so frame the teaching situation that students are supported and feels that they are supported. The student can be likened to the bungee jumper (Barnett, 2007: 1), being urged to leap, to have courage, while knowing that the risk is limited. The jump may even be exhilarating.

Third, teaching in higher education has to be understood as a matter of *energising* the student. Whereas affirmation is a *response* to the student's necessary phenomenological state, and whereas support is an *anticipatory* movement to ensure that the element of risk is maintained at a tolerable level, *energising* is both necessary *and* is contingent. Unless the educational process is imparting in the student *a will to learn* (Barnett, 2007), we cannot be in the presence of a genuine higher education. This is *necessary* if students are to form their own claims, their own judgements, their own actions, for which they take responsibility. It is *contingent* because students will differ in the intensity of this will as their course proceeds (as other aspects of their lifeworld take hold). This energising therefore is in part that of *provoking* the student's will, as much as it is enabling it to spring forward.

Energising is also a matter of *in*-spiring the student, of imparting air to the student (cf. Derrida, 1991; Irigaray, 1999), and this is a necessary part of a genuine higher education. Through it, students take on new life and new vitality, and come into themselves, propelling themselves forward with élan. Such a conception of teaching, of imparting new spirit, is ontologically demanding on the teacher, who has to give of herself. The enthusiasm can be infectious, and it can be caught by the student.

Teaching and research

The relationship between research and teaching has attracted much attention, and a whole battery of terms have arisen, such as 'research-led' teaching, 'research-informed' teaching and 'research-based teaching' (Healey, 2013). These phrases indicate a contested space with markedly different pedagogic intentions at work. Three options stand out.

One option is that of research being seen as giving command over a discipline. What counts, so far as learning is concerned, is informed knowledge, drawn from the latest research in a field. Here, the educational situation will give students a heavy exposure to primary texts in the academic literature. They will be expected to grapple with key papers in the academic journals and form their responses.

A *second option* is to enable students to take on something of *the sheer being of researchers*. Students might be given problems to be found in the research field – and they could be historical examples – and challenged to respond. They might even be encouraged to read biographies and autobiographies of key figures in the history of their discipline. In this way, they can acquire the mode of experience of being a researcher. They come to *embody* what it is to be a researcher.

The *last option* is that of enabling students to acquire *the skills of research*. Here, they would – for instance – undertake literature reviews, set up and run experiments or draw up questionnaires and administer them, conduct small projects, generate and interrogate data, offer some conclusions and 'write up' an ensuing report, or, they might, say, examine online and interpret original historical documents. In this way, students would be acquiring the wherewithal to conduct investigations of their own in the wider society.

While these three options carry the same label – effecting a close relationship between research and teaching – they are quite different ways of construing the research–teaching relationship, and they bear witness to fundamental *schisms* in higher education pedagogy. Respectively, we may term them (a) *episteme* – a focus on knowledge and its acquisition; (b) *ontologico* – a focus on a way of being and seeing the world afresh; and (c) *praxis-techne* – a focus on the skills of being a researcher.

Each of these options has its *pathology*: (a) *episteme* can tip over into the student becoming a sheer repository of knowledge of a field but unable to see the field synoptically. (b) *Ontologico* can become dilettante, with a student thinking that they are a historian or scientist in the making but lacking the necessary substance. (c) *Praxis-techne* can result in a student acquiring disparate research skills but unable to wield them together, still less to put new ideas into the world. Respectively, these are pathologies of a *lack* of (a) vision, (b) substance and (c) creativity. It is evident, then, that the relationship between teaching and research easily gives rise to *limited and pedagogically dangerous paths*.

Some may say that any teacher worth their salt would opt for an approach that draws on all three construals of the relationship between teaching and research. There is, though, an elephant in the room. Research plays only a minor role in most of the twenty-five thousand universities in the world, so an anticipated close relationship between teaching and research would exclude over 90% of teachers in higher education. What is needed is a more generous conception of the relationship. This leads us to the teacher as scholar (cf. Boyer, 1990: 23–24), taking a broad and lively interest in the field of study, seeing its connections with other fields, understanding its key texts and theories, and disinterestedly leading the student on. *This* conception of higher education would put teaching and research into a definite relationship with each other, but it would place teaching *above* research for, *in the educational setting*, teaching is more complex than research. Research has to be on tap, not on top.

Some believe that an essential condition of teaching in higher education is enthusiasm for one's subject. That could imply that the dedicated teacher has simply to be a devotee of their subject and then the students will become enthused. However, this idea is liable to lead to another pathology in higher education, namely the teacher as messiah and the student as faithful acolyte, with the student mesmerised by the teacher's personality and intellectual approach. The wise teacher would deploy his or her knowledge with a light touch.

The end of critical teaching?

Critical thinking is a key concept in higher education – and we shall come to it more fully in chapter 12 – and there are contiguous matters here. Through some scholars in the USA – especially Henry Giroux (1983, 2012), Ira Shor (1992) and Peter McClaren (1995, 2020 – with Petar Jandric) – a loosely formed movement has long been sustained in favour of critical pedagogy, and often drawing on the work of Paulo Freire. A central idea is that since education has social, economic, political and ideological functions, is adjudged to be having deleterious effects in each of those respects and has its place in a world that is manifestly unjust, irrationally unequal and injuriously structured, education should confront these presences; hence, a programme of 'critical pedagogy' and preferably in a spirit of 'praxis' (Gadotti, 1996; Cowden and Singh, 2013).

A riposte to this whole programme of critical teaching has recently been advanced in '*Post-Critical Perspectives*', and a '*Manifesto*' is offered as well

(Hodgson et al., 2017, 2020). These authors have set up camp in higher education, the pitch being that there lies much that is already valuable – 'immanent' – within the educational practices and that philosophy offers resources to tease out those 'practices whose value we can understand in educational terms. That is, not for their political or economic or other purpose'.

We have here, then, two 'critical' conceptions of teaching in higher education, a *critical pedagogy* and a *post-critical pedagogy*. Like ships that pass in the night, they fail to engage with each other. A virtue of critical pedagogy is that it *starts from the external world*, which it sees as being democratically impoverished and socially despoiled, and couples to it a sense that education has been enlisted in the constitution of late capitalism. However, this critical pedagogy movement instrumentalises students, placing them in the service of radical ends that are not up for debate. (This point is noticed by those in the post-critical movement.)

Post-critical pedagogy, in contrast, is not oblivious of malformations in the world but wishes to home in on what is valuable *within* higher education. However, it runs the danger of harbouring a naivety, as if the valuable elements of higher education are there to be uncovered (with tools that philosophy has to offer). The name 'post-critical' is unfortunately apt, for this programme contains a rather limited degree of criticality.

Both programmes share a normative aspect, with each seeing higher education as having potential in bringing about a better world. However, difficulties flow on both sides. In being seized of the pathologies of the wider world, the critical pedagogy programme contends against ideology but *is itself ideological*. On the other hand, the post-critical pedagogues seek solace in higher education in its own right. It is as if they have succumbed to Derrida's (2001a) fantasy of a university 'without condition', separate from the world. But higher education is *always* saturated by regulations, audits, institutional histories, disciplinary interests, in-house conflicts, collective sentiments and sheer state impositions. It does not enjoy the pure 'immanent' space that seems to be assumed. On the one hand, then, the ideological overload of the Critical Pedagogues, overly sensitive to the *structures* that bear in upon teaching. On the other hand, the disinclination of the Post-Critical fraternity to engage with those structures, with its overreliance on *agency* within the pedagogical space.

Teaching as provocation

'Critical pedagogy is [then] dead' (Jandric and McClaren, 2020: 1471). So what is to be done? Let us acknowledge that teaching in higher education is multiply situated among knowledge structures, state requirements, regulatory frameworks, audit arrangements and funding policies. And let us acknowledge, too, that these structures are real and are not easily dislodged.

Higher education, whether in nanotechnology, management studies, nursing studies or social theory, slides on the surface of these structures. To put it formally, there is a deep ontology to teaching in higher education. And now let us suppose that teaching especially in higher education is to be understood as enabling students to form themselves in relation to the world and to be able and willing to make their own pitch on matters.

Each discipline has its own way of going on that reaches even into the formation of sentences and strings of notation; of speech; and of comportment (Foucault, 1977). Yet, characteristically, higher education has pools of freedom, even though it be coloured by culture, ideology, economic framing or nationalism. Teacher and taught bring their own presuppositions to the encounter and dance around each other.

In the laboratory with its dangerous instruments, in the great lecture hall with its serried rows of faces, on the geology fieldtrip, in the sociology seminar, in the music conservatoire practice room and in the webinar, there are pedagogical options. What move is to be made? The task is *not* to teach, if by that is meant to throw at the students a battery of material to be ingested and memorised or even skills to be acquired. It is to harry a little, to dislodge, to lessen the student's hold on their assumptions and to *in*-spire. It is to open to some play (Nørgård et al., 2017) and, rather like the magician, to hold the attention, and to divert it, to open new vistas and to provide a space for unsettlement in the presence of strangeness.

This unsettlement is not a psychological anxiety but is a phenomenological anxiety; a Kierkegaardian troubled unease (Chamberlain and Rée, 2001: chapters 4 and 7). Here, the student is enticed into a cavern of wonders but which is unsettling. Water may rush in, the rocks may be slippery, the tunnel may end in a cul-de-sac, there are rumblings, there is darkness (Bengtsen and Barnett, 2017). This is a darkness produced by a 'pedagogy of vulnerability' (Lysgaard et al., 2019) that not so much brings students to the edge (of the so-called frontiers of knowledge) but puts them *on edge*. In being dislodged from their hold on the world, students become aware that there is no stable place. It is an inner sense that there are always counter-positions and that for any challenging situation (in the clinical setting, on the field trip, in writing an essay) there is always more that can be said or done.

Among the fundamental set of planks in Roy Bhaskar's philosophy of Critical Realism is a 'Holy Trinity' (2010b: 150). Alongside (i) ontological depth and (ii) judgemental rationality was (iii) 'epistemological relativism'. However, talk of relativism brings an unhelpful element into proceedings, implying difficulty in arbitrating across frameworks of understanding. It is much better to imagine the student coming to a sense of epistemological *diversity* attendant on any topic, method, interpretation, conclusion. The student senses the presence of a world that she is trying to fathom – she is an *ontological realist* – but she is uneasy. Awkward questions are put to her, situations are difficult to comprehend, acts are expected of her that seem out of reach. However, this teaching does not leave the student bereft but brings her to a *judgemental rationality* (Bhaskar's third idea). The student is obliged to say or do *something*, while aware of its utter contingency.

There are, then, these *three essential components* of teaching in higher education: (ontological) disturbance, (epistemological) diversity, and (collective) judgmental rationality. A brilliant example of all three conditions together is the pedagogy of Michael Sandel, a USA political philosopher, who deploys – in an Internet setting – interactive technologies to develop a real-time Socratic dialogue (cf. Altorf, 2019) among students across continents over a controversial matter. Here we see *ontological disturbance*, as students are put on the spot and as Mary is confronted with Ahmad's viewpoint (and Mary and Ahmad may be bearers of markedly different cultures); we see *epistemological diversity*, as students are brought to confront rival ways of looking at a matter; and we see *collective rationality*, as the different viewpoints move towards a provisional judgement (even if framed by Sandel). This is a teaching driven by a sense of *teaching as provocation*. And it is also, we may note, a kind of digital 'critical utopia' (Jandric and McClaren, 2020), realising educational possibilities not available in a pre-digital age.

Conclusion

Is teaching in higher education mainly an epistemological or an ontological issue? In higher education, the ontological side is primary, *and triply so*. An educational relationship has to be sustained, such that the students will come to (i) acknowledge the presence of an external world that, to a large extent, lies hidden; (ii) possess the resources to maintain forward motion across their lifespan in peering into the world; and (iii) so go on forming themselves *in a world in incessant motion*.

This is not to say that ontology trumps epistemology *simpliciter*. It is a necessary and, indeed, vital condition that the teacher is on the inside of a domain of knowledge or professional field and has an intimate understanding of its character, its movements and its contemporary shape. Only so can a teacher entice students into a field, prompt a sense of wonders in and of the world to which it is connected and pose difficult questions. The epistemological component has to be in the service of the (triple) ontological components of the world and the student's becoming within it.

It follows that teaching in higher education cannot be a matter of letting students learn (as Heidegger put it); nor can it simply be a heutagogy, 'in which learners, facilitated by a mentor/teacher, determine their own learning' (Snowden, 2017; Glassner and Back, 2020: 2); nor can it be a matter of cocreation (cf. Bovill, 2019). Students have to be led and enticed, and standards observed, but what is key is that the students are brought to an *abiding state of unsettlement and yet gain agency in relation to the world.* Student and world co-emerge (Facer, 2019b), and this is so for the medical student in the clinical situation, the music student in mastering an orchestral instrument, or the economics student understanding a modelling technique. Students have to be put on edge and given a frisson of anxiety that should endure. Only so can justice be done to the triple ontological demand of a genuine higher education.

'Teaching' turns out to be an honorific and even misleading term in higher education, and we are better off without it. A better term is that of pedagogy (Walker, 2006; McLean, 2008; Nixon, 2012a; Peters et al., 2012), which obliges us to keep thinking about the educational practices and purposes that constitute a higher education. The practices include those of affirming, encouraging, persuading, destabilising, questioning, enlarging, darkening, dislocating, widening, deepening, intimating, amusing, showing, declaring, asserting, inviting, cajoling, guiding, unsettling and inspiring the student. In essence, teaching – if we are to retain the term at all – has to be understood as a matter of *provocation*.

10 Curriculum
Making it explicit

Introduction

For a long time, the curriculum was neglected in higher education. Initially, it was assumed that the curriculum was merely a kind of précis of the contemporary state of affairs in a discipline, as established by research and scholarship. This was a shopping-list approach to curriculum, simply listing the topics to be 'covered' (as it was said). As such, curriculum did not have to be understood for it was research that mattered: the curriculum in any discipline was simply an adjunct to a research-driven body of knowledge.

Such a view of curriculum had point when students were largely drawn from well-heeled backgrounds and universities were small in number and size. Then, in an elite system of higher education, there was a social and cognitive affinity among the faculty and the students – a shared cultural capital – and much could be taken for granted. It was only with the emergence of mass higher education – with its heterogeneous cohorts of students, new institutions of higher education and more practically focused courses – that the contents of students' studies gave pause for thought. Only then did such concepts of a programme of study, courses, units and course objectives begin to emerge. Even then, the term 'curriculum' was seldom to be seen, and that remains the case. And yet the very idea of curriculum has to be understood as central to higher education.

The law and lore of curriculum

A curriculum has two facets. It is an attempt to unfold and to make *explicit* the territory of the course of study into which a group of students is to be led. And it is *intentional*, stating the intentions of the teacher or teachers. Straightaway, a paradox arises since the curriculum is not so much hidden (Margolis, 2001; Hinchcliffe, 2020) but is *fictitious*. It stands in a twilight zone, hovering between a field of study and what it is that students actually experience, whether in the classroom, the lecture hall, the laboratory or the fieldtrip. It is barely more than marks on sheets of paper or texts on a screen. Its context is largely *itself*: it is its own *contextualisation* (Bernstein, 1996).

DOI: 10.4324/9781003102939-14

So our question remains: what is this curriculum? One answer could be that a curriculum is an attempt to spell out the contents of a course being undertaken by a *specified* group of students. But as soon as we are on sure ground, so it collapses under us. For we have just observed that the relationship of a curriculum to what is *actually* taught is tenuous. The idea that, in their teaching efforts, lecturers and professors in institutions of higher education are frequently taking their bearings from the stated curriculum, and spend time cross-checking those efforts, is far-fetched. So what is the point of a curriculum-as-text?

Different answers prompt themselves. First, a curriculum has to be understood in the context of the *power background*, especially the relationship between the state and its universities. If the state has the major part to play in framing a curriculum, it will have an interest in holding university staff to account, and having a written document is a means by which accountability may be enforced. If it is the faculty which has much freedom to determine the curriculum, their university will want to hold the teacher – or teaching team – accountable, and, again, the stated curriculum becomes a means of cementing such an accountability relationship. So a curriculum takes on a quasi-legal status. It is an instrument of law, within which the teaching staff are obliged to act. Textbooks on curriculum love to observe that it marks out a course of study (as in 'race course') for the students and it keeps the students on the rails, so to speak. Much less noticed is that it also keeps the teaching staff on the rails. A curriculum is a policing document; a disciplining document (Foucault, 1991).

In a milieu in which the wishes of the students are being accorded increasing attention, making a curriculum explicit is helpful also to the *students*. Often students are meeting a high course fee and may even be heavily indebted, and they have a legitimate wish to be clear as to the experience that their fees are likely to purchase. With a curriculum made explicit, they can readily see what is liable to befall them, the experiences that will come their way, and where they themselves will have to expend some effort. This amounts to a *consumer-information account* of curriculum, where the curriculum has the students as its intended audience. Such a sense of curriculum especially has point in a marketised system of higher education (Molesworth et al., 2011).

It is unlikely that many students will take time to read such a formal document. Nevertheless, in a marketised milieu, in which students' evaluations are given heightened attention, it is important to have some written testimony against which *student complaints* might be assessed. The law-like character of the written curriculum safeguards the interests not only of the student but also of the university. It is a risk-averse policy document on the part of the institution, warding off vexatious claims on the part of the students.

A written curriculum, then, has a legal character, 'legal' understood both with a small 'l' and a capital 'L'. It frames the educational situation, setting boundaries and markers to the way ahead (small 'l'), and it serves as a kind of contract, against which teachers and teaching teams can be held to account by the responsible agency (upper case 'L'). In possessing this dual legal status, the document acts as a form of quality assurance, assuring the institution's management team and the state as to what is being taught in what is otherwise, in higher education, a secret garden. The curriculum is a form of biopower (Foucault, 1980), a panoptikon that exposes and polices the teacher's activities *and* the student's experience even without state officials or university administrators being present.

These are all dismal readings of a curriculum in higher education, testifying to the regulated character of higher education. It is a regulatory environment that is part of the shift that Readings (1997) saw, in higher education losing its connection with culture and becoming subject to an ideology (not his term) of excellence (which *was* his term). The written curriculum produces a legal and regulatory space that acts to steer and *limit* pedagogical possibilities. This is deliberate, for any openness in a programme of studies is to be liable to a departure from the path. And going off-piste in this way is to invite risk, even danger.

A case in point is the inclusion in curriculum statements of 'learning outcomes'. In higher education, learning outcomes are especially otiose. A *higher* education implies an elevation of some kind – Newman (1976) spoke of a university education being an 'ascent'. To receive a higher education is to be dislodged, to be provoked (last chapter), to lose an enduring sense of firm ground and yet to hover over it. This 'higher' is not value-laden but is higher in that the cognitive space opened up always invites the question 'and is that so?' (cf. Leavis, 1969). 'Muhammad says this but Helena says that: what do others think?' It is this questioning that lingers over *every* pedagogical situation in higher education. There is *nothing* to be taught as such; or, when taught, has to be placed in the quasi-public pool of matters for consideration and questioning (Masschelein and Simons, 2012, 2018).

Learning outcomes contain a particular danger, of closing off debate, whereas a proper higher education has to be forever *pedagogically* open (Peters et al., 2012). Even in programmes of study where matters of life are directly at stake – in medicine, in the handling of dangerous substances in the laboratory, in social work, in law, in engineering and so forth – it must always be possible to ask 'and is that so?' The logic of this openness is that one *never* knows what may come forth. Learning outcomes truncate questioning, placing boundaries around the student experience. They even smuggle in a 'do not enter here' notice.

It will be said that there is no difficulty here for openness can be built into the curriculum. But the logic of that move is that *the curriculum vanishes before us*. If a mark of a higher education is a pedagogical openness, a conversation with a principle of 'anything goes' (Feyerabend, 1975), then any curriculum-*as-text* may have little or no correspondence to the curriculum-*as-experienced* (Barnett and Coate, 2005). Our earlier sense of the curriculum-as-text being fictitious is now reinforced because it is completely unclear – and *must* be unclear – as to the relationship between the curriculum as a text and the curriculum as it evolves in practice. And this evolution has two elements: an open conversation, in which the student can put searching questions to the professor and the whole class; and the professor (or course team) critically reflecting on the course while it is in progress and adjusting it *in situ*.

A work of fiction

The curriculum-as-realised is always in motion, on a weekly basis and a daily basis, and in the real-time micro-exchanges of the pedagogical settings; it is a process (Doll, 1993), and never quite fulfilling its possibilities (Carlin and Wallin, 2016). In contrast, the *curriculum-as-text* is frozen in time, at best a set of programme intentions before the event, and now left behind by the pedagogical events, as they unfold. And in that unfolding, other intentions may come into play, especially those of the students. Formalised commentaries from the students – 'student feedback' – are probably of little weight; more significant are the unrehearsed inflections from the students in their experiencing of their educational situations.

What value, then, may we place upon the curriculum-as-text? This curriculum, for all its artificiality, its twilight status, its counterfactual character and its sheer staidness, has value paradoxically as *a piece of fiction*. Like all good fiction, its drafting calls for thought and imagination. Stock phrases will be eschewed as a future programme of studies is envisaged. A glimpse of the breadth and shape of the territory to be covered; the educational aims steering the course; the qualities in students to be developed; some of the problems that will confront the students and the tasks that they may be asked to undertake; a sense of the pedagogical relationship at different stages; the admission process and the patterning of the students' examinations; the responsibilities of the teaching team and the responsibilities of the students: giving thought to these and related matters is all to the good.

The problem is that, as implied, the regulatory function of the curriculum-as-text will supplant its educational function. Once formulated and adopted, it becomes frozen. In having the law-like properties that we noted earlier, the danger is that this curriculum-as-text will ossify as it falls in with a standard format, and the drafters of the document will slip naturally into deploying standard off-the-shelf wordings, and will be subject to a straitjacket in spelling out a set of learning outcomes, with their bullet-point list of actions. The curriculum-as-text becomes an instrumental rather than an educational document.

Are there *any* conditions to be satisfied so as to derive a curriculum that is proper to a higher education? The question has almost run into the sand for several senses of curriculum have been intimated: curriculum-as-text, curriculum-in-motion; curriculum-as-experienced by-students; curriculum-as-observed (although the concept of observation is problematic for where is any curriculum to be observed and who is to do the observing?); and curriculum-as-audited-and-policed. This is a variety of *modes of curriculum*.

The idea of curriculum in higher education rightly, therefore, evokes a frisson of discomfort. It can reflect undue circumspection and can limit horizons. But it can prompt *imaginings* of educational spaces in which students may thrive, and can prompt new ways of realising educational possibilities and responsibilities.

A universal concept?

Might the concept of curriculum have universal applicability? Does a curriculum in quantum mechanics have anything of substance in common with one in anthropology or Japanese literature? In most higher education systems, there are formalities to be observed over the length of the modules or units, the format of the examinations or the hours of teaching. There may also be national expectations that curricula should include a statement of skills. And, as noted, increasingly curricula statements are required to specify the 'learning outcomes' that a programme of studies will realise. But these are all surface matters and our question remains: is there anything of substance that is *universal* across disciplines?

There are two answers on the postcard. The first is that this is not a philosophical matter. There is a raft of practical and policy-oriented issues here, and they can safely be left to the (increasing number of) curriculum specialists in institutions and national agencies. The second is that the curriculum has become a political document, reflecting – as noted – sources of power over the components of a course of study.

But for all that, there are universal features of curriculum in higher education worth noticing. A curriculum in higher education is an expression of *pedagogical responsibility*. It reflects the breadth of the territory within which choices are made. This territory will contain a *stretchiness*. There will be explicit and tacit expectations to be met, but, in most jurisdictions of the world, pools of autonomy are left open. Even where there is a heavy involvement by the state or an external agency or even the university itself, still those who teach tend to retain some degree of responsibility for the shape, character and content of the curriculum.

The curriculum, therefore, is a public statement about the *range of optionality* that informs its design. 'Design' is a legitimate term here, with its connotations of aesthetics, imagination, standards, care and craft (Staley, 2019). The curriculum has to be *imagined*. Given the circumstances, just what might *this* curriculum look like? And this imagination stretches beyond the text to considerations of the kind of graduate – the very *being* of the graduate – that is anticipated (in the programme and in the institution in question). Curriculum design, therefore, is a matter of pedagogical responsibility.

The concept of pedagogical responsibility is *ambidextrous*. On the one hand, it looks to authorities for legitimacy. For instance, a medical curriculum has to heed the contemporary requirements of the medical authorities. In several countries, too, the design of a curriculum has to fall in with the ideological expectations of the state. On the other hand, the design of a curriculum has to *leap ahead*, to carry a set of values into an imagined space of the curriculum as a set of educational practices. The stated curriculum is a chance imaginatively to open a field of pedagogic *possibilities*.

The curriculum, then, can unduly confine or can expansively open a field for the student. A danger is that, in practice, it suffocates the students, who can barely cope in assimilating what is put before them (cognitively, experientially, technically). Whereas it should open spaces, it presents closure; whereas it should provoke, it tacitly invites compliance; and whereas it should offer synoptic understandings that just might lead to some kind of wisdom, it fragments into piecemeal experiences. This pattern of closure is *explicable*. An opening of mind, of large vistas, is precisely *not* what it is wanted. The world is sleepwalking into a general 'stupidity', and academic institutions are in danger of enhancing this global malady. In this diagnosis, the French philosopher, Stiegler (2015) was surely correct.

Time for a synoptic view

For nearly a century, educationalists have been concerned about the narrowness of the higher education curriculum. As a young leader of the University of Chicago, Robert Hutchins (1936) introduced a 'Great Books' curriculum. The idea was that all students of the university should be put in the company of the canon of work that was adjudged to constitute the finest expressions of modern civilisation. The idea has been pressed from time to time, not least by Bloom in his (1987) succès de scandale, *'The Closing of the American Mind'*. Hutchins' programme can be praised for its ambition to find a broad curriculum, so that students might emerge as part of a citizenry, sharing and taking forward a common heritage. It also served the purpose of bringing a common cultural capital to students from diverse backgrounds, as the first movements towards mass higher education were beginning to form.

The programme, however, ran into severe problems, problems that have only intensified over the subsequent years. The canon begged questions: who was drawing it up? On what basis? Was it not unduly selective and did it not betray biases? After all, it seemed to include few if any women, or people of colour, or critics of modernity. It was imbalanced too, in not sufficiently provoking students; it was an unduly safe curriculum.

The Great Books curriculum was an effort to construct a cultural edifice in society and deliberately to enlist academic institutions in that enterprise. It was an ideological project, being loaded with a preponderance of largely white, male and Western (especially USA) accomplishments. That it has failed speaks to large counterforces at work. The state and its agencies look to higher education to advance an agenda in favour of the knowledge economy, and the academic community has become even more fragmented, so making efforts in favour of a common curriculum even more difficult.

However, attempts continue in confronting the perniciousness of disciplinary boundaries. In United Kingdom, a clutch of new universities were established in the 1960s, and much effort was spent in bringing disciplines together, not least so as to give the students a broad curriculum. The cry went up in one of those universities 'to redraw the map of knowledge' (Briggs, 1964). In the end, those more epistemological ventures foundered, as the disciplines reasserted themselves. The idea of general education refused to die, however, a cause into which Habermas has been enlisted (Howard, 1991).

So-called liberal arts programmes are to be found even opening up, both in Asia and in the West. At the same time, multidisciplinary programmes of study are springing up, in which disciplines are brought together to direct attention to a cluster of problems in the wider world. There is a new sense developing that a higher education curriculum, built narrowly around individual disciplines and fields, cannot provide the more synoptic capacities that the world calls for (Berlin, 2000: 214–223; Auxier, 2017; MacIntyre, 2018).

It is one of the features of the new realisms to remind us of the interconnectedness of entities in the world and, that being so, a presumption emerges that higher education should also incorporate elements of interconnectedness. Calls for multidisciplinarity and interdisciplinarity have been made for decades (Klein, 2008), but efforts are now being seen to advance a philosophically backed movement in favour of transdisciplinarity (Lake et al., 2018). A problem facing such efforts is this: what might be the connective tissue between the disciplines (when brought together) *and* the world (since disciplines are *not* part of the fabric of the world but are human inventions)? Some wish to speak of a transdisciplinary ontology (Gibbs and Beavis, 2020; McGregor and Gibbs, 2020), but such an idea runs a risk of confusing the issue. Roy Bhaskar warned us against committing the epistemological fallacy, but this move would commit an *ontological* fallacy, reading epistemological aspects (namely transdisciplinarity) into the world as such. Nevertheless, these matters of interdisciplinarity and transdisciplinarity are vital for the whole world and warrant continued examination.

Much experimentation can be seen around the world, but a fundamental issue remains. On what basis might an organising principle be derived for a higher education for the twenty-first century? *Perhaps*, especially against the background of an increasing nationalism, the curriculum should enable students to become 'global citizens' (Nussbaum, 2010). *Perhaps* – the relationship between humanity and nature having been severely mal-aligned – students deserve a broad curriculum in favour of sustainability (Bartlett and Chase, 2013; Ryan and Cotton, 2013). *Perhaps* the curriculum could represent more of a balance of interests with the wider world, with internationalisation at its centre (Leask, 2015). *Perhaps* being a person in the twenty-first century calls for a wide array of sympathies and modes of being in the world (Latour, 2013). *Perhaps* a curriculum of posthumanism can be worked out (Braidotti, 2013, 2016), but, if so, it would need to transcend the humanities and start from a sense of the totality of the world and be designed not just for the world but *from* the world. It would be a *'non-human curriculum'* (Lysgaard et al., 2019: 114 [RB's emphasis]).

Whatever their aspirations, any general curriculum is going to have value, for it will *provoke students* into unsettling spaces, as they are jostled across disciplinary boundaries, practices and experiences. It will also *provoke the host university* into thought about the ordering of knowledge. (Do academic departments serve any useful value?) And it will *provoke academics* in their roles as teachers over the themes, clusterings and intended experiences for the students.

General curricula are multiplicities with intensities, pacings and spaces in tension within them (Deleuze and Guattari, 2007). To draw on the fundamental schema here (page 34), such curricula move on different planes simultaneously and reside at both their real and their imaginary poles. Such curricula are unstable, and they *generate* instability. This is all to the good, for they mirror the instability of the world. But they are liable to fall below their optimal level, not least so far as their educational possibilities are concerned.

Three questions have emerged to confront those who would champion general education: (i) what precisely is the dominant concern that animates any such programme? (ii) What is the relationship between knowledge and the world that the programme is intended to promote? And (iii) what kind of human *being is* being sought through the education that the programme will offer? Unless these three questions are explicitly addressed, any programme of general education is liable to contain confusions, epistemologically, pedagogically and ontologically.

A curriculum for the world

A profound revolution has befallen the curriculum. From a tacit mantra of 'knowledge, knowledge, knowledge' to a quite explicit mantra of 'skills, skills, skills': this has been the general direction of travel, and, in that vein too, and in many countries, 'employability' has emerged as a dominant trope. Certainly, there have been many paths opening along the way – marked by considerations of decolonisation ('Why is my curriculum so white?'), ideology ('Why is my economics curriculum an apologia for neoliberalism?') and epistemic narrowness and specificity ('Can a curriculum be designed "for a wiser world"?'; Maxwell, 2014). But the dominant pattern has been that of positioning the curriculum so that it is a space for the acquisition of skills.

'Employability', we may note, is an even more questionable trope than 'skills'. It not only frames a student, but it does so by seeming to place a student in the world of work and action (Arendt, 1958). But *work is not valued in itself*, for what is tacitly in play here is a selected portion of the labour market, namely high-earning and productive parts of the labour market. Descartes' 'I think, therefore I am' (admittedly always problematic) has here been replaced not even by 'I act, therefore I am' but by 'I generate high economic value, therefore I am.' However, privileging employability neglects the potential of the curriculum as a space in which thought, critique and imagination might be nurtured.

Responses to points of this kind tend to take two directions. First, curricula should incorporate *transferable* skills so that graduates can transfer their skills across settings. But are there *any* really transferable skills? Are the lawyer's communication skills at all comparable to those of the surgeon, the civil engineer or the orchestral player? Skills are not just context-specific but have their home in kinds of *habitus*, and are not good travellers. However, even if we are charitable towards the notion of transferable skill, there is little agreement on what is to count *as* a transferable skill. Is learning how to learn a skill? Can there be such skills as 'complexity skills'? This difficulty has come about because the term 'skill' has become so dominant that it has been stretched to a point of utter thinness. It is an empty but still powerful signifier.

It is evident that thinking about the curriculum in higher education is in a mess. It has grown chaotically. Rather like the rhizome depicted by Deleuze and Guattari as an emblem of the world, the modern curriculum is formless, going this way and that, adding on elements here and there, and seeking sustenance wherever it may be found. Its chaotic form justifies the title of 'assemblage'. But it has grown especially in the direction of *performativity* (Lyotard, 1984: 48), with the tendrils marked 'knowledge' fading, while those marked 'understanding' are now invisible. There are, too, absences of those marked 'thought', for thinking is hardly any longer prized. Problems are to be 'solved' rather than worried over.

This is, then, a misshapenness in curricula, wandering in some directions and leaving others alone. However, the rhizome metaphor itself is problematic, being unduly static (chapter 1). Even if the largest sense of both knowledge and skills is included, there would remain a gross deficiency.

Left out – and this is the *second option* – is the matter of sheer *being*. It is the student who knows or does not know; it is the student who acquires skills or does not acquire skills. It is the student who decides in a situation whether and how to deploy her or his knowledge or their skills, and there is continuous motion here, to which the concept of life-*wide* learning is testimony (Jackson, 2011). Simultaneously, the student engages with learning networks that reach into and across the world, of which the university programme is but a part.

Heidegger (1998) spoke of being as 'being-possible'. Being is only *being* insofar as it has possibilities. But the possibilities are often unknown and have to be eked out as best they may and the student's being extended accordingly. It follows that we need metaphors of motion *and* the idea of becoming: the student has her *being-in-motion* and is always a *becoming-student*. In unfolding in multiple and sometime antagonistic directions, the student is in a state of perpetual becoming.

Knowing, acting, being

The higher education curriculum, then, has three educational moments: knowing, acting and being (Barnett and Coate, 2005). In *knowing*, the student in higher education develops an understanding of knowledge that she encounters. The concept of understanding is vital but has seldom been properly addressed (cf. Elliott, 1975). In coming to an understanding, the student makes the knowledge encountered her own. She brings it in from the cold and tends it, going inside it. This knowledge is no longer inert but comes alive. She allows it to come into her being and assimilates it, but then accommodates to it, forming it to some degree within her own schemas of the world (Piaget, 1972). Finally, she surrounds it, becoming comfortable with it. But it is an unstable comfort, for this understanding understands that understanding can never be exhausted.

In *acting*, the student is able to deploy her knowledge, especially her tacit knowledge (Polanyi, 1966, 1978). Her understanding gives her authority to engage in epistemic and practical acts. She is able to form judgements, to place them into the world, to give them voice. The term 'skill' is inadequate here. In these epistemic and practical acts, whether in the performing arts, in civil engineering, in philosophy or in pure mathematics, the student puts herself forward, accepting responsibility for those acts. She embodies her understandings. More than a reflective practitioner, she is a philosophic practitioner (Tribe, 2002), able to reason about her actions and place those reasons against a horizon of the world. And in *being*, the student's self is always in motion but yet is able to find an occasional resting place to form judgements and to act. The student moves into that uneasy but yet assured space of 'authoritative uncertainty' (Goodlad, 1976), gaining a new relationship with the world, and even with herself. She come into herself.

These three moments of the curriculum – knowing, acting, being – are central to the idea of higher education. But over time, the balance between the three moments has varied considerably (Barnett et al., 2004). There is always a tendency for one of the three moments to be dominant (and the hierarchy differs *across the disciplines*), so leading to a lopsided curriculum. *Knowing* becomes mere memory-within-silos, *acting* in the world is reduced to a mere performance of skills-for-employability, and *being* is placed in jeopardy, locked into frozen stances in the world.

Conclusions

Curriculum is a central concept of higher education but is seldom interrogated. On occasion, matters bubble up. What part are skills to play? To what extent can a curriculum incorporate action elements, whether on campus or in the community? What is the relationship between knowledge and practice? Can there be an overarching transdisciplinary framework? Is it to be a problem-solving *or* a problem-*based* curriculum? (Savin-Baden, 2003). But even where there are responses to such questions, the curriculum-as-stated is necessarily fictitious, as the curriculum-in-practice unfolds. And in that unfolding, the *three moments of knowing, acting and being are always in motion*, weaving in and out of each other, conceptually and practically.

The higher education curriculum is elusive. It cannot be caught; the butterfly always escapes the net. It has an invisibility attaching to it. Perhaps, then, talk of curriculum should be abandoned. But there remains value in holding onto the idea of curriculum and in trying to make explicit the intended and *imagined* component parts that are to form the envisaged assemblage and their interrelationships. In thinking about the curriculum, spaces may open that may bring into view never-glimpsed possibilities and so pave the way for entirely new relationships with – and *for* – the world.

11 Being a student

A committed uncertainty

Introduction

What is it to learn and what is it to be a student in higher education? For many, these matters lie at the heart of any philosophy of higher education. However, just as with the term 'teaching', we must pose the question as to whether the very term 'learning' has much of a place in higher education.

My argument in this chapter is as follows. The world is in motion. All the entities of the world – viruses, glaciers, human beings, technologies, social institutions *and our knowledges of all of these entities* – are connected. Moreover, they are *inter*-connected, influencing each other and always on the move. What it is to learn at the highest level, in these circumstances, is to come into an awareness – however hazy – as to the interconnectedness of matters-in-motion and to a state of *reasoned disequilibrium*, all the while unstable in a perplexing world. It is a task of higher education to help to bring about in students this state of *reasoned-and-discomforted-but-not-overly-discomforted disequilibrium*.

Disciplined excitation

What is it to learn in the university in and for the twenty-first century and beyond? The clues, as they say, are in the question. In that phrase 'in and for the twenty-first century and beyond', the 'for' is vital, as is the 'and beyond'. On the latter point, we might observe that a large number of the students entering higher education at the end of the first quarter of the twenty-first century will be alive in the twenty-second century, and they will encounter and be involved in many matters across their lifespan. Higher education, therefore, has a responsibility to provide its students with the resources to live lives constituted by projects and interests that have enduring and intrinsic value *and* which elicit personal – and ultimately worldly – vitality (Ortega, 1946), and so assist not just their lifelong learning but also their life-*wide* learning (Jackson, 2011). Students' formal learning takes its place *alongside* a welter of informal learning processes in their family, recreational, work and social lives.

And what of that 'for' in 'for the twenty-first century'? What is it that the twenty-first century calls for? Matters of ecological devastation, global

DOI: 10.4324/9781003102939-15

conflict, pandemics, nuclear arms, inequality, undue nationalism and governmental legitimacy might come to mind. But these matters hint at even deeper issues. What is it to *be* in the twenty-first century? How is the relationship across peoples of the whole world, and to the whole Earth, to be construed? What place should be given to the economy? What are the possibilities of knowledge and where might it be its limits? Are there epistemic virtues that may help to provide an authentic grasp of the world and which may also help students in making their way in the world?

The world is in motion, and it is unstable. Human beings affect glaciers, and (the receding of) glaciers affects human beings. There is interaction here between thought and the world – not only that the world presses on thought but that *thought can affect the world*. Rarely, however, are we invited to consider the ways in which those two worlds interconnect. The modern realists want to remind us of the presence of the Real, a world that is *there*, independently of humanity's feeble attempts to gain an understanding of it (Ferraris, 2015; Harman, 2018), but they accord scant attention to the *interplays* between human knowledge and the world. The world always remains elusive: there is always more that lies in front of thought. But, and in part *precisely because of its limitations*, thought can and has wreaked havoc in the world, and the world, in turn, exerts its powers on human life.

How does this impinge upon learning in higher education? Profoundly, and at different levels. At the surface level, legitimate questions may be raised, for example, about the comparative pedagogical cultures in different parts of the world and their tacit conceptions of the pedagogical relationship. Dare the student voluntarily ask a question of the professor? In some cultures, probably not. But, at deeper levels, more awkward matters arise.

The world is in motion. The Real of the world, both the natural and the human worlds, is never stable, and human being has to find a way of accommodating to this instability. Our learning is but a feeble attempt to adapt, to bring about a new relationship with the world, so that we are better placed in this changing world. And humanity has derived various ways of widening its modes of knowledge, both in knowing how matters are and how to accomplish matters. *By sheer luck*, the formal knowledges associated with higher education – the 'disciplines' – turn out not only to illuminate our grasp of the world and our powers over the world but also to possess educational properties and powers to change the knower.

This ontological property of knowledge – its capacity to change human being – was recognised in the early nineteenth century by German philosophers and came to be codified in the educational idea of *Bildung*. Certainly, there are educational problems over knowledge. Are some knowledges more powerful than others? Does practical knowledge have similar powers to that of theoretical and empirical knowledge? Is tacit knowledge even more powerful than explicit knowledge? We can sidestep those matters here. What can be said here is that the forms of knowledge appropriate to higher education may – and should – profoundly affect one's being in the world, and so produce a battery of 'modes of existence' as Latour (2013) has called them.

But not one of the knowledges – appropriate to higher education – or any of their sub-forms is stable: they are always changing. If they were not, they should not be candidates for inclusion in a higher education curriculum for they would then be ideologies.

So we have now *a triple instability – of and in the world*; in the *accumulated forms of knowledge* of the world; and in our adjustments to the world (our *being*). This set of reflections prompts a *three-world thesis of learning* in which learning in higher education involves a *triple excitation*: an excitation in the *student* in response to an excitation in *knowledge*, which is itself a response to excitation in the *world*.

The idea of supercomplexity

Supercomplexity is not a concept of learning, but it forms part of the *immediate and crucial* background of learning. Supercomplexity straddles the worlds of the Real (the way the world is), and the responses of human beings to that world, and it has ontological, epistemological and phenomenological aspects.

Supercomplexity is located by *four sub-concepts*, those of uncertainty, unpredictability, contestability and challengeability (Barnett, 2000). Each is both real and phenomenological (they are both in the world and they are in *us*), and they interact with each other. We may locate the four concepts in a table:

	World	Ontology	Self	Epistemology
Cognitive	(a) *Unpredictability*	Ontology of the world	(c) *Contestability*	Epistemology of the world
Experiential	(b) *Uncertainty*	Ontology of the self	(d) *Challengeability*	Epistemology of self

It may seem from this table that its key terms occupy fixed and discrete positions but – to the contrary – *each one spreads dynamically across the table*, and hence the dotted lines.

The table points to the world's *indeterminacy*, a global virus and the ensuing pandemic being a striking example. The openness of events in the world is real, and the virus exhibits *unpredictability* (quadrant [a]). The felt *uncertainty* is a response to such unpredictability in the world (quadrant [b]), giving rise to raw emotions, even to fear. This uncertainty is compounded by a sense that, while the phenomenon of the virus can be examined, rival theories of it may emerge. The coronavirus is *contestable* (quadrant [c]), not that it does not exist (as some would have had us believe) but in the sense that its character can always be better understood, no matter where current understandings lie. Lastly, out-of-the-blue, the virus arrives – it is not just in our imaginations – and is unsettling. It is accompanied by drama, flowing from its *challengeability* (quadrant [d]): human life is severely challenged.

Learning characteristic of higher education is *an opening of oneself across all of the four quadrants*. It is to open oneself to an (a) *unpredictability* in the world, (b) *uncertainty* in our sense of ourselves in relation to that unpredictability, (c) *contestability* in our representations of the world and (d) *challengeability* in one's own understandings of the world, including of oneself. It is to come to a sense that the world is in flux and that our knowledge of it is always unstable and that *we* are in motion within the world. It is also to open *oneself* to being dislodged (in recognising both that the world itself is changing – the virus mutates, democracies turn into dictatorships, personality disintegrates – *and* that one's understandings are unstable). *And* it is to form authoritative *responses* to this world, in all its motion and multiple complexities.

Troublesome knowledge

Pertinent here is the matter of troublesome knowledge (Meyer and Land, 2005; Johnson, Murphy and Griffiths, 2019). There is dispute as to whether this troublesomeness is epistemological or ontological. Does the troublesomeness arise from features in the knowledge that have to be mastered, certain concepts being foundational to disciplines? In this case, troublesomeness is inherent in learning. Or is the troublesomeness more a contingent matter, as to how different students respond to the difficulties that confront them? Given the schema proposed here, it is evident that troublesomeness in higher education has *both* moments, it being necessary *and* contingent.

The grid of supercomplexity can be considered to be a grid of troublesomeness, for troublesomeness characterises *each of the four quadrants*, a sense of the *unpredictability* of the world, a realisation that accounts of the world are always *contestable*, the *challengeability* to one's own comprehensions of the world and the *uncertainty* that thereby ensues. This is a *complex of troublesomeness* that can constitute a severe dislocation of self. And this exposure is ratchet-like. Once one has come onto this grid, once one has formed these senses – of a world in motion and our accounts of it being always insecure – this dislocation cannot be undone. The grid amounts to a *constellation of fragility* that is inherent to higher education.

It follows that troublesomeness is not a moment, not a feeling, not an educational situation that has to be overcome, but is both a natural part of the idea of higher education and is required, and is to be actively *encouraged*.

What is it to be a doctor? It is to be faced with a surfeit of demands – too many patients, technologies to be mastered, an unceasing flow of new drugs (with their differential efficacies), changing procedures and technological possibilities, new findings in medical science, audit procedures, heightening expectations from increasingly diverse patients, the political sphere and national agencies, *and* insufficient resources in responding to this panoply of impositions – *but still possess the wherewithal to make authoritative interventions*. The doctor is but a node amid huge and colliding assemblages of knowledge, social institutions, markets, personal identities, technologies, algorithms, communities and the economy and yet is all the time being *agentic*. No wonder that some in the medical profession experience burn-out.

But the doctor has *also* to live in the world amid supercomplexity. Supercomplexity is marked by the question 'What is it to be a doctor in the twenty-first century?' Only a string of responses can be offered, invoking knowledge, technique, care, standards, reflection, health, wellbeing, ethics, professionalism, embodiment, compassion, healing, life, death and so forth. There can be no answer that yields *any* stability. To the contrary, the very asking of the question, and efforts to respond, will serve only to furnish *additional and competing* categories through which the question can be interpreted. *The doctor has to practise* as *a doctor without any prospect of pinning down what it is to be a doctor.*

A medical student, accordingly, is heading for a world both of irremediable complexity *and* supercomplexity, in which both the Real – independent of our doctor – *and* the categories of being a doctor are destabilised. *Troublesomeness is of the essence* of what it means to be a doctor. It is not a malady to be overcome. It has to be *lived with*, not as penance but in a state of contentment (Gibbs, 2017), the student acquiring resources to accept troublesomeness.

In the previous chapter, I suggested that the term 'teaching' should be abandoned. So now 'learning': the term misleads, implying some kind of settled new accommodation to the world is possible. However, a world of complexity and supercomplexity, and an abiding sense of troublesomeness as a necessary feature of higher education, leads to a goal of *un*learning; of a shedding of any definite understandings. Now, higher education promises a journey into a state of excitation, wonderment, puzzlement and disconcertedness at the world in its *unpredictability*; the *uncertainty* that that unpredictability prompts; the instability that arises in the face of the *contestability* of accounts of the world; and the intuition that one's state of being is always *challengeable*.

Dispositions *and* qualities

What implications arise from these considerations for higher education? We have noted that the two traditions of 'liberal education' and 'Bildung' have been influential, and even beyond Europe: however, neither is adequate to the twenty-first century. Under conditions of complexity, supercomplexity and a world both hyper-connected and in motion, to be a student in higher education is to be on a voyage that experiences continuing and stratified instability, with little in the way of a secure hold. The student is in motion, amid knowledges and practices that exhibit turbulence, in an institution that is being buffeted, and in a world and on an Earth that is profoundly unstable. A proper higher education has to have a strong ontological character, taking its bearings from a sense of the Real of the world.

We can, I think, meet this challenge through an educational theory of dispositions and qualities: both are crucial and neither is reducible to the other.

There are *six and only six* dispositions that should characterise the learning space of higher education:

- A willingness to hold oneself open to experiences, to encounter the world
- A preparedness to listen to the whole world
- A will to learn *and* to unlearn
- A will to engage
- A criticality (next chapter)
- A determination to keep going forward, to explore.

In contrast, there is a *multitude of qualities* that can legitimately be developed in higher education. Here are just *some* of the more obvious ones:

- Courage
- Carefulness
- Truth-seeking
- Integrity
- Self-discipline
- Respect for others
- Quick-wittedness
- Inventiveness
- Pragmatism
- Skilfulness
- Energy
- Kindness
- Thoughtfulness
- Quickness
- Empathy
- Steadfastness

So understood, *dispositions and qualities are radically different*:

- Dispositions generate forward motion in human beings, whereas qualities are aspects *of* that motion.
- Dispositions are limited in number, whereas qualities are numerous and extendable: there is *optionality* in the qualities and *none* in the dispositions.
- The six dispositions are *universal*, applying to *every* programme of study, whereas qualities are *more specific* to disciplines and programmes, and even institutions of higher education may have their favoured panoply of qualities.

- Every student in a programme of study should be expected to take on and exemplify the six *dispositions*, whereas each student, even in a small class, will take on his or her own palette of *qualities* (provided that the pedagogy encourages that difference).
- The six dispositions are vital in becoming a human being in a complex world, whereas the qualities constitute a student's *individual* character. It is the latter that tutors try to recall – the individual student's qualities – in writing a reference after graduation.

The six dispositions are fundamental to what it is to gain a higher education: they are *necessary* conditions of *being* in an age of complexity and supercomplexity. They are ontological conditions: unless students emerge in possession of each of these dispositions, they have not gained a genuine higher education and will not be equipped adequately to prosper in, and contribute to, a world that is in incessant physical and ideational motion. *The dispositions* impart a motion to the student that is fitting for the motion in the world. *The qualities*, however, are the ways in which students derive their own individual character and form the basis on which they can forge their own way through life.

This educational theory of higher education solves an old problem and opens another. Given the differences across disciplines and institutions *and students themselves*, is the educational task common or context-bound? Universalism or particularism? It is *both*, the dispositions being universal and the qualities being particular. The *universality of the dispositions* is required since the (ontological and epistemological) character of the world has universal features – of complexity and supercomplexity – to which higher education has to find an adequate response right across the world, and which can hold across all disciplines and all students. The dispositions begin not from the student but from the way the world *is*.

The qualities, on the other hand, are centrally concerned with the individuality of the student as a developing subject, in command of their own agency. This sense of *qualities* is in accord with Biesta's (2006: 148) sense that education should not constitute an attempt 'to produce a particular kind of subjectivity'. *However*, alongside the particularity of the qualities, the idea of dispositions situates higher education against a horizon of the totality of the world and seeks an adequate and *universal* educational response *to* the world. Through this juxtaposition of dispositions and qualities, we may hope to derive a higher education that is adequate to the universal challenges that the world brings *and* which just may help to develop individuals' individual agency in possession of their own causal powers (cf. Scott, 2019). We can have both universality and individuality: it is not a zero sum situation.

But now a new problem arises. There has been much discussion of *epistemic virtues* (e.g. Brady and Pritchard, 2003; Greco, 2011; Morton, 2014), these being virtues that come in the wake of serious efforts to understand the world. However, the theory of dispositions and qualities being proposed here – which is a variant of virtue philosophy – poses the issue as to whether each disposition and/or quality is an epistemic virtue or is simply a human virtue. And *then* arises a yet further issue as to whether bringing on such virtues is a matter of the educational process *or*, whisper it softly, is much more a function of the university as an *institution* with all of the extraordinary experiences that it offers.

Authoritative uncertainty

'Authoritative uncertainty' is a term introduced by the English educationalist of higher education, Sinclair Goodlad (1976), and it is much in keeping with the spirit of the analysis here. Given a sense of the complexities of the world, and an ensuing acute sense of supercomplexity, uncertainty is of the essence in higher education. As intimated, there is a triple uncertainty – of the world, accounts of the world and our anchorings to the world.

It may be that part of school teaching, ordinarily conceived, is to bring pupils to some points of reasoned security in the world: they are required to know things. On the basis of being secure, so pupils may go into the world and prosper. But higher education is precisely not of this character. It is to perplex, to unsettle, to provoke, to discomfort and to destabilise. It is to make strange that which is familiar, *and* it is also to approach a place of reasoned *in*security. This difference helps to explain why some university professors will advise – or require – their new students to disregard all that they have learnt in school. A proper higher education is a matter of both epistemological and ontological *dis*comfort.

Talk not only of discomfort but also of troublesomeness, excitation and strangeness – to pick out some of the other concepts here – could point to a fragmentation of the student's *being*. And, as a matter of fact, across the world, higher education systems are characterised by rising student non-completion (attrition) rates and concerns over student suicide. Being a student in the twenty-first century is a challenging matter. Doubtless several matters come into play in this situation, but we may conjecture that a growing instability arising from students' programme of studies may be part of the story.

What is extraordinary is that, *at its best*, higher education empirically seems to bring students on so as to attain some stability. They reach a place where they *are* able to live with uncertainty, in all of its forms. How might this be? It might be tempting to respond with the suggestion that it is a matter of social and cultural capital. Students from certain kinds of background – family, home, schooling, networks – have inner resources with which to tolerate the ambiguity that this pedagogical uncertainty brings. There may be something in that – we may leave it to the sociologists to unravel the matter – but it cannot provide the entire story.

In an empirical study, I can recall interviewing a student who had just graduated from one of England's ancient universities, and the student admitted her difficulties in striking out on her own in her essays; so she tended to play safe and frame her texts around what others were saying in the literature. This was probably a student with much in the way of personal resource but who nevertheless struggled to express her own point of view in her essays. On the other hand, I can also recall interviewing a student at a new university – the first in her family to go into higher education – who was brimming over with commitment and enthusiasm, and very conscious that her positive spirit owed much to the motivation that she had derived from the encouragement of her tutors: 'when you get someone who really believes in you, you know, it's really inspiring.'

What is at stake here is a self-belief in one's capabilities in grappling with a tsunami-like flow of (cognitive and experiential) unsettlement. The social psychologists term this 'self-efficacy' (Bandura, 1977), implying a capacity to direct oneself with both efficiency and effectiveness, but it does not fully meet the bill here. The self-belief of which I speak is the extraordinary achievement that higher education holds out, that it is possible for someone – often in transit to adulthood – to come into a space of security even amid turbulence and difficulties. It is akin to the potholer who has burrowed through narrow gaps in enclosing rock formations, almost completely in the dark, only suddenly to emerge into a great cavern, that even has some lighting and is replete with amazing crystalline forms. One is perpetually in the dark, but the cave offers transitory shafts of light. All too soon, one is plunged back into utter darkness (Aaen, 2019; Dall'Alba and Bengtsen, 2019), but our intrepid explorer has an inner assurance and confidence to keep pressing on.

More than self-efficacy, this is *self-possession*, but it is not hubris. Rather, it is a self-possession that emerges in an awareness of the world and its unpredictability, of contestations about accounts of the world, and even of oneself. A medical doctor is aware that viruses mutate and that they are not always well understood, and that there are many rival accounts of them, and that what is it to be virologist is itself unclear: in the evening, the phone call may bring an invitation of an interview on national news tomorrow, with the many and conflicting expectations that will accompany that. The doctor knows that there is no firm ground to be had; furthermore, she or he knows that the territory is conflicted and potholed. But there is a confidence to go on and act professionally even while living with that quadruple uncertainty.

Jouissance amid difficulty

Goodlad's phrase that we encountered earlier – 'authoritative uncertainty' – beckons again, but now it can be finessed. Uncertainty is central to the idea of higher education that I am proposing here and multiply so – in relation to the world, to accounts of the world and to one's own accounts of the world and ultimately, therefore, to oneself. It is a personal multiplicity of uncertainty, of fact and value, of thought and action, of doubt and will.

One's being is now on edge. 'Uncertainty' is present but 'authority'? Instances are common of individuals who have accomplished much in their lives but who wonder when they are 'going to be found out'. The more that is accomplished, the more the sense of the fragility of the ice upon which one stands. The further one moves on, the more one sees into matters and becomes sensitive to the widening pools of uncertainty.

Instead, therefore, of an authoritative uncertainty, higher education offers the prospect of an uncertainty that is not just tolerated but even *enjoyed*. One comes to live amid pools of uncertainty, in the Real of the world, in judgements about the world and in oneself. Better to be Socrates dissatisfied than a fool satisfied, as John Stuart Mill remarked (1964: 260). The triple destabilisation – the world, truth claims and self – provides the basis of *self*-sustainability. One acquires a little separateness from the world, from claims about the world and about oneself, and one is able to make informed judgements, however tentative, however ephemeral. One is now one's own person, thrown onto one's resources *to determine how to respond to the pools of uncertainty that confront one*. Certainly, these powers of judgement are heavily circumscribed; that is understood. But possessing a sense of there being boundaries to the spaces in which one can exercise judgement adds to the self-confidence. There is security *within* the insecurity.

In many countries, students' success at the end of their programme of studies is marked by a glitzy academic ceremony, full of ritual, solemnity and huge pleasure, and even some fun. The formalities are usually followed by an informal get together over tea and snacks, where – with everybody happy and photographs being taken – students not untypically introduce their professors to their proud parents. At such events in the United Kingdom, I have *not* overheard a student say that 'being here I have gained a lot of knowledge' or 'being here, I have acquired many skills.' I have, though, overheard a student say on these occasions something like 'Being here has changed my life.' And in so saying, students exude self-confidence while now knowing that any thought that they have, anything they put into the world, anything that they say, any claims that they encounter, any stance that they take up, is marked by instability.

A genuine higher education does not, *in the first place*, stand in the realms of epistemology or in techné, although *both have their crucial parts to play* – but in the realm of ontology. This is the wonder of a higher education, that it can change one's being and one's hold on life and the world. The student comes to recognise and to live purposively with uncertainty.

We can continue with Goodlad's phrase of 'authoritative uncertainty' but perhaps a happier phrase is '*committed* uncertainty'. This phrase reflects the extraordinary accomplishment that is testimony to the possibility of higher education, that individuals can be brought to a radicalised sense of the instability of the world, of accounts in the world and of oneself, and still have a commitment *to* the world (Wyatt, 1990). One is profoundly sensitive to the uncertainty of the world and to one's hold on it, and yet one is not paralysed into inaction. To the contrary; one is stirred into inquisitiveness about the world, about accounts of the world and about oneself in the world, and even to responsibilities that flow therefrom.

One of Chopin's preludes (opus 25, number 4) is marked as 'agitato'. That seems to me to be an admirable term here. The task and the achievement of a genuine higher education is to encourage the unfolding of the student into a state of agitation. One is always restless, never quiescent, and is in a state of *disciplined excitation* that is at once cognitive and experiential, and at once epistemic and ontological. One always has a will to learn.

Conclusion

Just as with the term 'teaching', so too the term 'learning' has to be ditched in the philosophy of higher education. This is not to repudiate either knowledge or skills that one may 'learn'. Both are necessary components, but they are not part of the meaning of higher education. It is in part like going from London to Paris by rail. One needs the rail system and all that is attendant on it, including the systems, knowledges and services, but the purpose of the rail journey does not lie in those systems, knowledges and services, crucial as they are. The purpose of the journey is to emerge from the tunnel under La Manche and arrive in Paris in good heart, ready to face what is in front of one in that extraordinary city. And on emerging onto the streets of Paris, one's demeanour may even differ from how one was on leaving London, perhaps a little uncertain as to how the day might proceed, but nevertheless intent on going forward in a positive spirit.

Learning in higher education has all of these components but more so. One emerges not – a là Plato – from the darkness of a cave blinkingly into daylight. Rather, one comes into a spaciousness that is fraught with uncertainty and even some *continuing darkness*; uncertainty as to what the world is like, how the world is seen by others and how – therefore – one is to understand oneself. And yet, somehow, one has acquired the dispositions and one's own qualities to go on amid uncertainty and amid the complexity and supercomplexity that contribute to that uncertainty. This is an uncertainty of being in which one can yet commit oneself, can venture forward, and in which one has an abiding and optimistic will to learn. Being a student in higher education, therefore, is to come into a state of *committed* uncertainty.

12 Critical thinking
The three crazy escalators

> Thinking provokes general indifference. It is a dangerous exercise nevertheless.
> (Gilles Deleuze and Félix Guattari, *What is Philosophy?* 2013: 41)

Introduction

The current age is one of mis-trust. The political sphere, public institutions – including universities – and the mass media are distrusted; statements are met with the accusation 'Well, he would say that, wouldn't he?,' and we are warned not to trust experts. In 2016, the term 'post-truth' was the Oxford English Dictionary word of the year, a reflection in part of the free-for-all that social media – with its light regulation – became. Culture wars break out, with those on the left taking succour from postmodernism and segments of critical theory, while those on the right complain that universities are dominated by socially liberal or even left-wing sympathies. Mistrust became a strong feature even within the academic world, a large segment of which took up with alacrity Ricoeur's neologism of 'a hermeneutics of suspicion' (the phrase was actually abandoned by him (Scott-Bauman, 2009)): all was suspect, seemingly being mere ideology or false consciousness (Rosen, 1996).

Given all of this, it is apparent both that the need for critical thinking has never been higher and that the connection between universities and critical thinking deserves at least to be restated, if not fundamentally to be rethought.

The territory: unclear options

Critical thinking might mean the capacity:

(i) to interrogate texts for their logical validity, the critical thinker being essentially a logician (able to detect departures from *modus ponens* and *modus tollens*);
(ii) to evaluate a text against relevant standards, say of a discipline;
(iii) to bring wide frameworks of understanding to bear in evaluating a text;

DOI: 10.4324/9781003102939-16

(iv) to assess one's own work ('critical *self*-reflection');
(v) to assess and evaluate a situation into which one is thrown (e.g. a clinical setting);
(vi) to form one's own ideas (authenticity);
(vii) to be *disposed* autonomously to think critically;
(viii) to be willing to act out one's critical judgements, especially in difficult situations (the whistle-blower engaging in critical action);
(ix) to be disposed so as to detect distortions in the frameworks of the wider society and to take action ('ideology critique');
(x) to critique frameworks of thought and action from alternative viewpoints ('critical interdisciplinarity');
(xi) to have the courage to contend with power (speaking 'truth to power');
(xii) to be active in cultural debates, even in culture wars, as critical intellectuals.

It is immediately evident, from this classification, that 'there has been a tendency to define [the idea of critical thinking] far too narrowly' (Davies and Barnett, 2015: 12). This classification indicates that the idea can be interrogated for its breadth, levels, skills, implications for judgement and for action, and the extent to which it places demands upon human being as such. Furthermore, there are many possible combinations in the one student and there may be tensions. Critical thinking is susceptible of multiple *legitimate* interpretations,

Imagine the following situation. In a pedagogical setting, students are presented with a text from an article or a newspaper item or, say, a video of a clinical or a laboratory episode or a historical event or an incident in an indigenous culture and, in each case, the students are invited critically to examine what is put in front of them. Superficially, there is a single logic at work, across the disciplines. In each situation, we have (a) a group of students being presented by (b) the professor with (c) a specific piece of text or a particular incident and (d) the students being invited to examine what they see. The professor might even instruct the students to (e) 'be critical' of what is before them. The pedagogical situations bear the same superficial logic, with at least five common components, but there are profound differences between these educational settings.

Just some of the responses called for here on the part of the students are those of interpreting movements on a screen, having empathy, discerning patterns in a text, imagining other possibilities, glimpsing hidden interests at work, scrutinising with care actual words used, examining the logic of an argument, interpreting actions, placing what is encountered in a wider background and analysing themes in an account. The term 'critical thinking' turns out to be an umbrella for a very wide range of meanings *and* educational interests.

We can sympathise, therefore, with the student who, having submitted their essay or project report, is faced with the instruction from their professor to 'be more critical' (doubtless now a margin comment online). Even in the context of a particular essay on a particular topic, and even in relation to a particular paragraph that the student has written, the phrase 'be critical' is disturbingly nonspecific. The student can justifiably wonder just what she or he is now to do to improve their essay or report. Which of the many possible kinds of response is being sought from the professor? It is completely unclear.

Openly critical

We may press the matter even further, and in *four steps*. Although I have just identified a wide range of examples of critical thinking, they possess a limited range. A *first step* is to recognise that all those examples possess a set of *similarities*: (i) a student in any of the disciplines just implied – medicine, cultural studies, history, philosophy, chemistry, sociology and anthropology – is being *presented* with an exhibit by a professor. (ii) Each such instance of critical thinking is *invitational* within a pedagogical situation. The professor presents the exhibit and asks the students to response (albeit critically). (iii) It is a bounded – and so a *near-closed* – educational setting with a strong requesting element written into it. (iv) The students are being invited to display their *skills* of critical thinking.

Now, let us move to *stage two*. Imagine students from each discipline are working much more under their own steam. They are working on experiments in the laboratory or are reading academic texts in the university library (or elsewhere) or are engaged on a mini-anthropological project. Perhaps in the laboratory, a professor is hovering, but by and large, the students are making progress by themselves. In all cases, the educational situation is quite open. In *no* case is a student being given an instruction by the professor, to 'see what you make of this', and still less to 'be critical'. In every case, the student is largely being accorded pedagogical space to attend to the task in hand, form their own responses, and make their own judgements. What is in question here is *not* the students' critical thinking skills in *response* to an instruction but, rather, their preparedness to be spontaneously critical, when faced with academic material in an *open* educational situation. (This distinction between closed and open pedagogical situations is *crucial* in higher education.)

In the language of the literature on critical thinking, the issue here is that of the students' *dispositions* (cf. Ennis, 1985). Are they, in their very being, *disposed* to being critical? Faced with the kinds of material or experiences that they experience in their programme of study, do they respond *unprompted*, and *unbidden*, with a critical eye? If yes, then they are responding critically of their own volition. Their very Being takes on a *critical orientation*.

However, now we move to *stage three*, for there are potential *depths* to having a critical orientation. A student in the physical sciences may go about her practices in the laboratory with a critical eye. She is critical of the way the instrumentation has been assembled for her experiment, and she is critical of the ensuing data: do those data have prima facie plausibility? But she might also begin to wonder about the societal interests that lie behind the investigations in which she is involved (her experiment, for instance, being linked to a line of funded research on which her professor is leading). She might become aware of, say, petroleum or pharmaceutical or bio-informational companies being involved in that research. And she might also reflect on the ways in which knowledge is motivated in those fields or on its significance (economic, political or ecological or whatever it may be) in the wider world.

In short, our student's being critical may have *depth* to it, attending to foundational and hidden matters about knowledge and its rootedness in the world. The idea of critical thinking as being interpretable in either a strong or a weak sense invites itself (Paul, 1981), and if we put that idea together with the observations just made, we alight on the following theorem: *the greater the depth, the greater the strength* of the student's critical thinking.

Moreover – *stage four* – critical thinking has *horizontal* possibilities, bringing a range of perspectives to home in on a problem and so exemplify *critical interdisciplinarity*. These *horizontal possibilities* allow one to be critical in quite different settings and generate varying complexes of thought and action. We have just noted that the *possibilities of depth* allow one to delve beneath appearances that immediately present themselves and allow one to discern the interests on the basis of which the presenting situation has arisen. It is at this point – bringing depth *and* breadth together – that critical thinking becomes *critique*, the power to discern that matters might have been fundamentally different, to bring to bear alternative frameworks and further to imagine plausible ways in which matters could evolve.

The significance of dispositions

There is, emerging here, a fundamental distinction between critical thinking *dispositions* and *skills* of critical thinking (cf. Facione et al., 2000), although they often come into play together. Being *disposed* to think critically, the student deploys her critical thinking *skills*. However, *there is no necessary link here*: she could possess *skills* of critical thinking but need not possess the necessary *dispositions*. She knows how to interrogate a piece of text (according to the protocols of her own field of study), but, left to her own devices, she fails to do so because she lacks the dispositions to be critical. Lacking those dispositions, she simply reads a recommended text to assimilate it, and she fails to bring her critical thinking skills to bear. *She has all of the skills of critical thinking but she lacks the dispositions of critical thinking*: she fails to respond critically of her own volition to situations that she encounters.

This is a complicated matter. The critical thinking dispositions energise the skills and bring them into play. And, in reverse, the skills heighten the dispositions. The effective deployment of her skills gives the student an awareness of the powers that those skills bring and so can lift her interest in critical thinking. The skills and the dispositions are *mutually* helpful but, still, this fundamental distinction between skills and dispositions remains.

To speak here of a fundamental distinction is *not* to point to an analytical distinction but to a deeper distinction, that of *being*. Critical thinking skills *are inert in themselves*. I might possess all the critical thinking skills in the world but never use them. It never occurs to me to use them, or I find the world entirely congenial or using them calls for too much effort or their deployment calls on me to put myself forward, not least in making judgements, and may even generate some personal risk. In short, although I possess critical thinking skills, I never actually exercise them. No one would even know that I possessed any critical thinking skills.

We should note, by the way, that the phrase 'critical thinking skills' is itself problematic. One issue is overriding: are any such skills universal? Are they not all context-specific? (McPeck, 1981; 1990). After all, making inferences, drawing conclusions, and formulating an argument take on their own hues across disciplines (cf. Foucault, 1977), and, therefore, evaluating, judging and being critical has to be sensitive to the form of understanding in which one is working. Even if some critical thinking skills can be identified that are transdisciplinary, it remains the case that critical thinking contains a strong sociocultural dimension (Davies and Barnett, 2015: 9–10), and it is in such contexts that the dispositions of critical thinking are exhibited.

The *dispositions* of critical thinking are, therefore, fundamental in that it is through them that one's critical thinking skills are properly exercised, and it is *in* them that critical *being* as such is revealed. The student may be willing to use her powers of critical thinking in the set task and even to reveal them in examination conditions, but, left to her own devices, she fails to exhibit them. We may say that she is *not a person who thinks critically*. She *can* be critical, but she is not critical as such. And she does not – because she cannot – *act* with a critical eye.

Our student happens to be a geology student, and she goes about her fieldwork rather unreflectively, hardly pausing to bring her critical thinking skills to bear. She makes her sketch-book drawings, collects rock samples, walks through an indigenous community in the locality and – with her tablet – reads academic material that speaks to the situation in which she finds herself. However, she fails to draw together the experiences she is having and insufficiently asks searching questions of those experiences *spontaneously*: why this coloured stratum? Why this shape? Why is this community here? Working by herself in the field (and so in an *open* pedagogical setting), she fails to exercise critical thought even though, in the classroom, when placed in a structured pedagogical environment, and when asked to be critical of what she is experiencing, *it appears* that she possesses an appropriate set of critical thinking skills. But such a student would not *be* a critical thinker; still less, a critical *being*.

We can say that our student is not being critical in the way she is *in* the world. If she shows no sign of being critical as she goes about her tasks within her programme of study, it is most unlikely that she will do so unprompted in her encounters in the wider world – say in social media or in a work setting. This is highly significant because, in her examinations, when confronted with situations – questions or events – to which she is asked to respond, she *does* display her *critical thinking skills* (and may even receive high marks for them) but, by herself, when acting and thinking autonomously, she fails to do so because she lacks the dispositions of critical thinking. Simply put, she lacks *the will* to be critical.

The dispositions of critical thinking, therefore, are fundamental in that they provide *inspiration* for the exercise of critical thinking skills. They provide the will such that the student comes to be a person who is *inherently* critical of that which she encounters. She is not critical of everything all the time; that would presage a disintegration of one's personhood. But she is *disposed* to be critical. She is always on the edge of being critical and naturally allows her *critical powers* to express themselves. Her predilection is to stand off from much of what she encounters rather than be totally consumed by it, and always to be ready to bring into play her powers of critical evaluation. Her inner antennae start quivering at any moment where a critical response might be helpful or particularly insightful.

Where critical thinking becomes critique

The dispositions of critical thinking are fundamental in a second way. It is via the dispositions that the critical mind can reach beneath what is immediately on view and inquire into the *conditions* that have led to the visible situation. This is the matter of depth on which we touched before, and it is where critical thinking becomes *critique*.

This step is important not just to the matter of critical thinking but to the very idea of *higher* education. In 'critique', the student exemplifies capacities to stand off from a matter – an experience, an entity, an event – and place it in a wide context, and peer into the conditions of its emergence. Especially in anything with a social dimension to it – including science as an organised body of knowledge – one can inquire into the *causes* of a situation. This is what Roy Bhaskar – in his (2008b) philosophy of Critical Realism – termed 'explanatory critique'. Both breadth and depth are here. That geology student sees an indigenous community and starts to wonder why is that community there. What is its relationship to the surrounding geological landscape with its surface fauna and flora? What is the mode of living of this people here in this landscape? What is their form of knowledge and how do they understand their relationship to the world in which *they* live? What technologies have they been using and how do those technologies compare with the technologies of oil and gas extraction that may be here in a year or two? Might those processes of extraction of the underlying deposits lead to a displacement of that community? Might another option be imagined?

Such a line of questioning is critical in several ways. First, it goes beneath the surface appearances which it, therefore, displaces to some extent. The student distances herself from her immediate circumstances. Second, it sensitises one to the *'necessity of contingency'* (Meillassoux, 2014) and the changingness of what one experiences. Nature, knowledges, cultures, social forms, technologies are all opened up as regions that are in motion and of which critical questions can be asked. Searching questions can be posed not only about hidden geological structures and their changes over tens of millions of years but also about the ways in which humanity has been altering those forms within the natural world. In turn, the student is led to *imagine alternatives*. To bend ideas of Castoriadis (1997: 369), this would be to step outside of the *constituted* imaginary of the immediate discipline and to enter a *constituting* imaginary. The structures of the world just might be different.

This is, perhaps, the most significant prize that higher education has to offer students, the beginnings of capacities to imagine the world differently, and an imagination that is built on deep perceptions of the way the world is and the conditions of its continuing emergence. Here lies *the prize of critique*, that it is a space into which students can move so as to begin the task of helping to change the world and for the better.

Biesta (2016) has spoken of the beautiful risk of education: here we glimpse the *hopeful risk of critique*, a critique that leads to imaginings of alternative and better worlds. It is risky for who is to say what constitutes a better world and where critique will lead: the student senses that her critiques come laden with uncertainty and risk. It is hopeful because, as we see – not least in the animated pleasure of students on graduation day – the student may come into herself. Never fully formed, the student is always *self*-provoking with her critical questioning and her imaginative and constructive critiques in and of the world.

In the words of the poet Yeats (*Easter 1916*), here is possibly a 'terrible beauty'. Consider the whistle-blower in professional and corporate life. A very large proportion of graduates proceed into public and private sector organisations, and characteristically those occupations play significant roles in the economy, the health and educational services, and the environment. Not infrequently, professionals spot arrangements, systems and practices that they judge to be awry. The interests of patients, clients, consumers, organisations and even the wider public (the 'public interest') are in jeopardy. Our graduate professional, now possessing not only the *skills* of critical thinking but moreover the *dispositions* of critical thinking *and the powers of critique*, comes readily to form just such judgements. She is possessed of the capacity for standing back, of displacing herself from her situation, and seeing beneath its immediate form and asking searching questions of it, and even glimpsing alternative possibilities. She needs no prompt to do any of this; not even from her professional body. She brings her critical powers to form judgements not just of what is said or written but of social practices in organisational life.

Note that this moment of critical judgement contains the vital element that *matters could be otherwise*. Our graduate professional *imagines* new kinds of arrangements. Different procedures could be in place, alternative criteria could be adopted in the audit in question, contrasting admission arrangements could be in place and so on. Indeed, the critical judgement only has point in the company of a sense that *matters could be otherwise*, and some intimation as to how those arrangements could be otherwise shaped. Perhaps an interest in social justice is guiding this exercise of critique (Shpeizer, 2018). It follows, once critical thinking takes on its more powerful cousin of critique, that the imaginatio*n has* to come into play. Critique is not criticism 'for its own sake' but incorporates an imaginative aspect that perceives alternative possibilities. (This is not the tradition-bound idea of imaginary that Charles Taylor (2007) drew out but is much more the transformative imaginary that Satre (2004) advocated.)

This is of vital importance for higher education. Higher education may develop a range of critical thinking skills in its students, but it has very rarely sought *explicitly* to develop these dispositions of critical thinking, the powers of critique and the resources of an accompanying critical but constructive imagination and, still less, to inject a 'moral and ethical dimension' into its pedagogies for criticality (Davies and Barnett, 2015: 16).

Critical action

There are further elements in the position of our whistle-blower. The clue is in the name. In blowing a whistle, a referee brings proceedings to a halt. The idea of the whistle-blower is that of an individual who discerns that matters are going awry, and senses ways in which they could be improved, but then puts those critical judgements into *action* and, in the process, expresses herself as a citizen (cf. Arendt, 1958). She bridges the gap between critique and action. Not for her the dictum that there is 'no ought from is'. To the contrary, not only can she espy matters that are awry, but she takes steps to try to redress the impairments in the situation (say in global warming or corruption), and she does so by calling attention publicly to the matter. She may even speak truth to power (even while still enrolled as a university student) and put at risk her own career, if not – in some countries – her very life.

Here we have critical *action*, which is an assemblage of experience, evaluation, imagination, discernment of possibilities, political nous, human qualities and *will*. Philosophers speak of epistemic virtues but what we have here are *ontological virtues* – of courage, political nous, diplomacy, resilience, steadfastness, care and stewardship. *These* virtues – of professional ethics – are expressive of having a care for what is held to be good in the world and could be better. And they are doubly ontological in that they express the student's very being, and they are attendant on the way the world *is*. For Heidegger, being was a matter of 'being-possible'. These students, on the streets of Santiago or Hong Kong, or in the trees, preventing forest destruction, are living out their possibilities of 'transformatory critique' (Davies and Barnett, 2015: 17–20), not least in glimpsing a new societal and even worldly order.

The three crazy escalators

In its ultimate form, then, critical thinking rests on three moments, of dispositions, action and being. At one time (Barnett, 1997: 115), I depicted these three aspects of critical thinking as three pillars, overlapping, and each with its own levels. I retain much of that depiction, namely there being three moments of critical thinking, with those three moments each possessing a layered depth, of their being interconnected and overlapping. I still hold to my earlier suggestions, accordingly, that we should displace the term 'critical thinking' with the much larger terms (that I proposed) of 'criticality' and 'critical being' (Barnett, 1997). What is on view when realised in its highest form is a complex of the three moments – mind, techné and sheer active Being – all working together to form persons as critical beings, possessed of criticality and with agentic *powers*. However, that metaphor of three pillars, I now regard as too regular, too narrow and too static. Another metaphor, more suggestive of unpredictable motion, is needed.

Against the horizon of this book, marked out by such concepts as motion, indeterminacy, complexity and emergence, we may see the three moments of criticality as standing in a hierarchy, but it is a set of hierarchies more like those of the interrelated staircases depicted by the Dutch artist M.C. Esher, where each staircase stands in different planes and sets up counterintuitive possibilities for movement. And, at any one moment, one staircase is both superimposing on and supervening on the others.

The skills lead to the dispositions, and the dispositions lead both back to the skills and onwards to action, which leads on to new skills, which turn in a new direction. Movement up one staircase suddenly shifts onto one of the other staircases, but now leading to a different plane and offering new insights. Unlike the M.C. Esher etching, these staircases are in motion, like *escalators*, and continuously moving at crazy and changing angles in relation to each other. *Simultaneously*, the skills of critical thinking may lead one forensically to focus on the minute details of a presenting text (say its argumentative logic or lack thereof), *and* to stand back from it, and see the text synoptically in an ideological context, inflected with powerful interests; and immediately, to leap, in one's imagination, onto a contiguous plane of action, envisaging a way of taking up the cudgels in combating the malign forces at work.

And each escalator, in its crazy motion (moving both up and down), opens possibilities for breadth as well as height and depth. Using one's skills to examine the logic of the text in question may prompt a separate inquiry to peer into the metaphorical character of the text, that inquiry sparked off by wondering about the text as ideology. And then, its metaphorical structure may in turn suggest a different tack for critical action, as a terminology and ideational structure are revealed that point to a deep connection with particular interests in the world. The three components of critical thinking – of techné, mind and Being – are *interfused*, dancing in and out of each other. And all the time, any one of the three components is liable to leap riskily onto another plane, seeing new avenues for judgement (for critical thought and critique), new possibilities for action in the world (for critical being) and new options for the deployment of one's skills (for critical thinking skills). Sometime, the escalators go into reverse, their negations leading to further negations but also possibly opening to entirely new movements (Guattari, 2016).

Conclusions

At one time, critical thinking was integral to the idea of higher education because it was understood that critical thinking was associated with a student's becoming as a person. In becoming a critical thinker, the student was achieving autonomy in her sheer Being. She was able autonomously – without any prompting from a professor – to size up her experiences and form her own judgements, and this evaluative form of life would carry over into her professional world and, indeed, her lifeworld.

Now, however, our dominant conception of what counts as critical thinking in higher education is hopelessly impoverished. *Impoverished* because it is narrow, superficial and mechanistic; *hopelessly* because it lacks hope and neglects the potential of higher education. As higher education globally has been drawn into serving cognitive capitalism, and patrolled by the state and epistemological police, critical thinking has *not* been outlawed; quite the reverse. But the danger is that critical thinking has been reduced to being just low-level skills of critical thinking to aid 'innovation' for the fourth industrial revolution (4IR) and which show themselves only in responding to set tasks (Mathews, 2017). Far from critiquing ideology, this critical thinking functions to *endorse* ideology. No boats will be rocked by this critical thought.

The twenty-first century, however, calls not for its earlier ideas of critical thinking to be restated but to be substantially *widened and deepened*. It is a world that is saturated with proliferating and rival accounts, and the peoples of the world are thrown into this situation and are having to make sense of it. Moreover, they will often be faced with unduly confined and even malign situations, whether in work, the political sphere or the public sphere. Graduates, having enjoyed higher education, could be said to have a particular responsibility not merely to size up situations but to intervene; to put themselves forward – often with some courage – to act critically; and to 'tarry with the negative' (Žižek, 1997) and speak truth to power.

It was this expanded conception of critical thinking – as a complex of critical thought, imaginative critical action and critical being – that led to the term 'criticality' being formed (Barnett, 1997); an idea possessed both of breadth and depth. Admittedly, formidable challenges lie ahead in working out the implications of such ideas for curricula and pedagogy in higher education (Johnston et al., 2011), challenges heightened by encouraging dispositions for criticality in *open* pedagogical situations. What criticality amounts to is nothing short of the formation of *critical citizens*, to be critical through their very being (running like the words through a stick of children's rock) and who are *disposed* to carry their criticality into and across the world, sizing up matters of their own volition, discerning alternative arrangements and working for them and so promoting a *critical public sphere*. The idea of criticality, therefore, is entangled with that of democracy: each is necessary for the other.

This much-expanded idea of critical thinking into criticality and critique and the formation of critical citizens as critical beings is bound to produce a nervousness in some quarters. After all, when carried into the professional, political *and* public spheres, this criticality is liable to be felt to be dangerous. And that is why it is needed all the more.

Part IV

The university as an institution

13 The place of the university

Introduction

The title of this chapter is intentionally ambiguous. I want to examine the university as a place, as a physical entity, as a set of buildings, that becomes familiar to those who frequent it *and* that generates emotional responses of pleasure or intimidation or whatever it may be. Around the world, the university has a phenomenological presence, having a particular place in the minds – and even the hearts – of those within it and around it. And I want also to reflect on the place of the university as it lies in different *spaces* across the world.

Noticing the university

Whereas the mediaeval town sought to construct a towering cathedral, the nineteenth-century town erected a grand railway station and the mid-twentieth century built its imposing shopping mall, the city of the twenty-first century is incomplete without its university. *In each case*, the architecture of the building characteristically soars upwards, often with pointed spires and large canopies. There is a strong identity between town and building. The modern university plays its part, with its atrium and its spaciousness and its newly built learning centre; but it also exhibits *separateness*, with its security guards and turnstiles, and lanyards or other distinguishing accoutrements, to mark out those entitled to be on the campus.

Now, the university occupies an 'in between' space (Nixon, 2018). It is strung between the pillars of reason and capital and – to steal from Italo Calvino (1974: 75), that poetic writer of travels – the university is 'suspended over the abyss'.

The university is a large and complex institution, with a real presence in a community, and it harbours nooks and crannies, of intimate and even of emotional spaces. It lives in the here-and-now, but it lives also in a timeframe that may stretch back for hundreds of years, and it has plans for its future for at least decades ahead. (Its estates officer may have a thirty-year horizon, as the whole estate of the university unfolds over time.) It is *here*, in this physical space or set of spaces, with buildings that dominate a large portion of a city, and yet it lives globally, with its synchronous – and asynchronous – communications across the world.

And so the place of the university gives rise to enduring issues: how might we understand the category of place in relation to the university? What *kind* of place is it? To address these questions, we shall have to dip our toes into matters of space, rhythm, movement, time and planes. Although there have been reconnoitres in some of these directions (Goddard and Valance, 2013; Cochrane, 2018; Meusburger, 2018; Brennan and Cochrane, 2019), it is a territory that is largely unexplored.

The university as a place: topology *plus* geology

The story is told of the Oxford philosopher, Gilbert Ryle, being stopped in the street by an international tourist and being asked if he could point the way to the university. What is the philosopher to reply? Does he point to the adjacent university buildings: is *that* the university? Does he single out one building – the Bodleian Library perhaps – as representative of the university; or its new department of nanotechnology; or its administrative offices, situated in a definite part of Oxford? Just where is the university?

Similar questions can be put to other organisations, particularly those that are knowledge-based. However, the matter is especially complicated so far as the university is concerned. *First*, it is loosely coupled (Clark, 1983), its constituent parts having highly varied worldviews. Its academic tribes live in different epistemic territories, have little interaction with each other and exhibit contrasting forms of life (Becher, 1989). *Second*, it is local, national and global – 'glonacal' – all at once (Marginson, 2010b). *Third*, it possesses an extraordinarily long-term horizon. *Fourth*, it is increasingly 'deterritorialised' (Deleuze and Guattari, 2007), as it swims in the digital ether. Consequently, the university is a strangely *ephemeral* entity, an ephemerality that accounts in part for Gilbert Ryle's difficulty.

It is a commonplace to observe that the very idea of the university is in dispute. Books have appeared bearing the title of '*The Idea of the University*' – or something very similar – for nearly two hundred years. Each age forms new interpretations of the idea, prompted by an unsettled sense that past ideas of the university no longer bear much weight. In the middle of the nineteenth century, Newman (1976: 5) felt that research (the 'advancement' of knowledge) was not strictly part of the idea of the university. Today, the university is seen both as being too separate from its region and the wider society *and*, on the contrary, too much bound into the world. The shapes of the university's spaces are in motion, and with this movement flows the university's ephemeral qualities.

The place of the university is an elusive matter. The university has a physical presence and lives amid digital (and even 'post-digital' (Jandric and McClaren, 2020)) flows; it has an ambiguous set of relationships with the world, both servicing the world's expressed needs and – where it may – acting as a critic of society, and it is connected with its immediate region, its nation and the global setting. A university rector, with an eye on world rankings, may feel that that university has no place in its immediate locality, despite that university being the largest employer in the town. Another rector, in a smaller university in the same town, may be working furiously to develop good relationships with local leaders in the business and civic communities, oblivious of many of its academics having their identities in global epistemic communities.

The idea of the university as a *place*, therefore, is problematic. Should the idea be abandoned? Are we to say that the university is an institution of *no-place*? That would be an error, for the concept of place is crucial to any satisfactory understanding of the university.

As an opening gambit, let us say that the university is *multi-placial*. Simultaneously, it lives, in many places, places that are both real *and* are in the minds of its beholders. The real and the ideational interact; there is even a 'tension' between them (Cochrane, 2018). The rector with an eye on world rankings seeks to displace the gaze of that university from its region *to* rival institutions even in far-off lands. Here, place becomes space, and it is ontological, for it invokes the university as a set of structures across the world, *and* it is phenomenological, concerning the ways in which the university – any particular university – is framed by those both who both know it well or very little. Its students may be profoundly affected by it as a place (Hajrasouliha, 2016). The university exerts a 'power of place' (Gettler, quoted in Jump, 2020). More diffusely, a university attracts a worldly imaginary: it is, for example, reported that data modelling at Johns Hopkins University is producing real-time calculations of Covid-19 infections in the world, and so images may result in minds around the world of *that* university and its character.

The place of a university is not just given to it. We can call to mind a particular university, locating it in its age, its size, its epistemic character (it is 'strong' in life sciences or the humanities perhaps). It has especially lively connections with its region and has a concern to recruit its students from a wide socioeconomic and ethnic base, and we understand that it has its place within a national policy framework, where it enjoys a certain level of public funding and even has multiple income streams. We place the university in a network of universities (Standaert, 2012), and intuit that this place is not just the set of structures that condition the university, for the university possesses *powers to affect its place* in the world, in its locality and in people's minds and hearts.

In getting to know a university, we might seek to understand it by looking at the range of its activities, its people and the networks in which those activities and people are located. And we spot profound differences across the university's departments. It has a *topology*, and an *uneven* topology at that. Some of its surface features bobble up and take the high ground. Others are barely visible (its live animals are hidden away). But this uneven terrain is indicative of large underlying forces at work and which are liable to produce crises on the surface. And so we need a *geology* of place, to peer into and assess the underlying structures and forces at work. And it is only with both approaches – *topology-plus-geology* – that we can seriously imagine how a university might edge into a different configuration.

The phenomenology of university space

Is it not the case that, for many fortunate to have been a member of a university, it is one or two intimate spaces that – many years later – are especially recalled? Each day, the student padlocks her bicycle and makes her way into the 'learning centre' and finds her customary place in a far corner of its upper floor. The desk is by a window, and looks out to a tree in an open space, and students and others can be seen circulating; and the leaves and blossom on the tree change with the seasons. This is *her* place in the university, and it imparts even her 'sense of identity' (Ossa-Richardson, 2014: 150). And when a university is recalled some years later, it is that scene that comes to mind; perhaps it is a particularly wind-swept and exposed corner of a building, remembered from snowy evenings, or perhaps again it is a critical judgement or unwanted request or encouraging endorsement from a teacher.

There is, therefore, a poetics of university space (cf. Bachelard, 1994). A particular university is recalled, positioned, accommodated, repressed and bracketed. The part it plays in one's trajectory is weighed and gives rise to gratitude and even awkwardness. The phrase 'alma mater' (used especially in the USA) – 'bounteous mother' – is connected to one's college or university and is testimony to a sense of beneficence, of a cornucopia of personal benefits that one's university has bestowed upon one; and it indicates a gratitude, a perpetual debt that can never be fully redeemed. One has been given more than can ever be repaid.

In this *debt relationship*, the real, the cognitive, the felt and the imagined all come into play. What the university bestows flows from its real position in the hierarchy of universities. The sentiments are a complex of cognitions, of personal remembrances and assessments of the university in one's life. One has invested much in it – whether as a member of staff or a student – and so one searches for signs that that investment has paid off, and a palette of values are on hand by which to assess that personal investment.

In these assessments and recollections, the university is *imagined*. A semi-fictional university is conjured. But it is a depiction that makes sense of the experiences, varied and contradictory as they are. It is a personal narrative that both offers an accommodation to experiences and allows for an assimilation into one's own schemas. And this process of accommodation and assimilation (Piaget, 1972: 75) may continue through a lifetime. One's experience of a university – of a particular university – is always in motion, even decades after the event. It may have a firm place in one's self-understanding or be absent or evoke resistance, and all of these relationships are possible and change. The manifold of experience – its shape, its contours – varies over time.

The university, therefore, offers an exceptional pedagogical opportunity to take advantage of Jan Masschelein's (2019: 201) idea, 'the university as pedagogical form'. Just as students can encounter a city anew through walking in it, so the university could be treated in similar fashion, its shapes and configurations examined for the narratives that they may yield. Such 'designs' could be ventured by students in *every* discipline that a university has to offer: the university could be turned into a 'public design studio' (203). And a pedagogical venture of this kind could provide a means of concretely effecting a *socio-material-phenomenological* transdisciplinarity, uniting body and mind, thought and action, individuals and collectives, the sciences and the humanities, and the physical world and the world of imaginative ideas. This would be an 'uncomfortable' (201) pedagogy, not least since conflicting imaginaries of the university – of market interests *and* the public interest – would have to come into view.

Rhythms of university places

As a place, the university has rhythms. We might even attempt – to use a term of Lefebvre's – a 'rhythmanalysis' of the university as place. Lefebvre (2004) observes that, for a rhythm to be recognised *as* a rhythm, it is helpful if there are contrasts in rhythm. Furthermore, rhythm has to be 'grasped'. This university has a surface busyness, as its staff and students hurry to their classes, their meetings, their laboratories and their computers. There is a freneticism here. But the micro-places of the university have their own rhythms, and intensities. The laboratory processes proceed in a measured way; the paper takes a certain time to compose, for the seven thousand words have their rhythm; and the class has a timetabled time, the interactive sessions possessing rhythms of their own.

Neither time nor rhythm nor intensity are given in this place, being – in part – dependent on energies. When the manager opines that 'we must work smarter,' an implication is that more can be achieved in the time available. The level of efficiency can rise, and this efficiency comes at a cost. There is an increase in performativity, to follow Lyotard's (1984) use of the term, namely the ratio between unit costs and unit outcomes. *That* performativity was – for Lyotard – a sign of postmodernity and was a telling symbol of the loss of 'grand narratives'. There are, though, material implications.

A culture of performativity is accompanied by a rise in decision-*ism*, where actions are performed with little forethought. This decision-ism seeps into academic life: the 'send' button is hit impulsively; the scanning of abstracts in papers substitutes for reading; the committee has too many items in its agenda to give each its due consideration; management decisions are made precipitately on the basis of inadequate data, without due regard for human and societal consequences; and the risk analyses conducted by the administrators are perfunctory, not least because risk to the university cannot be computed.

Performativity also has human costs, which arise in part from the awkward juxtaposition of humans as analogue beings being required to accommodate to a digital world (Hassan, 2003). Increasingly, this limitation is recognised, but in contradictory ways. On the one hand, the emerging industrial revolution four (IR4), a world dominated by artificial 'intelligence', Internet of Things, algorithms that smuggle in partial assumptions, and robots and cyborgs: all give rise to contrasting views, from fear to approval. On the other hand, resistance grows in favour of attentive 'slow' processes and activities, and the reading of the book and writing and poetry are celebrated, at least in some quarters.

So understood, the university is a *space of spaces*, with their own rhythms. Characteristically, a quickening of pace is ubiquitous across a campus, not least as the audit and managerial requests flow in email attachments. The urgent takes priority over the longer-term, and the urgent has its own quick rhythms. But, still, the micro-spaces of the disciplines – the music department, foreign languages, business studies, law and civil engineering – have their own rhythms. Of course, these local dynamics are not fixed, being inflected by hidden inducements to press on. There are always more data, another meeting, an additional health and safety consideration, to which to attend. And the texts emanating from the disciplines differ in their rhythms: compare those of economics, mathematics, history and geology, and the pacings implicit even in the length of their paragraphs (not to mention their use – or not – of bullet-points). The temporal structure of their utterances has *epistemic specificity*, and yet there is (just) time for a coffee on campus, where another tempo can be found.

In this place we call 'university', therefore, rhythm is a pool of rhythms, flowing across each other, with deep forces at work, producing great currents that wash through university life. Some disciplines live in the here-and-now, and some venture future scenarios; others live hundreds, thousands and even billions of years in the past. These temporal *epistemic landscapes* are not well understood, although work has begun (Gibbs et al., 2015). Amid huge waves that stop for no one (the audit is in one month's time; the examination is next week; the deadline for the submission of abstracts in response to a call for papers is tomorrow), still there is time for a snatched corridor conversation. A few years back, that conversation could have happened in the departmental kitchen, but that was taken out in the building's 'refurbishment'.

There is *real time*, then; the time imposed by epistemic structures, by the apparatuses of the state and by market forces. These are real forces. But, still, time can be bent a little, and it can be *constructed* to some extent. A reading group chooses to read carefully a paper from the academic literature, a group of students resolves to arrive for the class a half-hour early and (assuming that they can gain access to the room) work through some issues that have recently arisen in the programme, or a middle-manager – over a sandwich lunch – invites a few academic colleagues together from different departments and who do not know each other to explore a possible collaboration. For all the intensity of this place, new rhythms can still be injected.

Planes and trajectories

The university is in motion, and with a will o' the wisp character. No wonder if Gilbert Ryle was a little flummoxed in being asked to locate a particular university by a visitor to Oxford. It was not just a matter of pointing to particular buildings or even the activities within them, or even how the university was perceived by those beavering away in its laboratories, lecture rooms, library and at their personal desks. The place of the university is even stranger. For Gilbert Ryle could have turned to his inquisitors and said to them that 'The University of Oxford is within yourselves!' This is *not* to dissolve the university into mere constructions of it but to acknowledge that perceptions of a university are *part* of its being in the world.

How a university is perceived as a place – in its locality, in its nation and in the world – affects its possibilities in the world. We learn, for example, that perceptions of a university's departments vary according to the distance across the world involved: harsher judgements may descend on a university's humanities departments from the home nation than from the other side of the world (*Times Higher Education* magazine, 2020, 12 November: 21).

The place of the university is both real and phenomenological, therefore, and both moments are conjoined and are in constant motion. A new ranking position produces a reassessment of the place of the university in the panoply of universities. And in these (local and global) geographies of universities (Meusburger et al., 2018), an individual institution possesses, we have seen, both a topology and a geology. Deep and hidden – and even somewhat dark – forces are at work that profoundly affect its surface features.

Let us now place these reflections in our earlier *schema of the three planes* (p34) in which a university and higher education are positioned:

Plane one: a university as institution and a university as idea

Two universities in a town sit alongside each other but differ profoundly. Their size, their research intensity, their epistemic range, their penetration into the wider society and their global reach vary enormously. The plaques on their buildings in the town – bearing the names of their departments, research centres and administrative offices – are different in tone and in their branding (one of the two universities even still uses a serif script to help denote its longevity). The two universities have markedly different impacts on their town, architecturally, civically, economically and politically. Universities move – especially at the urban level – in a 'politics of space' (Lefebvre, quoted in Neary, 2014: 207).

But for all their differences, the two institutions are still 'universities', conducting themselves within a more or less common imaginary as to what counts as a university. Both institutions are 'inclusive' in their admissions policy and have a care towards their students; at least some of their staff are engaged in independent scholarship or research; they have connections with the wider world; they see themselves as contributing to the public good; they claim that truthfulness, academic freedom and open dialogue are fundamental values of theirs; and they look to offer enlargements of their students, and society.

Wider still, on the global stage, and despite considerable differences between national higher education systems, the ministers of higher education can hold joint conferences. Not only is there considerable overlap in the character of the institutions termed 'university' but it turns out that, amid globalised knowledge (Kennedy, 2015), universities across the world face contiguous challenges. And so our two universities are not to be mistaken for any other kind of institution. They are neither knowledge-based private corporations, nor schools for the compulsory education of adults, nor casinos, dealing in risky life chances. They are manifestly instances of 'university'.

Stretching back for over two hundred years, there is much debate worldwide about the very idea of the university. Over the past fifty years or so, scores of ideas of the university have been proffered (Barnett, 2013). Some ideas point to the desirability of establishing new institutions with an independence from a nation's system of higher education and enshrine the idea of a university as a 'cooperative' venture (Wright and Shore, 2019: 18–20). Others seek to move the university into a new global space by associating it with the United Nations' Sustainable Development Goals. Others want to give the idea of 'the civic university' a new lease of life, locating the university as a kind of civic resource (Brink, 2018). Yet others want to pump up the idea of community as offering an anchor amid academic motion. Ecology, too, has emerged as a strong theme around which imaginative thinking of the university has been developing (Barnett, 2018a; Goodyear and Ellis, 2020).

It follows that even within a near-universal understanding of what it is to be a university, there may turn out to be then, a surprisingly large degree of spaces (plural) for a university to affect its place in this ideational universe. After all, those two universities owe their origins to quite different sets of ideas. One was founded to meet the needs of nineteenth-century manufacturers in the immediate region, and the other was established by a religious community, with its eye on training schoolteachers for its own schools. Perhaps now, each can be oriented towards new sets of ideas, fitting for the century ahead.

Plane two: a university in time and space – a university in its possibilities

We see one of the two universities, its buildings sprawling across a town. We may even have some familiarity with it, and know of its local geography, its layout, its reception desk and the large lecture hall that it uses for its ceremonies. We intuit that it has a history, but that history is largely unknown to us. Its buildings may be largely modern, and we find that it has moved to this site comparatively recently and has over a hundred years behind it. Still, we sense – perhaps misguidedly – that this university is here to stay, at least for some time to come. But we also understand that it has international connections. We might be surprised to find that it has active collaborations right across the world, but we can see its students who appear to be drawn from many nations. (Of course, they might actually be resident in the host country.) So this place is an extended place, extending in time *and* space. And its places and its spaces not just affect each other but reach into and profoundly affect its learning and research practices and, ultimately, its institutional effectiveness (Temple, 2018).

So much for the left-hand side of plane one, the real of the university; but now let us switch to the right-hand side of this plane, the possibilities that might be imagined for this university. The other university in the town jostles right next to the university in front of us. The taxi drivers call this one in front of us the 'new university'; the other one, the much older university, is simply 'The University'. The two universities are rather different, having different trajectories, different possibilities. While being in largely the same place, they move in radically different spaces. And, for those in the know, the older university is regularly to be found among the top one hundred and fifty universities in the world rankings, whereas this smaller university in front of us has an inauspicious position several hundred positions below (if, indeed, it figures on the rankings at all). Their epistemic, student and staffing profiles overlap only a little. The two universities occupy quite different places in the firmament – the spaces – of universities, and their possibilities stand in marked contrast to each other, and, in turn, *their possibilities differ* substantially. One is seeking to become a university for the community – a 'communiversity' (Lessem et al., 2019) – while the other seeks to become a new kind of eco-university for the whole world.

Plane three: a university in its particularities – universals of the university

It might be felt possible to produce an inventory of the particularities of a university. The inventory would include all of its tangible and real assets – its buildings, technologies, legal agreements, finances, materials and so forth – and its less tangible assets, such as the minds of its staff and students, its epistemological resources, its reputation and its networks. It would be a very long inventory – approaching infinity – but, still, it would amount to a specification of a single university. But as well as consisting of its own set of discrete *particulars*, the university stands in a sea – a space – of *universals*.

Crucially, 'universal' here does not mean agreement on the meaning of any such large term. It refers, rather, to a concept that provides an umbrella for universal dispute (Butler et al., 2000). A university is an institution that we recognise through its association with concepts such as inquiry, knowledge, truth, education, scholarship, liberty, disinterestedness, public sphere and so forth, even though there be no agreement as to any of these concepts.

This cluster of universals is not fixed but is in constant motion. Some concepts – such as knowledge, truth, freedom – recede a little, while others – such as work, employability, skills, innovation – emerge and even take on a prominent position. But this suggests that there is room for yet other large concepts – say, wisdom, ecology, social justice, public sphere – to become part of this constellation of universals.

The university, therefore, moves in turbulent (real) spaces but has its own place in them, and it has its own possibilities in the world, seeking accommodations in its ever-changing situations, both ideational and institutional. The spaces of the university are both personal and public, and both open and closed, and have multitudinous lines of connection, sometimes quite steep: its 'couloirs' both encourage but all too often frustrate social and intellectual traverses (Temple, 2021). It has to be 'down to earth' while having its sights on distant horizons. It is, at once, in the world, of the world, for the world and from the world: it is a 'worldhood' university (Nørgård and Bengtsen, 2018b).

Conclusions

Any university has its place both in the spaces of the minds of people *and* of the Real of the world. These spaces flow into each other. Perceptions of the university affect actions and policies in and towards universities, and universities – as complex and sometimes massive institutions – exert not just influence but real force in the world, not least on the life chances of individuals and the wellbeing of regions and nations. Collectively, universities form a 'hyperobject' (Morton, 2013), and yet each contains very particular particulars, not least as individual students work on their own activities. The university, accordingly, lives in *multiple places within multiple spaces*. There is a multiplicity here of the university, with different rhythms, flows, intensities, timeframes and interconnections with the wider world.

Three planes configure the spaces of the university: (i) a university as an institution and as an idea; (ii) a university in its present time and space, *and* in its possibilities; (iii) a university as a set of particulars, and as nestling within a constellation of universals. The university is in motion between the two poles of each plane *and* between the three planes. The geography of a university is on the move, locally and globally, moves reflected in its changing positions in rankings. Governments modify their higher education systems, with profound consequences upon institutions worldwide. Ideas can inspire new universities: groups of individuals can and do establish new institutions. Both the topology and the geology of the university are on the move and are subject to violent disruption, as ideas and structures co-mingle.

The place of the university is not given, therefore. While there are huge forces at work, which exert real constraints, still the imagination can work to discern possibilities in the space(s) in which the university moves. The question to be confronted is this: what room is available to each university to move into a different place in the local and global spaces in which it finds itself, perhaps with different rhythms, lesser intensities and a collective sense of possibilities *and* responsibilities unfolding into the future? The structures of the world are corralling it into constrained places in those spaces, but perhaps there is more room for manoeuvre than is often recognised for the university *agentically* in framing its own future.

14 The spirit of the university

> There are many heavy things for the spirit, for the strong, weight-bearing spirit in which dwell respect and awe; its strengths long for the heavy, for the heaviest.
>
> Nietzsche (1969: 54) 'Of the Three Metamorphoses', *Thus spoke Zarathustra.*

Introduction

The matter of the spirit of the university is almost entirely absent from the contemporary literature on higher education, and yet it is fundamental to any serious understanding of the university. Without spirit, there is no university.

A university and its central activities – in teaching, inquiry and its connections with the wider society – are not just *there*, but are infused with some kind of spirit. That vague phrase 'some kind' is important, for spirit can be positive or malign (the latter notoriously present in Heidegger's reference to the university's 'spiritual mission', in his acceptance address as Rector of Freiburg University, 1933 (Heidegger, 2018:95)). The philosophy of higher education has a responsibility, therefore, to include the matter of spirit. Certainly, spirit presents formidable challenges, it being notoriously difficult to conceptualise and theorise, but those difficulties should not stand in our way.

Recognising a diffidence – or three

Across the scholarship on higher education, the matter of spirit shows itself occasionally. Jaspers (1965) touched on it in his book on *The Idea of the University*, produced at the time of the Second World War, and, very recently, spirit was a topic for the French philosopher, Bernard Stiegler, in his (2014a, 2015) concerns over the place of the university in a world being shorn of spirit. The kindred concept of vitality was, too, present in Ortega's (1946) *Mission of the University*, Ortega seeing university education as an engagement with 'the vital system of ideas' (44). But these are rare exceptions: mostly, there has been a marked silence in regard to spirit in the university.

How might we account for this diffidence about speaking of spirit? Perhaps, it is too close to matters of spirituality (Robinson, 2005) or the spiritual (Sheldrake, 2012), and the university largely wants to divest itself of its religious heritage or, at least, keep that heritage at arms-length. In work on higher education that emanates from religious traditions, especially the Christian tradition, we do see a continuing willingness to speak of spirituality (Astley et al., 2004) or of Spirit – with a capital 'S', as in the Holy Spirit – (Higton, 2013), but the matter of spirit as such remains largely untouched even there.

Perhaps, secondly, this absence reflects a distrust of Hegelian metaphysics, with its belief in the unseen presence of a global and totalising *spirit of reason* at work. This distrust has pretty firm foundations: 'until Spirit has completed itself in itself, until it has completed itself as world-Spirit, it cannot reach its consummation as self-conscious Spirit' (Hegel, 1977: 488). Such totalising sentiments – with its upper case 'S' in Spirit – run against the tenor of this age, with its sensitivities towards difference, fragmentation, dissolution of universals, particulars and so forth. But it would be unwise to dismiss Hegel here, not least because he detected an interweaving of knowledge (or 'science') and spirit: 'Just as Spirit in its existence is not richer than Science, so too it is not poorer either in content' (ibid: 491). It is separate from knowledge, but it is not to be reduced to an inner experience, as some imply (Jay, 2005: 74). Spirit inspires the quest for knowledge, for truth and for understanding, all of which require will, energy, courage, fortitude and resilience.

A third possible explanation – for the neglect of the matter of spirit in the university – lies in the philosophical materialism that pervades the current age. It is what is tangible, real and durable and that is open to empirical inquiry that counts, and, indeed, as if to reinforce the point, newer – albeit softer – materialisms have been arriving (Coole and Frost, 2010). Admittedly, there are connections between materialism and realism, which provides much of the ballast for this book; but the two philosophies differ. It is striking that Roy Bhaskar, the founder of Critical Realism, advanced a philosophy of metareality in which – drawing on Eastern philosophies – the concepts of spirituality and even spiritualism played a significant, albeit 'quotidian', part (Bhaskar, 2002b: 116, 2010a). Still, diffidences over the sheer mention of spirit are present and so we shall have to tread gingerly as our discussion unfolds.

Locating spirit

Spirit is elusive and yet ubiquitous. Every university is pervaded by a spirit of some kind; spirits indeed. Spirit is not to be associated with any definite intention or aim; indeed, to the contrary. Like Schopenhauer's will, it is an expression of 'the force exemplified in the constitution and motion of everything in the universe' which is expressed in humans as 'simply the will to live, ... to keep going' (Magee, 1987: 142).

Spirit shows itself in inorganic matter just as organic matter, but in organisational life spirit brings additionally a will to keep going *in situ*, in this university, in academic life, in one's career. The question is: *what kind of spirit is in this university?* Look at it in a set of paraphernalia: are there noticeboards in the corridors? Are they kept up-to-date? Are they fronted by glass panels, their contents out-of-date and changed only by certain administrators with keys, or are they open to all, serving as a community noticeboard for collective exchange? Look through the glass panels of the doors to the teaching settings: are the students animated? Are they engaged? Is there a liveliness in the classroom?

We have already drawn attention to the existentialist philosopher, Karl Jaspers. His small book, *The Idea of the University*, ranged widely and, in his comments on spirit, we receive but the sketchiest and most tantalising of notes; indeed, he himself calls them 'dogmatic remarks', but they contain some nuggets.

In a section entitled 'Spirit, Human Existence, Reason', Jaspers suggests *en passant* that 'the idea of the university ... is characterized by the spirit of scientific inquiry' [that is, knowledge inquiry; RB]. He proceeds in this way: 'Spirit is the potentiality and power of ideas.' Furthermore, '[s]pirit lives and moves wherever our striving for clarity is a striving for fullness of insight.' It 'is the power of creative intuition: without imagination, science remains sterile.' Not only are 'Spirit, human existence and reason ... foundations of the scientific outlook' but also 'Spirit, personal commitment and responsive reason make us aware of the broader context of ...possibilities in our lives' (44–45).

As well as that of spirit, key concepts in those few paragraphs include potentiality, power, striving, creativity, intuition, imagination, commitment, vitality and passion. For Jaspers, components of spirit, therefore, are that it is a power that is alive and has 'vitality' wherever there is an interest in systematically understanding the world. This spirit is a necessary condition of any advancement in understanding and so should characterise the university.

There is, however, a misleading aspect of Jaspers' treatment of spirit here. One could be forgiven for thinking that, in his mind, spirit is an attribute of *individuals*. (After all, Jaspers was an existentialist.) Indeed, he points deliberately to its association with 'personal commitment' and speaks, too, of 'innermost beliefs' and of 'the function of mind' and states boldly that 'ideas impel us from within.' Yes, there is mention of 'the scientific outlook', but the predominant reading of these passages must be that, for Jaspers, spirit is a personal quality. That spirit is a collective entity is for Jaspers, at best, only, a residual matter.

This is surely a misguided way of looking at spirit in the university. There, spirit is, first and foremost, a *collective* matter. The matter of spirit as a *personal* attribute is intriguing and significant. It can be present on its own account, but it can be substantially infused by the spirit of a person's university and, so too, it can be diminished and harmed. When we see increasing rates of student 'attrition rates', or rising levels of staff's low morale or dissatisfactions with the administrative burdens of university life, we sense a diminution of the *collective* spirit of a university. Unwittingly, the university can act to dampen spirit.

A spirit analysis

What is opening here is an analysis of spirit in the university; a *spirit-analysis*. Spirit in the university possesses both collective and individual expression. But spirit in the university also has *range*: it can be confined to inquiry and teaching and it can be much more encompassing, and the spirit of the university can exude into the wider community ('the broader context', as Jaspers put it).

A yet further axis is formed by the relationship between teaching and research: we can imagine universities where they are characterised by a collective vitality in relation to research but where it is almost moribund where teaching is concerned. Staff go through the motions of teaching, seeing it as a hindrance, with their eye on extending their publications in 'world-leading' journals. On the other hand, we can envisage institutions that are almost entirely focused on their teaching functions. The staff, by and large, are uninterested in conducting research. These different relationships between research and teaching and the spirit that they build may be found *within* a single large multi-faculty institution. In one department, the spirit of research may be almost touchable, with its frequent guest academics giving seminars, its celebration of its funded projects and so forth, while in another department in the same university, the dominant spirit is one of regard and care for the students. In the one, a spirit of *inquiry*; and, in the other, a *pedagogical* spirit; and all within the same institution.

A lesson may be derived that is crucial for a philosophy of higher education. Talk of spirit – and for that matter of vitality (as in both Jaspers and Ortega) – is not to be thought of as lying in an entirely separate domain from that of the intellect. Quite to the contrary: the intellect needs spirit, draws on spirit and can be energised by it. How else do we account for the collective energy in a classroom or in a laboratory?

This was a cardinal point for Henri Bergson, in his vitalist philosophy. Bergson stressed that the intellect and spirit were not 'isolated' but were intertwined and that science (that is, organised knowledge) should have a 'resolve to [place] the life of the body ... on the road that leads to the life of the spirit' (269). 'Thus is revealed the unity of the spiritual life' (268). There is a double movement of spirit here – again crucial for our purposes. 'Let us try to see, no longer with the eyes of the intellect alone, ... which looks from the outside, but with the spirit, ... which springs up ... by the twisting of the will upon itself ...' (250). There is 'an impetus of life' that is inherent in all matter, and there is the spirit of the inquirer who, in the process of inquiry, 'springs up' and energises her or himself. Do we not see this double vitality – of a world in motion and the efforts of the inquirer – over and over again in universities, whether in the educational process or in research?

This double sense of vitality – in *the world* and in the *inquiring human life* – is found in Jane Bennett's influential (2010) *Vibrant Matter: a political ecology of things*. Among the many virtues of this text, Bennett explores the relationship between the two vitalities and does so via the idea of ecology. Not for Bennett the idea of some realists that all the entities in the world are on a level, for the vibrancy of inquirers has a power to affect the lives of other vibrant bodies (animals, plants and other humans): 'while every public may very well be an ecosystem, not every ecosystem is democratic' (104). Spirit does not flow evenly across the Earth, and it therefore behoves inquirers to be attuned to the possibilities of their knowing efforts to distort life flows. Spirit in the university and higher education, therefore, can thwart life, and we see this daily, across the academy.

Spirits of the university

To speak of the spirit of the university is not to assume or to try to point to a singular spirit; on the contrary. We have already observed how the spirit of one department may be quite different from that of another, even in the same university. And this is not just a theoretical matter. At one time, the department of philosophy in the University of Sydney split into two departments because the warring tribes within it – of analytic and continental European philosophy – could not find common ground (Critchley, 2001: Preface). And so spirit can be full of conflict, colliding spirits and even division. And is this not the case with universities in general, that each one has different flows of energy within it, moving in different and often opposed directions?

What are we to make of this differentiation, of this collision of spirits, even within the university? Is it to be deplored or celebrated? It is not just that the world is characterised by multiple movements, and clashes of ideologies, but that the university is now faced with the near-impossible task of incorporating warring ideas and outlooks. And so a differentiation of spirit within the university is not just inevitable but is *desirable*. This *splitting and even opposition of spirit is inherent in what it now means to be a university*.

In this splitting and differentiation of spirit lie opportunities for voice and identity. Voice is a complex. It can be vividly present or it may be subdued, waiting to be uncovered. A mediaeval historian beavers away in her department, largely unnoticed in her university and even in her department, but then, following a 'find' in a local archaeology project, is suddenly recognised and is granted a voice. Spirit moves this way and that in the university, closing and opening spaces.

But voice can also be gained (Batchelor, 2014). A new head of department is appointed and a new spirit blows. In turn, a young academic begins to speak in departmental meetings and not just finds her voice or uncovers it, but gains it. Her voice develops, like an opera singer in the hands of a good teacher. Correspondingly, the hesitant student, lacking much in the way of a positive self-image, is faced with a teacher who is full of energy and marked by a spirit of affirmation, and the student finds herself gaining self-confidence. Now, there is a teacher who believes in her, and the student now flourishes in this particular pedagogical spirit. So there is a vitality that attaches to spirit. Spirit breathes life into the university; in-spires it. Spirit begets spirit.

A large empirical literature has grown up which has been examining academic identity, but it has not much touched upon the matter of spirit (only partly because spirit resists empirical inquiry). And yet spirit is literally vital to the matter of identity in universities. Without spirit, identity is unlikely to unfold as it could. Identity *is* spirit. So spirit (of the individual) flows with the impulse of collective spirit in the immediate environment. It is astonishing how academic identity can emerge, given an affirming and encouraging collective spirit; and that personal identity is always in motion, unless it be moribund. It is a function of spirit.

These flows of spirit may add to energies but can thwart life. Students and academics even take their own lives, under the duress of the negative energies that they face. It is part of the task of academic leadership, therefore, that it engenders a positive spirit, indeed 'raises spirits'; and even – whisper it – to encourage the formation of 'free spirits' (although this latter is admittedly a problematic phrase being prone to 'misuses'; Nietzsche, 1988: 53). Unfortunately, in academic life, spirit is often dull and not infrequently has negative energies within it and morale is lower than it might be. All too often, the university exhibits a state of entropy, in which spirit is depleting over time: 'our universities are ... the actual forcing-houses for this ... spiritual instinct-atrophy' (Nietzsche, 2003: 73).

This spirit is not unitary. Disciplines vary considerably in the character and direction of their spirit, and there is more at play here than the familiar science–humanities divide. Spirit works into crevices of academic life, into the students in a class, in the use of footnotes, into the mode of dress, literally into the style of movements in the laboratory, across a well-handled online discussion, and into the conventions of the seminar room, not to mention the cafés in and around the campus.

Spirit is not easily containable in academic life. The spirit of the university flows *outwards into society*, and so there are questions to be posed about the nature of that outward-flowing spirit; but then spirit may also enter the university. And those inward flows of spirit may galvanise the university into a new direction; perhaps to address its possibilities in responding to the United Nations' Sustainable Development Goals. But that inward spirit – in a consumer-led market-driven society with its interests in personal goods – may be damaging.

However, it is not unknown for individuals whose voice and identity is suppressed in their home institution then to find sustenance in their membership – formal or informal – of external groups and associations in the invisible colleges that constitute much of the structure of academic life, nationally and globally. There, a positive spirit may be found according not only voice and identity but a quite new level of recognition. As they circulate within, across and beyond institutions, individuals and groups live uncomfortably in markedly different flows of spirit.

Spirit in the university moves in mysterious ways, and this is inevitable for there are *multiplicities* (Deleuze and Guattari, 2007) involved. Spirit moves across epistemic structures (disciplines and their numerous offshoots), across the formation and – unfortunately too often – the dissolution of identities, across administrative arrangements, across allegiances and so on. To speak of a multiplicity of spirit, therefore, is to draw in a sense of *multiple* multiplicities; of intensities, rhythms, timeframes and power. Through spirit, the university is always in motion and can never be pinned down. Do its inhabitants not feel this, even though spirit cannot be touched? The students arrive for the lecture and hover outside the lecture room animatedly: does that vitality disappear on entering the room?

The academic attends a committee meeting in one room and moves to a second meeting in another room, and the tone, the atmosphere, changes. The intensities change, being dominated in the one instance by an interest in measurement and targets and in the other instance by a lively interest in a research topic (cf. Deleuze and Guattari, 2007: 534). There is a different circulation of spirit in the two rooms. The university is, therefore, always in a process of becoming, or, where spirit regresses, of an *un*-becoming.

Infusing and *de-fusing* spirit

Spirit in the university can energise or deflate, can uplift or suppress. If we think of spirit as motion, we would have to say that motion in the university can become more excited or more quiescent and even turgid. This spirit is both horizontal and vertical. The horizontal movement of spirit in a university is notoriously blocked, both by epistemic borders and administrative silos. Attempts to take down those boundaries can often be met with hostility. So long as they feel secure in their own quarters, the philosophers and the sociologists – or, for that matter, the administrators and the academics – will turn away from each other. The vertical movement of spirit also faces its difficulties. The management workshops may speak of 'top-down' and 'bottom-up'. What is in question here are the vertical flows of spirit: are they moving in both directions? And is there a negative collision of spirits, as the managerial clashes with the collegiate? We should not be surprised at any clash of spirit in higher education: after all, 'there is no [positive] spirit without spirits

[as] obscene ghosts. [S]pirit is forever haunted *by* spirits' (Žižek, 2013: 354 [RB's emphasis]).

Pedagogically, too, interruptions to the flow of spirit can also be detected, and again both horizontally and vertically. The horizontal flow of spirit has nothing per se to do with students working in groups, but it is a matter of students' receptivity to and endorsement of *each other*. Increasingly, students in a class are highly heterogeneous, and so there is a question as to the extent to which they acknowledge each other. Are the international students largely left to their own devices? Is the spirit of the classroom impeded? Is there room for the quieter students to speak up, even when working in small groups? Or is there such an enveloping spirit that it sweeps over all, compelling apparent assent?

Spirit is pretty well everything in the educational process. It is not a matter of letting learn but of *enlisting* learning. It is a matter of engendering a spirit of learning, and that spirit calls for affirmation. In the student being affirmed, *spirit* is engendered in the student.

There is an issue here. I have indicated that spirit may be malign, even corrosive, and we see this all too often. But spirit, I would also want to say, cannot be imposed. So how can it be that a spirit can be both malign and yet it cannot be imposed? The answer is that this apparently paradoxical situation comes about as a result of the multiplicities of the university (on which we touched a moment ago).

A head of department, say, decides not to help to advance a member of staff in their career, requiring that they invest their time in teaching, and desists from giving them support for their research. Hitherto, judged on the 'performance indicators', our member of staff has failed to achieve the necessary research outputs to warrant a research allowance. It is not so much that a managerial spirit is being imposed on the staff member but that the manager has been so incorporated into a spirit of managerialism that deleterious decisions follow that depress the energies of our staff member. There are here cross-flows of spirit with differential weight and force. Our beleaguered staff member does not take on the managerial spirit; on the contrary, tries to block it, and even resist it. As a result, *both* her teaching and research suffer. Spirit, her spirit at least, in not infused but, rather, is *de*-fused.

All this testifies that while spirit in the university may be malign, it can also *in*spire. Spirit may produce more air (Derrida, 1991; Irigaray, 1999), more air to breathe, more air to imagine, more air to become.

Increasing the value of spirit

To some extent, a spirit of higher education flows among universities across the world, but, again, different energies can be seen, not least between the Global North and the Global South. Each university possesses its own amalgam of spirit, depending on its geopolitical position and its epistemological spread. There are complex *spirit flows* between universities and the wider world. Spirit can even be said to be a political concept (Abbinnett, 2015).

A rare instance of the matter of spirit and the university being taken up is to be found in the work of the French philosopher, Bernard Stiegler. Stiegler at least was not shy of speaking of spirit. One of his books even has the subtitle, '*The Value of Spirit Against Industrial Populism*'. For Stiegler, society – 'the informatized society' – in the contemporary age is in a state of entropy and is fast losing its energy, or spirit, and the university is implicated in this change. However, unlike (say) Readings, Stiegler sees the possibility of 'an increase in the value of spirit' and a 're-enchantment of the world', and also sees the university as playing a part in this process. This increase in spirit Stiegler labelled 'negentropy' (2014b: 46).

Spirit is not easily caught. It is not just a matter of creativity: indeed, creativity may simply amount to smoothing out a system, and to a process merely of 'entropic adaptation' (Stiegler, ibid.). Such 'creativity' will work only to delimit and reduce the energy in the system. What is needed, instead, is a disruption, and the injection of new energies and on a collective scale.

Knowledge, life, the body and institutions harbour spirit. However, in all of these presences, spirit is being diminished and so 'a question of the ecology of spirit presents itself' (Stiegler, 2014a: 88–90). In the university setting, ideologies, regulatory systems, systems of surveillance and undue competition suppress and even exhaust spirit. An academic will send the academic in the adjoining room an email rather than put his head around the door. After all, conversation has its own spirit, and it may take off, demanding more energy in return. It is the total ambience of a university that is in question.

One reason, perhaps, for a diffidence about spirit in higher education is that it runs counter to a regulated system (characterised by 'learning outcomes', 'performance management', rankings, and so on.). Spirit can catch fire and run against regulation and control. There is a *phenomenology* of spirit in which the exterior is internalised, and where the internal knows no bounds except that it has to subject itself to an external test (whether the student or the academic). This spirit strives for accomplishment, for achievement, for affirmation. It is restless. It is its own movement. Its standards are its own (even if they were exterior originally). It is always in tension, therefore, with the systems that confront it.

Stiegler opens for us a structural sense of spirit, it having as its context the contemporary character of the world, configured both by a digitised knowledge economy and by the nature of digital technology as a force in its own right. '[A] major crisis of educational systems is a necessary result: the ecological crisis of spirit translates itself in the first place as a crisis of education' (Stiegler, 2014a: 90). In the university, spirit is liable to suffer depletion.

To this diagnosis, Stiegler applies a 'pharmacological' perspective, seeing both poison and cure. Spirit can be poisoned, but there is still potential for cure, for a new spirit. The university is critical: it can either succumb completely to the irrational forces of digital nonreason or it can seek to engender a new spirit, infusing new desires. Spirit here is not simply the outcome of irrational forces but can be worked at, as 'labour of spirit' (Abbinnett, 2015). For example, in pedagogy, this would entail deep reading, textual care and a preparedness seriously to engage with the ideas of other students.

Despite seeing universities as complicit in a generalised 'stupidity', Stiegler is by no means entirely pessimistic and sees universities as galvanising a new spirit not just within universities but across society. Hence, Stiegler's phrase of an 'ecology of spirit'. We can only suggest, but it might entail a heightened public interest in forming well-founded understandings, a collective spirit – reflected, for example, in the phenomenon of Wikipedia – and new relationships forged with the state, the wider polity, publishing companies and social media – and all oriented towards *mutual* enlightenment. And so Stiegler can speak of the emergence of '[t]he digital public mind and spirit [which] opens up … new forms of scholarly or scientific society' (Stiegler, 2015: 191). In Stiegler, therefore, we find a 'utopian thinker' (Bradley and Kennedy, 2019), in envisaging the university putting the digital sphere to work so as to inject positive spirit into a world whose energies are fast dissipating.

Conclusions: leading spirit

One can feel spirit, and even see signs of it, but it is elusive, and mention of it produces a nervousness. It is, though, literally a vital part of the university, as air and oxygen are to the body. Spirit is part of the university being in motion, and within a university and across universities, and in their inter-connections with the world, spirit is an interplay of multiple currents, moving in conflicting directions. Spirit clashes with spirit; it can be positive or negative. In its malign forms, there is a brokenness of movement; energies are diverted wastefully or even dammed, unable to proceed, and dampened spirit can point to unmet aspirations. The young lecturer has an idea for a new project that warrants some pump-priming funding from the head of department, but the idea simply does mesh with the stated priorities. The student sees a way of moving her essay into a new multidisciplinary direction that is out of favour with the confined disciplinary position of her tutor, and is de-energised. The total energy level and, so, the spirit of the department or educational setting, is depressed.

The university and higher education are respiratory systems, converting air into energy. The more air they have, the more energy they exhibit. This energy is converted into spirit, and it can be contagious, but the air supply may be defective. Spirit moves with a power that can overpower another spirit, this power reflecting deep structures of power and ideology in which the university is positioned. However, there are spaces for the injection of new spirit whether pedagogical or in research and scholarship, and at all levels of an institution.

It is here, in the elevation of spirit, that leadership can come into its own. Whereas management (quite legitimately) seeks to find means to ends, leadership finds new ends but it knows too that those new ends have to find responsive energies in the university. Beneficial leadership expands energies; it *expands* spirit within the university. Unfortunately, having been overtaken by the managerial impulse, spirit is often depressed in universities. There is no fixed sum of spirit in a university: spirit can be subjugated by spirit, but it can also be enlivened and even come into being *through* spirit. The central task of university leadership, therefore, is none other than the *recovery* and enhancement of a spirit-enlivening spirit. Spirit has to go on being continually sustained and created.

15 Academic leadership and management – and keeping clear water between them

> It is time to look for new ways to conceptualise and understand leadership beyond our twentieth century frameworks.
> (Simon Western and Éric-Jean Garcia, *Global Leadership Perspectives: Insights and Analysis*; 2018: 288)

Introduction

Some may say that the topic of academic leadership has no place in the philosophy of higher education. It is more a function and cannot bear the scrutiny of conceptual inquiry. Indeed, the world being so turbulent, the vision sometimes associated with leadership is otiose. Rather, what is needed is adroit management, able to respond quickly to situations and keep a university above the water-line. I disagree. It is precisely in a situation that is replete with indeterminacy and conflicting currents that leadership is required. If today is like yesterday or even like last year, and the future will also be like today, there is little need of leadership. It is when the waters are frothy and unsettling that leadership comes into its own.

However, the concept of leadership is far from clear. Is it to glimpse *possibilities*? Is it to *orchestrate* proceedings? Is it to inject new *energies*? Is it to develop the *value base* of an institution? Is it to hold an organisation *together*? Whatever it may be – and it is a mélange of all these – academic leadership raises a gamut of issues, many of which are addressed elsewhere in this book, and I allude to some of those other discussions as we proceed here.

In speaking of leadership, I shall mainly have in sight the top brass, the senior management team, although leadership is to be found throughout any complex institution. Indeed, there are particular challenges of leadership in the lower and middle tiers of universities (Butler, 2020). Just how my thesis here might play out across a university is a matter for another time.

My argument is that the role of leadership is to assist the university as an *organisational agent* in venturing forward in the world. That said, further matters spring forth – what it is for a university to be an organisational agent, and for a university to venture forward, and what is meant by the phrase 'in the world'. There is much ahead of us.

Leadership and management

An immediate matter is the relationship between the concepts of leadership and management. In understanding the university, *both* concepts – 'leadership' and 'management' – are vital. However, they differ profoundly. They are intimately connected but *neither is reducible to the other*. In brief – as one political leader was alleged to say of the generals – management should be *on tap and not on top*.

Management is that set of activities intended to organise systems such that a university might best achieve its purposes. Since a university is a complex organisation with conflicting centres of judgement and interests *within*, and numerous stakeholders *beyond*, charting a way forward is fraught with difficulty (Cutright, 2001; Marion, 1999). *Management* is the task of finding ways through complex situations with the least disturbance and maximum benefit. *Leadership*, in contrast, has the roles of *fermenting* a university's purposes (and sorting out what 'maximum benefit' means for a particular university), of enlisting some measure of support from significant others (the Trustees, the State) and enabling the members of a university in helping to forge a set of purposes and to work together against the horizon of those purposes. Compared to management, leadership is built on flimsy bases: *if management is the art of the possible, leadership is the art of the impossible*.

Leadership is the discernment of possibilities for a university's future. It is to identify options and shape priorities for the way ahead. But such a view, *large as that observation is*, sells leadership short. For what is the range of options that might be pursued? Are they to embody concerns with the voiceless, and/or with the totality of the Earth's entities? What are the values from which options and priorities might emerge? In which ways might leadership be associated with critical thinking? (Jameson, 2019). (Perhaps the juxtaposition of leadership and critical thinking is even an oxymoron (Barnett, 2019).) Quickly, therefore, leadership opens to philosophical questions of conceptual and ethical weight.

Just what qualities might be sought when looking for a new rector or vice-chancellor? The university is in motion in a world that is itself in motion. Sighting landfall, maintaining one's bearings, charting the rocks and the storms, being aware of the conflicting currents: meteorological and journeying metaphors seem apt, with their unpredictability. But *landfall is never made*. Moreover, the crew of the university are disputatious, for that is their calling, and (in most jurisdictions) they are able directly to transmit messages to the world, and those messages may run against the grain of the university's official position. Even a sigh in a meeting can seem threatening (Mathews, 2014).

To change our metaphors, Deleuze and Guattari (2007) spoke of striated and smooth surfaces on which life takes place. Are there ever *any* smooth surfaces for leadership? Is it not all striated; all is undulated?

Consider a new rector or vice-chancellor assuming office just as a global virus descends upon the world. It is evident that most of the teaching has to be shifted to an online mode and that has to be *managed* adroitly. Looming, too, are large challenges to the university's finances. Whether borne largely by the students or by the state, it is doubtful that the fee income will be maintained since the student enrolment is itself in doubt. Our new rector or vice-chancellor was recruited, having shared with the appointment panel his or her ideas – 'vision' even – as to the possible directions that the university might take. Now, however, there is the immediate challenge to his or her *leadership* in maintaining 'a spirit of willing cooperation' (Redding, 2019b: 171) right across the university, both staff and students.

These undulations move on *multiple* planes (chapter 2) of the university as an institution *and* the idea of the university: of the *entities* of this university here-and-now and their possibilities (chapter 1); of the *value structure* of what it is to be a university (chapter 3); and of the *temporal frame* of the university, with its past, present and possible futures (chapter 16). Values, structures, particulars, processes, possibilities and design: all jostle. A task of *leadership*, then, is to live not only practically among these intersections but imaginatively too; it is literally to make *some* sense, *and* to glimpse new *feasible* possibilities, and for and with *multiple* audiences. It is to construct collective meanings, within a sense of the real forces at work. It is also to *uplift* the spirit of the university (chapter 14).

A task of *management* is to live *operationally* among these intersections; to find ways through the hazards. In a turbulent world, a related task for management is that of identifying and calculating the risks attaching to any policy, and several kinds of risk are present in the university environment (Hommel and Stévenin, 2020).

To draw on an earlier distinction (chapter 14), *management* moves on the level of *topology*, whereas *leadership* moves on the level of *geology*. Management moves on the surface, planning, strategising and orchestrating movements. Leadership, in stark contrast, delves beneath, to unseen strata where there is turmoil and tension, to form a sense of the forces – and the conflicts – at work and to discern the possibilities. University leadership is always a process of its own 'becoming' (Davids and Waghid, 2017). It never quite succeeds; it is always falling short of its potential, not least because it holds within it its own undisclosed and unacknowledged 'symptoms' (Western and Garcia, 2018: 288).

A further way in fathoming the difference between leadership and management lies in the matter of organisational learning. *Management* relies on *single-loop learning*. It effects change, assesses the outcomes and makes further changes as necessary within the presenting territory for action. The changes, their implementation, their evaluation and their design take place within a (more or less) closed learning space; a single-loop learning circuit. *Leadership* assesses and evaluates that learning circuit and questions its basis, including its implicit values, purposes and effects on the totality of the university's environment. Leadership *changes the territory on which the action is played out*: this is a *double-loop* form of organisational learning (Argyris and Schön, 1974).

The systems of the university are, in the technical sense, *complex*, possessing qualities of unpredictability and emergence. Securing a low-risk way through is part of the challenge of management, even if it leads to the formation of yet further systems, which act as yet further layers of *complexity* and so forth. Management, therefore, is the art of managing *complexity* (or, the cynic might say, of creating complexity). Leadership, in contrast, is the manoeuvring through competing discourses of the university, which are characteristically competing with each other: culture or industry? Values or performance? Sustainability or rankings? Civic contribution or global recognition? This is *supercomplexity* (pages 133–34 above and Barnett, 2000), where there are no secure answers to fundamental questions. There are always contested spaces and rival groups (Brannmark, 2019), and living with this supercomplexity is part of leadership.

Both concepts – leadership and management – may be exemplified in the same *event*, but they are separate and call for differing dispositions. A good leader is not always a good manager, and *vice versa*. Indeed, the necessary qualities are often in tension.

Learning analytics

Let us look at learning analytics so as to put some flesh on these schematic reflections. Learning analytics are being instituted by universities across the world in monitoring student behaviours and generating management information, both at programme and institutional levels (JISC, 2017). The *managerial* approach is to see the worth of such systems in the information that they yield on students' movements within learning environments. It will also oversee the design of the digital systems, especially the algorithms that generate the desired information. Such information promises improved learning and student 'throughput' efficiency: unwanted patterns can be identified and addressed, the student's likely completion will be more assured and the total system more efficient and more effective.

A *leadership* approach will be different. Instead of treating students as means to the greater efficiency of the university, it will see students as ends in their own right. It will concern itself with the *judgements and the values* that inform the design of the algorithms and the digital processes being put in place. It will seek to open a dialogue with the students and *co-develop* a set of agreed ethical principles in any adoption of learning analytics. The principles would necessarily include openness so that the means, the purposes and the particularities are made transparent to the body of students.

The legitimation of learning analytics lies in the claim that they offer a means by which a university can attend to the needs of its individual students. Very well then: let this 'individuation' (Stiegler, 2015) demonstrate itself. For example, there is much talk about curricula being co-constructed, and here the idea of a system being *co-constructed with the students* becomes attractive. The voices of the students would be heeded *above* any proprietary controls that private companies may seek to exert over the design of these systems and their algorithms.

This process of transparency would be conducted knowing that students' understanding of the indicators and the algorithms will alter their behaviour. If students know that their presence in the library is to be a factor in monitoring their movements, then, they are going to be more present in the library, even though no additional thinking takes place on those more frequent library visits. The matter would be treated as having both ethical and educational aspects, its educational potential lying in promoting a self-learning pedagogy.

The management of the system has to be *preceded* by leadership, by the asking of awkward questions: does this university *need* a system of learning analytics? Which interests would it serve? Will it actually *improve* students' learning? Will it unwittingly 'drive student behaviour towards a statistically measurable norm that is unlikely to represent the best learning path for [the students]'? (Wilson and Watson, 2017). What part might students play in its design? What rights might they have (for example, *to opt out*, or to view their own learning profiles)? Only when such leadership questions have been addressed can the more managerial matters of design, orchestration and implementation come into play. (A review of the empirical literature on the orchestration of learning analytics found little evidence of learning improvement or of attention to ethical issues [Viberg et al., 2018].). The temptation, however, is to jump to the managerial issues without posing those more critical questions from a leadership perspective.

A learning analytics system could be designed – *together* with the students – that takes due account of social class, gender, ethnicity, disability, subject of study or age of student, and, instead of there being a uniform system across a university, a *localised* set of systems could be instituted, systems with inherent *educational* characteristics. It would be a system that put the interests of the students *before* that of the university as a managed system.

Moreover, many universities have student counselling, support units and faith centres, and a leadership of care would include conversations with those colleagues. Such professional people, after all, are at the sharp end of seeing student anxiety, and they may well be able to discern potential human and ethical *pitfalls* of a learning analytics strategy.

Management, then – being largely a matter of means – *should be in the service of leadership*, with leadership being construed as a *collective* construction of ends *and* the framing of an imaginative environment in which those ends might be realised.

Communication

The concept of leadership is contiguous with that of communication *and* the communicative flows within and beyond a university. Communication is a necessary condition of leadership.

A key distinction is that between non-deliberative and deliberative communication (Englund, 2008). 'Deliberative' leadership is not necessarily a matter of decision-making. Deliberation can come into play in assessing the *shape of the context* in which a university finds itself; or in considering where a university might seek to position itself in the *space of values*; or in weighing the *comparative claims* of financial management, institutional reputation, civic recognition and global positioning; or having a concern for the *emotional states* of the university's members; or helping staff of a university to have a wider sense of themselves and their possibilities.

In both sets of instances (deliberative and non-deliberative), certain *communicative conditions* have to be upheld for us to be in the presence of academic leadership. These include being heard, being listened to and being understood. With understanding comes levels of understanding *and* forms of understanding; understanding can be both rational and *felt* and both explicit and intuited. With understanding, too, comes *appreciation*.

Appreciation is not assent. I can see that your message springs from an attempt to place the university in a broad context and is proffered with the best interests of the university at its centre; I *appreciate* what you are saying. But I think that your prognosis of the university's situation and your proposed course of action are misguided, and so I withhold my assent. (I might not show this unwillingness to extend my assent, but that is a further matter.)

Deliberative and non-deliberative leadership are united in one respect, since an academic environment is characterised by being a space of reasoning (chapter 8), argument, dissent and critique, all of which – quite legitimately – contain a-rational elements. University leadership plays out in this querulous space, which takes on a particular shape for each university. It follows that leadership has to be spacious, generous and affirming, even while also decisive in its managerial leanings. The term 'body language' is potent, for there are languages spoken through the body, especially the face. Non-deliberative leadership has a strong nonverbal aspect (Beyes and Michels, 2014).

The academy is a particularly *writerly* institution, and so leadership has to pay attention to the nuances of its written texts (especially those shared digitally). After all, its written texts are public not only within and across the warring tribes of its internal members but are liable to be seen by multitudinous external interest groups and – being shorn of body language – are especially liable to be misconstrued. Any written sentence is obliged to make some sense to multiple audiences. Any such 'sense' has to be created and sustained on a daily basis.

A university is now a proliferating set of cultures, often engaged in their own culture wars. Even within a single department, micro-communities may feel that they have little in common, and, over the past half century or so, in many countries, the numbers of support, administrative and managerial staff have grown such that they outnumber academic staff and form their own sub-communities. 'Third-space' professional staff (Whitchurch, 2012) have emerged, often possessing doctorates, and with hybrid identities, and tension between the academic and administrative cadres is sometimes not far from the surface.

All these communities possess their own identity structures and links to external networks. And some of their members will be even dallying with rival agencies, whether on the other side of the world or just down the road. In showing an attentiveness to the claims of the many communities in and around an institution, non-deliberative leadership is perhaps more significant than deliberative leadership. Emotional largesse can go a long way.

Collective and corporate agency

The concepts of collective agency and corporate agency are linked, but they differ. *Collective* agency can be ascribed to groups. The presence of a group – a department, a research centre, a course team, a committee or a working-party – does not as such possess agency. It may have powers but might not exercise them. It may be moribund, or be so riven with conflict that it is paralysed. Nor can agency be imposed upon a group. A group possesses collective agency when it forms and nurtures its own will; its own 'collective intentionality' (Brannmark, 2019). Does it meet spontaneously? Are its members happily communicating with each other? It follows that collective agency is always *informal*. This agency is a matter of a collective spirit and will, being forged and sustained. Such agency requires space in which its collective and autonomous spirit can flourish (chapter 14).

Assume some members of staff have come into contact across departments and even across faculties. No one knows everyone; the individuals do not yet constitute a group. One of the individuals comes across a new book on student learning and draws it to the attention of the other colleagues. Quickly, a nucleus of half-a-dozen colleagues forms with the idea of working through the ideas in the book. The group becomes a space for support and the sharing of pedagogical ideas on a cross-disciplinary basis; it may even give itself a name. It takes on *collective agency*. The Pro-Rector for Student Affairs hears about it and incorporates it as a working group within the university's formal structure. The question *now* arises as to whether this formalisation of the group will strengthen or weaken its collective agency and energy. Its collective agency is fragile and is easily dissipated.

Let us turn to *corporate* agency. This idea has emerged in political philosophy (List and Pettit, 2011) and has yet to be much taken up in higher education. It differs from collective agency: whereas *collective* agency can be found at all levels *in* a university – a group of students may form a collective, with a common interest in a topic – *corporate* agency is an attribute of the institution. It is a matter of the university's '*actorhood*' (Whitley, 2012).

However, a university as such does not possess corporate agency. It possesses corporate agency when its decisions and strategies carry a fair level of assent among its members. For such agency, what is required is the fulfilment of a *negative* condition: for any action x or decision y made in its name, a university could not be said to possess corporate agency if a majority of its members were to withhold their assent, *if* asked about the matter.

There are a number of points to note about this condition. First, a university may have agency *here* – in setting up a campus overseas – but not *there*, in accepting a gift from a dubious source. It is not a unity. Second, corporate agency can be assumed unless demonstrated otherwise. The decision to accept the gift – the painting or the grant for a new business centre – can be taken without consultation and assent can be assumed. However, *if* the decision is subsequently uncovered and assent is shown to be absent (the painting was accepted from a dictatorship, the funding for the new department was derived from investments in fossil fuels), corporate agency dissolves, but it may still be retained elsewhere. Corporate agency is, then, a bricolage of decisions, actions and presumed and actual assents, but it has its place against the horizon of the university's collective values. Consequently, there may arise a tipping-point where assent is withdrawn and, soon after, the rector may be invited to retire.

It follows that a university's corporate agency requires will, imagination and resourcefulness. Without these three conditions, assent is empty. *Will* imparts collective energy, *imagination* imparts a glimpsing of possibilities and *resourcefulness* imparts an adroit-fulness in the deployment of the university's resources (including its reputational capital).

Broadly speaking, then, a university enjoys corporate agency to the extent to which it carries the support of its members. Nice questions arise, some of which have empirical flavourings: how might assent be obtained or even measured? How much assent is needed for a *due* measure to be present? Over what range of decisions might assent be withdrawn but still allow a university to possess its corporate agency? When does agency become illegitimacy?

Such questions imply that *a university's corporate agency is a kind of fiction* for it is seldom *overtly* put to the test. The point is that a university's corporate agency ultimately lies in trust (Gibbs, 2004). Another difficult concept, trust implies at least a sense of *relying-on*. A university can be relied upon to have a concern for truth, its own wellbeing, the local community and the wider society. It is trust*worthy* (O'Neill, 2002). But perhaps its pressing financial situation or its relationship with the state may induce it to act counter-factually, out of keeping with its past. Trust has to be redeemed fairly regularly. The university's corporate agency is always fragile, liable to be knocked off-course.

Collective agency and corporate agency are both important, but they are irreducible to and are often in tension with each other. The challenge of leadership is to bring about *collective* agency across a university while also achieving its *corporate* agency; the freely imparted collective will *and* the democratically assented agency – it is an uneasy marriage.

Leading dispute

Universities are disputatious institutions, and higher education is a process by which students come to live with dispute. Dispute is part of the university's DNA.

However, if dispute is part of what it means to be a university, is it a responsibility of leadership to *ferment* dispute? Central to the medieval European universities was the practice of open disputations (Novikoff, 2013), where two scholars would pitch their arguments against each other. Now, academic dispute takes place in academic texts (in journal and books), in conference and seminar settings, and so forth, and it would form a nice empirical project to ascertain the extent to which the cudgels are explicitly taken up in contemporary academic texts. There is good reason to conjecture that the level of outright dispute is now at a very *low* level. Work in all disciplines is conducted largely within collectively accepted paradigms. Whether in physics or philosophy, only when the resources of a paradigm are exhausted does restlessness stir and hostilities break out.

However, comforting as this line of thought may be – for it offers 'consolations for the specialist' (Feyerabend, 1977) – it is awry. It can be conjectured both that the past *was* marked by acrimonious conflict within disciplines *and* that academic life is now so bound into national and global audit arrangements and hierarchical management systems that it exhibits a risk-averseness. Much better not to enter the lists but to keep one's head down in protecting oneself and one's work profile. There is a loss of vitality in the whole global academic world and at both the individual and the institutional levels.

Leadership, therefore, has to concern itself with the *collective* vitality of academic staff. This is not necessarily to voice an opinion, but it is to orchestrate debate within the university, so as to 'institutionalize dissensus' (Englund, 2008). This is far from easy at times, bringing together colleagues who would not otherwise speak to each other, not only across the disciplines but even within them (where the internecine wars may be particularly hostile).

But do not university leaders also have a responsibility to play a part in the public sphere and to contribute to debate on relevant public issues? After all, the university cannot but be caught up in contentious matters of democracy, academic freedom, human rights and major public issues of racism, ecology and so forth. Might a university rector have a *responsibility* sometimes to speak out? Some believe so (Galea, 2019), but others consider that the role of leader-as-public-intellectual is not readily available in the twenty-first century (Flier, 2018). Voicing a view in public on a sensitive matter is liable to invite flak from the powers-that-be (including the trustees or the board of governors). Moreover, it is not clear as to the authority on which any such speaking out might be based, whether as the voice of the institution or of the individual leader. However, if a university is to hold faith with values of truthfulness, inclusion and equality of voice, then it cannot – on occasions – *but* take a position. Doing so will exacerbate its difficulties and bring opprobrium upon it. Not to do so, however, will risk falling short of what it is to be a university, although this may be impermissible in certain regimes.

Raising the level of energy

A key issue is this: is the university a site of entropy or – picking up the neologism of Bernard Stiegler (2014b) – negentropy? Is the energy level of the university dissipating or increasing? For Luhmann (2018), organisations are characterised in being autopoietic, with capacities for self-reproduction even in difficult circumstances, and just this seems to be the nature of universities. However, despite universities' tendency towards self-reproduction, their energy level is falling – they exhibit less creativity (Murphy, 2018) – and it is a *task of leadership to raise the energy level*. 'We cannot infer structural conservatism from the concept of autopoiesis' (Luhmann, 2018: 32): that is so, but nor can we infer *structural vitality* from the concept either. There is no fixed quantum of energy in a university: it can rise or fall. Low morale is indicative of a lessening level of energy, and a challenge for leadership is that of raising morale – and so raising the institution's energy level.

However, the situation is complicated. A university can exhibit a lessening of energy *and* an increase in activity simultaneously. The hours of work lengthen, the number of students taught increases, the number of papers produced multiplies and the income from different sources rises. Activity increases but, as morale sags, energy decreases. A theorem even suggests itself: *the greater the felt intensity of a university, the lower the energy level*. The performance indicators, therefore, may be grossly misleading.

Stiegler may call for negentropy – that is, to combat the decrease of energy or 'entropy' – but one should be cautious of what one wishes for. A university rector may put in hand all manner of 'reforms' and 'innovations' and heighten activity, but unless that activity is accompanied by self-willed and cooperative action on the part of the university's members, the new intensity will be misleading. Just as Adorno observed that the negation of a negation may well be a further negation, so the leadership's attempt to negate a negative situation may lead to a *yet*-heightened level of *negative energy*. The task, therefore, is that of generating a *positive* energy; a *posentropy*, as we may term it. This is far from easy.

Conclusions: towards ecological leadership

Academic leadership is the art of the *im*possible. It is to live on the several planes of the university and in multiple timeframes (the history of an institution, its present, its tomorrow, its next year and its next century). It is imaginatively to glimpse possibilities for a university while heeding the circumstances in which a university finds itself. As well as observing the injunctions of the State, it is to be sensitive to an ever-changing sense as to what it is to constitute a university in the world. It is to be situated amid an ever-expanding cluster of universals – value, social justice, ecology, public good, freedom, public sphere, wisdom, wellbeing and life itself – and to be sensitive to all the particulars that constitute *this* university. It is to weave a path through the conflicting agendas and near-empty concepts of cooperation and competition; of networks and hierarchies; of the dubious claims of 'community', 'excellence', and 'world-class'; and of the press of the STEM disciplines while finding a place for the arts and humanities. It is – to recall the fundamental schema of the philosophy of higher education being contended for here (page 34) – to live, uncomfortably for sure, in the two worlds of the Real and of ideas.

This is a formidable set of challenges, but they are not yet the full story. The university spreads across several ecosystems, each one of which is in motion and each one of which affects the others. Somehow, a university has to effect a situation of *tolerable disruption* that allows it to strive in advancing wellbeing in an indeterminate world. It has to become a corporate agent in a world of risk, its agency put into the service of the whole Earth. It would be at once restless, energised and energising. It would be (to anticipate our final chapter) an ecological leadership.

16 Time, space and the digital university

> There is, then, above lived time, thought time. This thought time is more aerial and free....
>
> Gaston Bachelard, *The Dialectic of Duration* (2000: 37)

Introduction

As this is written, the twenty-first century is well-advanced and many reading this book will see the second half of the century arrive within their working lives; and many *present* students will live part of their lives in the twenty-second century. How might we understand the university against this background? What are the timeframes in which the university and higher education are to be understood? And which spaces? Just what might it mean even 'to be human in a hyperconnected era?' (Floridi, 2015).

The university started its modern history in the Europe of the Middles Ages when books were precious manuscripts forged by hand – not only the writing (with embellishments using pigments from different lands) but even the parchments themselves – and guarded in chained libraries (Ovenden, 2020). The university then *was* a place, and the scholars of those times would travel far to reach the place of their learning. Perhaps they wished to listen to a great teacher, such as Abelard or Erasmus. It is a world long gone, and despite Eco's (2015) protestations that '*This is not the end of the book;*' (and his semicolon was deliberate), the end of the book seems close at hand. The book is disappearing from university libraries, and this opens large issues about space, time and the digital university.

The coming of the digital university

Some consider that 'the singularity' – in which computerised technology becomes the main driver of change – is upon us (Kurzweil, 2006), and, more locally, it is argued that the university is an analogue institution living in a digital age (Hassan, 2003). In any event, an algorithmic world imposes itself

DOI: 10.4324/9781003102939-21

on the university (Peters, 2011b), not only epistemologically (in students' and academics' research endeavours) but also managerially, with bio-surveillance techniques, and performance management. The identity of each student and academic is being gradually digitised into a 'quantified self', a mere 'statistical reading' (Mosco, 2017: 101). The university is being shaped by digital technologies that 'go all the way down' (Gottlieb, 2018: 176).

Are some forms of this digital age so impinging on the university's functioning that the university's agency is being diminished? Or is it being *enlarged*? Each case would have to be assessed on its merits, but they include learning analytics, the dominance of the screen (its multimodal effects and its effects on brain functioning), the slide from knowledge and understanding to mere information and data-handling, the speed and multitude of messages (now generating calls for 'slow' activities), a dislocation of the relationship between being and nature, and the roboticisation of the pedagogical situation. The term 'hyperreality' can comfortably be used, for here are intertwined virtual reality, physical reality, human intelligence and artificial intelligence (Terashima, 2001).

In sight are fundamental disruptions in human understanding and communication, such that the university as a space of reason and authenticity of enunciation, of untrammelled and critical thought and of care between *human* beings are all in jeopardy. It is hardly surprising that the idea of the posthuman society has emerged (Braidotti, 2013; Herbrachter, 2013; Peters and Jandric, 2019).

This is not the end of the library;

If Umberto Eco can say it for the book, why not for the library? Let us entertain the idea that we are not quite witnessing the end of the university library, and let us use, too, the semicolon to register the sense that new life may open for the university library, not least as it changes from a set not of book spaces but of learning spaces (Cox, 2018). Let us hold onto that possibility, that a kind of 'postdigital' world may be before us (McClaren and Jandric, 2020), even as the university transports itself *into* the digital age.

Now, the library – once so significant on the campus – has become just a set of learning spaces, its books dispatched to invisible stores, perhaps miles away; or just taken out of the library stock altogether. The book spoke of a particular *pace*, but that seems passé. For some time, we have been told to entertain the idea of the digital library (Lesk, 1999). Now, too, complex international conferences can be held online (with break-out groups and plenary discussions), and the significance of the university as a physical place seems to dwindle. Universities spawn and harvest 'big data' banks, with computers unceasingly, in their global networks, exchanging digital messages. Students work in multimodal settings (Kress and Van Leeuwen, 2001) with many, if not most, becoming 'digitally tethered' (Savin-Baden, 2015). Epistemic acts abound in the digital manipulation and simulation of biomaterial, in the examination of historical data, and in computer-based modelling. Artificial intelligence is both a topic of academic research and an instrument for use in the university.

The academic world is actively involved in advancing this digital world. The university and its activities are in fundamentally new time-space configurations in which physical place seems to matter little. The university now relies on the digital in knowledge *production* and in *communication*. In many fields (genomics, building design, engineering, architecture, urban planning, medicine, biochemistry, performing arts, sports science), digital processing makes possible *representations and insight* simply not possible hitherto. The oxymorons of 'artificial intelligence' (Aoun, 2017) and 'digital reason' (Peters, 2015) beguile.

To press the points, the digital is (i) a *mode* in which knowledge and understandings are created; (ii) the *method* by which these understandings are communicated and discussed; and (iii) the means by which epistemic *communities* are created and sustained. Epistemology (the act of knowing), ontology (insights into the way the world is) and understanding (communication and mutual exchange) are all affected. Surely, the distinctions *between* and the jointness *of* these three moments have not been given the attention that they deserve.

A sense that there are changes underway that disrupt the academy is nevertheless abroad. For some time, there has been talk of the virtual university (Robins and Webster, 2002) or the digital university (Peters and Jandric, 2018). However as noted, there is also talk of *post*-digital education (McClaren and Jandric, 2020). In this nomenclature, the university as a place is being *re*-covered in ways that transcend the digital world. Perhaps the university library can be re-born as a place within spaces. Where a university takes seriously its civic possibilities, the library could be enlisted as a cultural centre, blurring the boundaries between a university and its civic environment, exploiting its resources for local *collective* events, and including exhibitions, talks and gatherings around large issues of the day and which could include digital communication with adult societies and local schools.

This is the paradox of the university in a digital age, of simultaneous closure and openness, of diminution and enlargement, of a loss of energy and of a new spirit, of civic contribution and global positioning. The stakes are high.

Times and spaces

In an open area on a campus, an academic sees a student over whom she has concerns, not having received an essay from him or not having seen that student in the laboratory, and stops gently to enquire how things are. In the encounter, the academic gives her attention to the student, listening to and sensing the student's here-and-now. But the academic was on her way to an urgent meeting about a research proposal involving collaboration with colleagues, with a deadline looming and the project intended to last for some years. The student, it turns out, has worries about one of his parents who is terminally ill and lives far away.

In this single *time-space encounter*, wide sensitivities are in play: the here-and-now jostles with distant-in-time and the distant-in-space. Being is in time, but this being-time relationship is now, in a networked and digital age, much more complex than Heidegger could have perceived (Gibbs et al., 2015). We should abandon talk of the university living and moving in time and space, for it lives and moves not only in *multiple* times (Nowtony, 1996: 74) but also *multiple* spaces, and these co-mingle, even in its micro-practices. Our single academic almost miraculously lives and handles multiple timeframes simultaneously (from the instantaneous to next year and for decades ahead and hundreds, thousands or even billions of years past, if she is a historian, geologist, or cosmologist or simply has a care for this Earth).

Simultaneously, the university and its practices have their being in multiple time zones and multiple regions of the world. The narratives of the university play out not only in time (Ricoeur, 1990) but also in space. The thousands of individuals who have much of their lives in a university are configured in *time-space complexes*. Their individual stories are actually a mix of stories, of time-space networks and projects, of commitments and responsibilities. In the middle of the night, a thought occurs about a project being conducted jointly with colleagues in a faraway country, and perhaps even a message is sent. Work and life-world collide across time-and-space zones. Bachelard's (2000: 47) observation in regard to time still holds: 'dialectic and not continuity is the fundamental schema.'

For most organisations, their worldliness and their multiple timeframes are contingent aspects of their existence. In the university, however, these features are *necessary* parts of its very being. Knowledge and understanding, after all, know no bounds, in time or space. The university is becoming de-territorialised as it becomes active – if only remotely – across the world. Concepts appear such as those of 'the borderless university' (Middlehurst, 2001), 'the edgeless university' (Bradwell, 2009) and 'the networked university' (Selingo, 2017).

A separate matter is the university as a place (chapter 13). Until recently, a university was co-extensive with a place. Many took the names of the towns and cities in which they were founded, and, as places, they supplied memories, affections and identity to their members, long remembered through subsequent life. That local relationship is problematic, as the university has come to live globally, and well into the future. (Many universities have corporate strategies for decades ahead and so are announcing their anticipations of their futures.) Recently, in social theory, there has developed a new appreciation of the significance of place; even of 'the intelligence of place' (Malpas, 2015). There is a prompt here, for the university disregards 'place' at its peril. Indeed, it just may be that a sense of the university as a place can be regained anew, and without nostalgia.

Institutional theory has recently taken a 'spatial turn', but 'there [has not been] much explicit theorization of space' (Gluckler et al., 2018: 8). Nevertheless, some points can be made in the present context. The university as a place and as a space should be distinguished, and both are significant (Temple, 2014, 2018). *Place* denotes the university geographically, whether a single-campus institution *or* physically distributed across the globe. *Space* is a quasi-metaphysical concept, and it takes on multiple forms, the university being situated in epistemic, cultural and social spaces. Until recently, the university occupied its own space, but the boundaries of that space have become porous.

In place, space *and* time, the university has been dislodged in ways that are, as yet, unclear. Perhaps, in understanding the university in this digital age, a kind of 'speculative topography' (Thrift, 2008: 2) can be developed, but we need to harness to it, too, a cosmology of the university, viewing it from a distance, seeing it not only as it was but also as it might become.

In the academy, space and time can all too easily *entrap*. A student, taking several units that run alongside each other, is overwhelmed with the load that several assignments – to be completed within pressing deadlines – are simultaneously imposing. An academic, having agreed to lead the development of a new doctorate programme, becomes aware of a time-sequence of audit dates, and little time-space is left for her other writing and pedagogical commitments. The analysts of time rightly distinguish between objective and perceived time: in the university, time *seems* to accelerate *and* it does (Vostal, 2016), but space should come into the reckoning too. *Compressed* time, with its quickened pace, can limit the space for being: the real and the phenomenological intermingle.

And pace is ideological. It reduces not just time for thought but thought itself. Not only is the amount of time for thought reduced, but, too, the time for deep thought is put in jeopardy. Time has its own quality, for thought, as we were reminded (Deleuze and Guattari, 2013: 41), 'is dangerous'. It is in the interests of the dominant powers that thought be limited in time and scope. The imposition of multiple *deadlines* does this, but the presence of multiple *timeframes* also achieves this state of *non-thinking time*.

This matter of the individual living within multiple timeframes simultaneously has only rarely been subject to reflective inquiry (Nowotny, 1996; Decuypere and Vanden Broeck, 2020: 604), and yet it is now a vital part of the lives of anyone in higher education (Marginson, 2010a; Gibbs et al., 2015). When human beings find their very being is straddling multiple and conflicting time-zones (today, tomorrow, next week, next year, several years ahead), priorities will be made. Typically, the immediate task wins the day: one opts for the short-term rather than the far-off or for the time-zone that is likely to provide a high rate-of-return. Either way, judgement is limited for the *time-context* is limited. Epistemologies turn out to be not just social but also temporal, and the temporal is political.

Digital epistemics – and the magpie tendency

The digital zone encourages magpie tendencies, including cognitive theft, scavenging and corruption. This will be felt by magpie lovers to be unkind for there is much dispute about the real-life character of magpies, many thinking that their reputation for robbery is undeserved. Others point to a wide set of antisocial behaviours among magpies extending to the downright murdering of smaller birds. Be that as it may, the digital territory harbours opportunities for antisocial behaviour on a grand scale. By and large, the academic world does not exhibit the intellectual property theft seen in the corporate world or in the behaviour of states, nor does it pursue the cyber-attacks committed by those others. However, the academic world is by no means immune to comparable practices.

Two patterns are evident. First, and as a sign of the significance of the academic world to the wider global knowledge economy and to state interests, the academic world is frequently assailed by cyber-attacks, and is open to intellectual property theft and the purloining – without the normal attributions – of its online materials. The cognitive resources of universities are now seen as valuable by many interest groups and even nations. In a world in which universities are hierarchically placed, universities as powerful organisations within cognitive capitalism become prime targets for digital disruption.

These are serious matters, but – and second – it is of even greater significance that the digital era exhibits intellectual sabotage from *within* the academic world. I use the term 'sabotage' loosely, for it takes a variety of forms, being conducted by different groups of actors – namely academics themselves, managers and students – and it is imbued with a sliding scale of intent and so, too, a sliding scale between being over and beneath the radar. For example, students and academics may deliberately resort to plagiarism, but they may also commit the crime *unknowingly and unwittingly* (Young-Powell, 2017). An idea, and even a single word, may have been created and put into the academic literature such that, initially its creator(s) receive due acknowledgement but that, very quickly, words pass into circulation and become part of the discourse of an epistemic community. Much like the creators of popular songs who end up without royalties while seeing their creativity unrecognised, so too the hapless academic whose only solace is that 'all news is good news.'

Admittedly, such examples are testimony to ever-present human frailties, but the digital era has tacitly encouraged such behaviours. Sometimes there is intellectual fraud present on a large scale where, for example, principal investigators in large projects manipulate data so as to buttress hoped-for results (such that later, the journals implicated are obliged to publish retractions and even withdraw the offending papers from the public record). At other times, the magpie pattern is much more subtle.

Hardly surprising is it then that the cry has gone up in some circles for research 'integrity' to be taken seriously and even the occasional suggestion that a universal academic code of ethics might be developed. And it is at this point that the largely empirical matters just observed take on philosophical overtones, especially the matter of thought as such: in this milieu, is thought enlivened, quietened or just utterly changed?

Raiding concepts, theories and ideas in one domain and transporting them into another is a valuable element in promoting the vitality of an epistemic field. In the process, there will be some corruption in the idea being picked up, 'corruption' shorn of its value aspect: an idea or concept will take on a different form in its new home, and that is *inevitable*. Its new home will accommodate to the idea at least a little, and it may even move towards a revolution (in Kuhn's terminology), but the idea will be assimilated and will take on a new shape, as it is incorporated into a new theatre of theories and concepts. This is all testimony to a liveliness in the knowledge ecosystem.

So the thieving and the magpie-like behaviours may – to use an old-fashioned sociological term – be *functional*. They may bring additional motion and energy to a field and enable it to flourish, and to say this is to import an ecological perspective. The Internet age heightens the likelihood of magpie-ism and so can strengthen the knowledge ecology as a whole and its sub-epistemic ecosystems. In the movement of an idea or concept from one field to another, the second field is not merely sustained but is given new life, new *vitality*. An idea – 'rhizome', 'ecology', 'performativity', 'entanglement', 'supercomplexity', 'criticality' – spreads and is taken up, and conferences, journals and academic communities and even reputations are born.

There is here, to draw again on one of Bernard Stiegler's ideas, a pharmacology at work. It is capable *both* of virus-like corruption *and* pharmacological therapy and health. Serendipity plays its part too. Browsing on the Internet, the student comes across a term that intrigues and imports it into her essay, even though its formal relevance is slim. But the student is suddenly inspired and her thinking takes on a new vitality, looking to see how the term might aid her approach to the problems before her. Thought can be digitally disrupted *and* prompted, and an *unintentional* creativity comes about precisely through the near-randomness of the data-flow. Magpie-ism can have beneficial effects, even if it also has some of which to be wary.

On digital identity

The world is digitally globalised and so are identities. Not least with social media, students have their being in an ethereal space, their followship communities spread across the world. Academics' identities are distributed around the world, too. A single academic – or, with social media, a single student – may have an identity in the USA, in Lithuania and in South Africa. The word goes around the globe of a person's qualities and cognitive interests.

Of course, it was always thus. The reputations of the great wandering scholars of the Middle Ages in Europe preceded them, as did those of the wise desert hermits even earlier (Williams, 2003). But the digital age provides a speeding-up, a quickening and a ubiquity: now – in an age of h-scores and citation indices – everyone has their global identity, wished for or not.

A key concept in the philosophy bequeathed to us by Roy Bhaskar (of Critical Realism) is that of absence, and it takes on a particular hue here. Now, *not* to have a global identity – whether as student or academic – is significant in itself. Not to have one's followers, not to be a recognised member of online communities, not to have an h-score or to figure in citations indices are tantamount to having no identity. Gouldner's rightly famous (1957) paper on locals and cosmopolitans has a born-again quality in a digital age.

Now, one can be both local and global *simultaneously*. One can be a member of a particular group or learned association that spans the world. It is local, in being very particular, having been formed around this or that theoretical problem or the work of a named luminary; it is global in spanning the world, its members drawn from all continents. However, whether it is cosmopolitan is a further matter. Behind the modern idea of cosmopolitanism stands the idea of a citizen of the world, for which we should thank especially Diogenes and then Kant, and others have developed that idea (Nussbaum, 1997; Delanty, 2001; Peters, 2018; Nørgård and Bengtsen, 2018a). The digital communities of the twenty-first century may be global, but they are often highly restricted and are by no means cosmopolitan. Awkward questions can be asked as to the extent they are open.

It is apparent that the spaces of digital identity move in conflicting ways. They widen and close spaces of thought. Epistemic communities can form within a few months. Global identities can blossom, as individuals can not only speak to each other but also see each other in Zoom-type settings. Energies can be *in*-spired. Those of a utopian bent might glimpse here the formation of a global academic citizenship, but there are traps for the unwary. There is increasing concern over 'epistemic injustice' (Fricker, 2010), and that takes on a heightened form in a digital age. In an online world, it is too easy for the academically disadvantaged to be neglected and further disadvantaged. To what degree can those of the Global South gain access to the digitised epistemic communities that are being formed (cf. Walker and Martinez-Vargas, 2020)? This matter plays out amid massively unequal power across the world's universities and centres of knowledge production and publishers. A global academic politics attaches now to the development of academic identity in a digital age.

There is a further matter in play, and it straddles the real and the imaginative dimensions of the academic world. It is sometimes observed that the digital world reduces an interest in knowledge to mere information and further reduces the significance of information to mere flows of data (Abbott, 1999). In these discursive movements, the human mind is rendered superfluous. All that is needed is large computing facilities to manage the 'big data' banks. It would be tempting to see here a movement from the wisdom of individuals to a kind of collective wisdom, but nothing could be further from the case.

What it is to know is being reduced to a mere accumulation of information or, more concernedly still, to the management of data, and the idea of knowledge as opening large windows on world – in helping humanity to understand the universe and humanity's place on Earth – is threatened. In this conceptual slide, university practices change so as to heighten epistemic hierarchies. Disciplines are judged to the degree that they are in command of huge databases, and the humanities fare poorly in this calculation. In turn, any association of higher education and the university with wisdom is lost (Maxwell, 1984, 2014).

The connection between these reflections and digital identity is disconcerting. To have a digital identity is liable to constrict even as it opens. Obviously, it relies on data handling, data resources and capability. But, more deeply, the identity is liable to become one which is supersaturated by data. The identity is enfolded by data, and data are multimodal. In this digital tsunami, in which a single essay, paper or project may move amid tens of thousands of papers and gigabytes of data, thought is thinned, and so too is creativity (Murphy, 2018).

Pessimists and optimists

Inevitably, there are pessimists and optimists. On the one side, we have Paul Virilio (2010), who espies 'the university of disaster' and, on the other side, we have Bernard Stiegler (2015), who sees – as noted – positive 'pharmacological' therapies to combat the 'stupidity' that he perceives in the knowledge structures of the twenty-first century.

The pessimists capture the high ground, for it is crises and malign events that make the daily news. We have reminded ourselves of plagiarism (committed both by academics and students), the easy sliding over complex material (as abstracts and summaries are barely scanned), the disruptions to conviviality in personal and social life (not least as the work-life relationship is unbalanced), and the flood of material that turns into mere data to be managed, such that a *general thoughtlessness* emerges. Students are expected to display the skills of handling data and even of producing 'innovative' patterns; much less in evidence are expectations that they might also take on the dispositions of carefulness, slow and deliberate thought, and the courage properly attendant on critical reasoning.

There are further matters that spring from the deep structures at work. That concerns arise over research integrity is not happenstance; rather, they are explicable, given that a global *digitalism* has emerged over the past few decades. In this academic competitiveness, universities are pitched against each other. Priority disputes are nothing new, but now they take on a public aspect, particularly in bio-fields where universities have 'collaborations' with big-pharma, research centres work around the clock to be the first to achieve a 'break-through', and the peer review system for assuring output 'quality' is put in difficulty. The scare quotes are justified, for the popular discourse of science policy deserves critical scrutiny. Amid globalised knowledge, made all the more intense by the digitisation of data, concerns over research integrity are inevitable. But note too that individuals are being asked to bear the *responsibility load* of the evolving research ethic.

In his book, *'The University of Disaster'*, Paul Virilio (2010) quotes the British astrophysicist, Sir Martin Rees, as saying this: 'I staked one thousand dollars on a bet: That by the year 2020 an instance of bioterror will have killed a million people' (130). Martin Rees made that projection in 2003 and a million deaths from the Coronavirus, Covid-19, were recorded in September 2020. Rees may have won his bet, therefore.

By that phrase, 'the university of disaster', Virilio has two missions in mind: the estimation of risk amid the 'accelerated reality' (123) that marks the new world order; and a charting of the linkages of science to human and global disaster. In this latter mission, there lies the faint hope of revivification with 'a more democratic approach to research and to scientific and technological development' (121), but Virilio seems doubtful. He is insistent that it is not a failure but the very success of science; 'the excess of its success', as he puts it (118), that has led to the present situation. 'You can't stop progress, they used to say. No, but today it has stopped by itself' (132). The university of disaster would be a kind of 'hospice', tending to the ending of the university and perhaps even to the end of the world, and this, Virilio wryly observes, would indeed be a paradoxical project (118).

Stiegler's analysis has much of Virilio's high-velocity critique of knowledge in the contemporary world: where Virilio speaks of 'madness' (124), Stiegler speaks of 'stupidity'. These are attributes of a world in which humanity long forgot and disregarded planet Earth. And it is the data-driven nature of the digitisation of knowledge that is responsible in large part in bringing about this situation. Stiegler, though, detects real potential. Yes, we are witnessing 'the destruction ... of theoretical knowledge'; 'it is in this context ... that there has emerged ... what the Slow Science movement refers to as fast science' (2015: 174). Crucially, however, for Stiegler, the potential for alternative modes of being lies not alongside the digital but *within* it: 'digital technologies are exceptional: their speed constitutes absolute shocks ... [such that] they also constitute a new associated, dialogical and retentional milieu.' This implies that 'the university must place the speed of the [digital order] in the service of peace.'

This is optimistic, but is it not *too* optimistic? For it is a characteristic of the digital that, far from offering a new form of memory and societal self-narrative, it tends to obliterate memory. Now, it is the instant and the future that are celebrated; archiving becomes near-impossible. In the process, the 'self' hides behind data and the image. But, on the other hand, the digital world offers new spaces for community, and this is evident in the academic world as new groups spring out, even with global aspirations. Some see in the digital the possibility of a new university, both public and creative all at once (Peters and Jandric, 2018).

Conclusion

In the digital age, the university is on a cusp. Longstanding tendencies towards academic competition and inauthenticity (among both students and academics), an over-bureaucratisation of academic life, a shift from knowledge to mere data management, and a diminution in being as such are all heightened by the power that resides in digital flows. Levels of anxiety rise too. But this digital age offers new resources for community-building; for narratives; for public understanding; for culture, scholarship and creativity; and even for new kinds of literacy (Aoun, 2017: 54–61) or 'iteracy' (Berry, 2015: 188). Identities, either in scholarly and research work or in student studying, can develop.

As our opening quotation from Bachelard intimates, wherever human being remains, so too does the possibility of thought and imagination. The keyboard offers – literally – untapped potential. Eco relied on his computer and word-processor even as he would have typed 'this is not the end of the book;' The semi-colon matters: especially in a digital world, there is always more that can be said.

Part V

Higher education and the world

17 Higher education and the university

Two very public matters

Introduction

The idea of 'public' has emerged as a way of putting the relationship between the university and the wider society onto a broader footing than hitherto. There is both pull and push here. The world wants higher education to play a wider role in society, *and* higher education is keen to demonstrate its capacities beyond the economic sphere. However, this 'public' gambit quickly runs into difficulties. Is it to be 'a public' or '*the* public' to which the university is to orient itself, or even public*s* (plural)? And, to pick up another set of variants, is it 'a public *good*' or 'public goods' or '*the* public good'? And what of 'the public sphere', 'the public interest', 'public spaces', 'the public realm' and 'public horizons'?

With the university, yet more questions hurl themselves forward. While 'the public university' is often advocated (Levin and Greenwood, 2016), with a *manifesto* being proffered for it (Holmwood, 2011) – even while the possibility of its 'death' is contemplated (Wright and Shore, 2017) – that very phrase carries its own ambiguities: is it to be a university *from* the public, *of* the public or *for* the public? Ambiguities lie, too, in the idea of 'the public mission of universities': we are told that 'a clear mission is vital' (Calhoun, 2012: 7), but is this on the cards? *Is* there a single public mission, or are there not multiple public missions across universities, and even *within* a university?

It is a commonplace to observe that this conceptual landscape is messy. To draw on a polarity of concepts by Deleuze and Guattari (2007), this territory is neither 'smooth' nor 'striated', for even striations have their order. Rather, this is a disordered, scarred, pockmarked and contentious region, with lines of flight across it (Guattari, 2016) in criss-crossing directions. There is no stability here. But even *if* this territory can be brought into some kind of order, who should heed these matters and why? For the good of the economy, society, democracy, personal wellbeing, the planet …?

In this chapter, I shall deploy two main strategies. I shall introduce what we might term the Arendt-Habermas debate, and I shall map that debate onto the three-planar depiction of higher education (which has run through much of this book).

DOI: 10.4324/9781003102939-23

Some distinctions

Let us clear the thickets with some distinctions. A first is that of *the relationship between higher education and the wider society* on the one hand, and *higher education in-itself* on the other hand. For example, if we speak of the public sphere, we should be clear as to whether we have in mind the public sphere in the wider society *and* the role of the university in promoting that public sphere, OR the university itself as a microcosm *of* the public sphere. Too often, these matters are conflated.

A second distinction is that between the concepts of university and higher education (chapter 2). With the concept of *university*, issues quickly arise about the public *sphere*: what might be considered to be the public sphere and what might it mean for the university to promote it? With the concept of *higher education*, that is, with the education of students especially in mind, the concepts of public *good* and public good*s* come more readily into view. In what way might higher education count as a public good? Which public goods are generated in educating students? Research seems – potentially – to straddle *all* of these notions of 'public': it could be assessed for its contributions as *a* public good, to *the* public good *and* in support of the public sphere.

How might we account for these different conceptual clusters? It is natural that the concept of public sphere – and the concepts of public realm and public space – attach themselves to 'university', for those concepts are pointing to society and the workings of its institutions. On the other hand, public goods attach also to persons, and so questions about *public goods* are happily clustered with *educational processes* and the benefits that *students* derive and carry with them into the society.

A third distinction is that between the private and the public spheres. Until relatively recently, for example, women's participation in higher education was felt to be a matter of personal choice and was relegated to the private sphere (and still is in some nations). However, over time, and in many countries, the matter of women being students and taking degrees has come to be understood as a structural issue in society and so is now rightly understood to reside in the public realm.

A *fourth observation* follows. It is understandable if those with a policy orientation are interested in higher education as a supplier of public *goods*, whereas those of a more philosophical orientation gravitate to the ideas of *public sphere* or public *realm*. The ways in which the student successfully completing a programme of study constitutes a public *good*, and public good*s* associated with higher education, possess an immediate policy aspect. 'Public sphere' and 'public realm', however, and – we should add – 'public space', are highly abstract concepts, and they are just the kinds of matters to keep the philosophers happy.

A final distinction is this. The ideas of public sphere and its conjoints – public space, public realm – are *critical* concepts. We may ask of any society: 'Does it really possess a public sphere?' 'To what extent does it provide genuinely public spaces?' Indeed, a public sphere *and* public spaces may be judged to be *absent* from a society. On the other hand, aspects of higher education as public goods, and as contributory *to* the public good, are *always* present. *These* latter two concepts – public goods and public good – do not have the critical bite possessed by the concepts of public space and public sphere.

The idea of the public sphere

The public sphere has spawned various interpretations. An early version was that of the Greek 'agora', a relatively open meeting-place where ideas could be exchanged and developed (Nowotny et al., 2003). Hannah Arendt developed this set of practices into an idea of the public realm as 'a space of political freedom and equality which comes into being whenever citizens *act* in concert through the medium of speech and persuasion' (*Stanford Encyclopedia*, RB's emphasis): central here is the notion of (free) action. For Jürgen Habermas (2005), the public sphere is marked by an allegiance to collective *reasoning*, a space separate from that of the State. For Alisdair MacIntyre (1990: 217), the public sphere rests on 'educated publics' which, as he sees it, have disappeared. Given these views, we may say – as a stipulative definition – that *'the public sphere'* is a non-instrumental space in society, of open and unconstrained communication, separate from the State, and especially for the exchange and development of ideas on issues of collective import.

In relation to *higher education as an educational process*, the public sphere suggests curricula that enable students to develop communicative – and especially reasoning – capabilities in public engagement and to become full citizens (even 'world citizens' (Nussbaum, 2010; Erguyan et al., 2019)). In principle, this curriculum orientation could be evident in every discipline; it need not be confined to the social sciences and the humanities (despite Nussbaum's efforts so to locate it). The science curriculum could include reflective and even controversial matters concerning science in the world. However, the educational situation itself could be orchestrated so as to constitute a public of sorts, for example, by including debates in classroom settings (as Michael Sandel, as 'The Public Philosopher' does so brilliantly, in using public broadcasting and on a world scale).

The university can – and now *does* – seek to develop public spheres (plural), (Volkmer, 2014) in the wider society by engaging with different communities in debates on complex issues. In this way, boundaries between universities and the wider society lessen, and we are seeing emerge 'universities without walls' (Finnegan, 2005). Here, certainly, we need to ward against any assumption of trickle-down epistemology, the belief that the university is all-knowing and that its public-sphere role lies simply in handing down the fruits of its intellectual labours so as to enlighten the public. To the contrary, society may be construed as sets of intertwined 'learning systems' (Habermas, 1987a) in which the university plays but a part. Nevertheless, in a digital age, opportunities are expanding for the university to reach into the public realm.

However, if the university is legitimately to adopt this role, it has itself to constitute something of a public sphere (Pusser, 2012).

Hannah Arendt and the public realm

Hannah Arendt is particularly associated with the idea of the public realm and threats to it (Hill, 1979), especially those arising from the emergence of mass society – a society that 'has conquered the public realm' (Arendt, 1958: 41). For her, the public realm was a sphere of action, in which citizens freely gave of themselves in collective action to address matters of common concern. However, in the mass society, 'behaviour has replaced action' (ibid), and so the public realm has been squeezed out.

In Arendt's thought, the public realm has two understandings. In her (1958) major work, *The Human Condition*, it 'was permeated by a fiercely agonal spirit' (ibid): this was a competitive arena, in which citizens would strive to be heard and to have effects on their fellow citizens. Elsewhere in her writings, Arendt favoured a more 'associational' reading, where 'men act together in concert'. This is not a space 'in any topographical or institutional sense … [Indeed] a private dining room in which people gather to hear a *samizdat* or in which dissidents meet … become public spaces' (Benhabib, 1994: 78).

So, two kinds of public space then: the space of the Oxford University Union debating chamber, of showiness, effect and rhetorical persuasion, *and* of the Quaker meeting room, of reticence, mutuality and a collective mood. Each has its advantages and its weaknesses. The agonal, striving-for-effect, space becomes a matter of show, devoid of moral compass but, yet, persuasion has a value. On the other hand, Quakerish reticence may lack a certain energy level, but, at least, the timid can more easily have their day in the sun.

I have been urging – in this book – a fundamental distinction between higher education as a set of pedagogical processes and the university as an institution. So far as the first is concerned, the idea of the pedagogical process as a public space has been much advanced by Masschelein and Simons (2012, 2018; also Biesta, 2012 and Ripatti-Torniainen, 2018). And, in their hands, *this* idea of higher education echoes Arendt's 'associational' space, for they offer an idea of teachers and taught coming freely together in the mutual offering of ideas and their collaborative examination. This would be a space not simply *of* freedom but a space 'where freedom can appear' (Arendt, quoted in Benhabib, 1994: 78).

Potentially, an even more powerful reading of higher education as a public space can emerge if we turn to the university as an institution. Here, Arendt's 'agonal' reading of the idea of the public realm deserves the palm. After all, the university is an institution that is both witness to the cross-fire of multiple global forces and subject to them, and even plays its part in them. This is a competitive marketplace of ideas, the *real* of higher education, shot through with power. For the university to enter these lists can be – to which the situation in several states bears witness – to jeopardise its very existence.

I have, then, posited two relationships, in picking up on the two ideas of the public in Arendt's work and two relationships with higher education: (i) *associative* – higher education as pedagogy and (ii) *agonal* – the university as institution. However, we can also insert the *agonal strain* into pedagogy. Students in a class could be positioned so as to vie with each other in projecting their own ideas; the kind of pedagogy that might spring out of a neoliberal and marketised higher education system. And we can also ally the university as an institution with the *associative strain*. A university could, for example, strive to work with communities in its locality to explore responses to an ecological crisis. Assessing Arendt's ideas of 'public', then, it is apparent that *both* pedagogy and the institutional aspects of higher education possess *both* agonal and associative potential.

There is a further issue lurking: what might it mean for the university *itself* to be a public space? Does a university have a societal responsibility to keep open its doors and to offer every seminar and other debates – indeed, *every* webinar – to the public? We should note that many apparently public spaces in the wider society turn out to be owned by corporations in the private sector, the spaces being subject to digital and human surveillance (with individuals being asked to move on if felt not to be in keeping with the desired ambience); and universities seem to be similarly heading, not least as they deploy proprietary software enabling data capture for management purposes (Komljenovic, 2020), and their grounds patrolled and their 'welcome' desks operated by outsourced companies.

Seyla Benhabib advances a set of pertinent commentaries. The idea of the public presupposes conversation among equals but two questions arise: *first*, who counts as an equal? Who is to be granted legitimacy in a 'public' space – are some to be excluded, their potential contributions down-valued?

Second, what gets onto the agenda? Are some issues to be designated as within the private realm or, say, as falling within labour relations (for instance, the university as an employer or the salaries of rectors), and so not warrant becoming matters of public concern. For Benhabib, this is exactly what Arendt unwittingly did, in drawing overtight boundaries around the public realm, a pattern – we may note – that is evident in some countries. What may seem to be a matter purely internal to the university may be legitimately be a matter for public debate in the public realm. Correspondingly, what may have been felt to be a matter just of wider national interest may be matters that deserve to form topics for university scrutiny.

Jürgen Habermas

It is tempting, at this juncture, to delve into an early work of Jürgen Habermas (2005/1962), '*The Structural Transformation of the Public Sphere*', it being a work of foundational importance (Calhoun, 1994). In it, Habermas surveys the emergence of a public sphere in European cultural and literary circles in the seventeenth century, especially in England and then its subsequent 'weakening' (p. 232), as both the State and the market grew in tandem. Habermas notes 'two competing tendencies' in the modern social welfare state: 'a staged and manipulative publicity' and 'a critical process of public communication'. These observations set up a question: 'What are the *conditions* of a public space in society in the twenty-first century?' But this philosophical question is not *explicitly* posed in that Habermassian book, the book being situated much more in social theory.

For work in Habermas' oeuvre that is of more help to us, we should turn to his most significant contribution to philosophical thought, namely his (grand) theory of communicative action (Habermas, 1984, 1987b). There, Habermas sought to discern the structure of rational communication, a structure that he claimed to be latent in human discourse. At its heart, Habermas saw human communication as harbouring an ideal speech situation, which presupposed three 'validity claims' of truthfulness, sincerity and appropriateness. The question for us is this: does this suggestion – of validity claims – help us in being clearer as to the meaning of 'public space' in relation to the university?

I think it does. Latching onto these validity claims, we may sense that a public space has to fulfil certain (necessary) conditions in order to count *as* a public space. The question now becomes: are the conditions that Habermas picks out also *sufficient* conditions of a space that is properly termed public?

It is surely evident that, in understanding the public sphere, Habermas' validity claims are *in*sufficient. They specify the conditions of a rational discourse once joined by the parties concerned. They are *internal* constituents of the conversation. We need to add conditions that are necessary for the conversation to get going in the first place. These include the familiar ideas of freedom of association, freedom to speak and freedom to dissent and to critique, and they *also* require the presence of *societally* generated capabilities (Nussbaum, 2011). There are many places in the world where these conditions are not upheld.

Since the university finds itself in situations shot through with undue power exercised by authoritarian states and global corporations, human qualities are *also* called for if a public space is to be sustained. For example, courage, steadfastness and political nous are needed and at both the university level and the level of the individual faculty and student member. Individuals *and* universities are continuously faced with forces that would curtail their agentic rights and possibilities. Steadiness under fire (literally so, on occasions) is necessary.

But there opens, too, as Benhabib observes, considerations of *different* public spaces: 'there may be as many publics as there are controversial general debates …' (87). Compare an academic participating in a public call-in radio programme, students protesting about a new government policy, academics contributing to the public proceedings of parliamentary committees, a research centre making its data freely available and engaging with citizen scientists (Arvanitakis and Hornsby, 2018), and a university co-constructing public town-hall events to consider its report on a major development project. These are all public spaces, but they differ considerably in the publics involved, especially in the degree of their openness and in their underlying norms of debate.

In other words, Habermas' conception of the ideal speech situation has to be given a pragmatic touch, given that the university finds itself engaging with quite different publics. Moreover, voices have to be not only heard but also *promoted*. This, as Benhabib observes, is one of the drives behind feminism, that the formal fairness of a speech situation can act to *depress* voice and (women's) presence in it may be near-invisible (cf. chapter 11's discussion of Fricker's idea of epistemic injustice).

Now, especially in an Internet age, there are multiple spaces and multiple would-be participants in societal spaces and with differential power in those spaces. It is all very well to notice that within the juxtaposition of the concepts of university and public stands a demand that the university makes public its utterances (Willinsky, 2011) but it may be that those utterances are unintelligible to various publics. At times, a university in possession of a public disposition may find itself having to *'convene' its own publics* (Facer, 2019a, 2020). Admittedly, this places the university in a perilous situation. On pain of being marginalised, it is called into public arenas but is then assailed for being active *and* for its pusillanimity.

A difficulty is that we lack a concept of what it is to be a public intellectual in the twenty-first century. Justifiably, the idea has long been in decline (Small, 2002; Posner, 2003) – it smacking of a unitary public and a *de-haut-en-bas* tone of superiority. Work has been undertaken to discern possibilities for the student becoming a citizen, especially in community settings (Arthur, 2005; Nussbaum, 2018), but much wider horizons are needed to articulate a sense of both academics and students taking on public responsibilities that heed callings of the whole world, including nature (Latour, 2004; Nixon, 2019). The very term 'public intellectual' should now be abandoned in favour of 'citizen of the Earth'.

Public good and public goods

Much acknowledgement of Samuelson's work (in economics) on public goods (Marginson, 2007) has been made. In this depiction, public goods are non-rivalrous and non-excludable: their value does not fall even as their distribution widens and their take-up cannot be restricted. This approach has its limits, not least in seeing knowledge as a quasi-economic good possessed by individuals, but, at least, it opens the thorny issue of 'who pays?' (Bou-Habib, 2010). If the goods with which universities are characteristically associated are public goods – their value neither being confined to individual buyers nor depleted by their use (actually to the contrary) – the bill is unlikely to be met by the market.

We lack an inventory of the full range of public goods that may come into the reckoning so far as higher education is concerned. *This is inevitable*. Each university, each department in a university and each discipline will be associated with its *own panoply* of public goods.

Moreover, any attempt to compile a list of the public goods in sight is shot through with difficulty, there being *controversy* over what counts as a public good. Is research for military uses a public good? Are skills that generate economic returns for individuals and corporations public goods? Is a *private* university with a medical hospital (with 'private' patients) contributing to the public good? No simple division can be made in the relationship between public and private goods (Marginson, 2012). After all, a good may be held in the public *domain* but not provide public *benefit*; another good may lie in the *private* domain yet provide *public* benefit.

We may discern groupings of public goods along no less than *four axes* that criss-cross each other in an intersectional space: (i) individual and collective; (ii) knowledge-based and based more in society; (iii) nation-based and of global reach; and (iv) short-term and long-term. Examples are not confined to any location, but spread *across* this space: the university-trained *individual* doctor provides healing to patients and is part of a community of health experts that enhances the public health of society; a university's orchestra provides heavily subsidised concerts to the local community; graduates are more likely to be informed, be active citizens and take a close interest in their own health and so sustain a high level of public health; students may develop lifelong dispositions in being concerned for the world; new ideas emerging from research in a specific university can circulate across the world.

Some public benefits have been subject to empirical examination, but that work is bound to be limited for many of the benefits just identified are long-term, global and diffuse and are not easily amenable to research. Ultimately, what counts as a public good is an ethical matter; public goods are always moral goods (Nixon, 2011). Suppose it turns out that a highly educated population is not only a phlegmatic population, but that its citizens also have a care for the good of society. Some would see this as a *eudaimonistic* society, with a heightened level of human flourishing; let's be like the Danes, some may feel. It follows that determining the public goods associated with higher education is irredeemably contentious.

If contest is present in relation to the public goods of higher education, so it is even more so in relation to the 'more normative' notion of *the* public good (Marginson, 2012: 11; Filippakou and Williams, 2015). Partly, this conflict is a natural outcome of the fuzziness of the concept that is reflective of the public good, it being a *hybrid* between that of public goods and the public realm. It pretends both to an easy empiricism *and* to a transcendental loftiness. The question is: can it be cashed out? Yes, but with some caution.

We may speak of the public good when we have in mind the *long-term* wellbeing of society taken in the round. *All three elements* should be present: higher education works for the public good when it is (a) of lasting value, has (b) wide societal reach and is (c) intimately connected with societal wellbeing. These three conditions – durability, society as such and societal wellbeing – are *necessary* conditions. But difficulties abound: how long-term is 'long-term'? What is to count as societal wellbeing? How extensive across society? The concept of the public good, therefore, is a universal – it can carry across nations and cultures – *and* it has global pretentions (Marginson, 2007, 2012), but it harbours much contention.

There is a further matter that even threatens to undermine this discussion. If higher education and universities collectively can be seen to add to *general* levels of considerateness, rationality, a concern for one's health, a reticence, care for disadvantaged peoples, propensity to exercise, participation in public debate, engagement with democratic institutions, an interest in Nature and so forth, are we not in the presence of *societal* goods? These are goods, after all, that benefit society. That there is now a tendency to label societal goods as public goods is testimony to thinking being bewitched by economic frameworks, from which the notions of public goods and public good have flowed. And this tendency to conflate social goods and public goods can be seen among both those who are involved in systems modelling *and* who critique that approach (such as Collini, 2012). A careful disentanglement of these two concepts – societal goods and public goods – awaits us, however.

The three planes

Let us return to the three-planar conception of higher education that sits at the heart of this book (page 34). It will be recalled that the three planes, and their poles, are (i) higher education as a set of *institutions* – as a penumbra of *ideas*; (ii) individual institutions in their *here-and-now* position – in the *possibilities* that might be imagined for each university; (iii) the *particulars* of higher education (its intricate activities and its micro-objects) – the *universals* of higher education. In coming at the relationship between higher education and the public realm, the public goods of higher education fall onto *the left-hand side of our three planes* – their ontological aspects. Here arise legitimate concerns about the extent to which the goods that derive from higher education are *actually* circulating in society. These concerns can be addressed *both* to the educational processes of higher education and to the absorption of graduates into society (do those graduates *actually* carry public goods with them?) *and* to the ways in which universities conduct themselves in their interconnections with society (which public goods do they offer to society? Do research and scholarship *actually* constitute public goods or do they rather further cognitive capitalism and the wealth of the few?).

And these questions – still on the ontological side – can be posed *on each plane*. For instance, on *plane (ii)*, we may ask of a university: to what extent is any particular aspect available to the public – its estate, its grounds, its seminars, its research, its teaching materials, its projects and so forth? It is on the basis of these considerations that each university in receipt of 'public' funds can be invited to identify the public goods that it is placing into society. Public funding deserves public accountability in the form of a *profile of each university's public goods – their specificity and the extent to which they are actually realised in society*.

The ideas of the public sphere and the public realm sit more happily on *the right-hand side* – the ideational side – of our three planes. Here, we may inquire into what might count as the public sphere in relation to higher education, but we can also peer into its *possibilities*. As noted, the public sphere is positioned as residing *either* in the wider society – and then the issues arise as to how the university might enhance that public sphere – *or* in the university – and then the issue arises as to what it might be for the university itself to be constituted as a public sphere. But these two depictions of the public sphere delimit the agenda. If we were instead to see the relationship between the universities and the public sphere as a matter of *public interest*, then the public as such can rightly become involved in influencing the relationship.

Conclusions

The idea of 'public' presents formidable difficulties to the philosophy of higher education, and we have touched only on some. The troublesome issue of the *public interest* could have come into view (is it *in* the public interest that public monies be devoted to the humanities even though the matter is not *of* public interest?). Matters, too, of democracy (Levin and Greenwood, 2016), citizenship (Ehrlich, 2000) and commons (Szadkowski, 2019; Szadkowski and Krzeski, 2020) could have come into the reckoning. Moreover, there is a geopolitics at play here: the public good and the public sphere differ considerably as between a liberal democratic state and a state-controlled setting.

Many of the difficulties arise because the concepts in question – public goods, public good, public space, public sphere, public realm, public interest and so forth – sit on *all three planes* of our general schema and *at the two poles of each plane*. They raise questions as to how, *on the one hand*, higher education and the university *are* and, *on the other hand*, provoke issues as to how we might *imagine* them.

Some of this territory is amenable to empirical inquiry (to what degree do graduates carry with them general dispositions of value to the wider society and so constitute a public good?), but some of it resists empirical inquiry. For example, if it be felt that virtues such as a heightening of civility, or sociality, or citizenship, or reticence, or wisdom contribute to the public good, how might such contributions be evaluated? Understanding some goods – perhaps the most important public goods – involves both facts and values, and their consequent neglect represents a diminution of higher education.

A realist approach requires recognition of there being different publics with which the university can engage. More and more, universities are reaching out locally in a spirit of civic construction; regionally, to indigenous communities; and globally, collaborating with transnational agencies in establishing eco-sensitive systems. An interest in the idea of public good must loom into view for academic leadership out of felt *responsibilities* to students, society and the wider world (cf. Solbrekke and Sugrue, 2020). The matters of engagement and responsibility, therefore, attract our immediate attention.

18 The lure of engagement
Traps for the unwary

Introduction

Over recent decades, there has arisen an expectation that universities should be more *engaged* with society. In the process, a welter of terms has arisen – 'third mission', 'enterprise', 'knowledge transfer', (a return to) 'the civic university', 'impact', 'the engaged university', 'service' and 'responsibility'. How is this discourse to be understood conceptually? It could very easily, and indeed it does, encircle the globe: a ring of engagement, indeed. *Conceptually*, then, how might we form a view of this complicated region?

Clusters of concepts

A number of clusters of concepts are present in this space. No less than eight are apparent, and they share something of each other's space, with some concepts situated in more than one cluster:

The cluster of engagement: the engaged university; knowledge engagement; civic engagement; engagement itself; knowledge exchange; knowledge activism; innovation.
The civic cluster: civil society; civic society; the civic university (with old and new variants); the concept of civic itself; service; citizenship; community.
The cluster of diplomacy: knowledge diplomacy; science diplomacy; public diplomacy; expertise.
The cluster of globalisation: global and local; the idea of 'glonacal'; globalisation itself; internationalisation.
The cluster of colonisation: colonisation; coloniality; decolonialisation; post-colonialisation; traditional cultures; indigenous cultures; 'epistemicide'.
The cluster of sustainability: sustainability itself; 'Sustainability Development Goals' (as advanced by the United Nations); 'the sustainable university'.
The worldly cluster: multiple worlds; plural worlds; common world; the commons.

In this galaxy of engagement, there are no timeless essences of concepts: all is in motion, both individual concepts and their clusterings, and the situations to which they refer. Gravitational pulls exert their influence on each other, with individual concepts being attracted to a neighbouring constellation. For example, *civic engagement* is a hybrid idea and has associations both with ideas of engagement and with civic ideas. For now, it sojourns mainly in the *engagement* cluster, as civic *engagement*, with its operational and policy overtones. The question arises, therefore, as to whether it might be lured more into the *civic* cluster – as *civic* engagement – and so be open to imaginative ideas about the whole realm of the civic in the twenty-first century.

These ideas about engagement constitute a vast galaxy, its concepts moving in all manner of directions and exhibiting differences across national systems. Is there a way of gaining some order? I suggest that we can do so by importing the concept of responsibility (from beyond the galaxy). To stay within due limits, I shall explore the relationships between the concept of responsibility and just two other concepts, those of service and engagement itself.

Planes and possibilities

It will be recalled that a three-planar schema has provided the foundations for this book (p 34). Each plane – it will be recalled – possesses an ontological *and* an imaginative pole; higher education both is in the world *and* is open to an imagining of its possibilities (in short, higher education as Real *and* as Idea). Here, on the ontological side – and in relation to the cluster of engagement – universities and their educational processes are engaged with people and institutions. These engagements possess ontological substance: they are real and have effects in the world, whether intended or not. That a university begins an innovative programme of study can – unintendedly – influence another university, even in another part of the world, as it revamps its course offer. And these engagements have depth: flows of students can be affected by dubious and barely seen geopolitical movements.

Straightaway, then, on the ontological side, we have four kinds of engagement. Some will be (i) *transparent and intended*: a programme of studies is deliberately designed to elicit students' engagement with a difficult public issue. Some will be (ii) *transparent and unintended*: a new pedagogical practice manifestly leads to a level of dissatisfaction among the students, the students becoming *dis*engaged, exhibiting a higher rate of attrition from the programme. Some will be (iii) *invisible and unintended*: despite many declarations of concerns for inclusion and life chances, institutions of higher education unwittingly reinforce socioeconomic hierarchies. And, lastly, some will be (iv) both *invisible and intended*: a university's Board of Governors assents to investments of dubious moral worth, and agrees to remain silent about the matter by, for instance, excluding mention of the particular investments in the university's annual financial statement.

All of these forms of engagement lie on the ontological side of our three-planar depiction of higher education. They are indicative of the *ontological complexity of engagement*. They are real (plane one); are of the moment (plane two) and involve micro entities within the university and its teaching practices (plane three). Some forms are proclaimed, and others lie hidden, below the surface, perhaps in murky waters. 'Murky', of course, is a matter of fact and of value. As *matters of fact*, forms of engagement may be difficult to discern, lying at a depth, and unbeknown even to those who are engaged in them (only subsequently might the practices come to light). As *matters of value*, some engagements are morally questionable. There is, therefore, an ethics that attaches to this whole matter (Tesar, et al., 2021). The point is that *both* fact and value are to be found on the ontological side of our three-planar schema.

On the other side of the three planes of our schema – the right-hand side – are the conceptual and imaginative aspects of higher education. Here is the world of debate, ideas and dispute. And in many universities around the world, there will much discussion about the legitimacy of particular forms of engagement that are being pursued. *On plane one* appear both pedagogical and institutional issues. There are concerns that students do not always engage with their studies as well as they might, but to what extent is it legitimate to orchestrate the student's engagement: shouldn't students be free to determine their level of engagement for themselves? Should a university engage with wealthy donors and accept donations from that quarter? Should it set up an overseas campus, given the conditions being imposed by the host state? Should an agreement be made with a pharmaceutical company, such that the university's research findings become that company's intellectual property? Each of these questions raises conceptual issues about the boundaries, conditions and limits *of* engagement.

Moving to *plane two*, we can inquire into the actual *possibilities* for engagement of any particular university. In teaching, educational possibilities will play out according to the epistemological geography of an institution, the technologies available to it and the pedagogical dispositions of its faculty, both in the near future and further ahead. These possibilities are not mere projections of the current state of play but are imaginative and creative discernments. New vocabularies may be drawn upon as, for instance, entirely new relationships are glimpsed between a university and the Earth.

On *plane three*, in moving to concepts that possess universal potential, the concept of engagement can be treated with even more high-minded seriousness. Can the militaristic sentiments within the concept (the armies *engaging* with each other) be reconciled with its conciliatory aspect (the couple becoming *engaged*)? Or is this a multiplicity, the idea of engagement moving with different rhythms, different intensities, different affordances? The men and women in the armies (that engage with each other) can be counted; the lovers who become engaged can only be wondered at. The engagements of the university can be glimpsed from multiple directions. The department of civil engineering engages with private companies, as they together seek to shore up the leaning tower of Pisa; the Pro-Rector for Enterprise engages with officials in the Ministry for Business Affairs; and the archaeology department engages with a local museum, hoping to develop a new kind of student programme. The sentiments and values beneath these engagements jostle with each other.

So what are the possibilities for the engaged university? Are there to be definite *rules of engagement*? Is there *always* to be some element of reciprocity? The gears mesh in their engagement, and perhaps they grind with some screeching. One cannot properly engage by oneself. But, then, the matter of *asymmetrical* engagement arises. Is not one party always more powerful than the other? A research-oriented university in the Global North engages with a university in the Global South. A memorandum of understanding is signed, even with a lavish ceremony, and hands are shaken, and there is talk of 'collaboration', but it is understood where the power lies (Walker and Martinez-Vargas, 2020).

Let us not talk – as many like to do – of 'lines of flight' but instead speak of *paths of possibilities*, with their lines proceeding in awkward, dog-leg, ways. That conversation between the local museum and the department of archaeology falters, but nothing ventured, nothing gained, and so the programme leader turns to a local archaeological society and the tourist board (which glimpses potential tourism opportunities) and new options open for the students' practical experiences. A path opens; a path of possibility. Intensities, magnitudes, quantities and qualities run into each other in these multiplicities of engagement.

Engagement then can be understood to be a universal but only insofar as it is also understood to offer an infinity of *conflicting* possibilities yet to be imagined, and glimpsed, in the real of the university. These are possibilities both of purpose and of procedure: it is all very well to advocate an openness in the circulation of knowledge – even a 'knowledge socialism' (Peters et al., 2012a, 2020) – but to what end? Especially in a digital age, there is a risk – in engagement – of 'mutation' and not just in the humanities and social sciences (Lévy, 2020). Tone is not everything, but it counts for much. With what nuance, with what empathy is any engagement to be entered into? Can the position of the other be taken? Does the university understand its powers as it seeks to engage with another party? Perhaps there is a *lack* of engagement, for the parties stand in different fields, really unwilling to engage.

Service, responsibility and engagement

For a long time, it has been part of the self-rhetoric of higher education in the USA that, alongside teaching and research, 'service' is a third arm. And recently, the idea of service has been promulgated in just that way, as one of (the) three arms of higher education (Bourner, 2018; Bourner et al., 2020). Played up in this way, we are not merely in the throes of an account of the way matters stand for higher education but of a spelling out of its responsibilities (Davids and Waghid, 2019). There is a strong 'oughtness' here.

We have, then, a local cluster of concepts: service, engagement and responsibility. A set of interconnections immediately suggests itself and a beguiling narrative: the total world – human and natural – is in a parlous state and institutions of higher education perceive that they have *responsibilities* in addressing the situation, in *engaging* with matters and in *serving* not just the public interest but the planetary interest as well. It is a conceptual story of this kind through which, I think, we can understand the way in which many universities across the world are addressing the United Nations' Sustainable Development Goals (Chankseliani and McCowan, 2021). In those responses, the three concepts of responsibility, service and engagement are in harmonious alignment, or so it may seem. However, the three concepts are moving in many directions and are often in tension with each other.

Does the idea of responsibility give a university direction? Does a university owe anything to its founders and the value base of its past? Or should it understand itself as having responsibilities to generations *ahead* and to conditions of the world that cannot be foretold? Responsibility, after all, is a temporal concept: it speaks of the past, the present *and* the future. But then, what might constitute a responsibility to serve? Who draws up the menu that will constitute the items in the service? And on which conditions is the university to serve? Perhaps there are *undue* conditions attaching to any responsibility that a university perceives itself as serving.

In picking up the idea of responsibility, we should distinguish between a responsibility 'to' and a responsibility 'for'. A university has a responsibility to X (a social class; the natural environment; its students; the standards inherent in disciplined inquiry) in order to do Y (improve life chances; expand the economy; assist in rectifying impairments in the natural environment; enable its students fully to become their own authentic and rational human beings; faithfully uphold disciplinary standards). *There is no responsibility in itself*: it is always a responsibility towards some or other entity and with some purpose in mind. And it comes into play in a situation of *absence or impairment* (a social class is not properly represented in the professions; the natural environment is in crisis; students do not fully possess the powers of criticality; there are signs of a lack of integrity in academic processes).

Correspondingly, service is always service in-context and it is – to draw on an overused term – a *relational* concept. A university serves Y. However, that relational dimension may be ontological or ideational. Ontologically, Y may take many forms: it might be a state, a locality, a group of students, a nation. Ideationally, too, a university's responsibilities (towards Y) can have a multitude of orientations, including freedom, justice, truth, equity or even a (presumed) national identity. The values implicit in such ideals may be served in contradictory ways, and the ideals may orient a university in multiple directions. Even if it wished to do so, the university cannot adequately serve all of its claimants, for their claims will be bound to conflict.

Responsibility and service, then, are not so much empty signifiers but are open-ended conceptual umbrellas, under which a multitude of claimants can present themselves. Even single entities – 'the student body' – present a manifold of claims.

The claimants to which service is to be legitimately given, and the responsibility to be discharged in that service, never announce themselves with unalloyed directness. Just as we learnt from Derrida (2001b, 2005) that friendship and even hospitality are never without conditions, so too service is always present on condition. The tutor gives unstintingly of herself to her students; she serves her students. But that idea of service is contained within a pedagogy at least of hope and even of expectation that the students in question will invest something of themselves not least in coping with difficult material or experiences.

Service with a smile, as they say, but on condition. The conditionality, though, points in multiple directions. Of course, conditions attach to the professor's efforts, but the students also have a responsibility to *themselves* to promote their own flourishing; they even have responsibilities to their teachers, their fellow students and their family and others who support them. Responsibility flows in ever-widening circles.

This service consistently presents ambiguities. Tutors, being seized of their interests in, and even their passions for, their subject will be continuingly weighing their responsibilities in serving the standards of their epistemic communities and in having an empathy for their students. A sense of responsibility is always liable to open the floodgates to a welter of expectations from contending parties. In an interconnected world, responsibilities have a propensity for never-ending expansion. Ideologies, epistemologies, sets of standards, truth regimes and blockbuster nostrums – care, skill, understanding, ecology and so forth – present their calling cards when the door to responsibility is opened. In principle, *responsibilities have no limits*.

There can be no clear direction, no signpost: neither responsibility nor service has a definite endpoint. To the contrary, the more a sensitivity to responsibility and service, the more the danger lurks of being paralysed into inaction. The siren voices – of equity and standards, of global citizenship and local community – speak across each other. The faculty member feels the pull of his or her institution, epistemic community, students and professional association and even his/her nation, and those pulls are in tension. How are the claims to be judged? Where lies any priority? Does the faculty member attend to the student's essay or laboratory project OR to the university injunction about online learning OR to the wider insistence that her publications' list be extended (and preferably through 'world-class' journals)?

Complexity and supercomplexity, again

The dilemmas just intimated are dilemmas of *complexity*. They speak to the interweaving of systems – of institutions, state bureaucracy, globalised academe, epistemic orderings and student markets – in which academics find themselves. This complexity – as observed in an earlier chapter – imposes real difficulties (that emanate from the *real* of academic life) and lead to stress. Just where is the academic's primary allegiance to be directed? Where are the main responsibilities to be felt? And just what level and quality of service is to be provided? But in addition to these dilemmas of complexity arise dilemmas of *supercomplexity*.

The academic life is one of responsibility. In it, one is called to serve. But by which creed? Of 'innovation'? Of academic freedom? Of truthfulness? Of ecological sensitivity? Of economic supremacy? Of national pride? Of work, the labour market and employability? Of care for one's students? Of truth-to-power? Of openness-wherever-it-might-lead or justice-for-the-oppressed? In higher education, responsibility plays out in a mélange of discourses that cut across each other. Even though we are in the presence of ideas, those ideas ride on undercurrents of deep-seated ideologies, which are the ground on which hostilities often break out. This is supercomplexity: a situation of proliferating and competing discourses.

It emerges, therefore, that not only are the concepts of responsibility and service intertwined but that the ontological and imaginative realms are frequently in tension with each other. And this plays out both at the institutional level and that of the educational processes that are termed 'higher education'. We may draw again upon the thinking of Bernard Stiegler here. The situation may be termed a 'pharmacological' situation, in which there is present both disease and restoration. Precisely in being responsible and in being willing to serve, the university and the teacher are liable to be corrupted by the forceful voices – of innovation, of nation, of publication, of student-as-customer – but spaces may still be glimpsed for alternative notions of *responsibility* and quite different forms of *service*.

So contextualised, *engagement* now becomes problematic. A proper engagement is reciprocal: the parties are more or less equal, and there is give and take. The two fencers joust: they *engage* with each other, as play and seriousness intertwine. But the two parties in an engagement – the armies, the lovers – can become locked together and enmeshed in each other. Suffocation threatens. The university, the student, the researcher, the scholar and even the 'third-space' administrator have to have space to *dis*engage as their sense of their responsibilities tilts or as new responsibilities appear. A particular service has to be ended, even abruptly. The 'guest speaker', having been engaged for an event, turns out to be an apologist for racism, and, after careful consideration, it is judged that neither the interests of the university nor the public interest would be well-served if the event was to proceed. *Engagement is a concept to be kept at arms-length*.

Traps for the unwary

The university is summoned to be engaged, but there are traps for the unwary. The university can find itself so enmeshed that it surrenders its autonomies.

Programmes of higher education and their students become so engaged that their spaces for independent critical thinking are severely diminished. Disengagement is not even considered for engagement becomes naturalised, a collective understanding of the university's natural mode in the world.

Moreover, the university and higher education are connected with the world in a multitude of ways: for hundreds of years, programmes of study have had more than an eye on the world. Law and medicine, which are bound up in the world, were significant constituents of the medieval universities, as their ancient buildings can still testify. (The epithet of the 'ivory tower' was always problematic.) The situation, therefore, is one of degree: at some point, connection becomes engagement. The problem is that that moment – of connection becoming engagement – can often be identified only after the event. It happens piecemeal over time and, then, if disengagement is desired, it may not be easily possible. Too much has been invested: the student flow from a particular nation can be stopped only at much cost.

And yet engagement is *inevitable*: the university cannot but be engaged in quests for understanding, in immersing itself in a culture of truthfulness, in having a concern for carefulness in utterance and in the essential conditions of respectful conversation. Those leading programmes of study and having a concern for students' unfolding cannot avoid being engaged.

And all the time, in the *real* of the university, opportunities for new engagements emerge. The Internet makes it possible for students on a course of study to engage over time with students on a comparable course in another country. Emerging concerns about racism, the Global South and climate crisis as well as a heightening of worldwide interest in particular social and global-political matters all pose awkward questions to universities as to whether they should explicitly engage in any of them. The university is called upon to declare itself.

Key in all of this, as intimated, remains the matter of responsibility, a concept with its own internal strands (Robinson, 2019). As part of its being in the world, does the university have a *responsibility* to engage as such? For those of a realist persuasion, the matter of responsibility arises where there are demonstrable and deep-seated injurious absences in the world that the university can naturally help to rectify (Nixon, 2019). Oppressions can be seen, exclusions can be identified, poverty can be recognised, physical and emotional hurt can be felt. It is presumably on the basis of the implied absences – absence of equity, of respect for persons, of a basic subsistence and of peace – that universities are turning to the United Nations' Sustainable Development Goals or join an international grouping such as the Talloires network of universities, with its interest in civic development (Watson et al., 2011). Institutions reach a point where they feel that they have a responsibility to deploy their resources in addressing the absences in the world. As Roy Bhaskar (2008b) might have put it, they embark on a strategy of 'absenting absences'.

In such moves, universities come to be haunted by absences in the world where they possess resources to make a difference, and it is understandable that, so moved, they seek to engage with the world, in addressing the matters in question. We may note that engagements such as these are situated both on the left-hand, the ontological, side of our three-planar schema *and* on the right-hand side, the ideational side. Being concerned about hurt and injury in the world, universities are engaging both with the real of the world *and* with ideas of the world. They even conjure visions of themselves for their future trajectories. (Plane two.) But the traps for the unwary still lurk. Engagement lures one in. The university overcommits to the UN's Sustainable Development Goals and then is unable to critique those goals. In the process, while it is seeking to *be* responsible, it *jeopardises* its *responsibilities* for its own autonomy and possibilities for critique. Paradoxes lurk.

The state and the university, and engagement

The relationship of the state and higher education in the twenty-first century is not well understood. There was a raft of work on the state-higher education relationship in the 1990s (by Salter and Tapper, 1994), including the idea of the 'evaluative state' (Neave, 1998) and other works (Green, 1990; Henkel and Little, 1999; Kogan and Hanney, 2000; Kogan and Marton, 2000), but that work did not always do justice to the idea of the state as such. That the state is a problematic entity needs to be recognised (e.g. the state as 'social relation' advanced by Jessop [1990] on the one hand, and the evaporation of the state implied by Hardt and Negri's [2000] theory of Empire). That whole story – of the state *and* higher education – needs urgently to be brought up-to-date, not least amid post-capitalism, a digital era, populism, state steering of public sectors, worldly disequilibrium, the global and hierarchical character of higher education, Agamben's (1998) idea of 'sovereignty' and theories of coloniality and posthumanism.

Without an adequate conception of the state–higher education relationship, the matter of engagement cannot be properly theorised, and still less, re-imagined. The general situation appears to be one in which the state is all the time trying to manoeuvre the university into being engaged but on the state's terms, such that engagement has its place against a horizon of digital surveillance, state audits and ideological constraint (which vary across nations).

What can be said is engagement pulls in conflicting directions. The trope of 'surveillance capitalism' (Zuboff, 2019) suggests that the university should be cautious of becoming overly *engaged* with society; it should sup with the devil with a very long spoon, despite – or because of – the largesse coming its way from the state. On the other hand, many consider – whether on account of the ecological crisis or on account of societal deformations (grotesque inequalities, nationally and globally) – that the university *should* be actively engaged in the wider world. But what might be the conditions of any such engagement?

On the theory of Hardt and Negri (2000), it can plausibly be suggested that the university has been co-opted – epistemologically, economically, technologically – into 'Empire' (a 'logic of rule' [page xii] beyond (declining) nation-states). But, yet, the nation-state persists, and higher education is – more than ever – part of an *epistemological state apparatus* (as we may term it, adapting Althusser [1971]). The university now constitutes a machine of the state in promoting STEMM (science, technology, engineering, mathematics and medicine [Cohen, 2021]) – and we see this particularly starkly in some nations. University engagement is now *compelled*: the university has received an offer that it cannot – or dare not – refuse.

There is a yet wider issue facing the university and the state. All universities – and their programmes of higher education – are, to a greater or lesser extent, creatures of their nations, but the very idea of the university implies a set of *universal* responsibilities. Some might consider that the university has a responsibility to engage with and in the interests of the whole world and even to help to forge a 'world community' (Bartelson, 2009). But that idea serve only to bring into play a raft of further issues, especially tensions between particularistic and universal considerations. To what extent might local considerations have to give way, if universality is to be forged? Indeed, it may be that 'the idea of a world community entails the assumption that human fulfilment is best achieved through the emancipation of human beings from belonging to individual communities' (ibid: 13).

This matter has taken on heightened urgency due both to states taking a closer interest in their higher education systems, seeing in them engines of state ideological and cultural ('soft') power, and to the onward march of the digital age, with its own universal algorithmic surveillance systems and in which the university is already becoming entrapped. In this situation, the concepts of responsibility, service and engagement are in danger of losing their traction: the university is supposedly more than an institution serving narrow and particular interests but is being deprived of a landscape in which universalism could make even the beginnings of some kind of sense. Perhaps a glimmering is opening, though: drawing on Judith Butler's thoughts, the university – we may say – is an institution that carries with it the force of nonviolence in a 'force field' of violence (Butler, 2020b: 40). Here – to be teased out – may be a way of redeeming an ethic of universality for higher education and the university.

Conclusions

Engagement, responsibility and service constitute a beguiling cluster of concepts for the university and higher education and their connections with the wider world. Which university wants to *disengage* from the urgent matters facing humanity and this Earth? Of which programme of study is it to be said that its teachers were *ir*responsible? Of which group of students would it be desirable that they graduate without any sense of *service*? Each of these three concepts (engagement, responsibility and service) draw one in. They demand a positive assent; they bequeath an 'of courseness'. But we should note that, in the company of the university and higher education, these concepts are aired by certain voices.

To rehearse a point that runs through this book, all is in motion – and conflictual motion at that – and, with it, the concepts of responsibility, service and engagement. Having their place both in the unstable worlds of the Real and of the imagination, there are no settled spaces for these three concepts. This is not to say that they should be abandoned or that they should be explicitly repudiated. But they should be treated cautiously, gingerly even, with a healthy scepticism that might encourage one to seek the origins of the discourses behind the concepts. Otherwise, there lies the prospect that these banners might be raised and, in turn, the university's *primary* obligations to truthfulness, autonomy of judgement and freedom of expression will be jeopardised.

The three concepts – responsibility, service and engagement – swim in each other's waters, but responsibility and service are minnows compared to *engagement*, which is a huge force of its own and is liable to eat the other two. The university *can* reach for *responsibility* and – with great care – to *service*; engagement, though, has turned out to be far too dangerous (despite its attractive aspects). Indeed, if the world is in a parlous state – and it is – the idea of responsibility *must* beckon. But to what should it beckon? To humanity or the world beyond? Or, more than to an ecology of others (Descola, 2013), perhaps to an ecology of all. This will be the final matter before us, but, first, matters of justice deserve our attention.

19 Social justice – and onwards to *ecological* justice

Introduction

I draft this chapter having just read two newspaper articles. One is about the participation of young black students in STEM disciplines in universities, and the other is concerned with the limited black and minority ethnic presence among the undergraduate students at the University of Oxford. These two articles, appearing on the same day, speak to the matters of social justice and fairness. These two matters, however, are (too) easily run together, and they *also* raise the *separate* matters of epistemic and cognitive justice.

Justice as fairness or justice *and* fairness?

The *issue of justice* speaks to this question: should higher education be available to all, whatever the circumstances of individuals? Is it a universal right? The *issue of fairness* turns on this issue: whatever the number of places available in a higher education system, how might they be made available fairly, such that no one feels or is disadvantaged? The failure to distinguish these two issues leads frequently to confusion.

Famously, John Rawls (1958, 1989) deliberately ran the two issues together in his political philosophy, *justice as fairness*. Importantly, Rawls did not claim that justice and fairness were synonymous or that one is more important than the other, but he did claim that 'the fundamental idea in the concept of justice is fairness' (Rawls, 1958: 164). Rawls reached this view with two principles. First, the liberty principle: 'each person participating in a practice, *or affected by it* [RB's emphasis], has an equal right to the most extensive liberty compatible with a like liberty for all' (165). Second, the equality principle: 'inequalities are arbitrary unless it is reasonable to expect that they will work for everyone's advantage' (ibid). To dramatise these principles, Rawls posited 'a veil of ignorance' in which individuals 'do not know how the various alternatives will affect their particular case'. The basic idea is to ensure that a fair state of affairs will ensue where no one knows how matters may play out.

Prima facie, this is a powerful set of ideas, not least in higher education, which is a significant player in the allocation of life chances. It has, however, been subject to a number of critiques, not only from political philosophers but also from educational philosophers and policymakers. The most influential line of counterargument has been inspired by Amartya Sen (2010: 12–13), who poses this problem. Suppose three children are arguing over who should have a flute: one claims it because she knows how to play it; another because he has no toys; and the third reminds the other two that she actually made it. In such a situation, 'justice as fairness' gives us no guidance for, in practice, different conceptions of the good life stand *behind* the veil of ignorance.

Sen's approach is to look to the capabilities that human beings need in order to realise their functioning as agents, and this entails enabling human beings to have choices, which in turn suggests the need for societies to provide all their members with the wherewithal to make the choices that enable them to realise those capabilities. At the root of society is not economics but the social good. Martha Nussbaum (2011) – whose work has contributed much to the philosophy of higher education – has developed this capabilities approach, distinguishing (ibid: 20–23) between 'internal' capabilities (those of an agent as such) and 'combined capabilities', which reflect *also* the societal spaces in which to realise one's capabilities. Nussbaum has spelt out ten sets of core capabilities. These include – as a single set – 'senses, imagination and thought ... informed and cultivated by an adequate education' (ibid: 33).

What are we to make of these ideas of social justice? Thomas Pogge (2011) has provided a comparison of the approaches of Rawls, Sen and Nussbaum, and he concludes in Rawls' favour, seeing Sen and Nussbaum as overplaying their hand. With a little correction, with account being taken of environmental diversities, the fairness approach still holds its ground, but the situation is rather more complicated.

Suppose we come at the matter crab-like, from the side. Imagine a couple, perhaps getting on in years but still living an incredibly rich life. They are privileged in that they have the resources to enjoy many and varied cultural events and travel to many countries to indulge their interests in opera. Over the years, they have acquired several languages, much self-taught, and their home is full of books that they value and enjoy. However, they did not go to university, and they neither possess a computer or smart-device nor have experienced social media or surfed the Internet and nor do they wish to. Are we to say of this couple that this is an *unfair* or an *unjust* situation? It is unfair only insofar as their own highly fortunate style of life is not available to others, but their life is not unjust, even though neither of our couple has experienced higher education and they lack what many would consider to be necessary features of effective functioning for twenty-first-century life.

There are, therefore, multiple conceptions of the good life, and standing behind a veil of ignorance cannot help us in determining *what* might be distributed or what it might be distributed *for*. Some say that higher education is necessary for human beings to function well, but our example suggests otherwise.

Educational justice

In sight is an idea of *educational justice*, a term that has begun to be used in relation to school education (Merry, 2020) but which poses particular difficulties in higher education. We may say that it is *educationally just* that a science student be permitted to take a programme in liberal arts, but if the student is restricted to a pedagogical diet that excludes examining the relationship between chemical engineering and climate change (Gutman, 2015: 15), we would then be in the presence of *epistemic injustice* (about which more in a moment).

Yet further twists suggest themselves. In most nations, higher education is a restricted good, not readily available to all. Does 'justice-as-fairness' suggest that (*option one – justice*) higher education should be available to all, or does it rather suggest that (*option two – fairness*) some equitable arrangement for the allocation of student places be provided? And how might these issues play across the disciplines? Suppose that I do not have the most rudimentary grasp of basic concepts in physics: how might then the matters of justice and fair allocation of restricted places play if I wish to study physics in a university?

Lurking here – especially in relation to *the justice option* – is the question 'who pays?,' and it has philosophical aspects (Bou-Habib, 2010). Assume that higher education can be made readily available to all. Nice questions then arise about the relationship between what is to count *as* a higher education and its availability. Are there limits to the concept of higher education (its 'standards'), or is it to be limitlessly plastic, moulding itself to the expectations placed upon it?

It is part of the argument of this book that the concept of higher education is extraordinarily pliable and should open to multiple new designs in the twenty-first century, *but* that the idea of higher education also possesses conceptual substance. That adjective 'higher' does conceptual work, and it imposes criteria which educational processes have to fulfil to warrant that appellation ('higher' education). Nevertheless, empirical matters matter. Social justice bears differently in nations that exhibit participation rates of 70% – as in South Korea – compared with low-participation countries.

On the second option, is a contentious-less means of allocating scarce places available? I suggest not. It would be readily granted that higher education heightens economic and social capital. The Peter principle is alive and well: 'To them that hath shall be given.' How then might higher education places be allocated? Having endured much pressure to reform themselves, some of the world's elite universities are making efforts to recruit students from socio-ethnic-economic backgrounds not much hitherto represented. But on what basis? A needs-blind policy? A policy that explicitly takes *past* disadvantage into consideration? A policy that tries to *forecast* the extra added-value in taking in student X as against student Y? A policy that *a priori* allocates a proportion of places to students who otherwise might not be selected or selects with a pin? (Each of these options have been suggested from time-to-time.)

What is evident is that, behind these matters of philosophical, conceptual and practical intricacy, there stands an unequal playing field, marked by the stratification of higher education systems, the weight given to the STEM disciplines, the relationship between inequalities in the wider society and their reproduction in higher education, and the regressive financing of an expensive good. *Justice* would suggest expanding the *total* system such that all can proceed to higher education without hindrance *and* be given the kind of schooling to proceed into such an expanded system. *Fairness* would suggest that the allocation of places across institutions *and* disciplines be such that there be no undeserved outcome across social groups, but then we get into awkward issues about the legitimacy of the practices and institutions in question. We see this in the debate over 'meritocracy' (Young, 1958; Sandel, 2020): fair access to an unjust society cannot lead to the good life.

Social justice and knowledge

Let us turn directly to the connections between social justice and higher education. A prompt here is the (2014) book by Jan McArthur, *Rethinking Knowledge within Higher Education: Adorno and Social Justice*.

Much debate has been concerned with injustice and lessening it. McArthur turns this around: can we *enhance* social justice? McArthur's surprising answer is that of knowledge. 'Higher education can contribute to social justice through its engagement with complex and dynamic forms that are … *not easily known*' (ibid: 50, JM's emphasis). As McArthur readily admits, 'At the heart of this argument is a paradox: a belief that complicated, specialist knowledge, … inaccessible to many in society and … fundamentally difficult *to know*, can be pursued in order to achieve greater social justice for all' (ibid). How might this paradox be resolved? How do we move from knowledge that is not easily known to social justice?

The move that McArthur makes is to observe that knowledge is not easily *owned*, or, at least, it *should not* be easily owned (ibid: 70). The problem is that knowledge, especially that associated with universities, *is* tied to ownership. In contrast, for McArthur, it is desirable 'to fundamentally rethink the nature of the knowledge engaged with'. McArthur offers us three key ideas for an open conception of knowledge: exile, sanctuary and diaspora. These ideas suggest knowing as a journey of separation, of hospitality and of community: an exile from self and convention; a safe but a public space; and a community finding a new home, which prizes the imagining of possibilities that 'transcend current realities'.

For McArthur, behind these ideas stands the stern presence of Adorno. McArthur observes. 'Adorno did not believe that "progress" was defined by integrating more and more people into the mainstream: progress was defined by *challenging* that mainstream' (139) [RB's emphasis]. However, an issue then arises. For McArthur the matter of access to higher education 'needs to be about far more than access: it needs to be about welcoming whole diasporas into higher education' (ibid). This is a somewhat troubling sentence, which – for all its virtue in having a concern for diasporas – goes directly against that previous sentence. There, Adorno is suggesting that progress is to be understood *not* by bringing more people into the mainstream but rather by '*challenging*' the mainstream. However, McArthur wants to integrate more people into the mainstream ('whole diasporas') but not to challenge that mainstream: *both* parts go against Adorno's advice!

Here, we can extend an earlier point. To focus on justice just as fairness (the Rawls' approach) unduly privileges a concern with the allocation of higher education as a social good and avoids attention to what counts *as* higher education. If we are not careful, we may end up with a 'fair' system which is tacitly supporting a higher education that limits the expression of critical voices, and this is a matter of epistemic justice.

Epistemic injustice

The term 'epistemic injustice' signals concerns with the marginalisation of voices. Perhaps the two most prominent arguments are these: Miranda Fricker (2010), in *Epistemic Injustice: Power and the Ethics of Knowing*, offers us a *conceptual* treatment of the matter, while in *Epistemologies of the South: Justice against Epistemicide*, Boaventura de Sousa Santos (2014) presents a *comparative sociological* account of the ways that, *globally*, certain knowledges exude power over other knowledges. In these accounts, each of the two social philosophers is strong where the other is silent.

It is surely undeniable that unequal patterns of social relations and social practices involving knowledge can be readily seen within academic life, between individuals, within universities, across national higher education systems and cross-nationally. These practices vary considerably: national research agencies may allocate their monies predominantly to particular kinds of institution; women academics – and not only those working in sensitive matters of ecology, feminism and identity – may endure prejudice in securing promotion; journal editors may show a pattern of rejecting submitted papers whose authors are from certain regions of the world; global rankings appear to favour universities in the 'Global North'; and research projects may be undertaken into indigenous cultures where little attempt is made to draw those cultures' representatives into dialogue in the design and prosecution of the research. Are all these to be considered examples of epistemic injustice?

Right at the outset of her book, Fricker makes a signal distinction: 'the idea of epistemic justice might ... prompt thoughts about distributive unfairness in respect of epistemic goods such as information or education ... [but], there is *nothing very distinctively epistemic* about it' (2010: 1, RB's emphasis). Fricker proceeds immediately to state that her book is concerned just with 'two forms of ... injustice that are distinctively epistemic [which consist] in a wrong done to someone in their capacity as a knower'. The two forms of epistemic injustice that Fricker picks out are testimonial injustice and hermeneutical injustice. *Testimonial injustice* occurs when the authority of a speaker's utterances is down-valued through a prior prejudice on the part of the hearer. *Hermeneutical injustice* occurs when someone is placed at an unfair disadvantage as a result of an impoverished set of 'collective interpretive resources' (ibid: 1): students who protest publicly against a narrowing of political rights may suffer where the state has a limited understanding of the idea of democracy.

Fricker has in mind, therefore, instances where an individual is wronged *epistemically*; and this is an approach that has been implicitly endorsed even by its critics (Nikolaidis, 2021; Grabina, undated). However, this individualist approach to epistemic injustice has two limitations, in leaving out of the reckoning injustice in the systematic *distribution* of epistemic goods and the conduct of *institutions and states* in upholding (or not) epistemic justice.

Both of these dimensions are, however, to be found in de Sousa Santos' book, albeit tacitly. de Sousa Santos is interested in institutional forms of cognitive justice (as he terms it), and the particular cognitive injustice that concerns de Sousa Santos is 'epistemicide'. By this, de Sousa Santos has in mind the epistemic power that – as he sees it – the Global North wields over the Global South. In exercising this power, the Global North exhibits 'abyssal thinking', declining to acknowledge the worth of the epistemologies of the Global South. This is an institutional, indeed worldly, form of Fricker's 'testimonial injustice', which 'occurs when prejudice causes a hearer to give a deflated level of credibility to a speaker's word'.

There are several problems with de Sousa Santos' account. First, he gives no clear definition of cognitive justice. He uses the phrase many times, but, on almost every occasion, contents himself with comments such as that 'there is no global social justice without global cognitive justice' (133) and 'social injustice is based on cognitive justice' (189). We need to know what is meant by social justice and by cognitive justice *and* their relationships, but we are told none of these. Note that in those two quotations, the relationship varies: in the first, cognitive justice seems to be a necessary condition of social justice; in the second, the relationship is looser, albeit with some kind of priority accorded to cognitive justice.

Perhaps more concerning is the broader argument. de Sousa Santos notes 'the internal plurality of science' and that the matter has been raised *in the West* 'by feminist epistemologies, by social and cultural studies of science, and by currents in the history and philosophy of science' (193). We can even add to these acknowledgements by pointing to the 'Mode 2' debate (Gibbons et al., 1994), ecological critiques of knowledge, especially from feminist perspectives (Warren, 2000; Plumwood, 2002), and Critical Theory, not least with its Marcuse–Habermas debate over the possibility of an alternative science (Habermas, 1970), and increasing recognition of indigenous communities and their knowledges (Manathunga, 2019; Stein, 2020). In short, *Western knowledge contains considerable reflexive resources within itself* such that it is continually changing, so the charge of its embodying cognitive injustice deserves more nuancing than in de Sousa Santos' account. And nor is there any consideration as to where China (now the producer of the largest number of scientific papers) sits, as to its role in global cognitive (in)justice (cf. Fredua-Kwarteng, 2020). The matter can no longer be caught along just a Global North–Global South axis.

What is to be done? de Sousa Santos says that 'it is important to build a truly dialogic articulation between knowledge considered Western, scientific, and modern and those considered traditional, native and local.' This articulation should evolve into an 'ecology of knowledges', built around 'knowledge-as-intervention-in-reality' which could include 'the preservation of biodiversity made possible by rural and indigenous forms of knowledge' (201). Some of this is already underway (Ahenakew, 2016; Keet, 2018; Manathunga, 2018; Dawson, 2020; Guzmán-Valenzuela and Gómez, 2019), but difficult questions have to be addressed if the argument is fully to hold water. Where are the boundaries of this ecology? In the operating theatre, what part – if at all – should indigenous knowledge play? So as to avoid undue epistemic hegemony, under which circumstances might one kind of knowledge give way to another? Simply to speak of 'articulation' does not, I fear, carry us very far.

If we place these two accounts of epistemic justice – of Fricker and de Sousa Santos – alongside each other, what might usefully be said? Strikingly, the academic world as such is hardly to be seen in either account, despite the questions that may very fairly be posed of universities in relation to cognitive injustice.

In Fricker, which focuses on epistemic injustice in social interactions, we are left without an account of *institutional* epistemic injustice: what might it be, for instance, for a university as an institution to take on board an agenda of epistemic justice? And in de Sousa Santos, where we receive a stratospheric treatment of epistemic injustice at the global level, in short supply is any examination of the kinds of educational practices that could begin to bring the global, institutional and personal levels together. For instance, there are nice judgements to be made as to where a sensitivity to coloniality should show itself; whether is it largely a matter of curriculum *or* pedagogy and whether it should differ across the disciplines. (In part, these omissions are now being rectified – see close of next paragraph.)

However, both accounts are joined at the hip, in that neither offers us an examination of the relationship between social justice and epistemic justice. It should not be assumed that both can be realised *simultaneously*. Epistemic justice has to contain a concern for truthfulness, and, on occasions, a tension may arise in relation to *social* justice. In an interview for university admission, social justice may reasonably trump truthfulness. How, then, might we depict this relationship? The two concepts are distinct: epistemic justice should be judged not as a *condition* of social justice but – on occasions – as its *rival*. Although scholarship is fast developing in this field (de Sousa Santos, 2018; de Sousa Santos and Meneses, 2020; Bhambra et. al., 2018), many of these difficult *conceptual* tensions await serious consideration.

Epistemic coloniality

Recently, the concept of coloniality has emerged (Quijano, 2000), which opens the matter of epistemic coloniality and the roles that the university has and is playing in it (Grosfoguel, 2007). Academic coloniality characteristically includes giving a low status to academics and universities in the countries of the Global South (which are former colonies); paying little heed to utterances and texts emerging from those countries; down-valuing epistemic efforts from other than 'white' ethnicities; holding at a distance (and treating as 'exotic') epistemic traditions of the Global South; and giving countries in the Global South a diminished role in research and other partnerships.

In this context, 'Southern Theory' (Connell, 2019: 92) has a hard time of it. This is 'a large field' (ibid) and includes 'indigenous knowledge formations', 'alternative universalisms', 'knowledge generated from the colonial encounter' and knowledge generated 'from postcolonial dynamics'. Questions arise as to the status of 'alternative universalisms', the extent to which these theories range beyond social and political spheres, and whether this is Theory *from* or *within* or *about* or *for* the Global South.

These variants of academic coloniality show themselves in the curriculum, the student's educational experiences, admission processes, examining, the evaluation of research projects, and the reviewing of academic texts. In short, academic coloniality plays out at the individual *and* the institutional levels. But this territory is more complicated still. Both nations *and* transnational corporations (especially those active in educational technology) have come to wield epistemic colonising power. In a globalised academic world, powerful states and corporations seek to impose their own imaginaries on the academic practices of others. This may be emerging from a state of cultural ignorance, but, more likely, it comes about as a form of cultural imposition.

But note, epistemic coloniality – and epistemic injustice – can be seen not only at the level of the state but *within* the state as well. They are evident in higher education; for example, in situations in which STEM-based epistemologies and methods are colonising other fields. These situations have added force where resources – at departmental or institutional or national level – are at stake. This is glaringly so in the disparaging of the humanities, but the general pattern can be witnessed at a *departmental* level, where an academic department has its favoured texts, methods and even ontological assumptions. Subtle and not-so-subtle efforts may be used to corral recalcitrants into the epistemic fold.

A double thesis is emerging here: (i) the 'epistemicide' of which de Sousa Santos spoke is an exaggerated term to depict the epistemological stance of the Global North towards the Global South. A happier term would be 'epistemic neglect' or, indeed, 'epistemic injustice' (and so extend the term beyond Fricker's sense of it). On the other hand, (ii) 'epistemicide' depicts a loss of epistemic opportunities in institutions of higher education, including the suppression of the humanities and cognate fields and methods, *within* the Global North (which now has to include China). There are certainly global epistemic hierarchies (cf. Connell, 2019: 91–93), but, alongside those in Global North–Global South relationships, they are also to be found in East–West relationships.

That second thesis, as to epistemic colonisation *within* the Global North, warrants our further attention. Alongside a domination of some disciplines and methods over others, it includes a limitation of life chances, suppression of and attempts to divert (academic) identities, undue use of resources to secure epistemic ends, and an othering of bona fide academic activities. In other words, the panoply of instruments normally associated with global colonisation can be found *within* universities, not least in the Global North. Indeed, the 'abyssal' tendencies and the ensuing invisibility on the global scale – of which de Sousa Santos speaks – can readily be found in the Global North. 'Academic narcissism' is ubiquitous (Nyawasha, 2020). Academics who are pursuing lines of research not in keeping with the mainstream can find themselves missing from the department's website: they become invisible and fail to count as departmental members. Some knowledges are invisible even within the Global North.

'Global cognitive justice' (Azumah Dennis, 2018) is, therefore, a fundamentally important concept, but it deserves the widest context. And efforts are in hand to 'gesture' imaginative possibilities for pedagogical and institutional decolonisation in the Global North (Stein, 2018), just one idea of which is that of the 'communiversity' (Lessem et al., 2019). However, this landscape of epistemic injustice is in motion. Central – as noted – is the hierarchy topped by the STEM disciplines, but this is already morphing, with an epistemic nexus of biomaterial, technology, digitisation, engineering, computing, nanotechnology, quantum mechanics and big data emerging as the dominant knowledge complex. Alongside and intermingling are other epistemic hierarchies in which gender, race, nation and corporation are evident. There is a multitude of global epistemic hierarchies, and intersecting with each other, and all on the move, like the child's kaleidoscope. Discerning their unstable patterns is far from being straightforward, and the pattern will vary according to the context.

But what is the context?

Around the world, some universities are selector institutions, being faced with more qualified candidates than they have places on offer for their higher education programmes. To accept one candidate is to reject another. Imagine that two candidates present with wildly different social, cultural, cognitive and performative capital, candidate A, from a privileged background showing considerable accomplishments and 'polish', and candidate B, from an impoverished background, showing much 'promise'. How to proceed?

All who plead the cause of social justice implicitly suggest that the context should be taken into account. But how? In our example, does one continue to add in pieces of context in order to bring the scales up on B's side? Does one even discount some of A's accomplishments precisely because of A's privileged context, and so depress the scales on that side? *Context* seems to work well when it increases life chances for the disadvantaged but not so well when it depresses life chances for the already favoured.

There lies here a most perplexing matter, to which Ernest Gellner pointed in a classic paper (cf. Hall, 2010; Barnett, 2020). Gellner (1970) observed that any serious interest in concepts had to take into account of the context, and this was the tenor of the later Wittgenstein (1978) in playing up of 'forms of life'. But, whereas for Wittgenstein, context supplied answers, for Gellner, context generated a problem: how widely or how narrowly should a context be drawn? Margaret Archer put the matter directly: 'Gellner is undoubtedly right that the difficulty of letting the context in … is the absence of flood gates. For there is nothing in the context itself which dictates just how much of it is relevant to any proposition, concept or unit …' (524).

This matter has profound implications for higher education policy and practices. In assessing a potential student for admission to higher education, just how much – *if at all* – should her or his context be taken into account? Or – another example – just how much context should the journal editor inject in determining the merits of a paper submitted from another part of the world (including the Global South) or from members within marginalised groups?

Significantly, social justice and epistemic justice pull in *different* directions. *Social* justice implies that one should pay attention to context in judgement. Even positive value could be accorded in some settings to hitherto impaired life chances. *Epistemic* justice comes into play more as a negative stance, in warding off epistemic *in*justice, in ensuring that epistemic judgements do not derive from social judgements. Context is pertinent only insofar as it may impair epistemic judgements.

This distinction – between social and epistemic justice – could suggest the following *principle*: in admissions policies, universities can legitimately – as a matter of *social* justice – take an applicant's context into account, but, in the examination of students (once admitted), it would be illegitimate – as a matter of *epistemic* justice – to take a student's context into account. But then a morass of further issues arise, both in practice and of principle, not least that of any '*pre*distribution' (O'Neill, 2019) required to bring about 'socially just pedagogies' (Bozalek et al., 2020). Gellner is right after all: 'it is probably impossible ... to draw up general rules for delimiting the legitimate and illegitimate uses of [context].'

Conclusions

Perhaps of all of the matters in this book, social justice is the most difficult in which to say anything of substance with any confidence. Even to say that 'it is a matter of context' may be true, but, as we have seen, that is an empty assertion. For all that, I offer some observations, recalling the three-plane schema that frames this book.

The poles of the three planes depict the space between the real of the world and ideas of the world. Social justice and its younger sister, epistemic justice, are both matters of the world *and* ideas of the world, and they *both* exert generative powers (Bhaskar, 2008a). Practices in, and around, higher education are affected by ideas of social justice and epistemic justice, and ideas of social and epistemic justice are affected by practices in the world, especially as they come to light, whether through social movements or empirical research. Practices and ideas swirl in and out of each other.

The three planes move on trajectories of increasing steepness and abstraction. On the first plane, we see *actual* ideas of social justice in the public realm having influence on social practices in higher education (of fairness, of equality, of recognition, and so forth). On the next plane, we might glimpse *possible* ideas in advancing practices of social justice in a particular institution, and examples can be seen around the world. And on the highest plane, we can try to *widen* the concepts of justice so as to change the *real* itself. Given this schema, it turns out that the concepts both of epistemic justice and social justice are *deficient*. After all, who speaks *for the glaciers and the rhinos*? Being part of the real, *do they not deserve justice in the university?* The concept of *ecological justice* beckons.

20 Beyond the Anthropocene

> The relationship between humans and nature will, in all probability, be the most important question of the present century.
> (Philippe Descola, 2013: 81, *The Ecology of Things*)

Introduction

'The Anthropocene' is a disputed concept, but it is central to the philosophy of higher education; indeed, perhaps the most important concept to the field. Originally emerging in the natural sciences, in the interplay between earth sciences, chemistry and geology, it contained the contention that, just as planetary phases of time are marked by layerings of geological strata, so the contemporary age is being marked by a new layering of the effects of humankind on this planet. It is a 'new epoch' (Hamilton et al., 2015). And hence the term 'Anthropocene', reflecting that the most significant element in this new stratum is humanity itself. This idea has since been taken up in social theory and ecological and environmental studies, and, in the process, the idea has undergone three shifts.

First, the concept has taken on an *evaluative* character, the Anthropocene being understood as the expression of deleterious effects of humanity, to which climate crises and ecological degradation bear witness. This situation cannot be undone: 'It is too late to avoid the Anthropocene' (Mickey, 2016: 88). *Second*, it has become a *linguistic banner* of an intellectual and practical movement. This banner – the capital 'A' is significant – heralds a value-laden and action-oriented project that unites scholars, researchers and activists. To place oneself under this banner is to signal that one's scholarship has already taken sides: the Anthropocene is a matter that *has* to be addressed. Usually, those in educational and social theory – in writing about the Anthropocene – regard themselves as engaged in a 'critical' study and often proclaim it as such (Stratford, 2018).

Third, the Anthropocene has become a reflexive concept. Through it, humanity interrogates itself and disparagingly so (Hamilton, et. al., 2015). It encourages knowledge about knowledge and harbours a self-distrust, sensing

DOI: 10.4324/9781003102939-26

that formal knowledge has helped bring about an impoverished situation. Mention of the Anthropocene announces a repudiation of the world's dominant knowledges (whether those of the 'West', the 'Global North' or 'modernity') – but it also prompts thinking about the nature of inquiry *within* the Anthropocene (Kuntz, 2019).

All this has come to pervade the university. Not only does it find itself situated in the Anthropocene but that, as a primary producer of knowledge, it is held to be in part culpable for the formation of the Anthropocene. There is a strong 'if-then' relationship at work. *If* it is the case that we can sensibly talk of the Anthropocene, *then* the university has a responsibility in addressing the malformations in the new stratum.

Several issues arise. To what extent does the term 'the Anthropocene' refer to real entities and formations in the world *and* to what extent is it a shorthand for certain ideas and values? To situate the question in our three-planar schema (p 34), does the Anthropocene sit mainly on the *real* side of the planes (it is real in the world) or more on the ideational and imaginative side of the planes? This is important, since practical implications flow. If the term 'Anthropocene' is really real, and is constituting the world, then perhaps the university's response lies more in new practices to elicit a different set of worldly formations. If, however, the Anthropocene is more a matter of ways of ideas in looking at the world, then perhaps the response of universities lies more in the raising of awareness of issues and the development of a new sensitivity to the world. I shall try to show it is both of these.

Conceptual clusterings

There is a raft of concepts in the company of the Anthropocene, and they constitute a massive constellation. The concepts that constitute the *immediate cluster* with the Anthropocene are those of ecology (and 'deep ecology' (Naess, 2012), Nature (with a capital 'N'), environment, anthropocentricism and sustainability. Further out are to be found concepts such as the Enlightenment (with a largely critical stance being taken towards it), knowledge (here stances are *both* critical of knowledge *and* seek to transform it), the Earth ('the Earth' being favoured over talk of globality), neoliberalism (which is a target of a scholarship of *resistance*), ecosophy (a term invented by Guattari (2000)), and transdisciplinarity (it being contended that joined-up inquiry is essential if it is to match the interconnectedness of Nature). Even further out but still with a gravitational pull can be seen the concepts of wisdom, spirit and religion (Mickey, 2016), as well as references to traditional cultures and indigenous communities (Plumwood, 2002).

What is apparent is that whatever Real presence it possesses, the Anthropocene has come to spawn its own *ideational* layer. A scholarly community has emerged with this battery of concepts and ideas, a community seeking not only to understand the world but also contending for the world's transformation. In the process, there lurk signs that this clustering of concepts and ideas is becoming an ideology, its key concept of 'the Anthropocene' being all too rarely questioned *within* the community (Hamilton et. al. (2015) and Charbonneau (2018) are important exceptions) and more serving as an umbrella under which this community drives forward in saving the planet. That its heart is in the right place is no reason not to pause and reflect on the matter.

Both higher education and the university come naturally into the sights of this community. Especially since the Enlightenment, the university *has* been marked by an *epistemological anthropocentricism*. Its knowledge efforts have overwhelmingly placed humanity as the centre of its epistemological universe. The humanities, the social sciences, professional studies and the study of societal systems have all taken humanity not just as their starting point but as their *raison d'être*. Major interests of theirs have lain in advancing human understanding of the human world and, implicitly, in deepening (*human*) culture. Huge swathes, too, of the natural sciences have been given over to inquiries into the *human* body. Other apparently nonhuman areas of study – such as mathematics, statistics, computing sciences and engineering – have focused upon human activities. And yet other areas, with no visible human element in their topics (the dance of molecules, the functioning of the rain forests, the combustibility of materials), can be seen to be fuelled – at least in part – by an interest in control over the human environment.

To all of this has to be added an instrumentalism: knowledge – at least the knowledge enshrined especially in universities – has been driven by a latent interest in control of features of the world. Remarkably, despite their evident differences (Ashenden and Owen, 1999), *both* (the early) Habermas and Foucault find common cause here. For Habermas (1978), an interest in control lay behind science: it was a 'knowledge-constitutive interest'. For Foucault (1991), science as a system, as a body of knowledge, bequeathed power and control; indeed discipline. On the one hand, an interest in power and control fuelled knowledge activity, and, on the other hand, a knowledge/power discursive regime. On both counts, knowledge, especially science, was integrated with technology, and the relationship has been dialectical, with each prompting the other. Knowledge – and the physical sciences in particular – became a force of production in its own right.

There are, then, two counts on the charge sheet: Western knowledge overly reflects human interests, *and* it possesses a thick stream of instrumentalism oriented towards power and control (Nelson, 2011). Knowledge is doubly in the dock and is guilty as charged. Its epistemologies are anthropocentric, putting the interests of humanity first and then sliding into an assumption that Nature is a resource on which science-based technologies can draw. Ecological degradation and climate change are inevitable outcomes of this *knowledge-power-environment* matrix of relationships.

It is against this horizon that the concepts of ecology and the Anthropocene came to public prominence. *Ecology* has had the longer innings, and it has subtly shifted over time. Originally, it was a concept four-square within the Earth Sciences but, as indicated, it has broadened to include a value-laden concern for the Earth. The *Anthropocene* is a depiction of a way of life on this planet marked by the imprint of humanity. The two concepts take in each other's washing: on the one hand, an inquiry into the totality of Earth-humanity relationships (ecology), and, on the other hand, the formation of a layering of human life and its impact on this Earth (the Anthropocene).

The idea of ecology

The word 'ecology' does duty for a penumbra of ideas that have fuelled a movement, with its own sects and lanes of travel. At its core stands a strong sense of interconnectedness, especially of the human and the natural worlds. However, ecology has also come to contain an evaluative strain: at its heart lies a powerful rebuke, that humanity has bespoiled the Earth. And that bespoiling, and the subsequent climate crisis, are natural outcomes of an instrumentalism built into dominant forms of what it is to know. To know the world, in this *Weltanschauung*, is to be more able to *do* things in the world, to effect change, to extract value *from* it, to show itself in *innovation* and to have *impact*.

It follows that, in the widespread taking up of the idea of ecology, we are witnessing much more than the formation of a cognitive culture. More, ecological movements have their eye not just on rectifying the malformations that they espy, but also seek to redirect knowledge itself, since knowledge is in the dock in being at the centre of the ecological crisis.

Ecology has developed two meanings that – for our purposes – just have to be distinguished. It has come, *first*, to stand for systems in the world that (i) hang together, (ii) are self-reproducing, (iii) exhibit a level of sustainability, (iv) are to a degree open and (v) fragile and are (vi) *inherently* worthwhile. There are many ecologies in the world, which fulfil all six of these conditions. 'Nature' (rightly) takes the palm here, and there is much public discernment of fragile ecologies in Nature; but importantly, too, ecologies have been identified in the human world (such as 'ecologies of knowledge' – de Sousa Santos, 2016) and 'learning ecologies' (Barnett and Jackson, 2020).

However, *second*, as well as ecologies being identified *in* the world, ecology is also the name given to a large group of *inquiries*. These studies are to be found especially in universities, and, while they are focused on aspects of the natural world, they often probe relationships between social practices and the natural environment, especially where it is felt that malformations in the environment can be attributed to certain kinds of social practices.

To use the language of Bhaskar's (2008a) critical realism, 'ecology' sits both in the intransitive realm and in the transitive realm. It points us towards real – and characteristically malformed – features in the world that stand independently of humankind's knowledge of the world (even though humankind's knowledge of the world has contributed to those malformations). In this sense, ecology sits in the *intransitive* realm, and it points us towards the *study* of those features in the world, in both the natural and the social world. All manner of programmes of study - often imaginative interdisciplinary programmes - have mushroomed across universities that bear the terms 'ecology' or 'ecological': this is the *transitive* realm.

This distinction – the intransitive and the transitive aspects of the world – grew out of Bhaskar's early interest in the philosophy of science: there, the distinction between the world-in-itself – independent of knowledge – and knowledge of that world arises fairly readily. When we include the human world, however, matters become more complicated. Knowledge especially takes on both *intransitive* qualities, standing independently of understandings and inquiries – Karl Popper understood this, in speaking (1975) of 'epistemology without a knowing subject' – and *transitive* qualities, involving increasingly complex processes of inquiry. Epistemology has *some* ontological properties, the intransitive and the transitive realms flowing into each other's waters.

This interplay between knowledge and the world is heightened in the idea of ecology and more so when we bring higher education into the picture. We have just observed that ecology can refer to systems *in* the world *and* to humanity's study *of* those systems.

Knowledge, for example, can be studied *as* an ecology. As a set of cognitive systems stretching across the world, it contains malformations, and yet is open to amelioration. It has become an ideology, exhibits gross and systematic inequalities (on institutional, national and global scales), is imbued with questionable procedures and is aligned with centres of power. The public understanding of complex matters may be fundamentally askew, either misunderstanding academic knowledge or not having had access to it (or both). How this *knowledge ecology* has come to be this way, with its distortions, favouring of certain interests, and splitting-off of some disciplines from others (including a tendency to consign the humanities to near-oblivion across much of both the Anglo-Saxon world and China): knowledge can therefore be studied as an ecology in the world.

Ecology, therefore, is an elastic term. It is *in* the world – the Real of the world – and is a knowledge *of* the world and is simultaneously fact and value and description and action. These binaries run into each other. In becoming alert to interconnections between the human world and the natural world, and especially to changes that human action has wrought upon the world, multiple connectivities become evident (knowledge-the world; human world-inorganic world; human world-organic and animal worlds; human knowledge-the external world). And in pursuing these connections, concerns are heightened about the deleterious effects of humanity's knowledges upon the natural world.

In these ecological concerns, the plaintive cries go up 'And who will speak for the glaciers?' and 'Who will speak for the rhinos?' It has become evident that organised knowledge has *antidemocratic tendencies* in the sense that much of the world – all the nonhuman entities in the world and many humans – are typically *excluded* from the framing of research endeavours (Latour, 2004); hence, the emergence, for example, of 'ecological feminism' (Warren, 2010), and, more generally, of an 'ecology of recognition' (de Sousa Santos, 2016: 177–178). The idea of *ecological justice* prompts itself, but to wait upon another occasion.

Ecosystems and ecologies: four zones

It makes sense to keep the two senses of ecology separate – of ecologies in the world *and* our study of them. Let us term ecologies as they are in-the-world '*ecosystems*' and reserve 'ecology' for *systematic inquiries into* those ecosystems. There are, though, other distinctions to be made.

As is apparent in his book's title, *The Three Ecologies*, Félix Guattari (2000) identifies three ecological registers (as he terms them): 'the environment, social relations and human subjectivity'. The totality of these three registers and their study Guattari wishes to term '*ecosophy*'. Three points can be made.

First, Guattari does not explain why, in picking out these three registers and quite justifiably going beyond the natural environment, he limits his registers to just three. *Second*, Guattari's phrase, 'the environment', is ambiguous. The phenomena to which Guattari points include culture, the economy, knowledge, politics (he refers to 'the State'), the law and so forth; but, then, that phrase ('the environment') is being overloaded. It is much better to identify these different systems each in its own right.

Third, and by extension, 'ecosophy' refers to all of these systems taken together. However, in keeping with our realist-ideational schema (page 34), it makes sense to distinguish, *on the one hand*, the many systems that there are *in* the world – natural and human – and, *on the other hand*, the *study* of those systems. If we reserve 'ecosophy' to this latter realm – the *study* of ecological systems and their interplay – then we can suggest the term 'eco-world' as that actual interplay of systems as they are *in* the world.

We have then *two levels* at which the ecological realm is at work and, at each level, two *ways of construing* the study of the ecological. This gives us *four ecological zones*:

(1a) Ecology as it is *in the world* – '*ecosystems*';
(1b) Our *study of* each of these ecological manifestations or ecosystems – '*ecology*';
(2a) The *totality of these formations in the world, especially in their interplay* – '*eco-world*'; and
(2b) The *totality of the study* of ecosystems – '*ecosophy*'.

240 *Higher education and the world*

Recognising the distinctiveness of these four zones is vital if we are to make progress in the philosophy of higher education. To tilt the field in this way would be to ally it to the 'geophilosophy' of which Deleuze and Guattari (2013) spoke or the 'ecophilosophy' of which Roy Bhaskar (2012) spoke, in concert with Nordic philosophers. Of these two concepts, the latter is surely more potent, with its explicit nod to the ecological realm, and its sense of 'laminated systems', causality and differential power, all of which fit with our three-planar schema here.

The university and higher education in an eco-world

Before us is nothing less than valuing the university and higher education anew and doing so with an ecological approach (Barnett, 2019b). Let us return to our reflection that Guattari failed properly to demarcate key ecosystems in the world, limiting himself to just three. There is an infinite number of ecosystems in the world, given the conditions of 'ecosystem' just proposed. However, our concern in this book is that of higher education and the university, and I suggest that there are no less than *eight ecosystems* that should especially come into view here, those of *knowledge, persons, social institutions, the economy, the polity, culture, learning* and the *natural environment* (Figure 20.1).

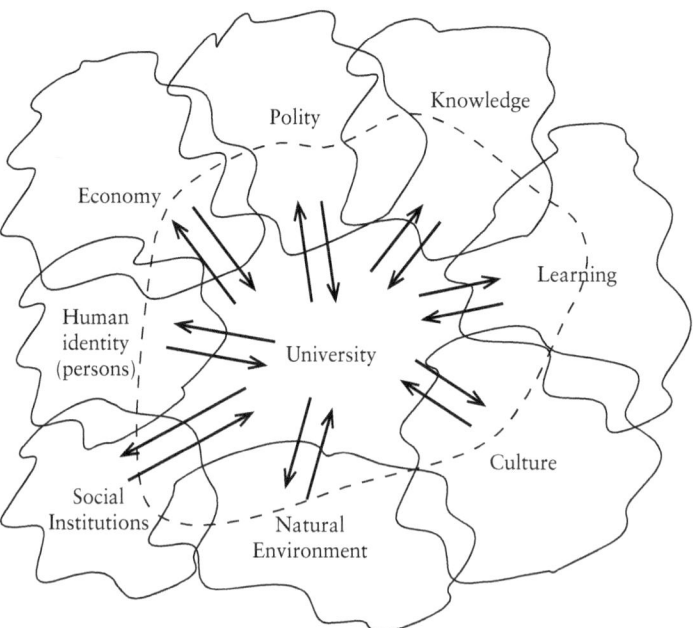

Figure 20.1 The ecological university, entangled with eight ecosystems.

From the mid-twentieth century, the dominant framing of higher education has lain in its interconnections with the economy, and it is right that the economy – as an ecosystem – should appear in this list; it is right, of course, that it be accompanied by the natural environment. In both cases, we can enquire into their territory, their elements and interconnections, their sustainability, their impairments, their precarity and wellbeing, *and* the humanity's impact upon them. *Both* the economy and the natural environment constitute ecosystems as I am interpreting the term here.

However, the university moves in and out of many ecosystems, and I suggest that the eight I have just picked out are so significant that, in the twenty-first century, the university cannot be understood independently of those eight. To say this is for the economy as an ecosystem to lose its privileged status (although it has to be retained). But note that, even though – in an ecological orientation – there will be an understandable tendency to give special attention to the natural environment, neither can that ecosystem be privileged. A proper attention to the natural environment calls for attention to be paid to *all eight* ecosystems. Not only is the university entwined with each of the eight, but its concerns for the natural environment calls also for each of the other ecosystems to be present in any single university's understanding of itself and the design of its strategies. An *ecological transdisciplinarity* calls.

This is a radical thesis, possessing several properties. *None* of the eight ecosystems picked out can properly be understood without also referring to higher education. Each one significantly pervades higher education, *and* higher education moves in each one. The term '*entanglement*' can legitimately be deployed (cf. Barad, 2007). *In each case*, both parties – higher education and the economy; higher education and culture; higher education and learning; higher education and the polity and so forth – are interrelated, such that the one cannot be understood without the other. For example, higher education cannot be understood without reference to the learning systems of society, and society as a learning system cannot be understood without reference to higher education. (Wals [2015, 2020] goes far in this direction but not quite far enough.) *Entanglement is mutual*. And these strong mutual interconnections hold across *each* of the eight ecosystems.

I am proposing here, therefore, *a radicalisation of Guattari's idea of the three ecologies* and in two ways. *First*, I have placed his idea of ecology in a broader framework, distinguishing the ontological and the imaginative-ideational *aspects* of ecology, *and* the *levels* of ecology, as between individual ecosystems and the interplay of ecosystems (the eco-world). *Second*, I have extended Guattari's three ecologies and, with an interest in higher education and universities, have picked out eight ecologies. (As stated, instead of the term *ecologies* here, I prefer the term *ecosystem* so as to distinguish the *real* existence of ecosystems from the ecologies that we form in *studying* ecosystems.)

However, we need to make two further moves. The first concerns the establishment of that *ecosophy* of which Guattari spoke. Universities are intent on studying ecosystems. Much of this is overt, with various forms of ecological studies being found in the biological, Earth and environmental sciences. But, given the idea of ecosystem sketched here, it is apparent that ecological studies are potentially present in *studies of* social institutions, the polity, persons as human beings, learning, culture, the economy and knowledge. In each case, inquiries could be mounted about the extent to which the domain in question – considered as an ecosystem – is sustainable, contributes to the wellbeing of the planet, interconnects well with other ecosystems, and is impaired (and possibly distorted). In other words, *we can pose awkward and even critical questions of each of the eight ecosystems.*

This would constitute the formation of that 'ecosophy' of which Guattari spoke, but now given substance as a collection – indeed, an assemblage – of ecological studies. This ecosophy is not yet fully with us, but there are sightings of it in embryo.

The coming of the Ecocene

If our first move in higher education is to put the idea of ecosophy onto a sound footing, our second move concerns the Ecocene. Both in the public realm *and* in the academic world, 'ecology' has grown into a project of global proportions. And we explain this phenomenon as a response to an awareness of the Anthropocene (even if the actual term 'Anthropocene' came some time later). Not surprisingly, if concerns can arise about the Anthropocene, then there are likely to be responses to it: hence the idea of 'the Ecocene' as that form of planetary being in which humankind looks to *recover* ways of living in harmony with Nature. It then becomes a natural extension of ecological studies that they turn their attention to the Ecocene (Kupers, 2020), spelling out its conditions and inquiring into its 'design' (Boehnert, 2018).

If we now put together the three ideas of (i) the university, (ii) ecosophy and (iii) the Ecocene, we can say that *the key challenge in front of the university (at least in the twenty-first century) is that it form an ecosophy – the study of ecosystems, natural <u>and</u> human – that can help to usher in the Ecocene.* There are a large number of suppositions here – of fact and of value – to be teased out on another occasion. But a few observations may serve to draw together some of the threads of this book.

I am proposing that the university should so orchestrate its disciplines and its inquiries that they constitute an ecosophy. This would entail its curricula, its teaching, its research and scholarly activities and its worldly engagements all having an explicit interest in ushering in an Ecocene, understood as that form of planetary being in which humankind recovers ways of living in harmony not just with itself (and that itself is a tall order; Facer, 2020) but directly with *Nature*. Its efforts, in teaching, research and outreach, would be oriented in favour of Earthly harmony and, to bring this off, the whole university would be imbued with an appropriate spirit (Chapter 14). *Then* we would be in sight of the *ecological university* (Barnett, 2018b). In teaching, this would point us in the direction of an *ecopedagogy* (Kahn, 2020), an idea that has to be treated in higher education with some care. Every programme of study – across the disparate disciplines – would have to have the planetary crisis in its sights, but, even to advance in that direction, it will have to be sensitive to *all* the eight ecosystems for they are intertwined.

Epistemological implications follow. It is increasingly recognised that the fissiparous nature of disciplines, with their tendency to split apart, is injurious to comprehending the world and that forms of interdisciplinarity or transdisciplinarity are required. Those two approaches warrant comparative evaluation (Klein, 2008), but the general sentiment takes on heightened significance and urgency. If the world is interconnected and in motion, then there is 'an ontological reason for interdisciplinarity' (Bhaskar et al., 2012; Høyer, 2012: 62). However, that idea has to be radicalised, not necessarily in the direction of an *ontological* transdisciplinarity (Gibbs and Beavis, 2020) – which has yet to be cashed out – but in the direction of a fleet-footed nomadic *cross-disciplinary* inquiry, able to pass across epistemological borders without hindrance by the epistemic border guards.

It is at this point that we can draw upon the concept of sustainability. *For a university to align itself with the concepts of ecosophy and the Ecocene would be to form an interest in the sustainability of the entire Earth.* But it is evident that we need 'new ways of thinking about what sustainability might be' (Hroch, 2016: 57; Sterling, et. al., 2013), not least when placed against a horizon of the Earth in its totality; organic and nonorganic; human and nonhuman; social institutions, communities and persons, and technologies; *and* ideas, knowledges and imaginings. This means that all of the knowledges of the university should be orchestrated as an ecosophy – in research, in teaching and in outreach – in favour of the Ecocene. But the Ecocene can only be imagined and conjectured. So, a university – as a set of inquiries orchestrated as a unified ecosophy towards ushering in the Ecocene – would be a set of practical and *imaginative* projects. Such a university, of and for the Ecocene, has to be designed (cf. Staley, 2019) and a suitable policy environment – 'policy ecologies' indeed (Stratford and Wals, 2020) – developed.

Each university – and each of its departments – would respond to this call in its own way, realising its own possibilities; there can be no isomorphism either within or across higher education systems. These ideas – of ecosophy and the Ecocene – would also be played out at the local, national, global and geopolitical levels among universities across the world (cf. Guattari, 2016). Of course, there are tensions here (Ruuska et al., 2020), but *imagine what it might be if all the twenty-five thousand universities of the world were to sign a collective treaty to harness their resources to form an ecosophy in favour of the Ecocene and they all worked in that direction.* (It would parallel the Paris Agreement among nations – on climate change.)

These ideas would also take form at the level of the individual student and the space and educational challenges being opened to them. The student's whole development as a human being within the infinite Real of the world is in question, and, as such, the concepts neither of learning nor of teaching are helpful to us (and both of these theses were argued in earlier chapters). What *is* in sight is similar to that of a plant as it flowers. It opens itself to the world and lives more or less in harmony with the world, and plays – within its fragility – its modest part in and for the whole world; the whole Earth indeed. An individual class of students can take this form, placing their studies against a horizon of the whole Earth, for example, in forming connections with another class of students in a quite different society.

And so the two concepts of ecosophy and Ecocene would be reflected in the university's research, teaching and outreach ambitions. Admittedly, this is to set up a set of 'wicked problems' (Keenan, 2020), combining the universal and the local, the epistemological and the ontological, the prosaic and the utopian. To crib Guattari's words, these suggestions call for efforts that 'in the short term, don't profit anyone, but in the long term are the conduits of a processual enrichment for the whole of humanity. It is the whole future of fundamental research and artistic production that is in question here' (2000: 65).

Conclusion

It is not enough for the university to be critical of the Anthropocene. Higher education and the university have to go beyond critique so as to imagine the university 'otherwise' (Amsler and Facer, 2017). Insofar as the concept of the Anthropocene has substance, the university has to admit '*mea culpa*': the causes of the Anthropocene can be laid partly at the door of the university in the alacrity with which it has assumed an instrumental and human-centred view of knowledge that has allowed it first to put the natural environment in jeopardy and then to threaten human life itself. The university, therefore, has a responsibility in deploying its resources to turn matters around. And since the Anthropocene is all pervasive, the task in front of the university is immense; nothing other than playing its part in the formation of a new Earthly stratum, that of the Ecocene, in which humanity finds ways of living in harmony not only with and *in* the natural world but also with *itself*. This is a considerable burden to place upon the shoulders of higher education and the university, but the burden is actually already there.

This is, of course, utopian thinking, and one should be careful what one wishes for: 'one person's utopia is often another's dystopia' (Stein, 2018: 152). It is, though, *feasibly* utopian: in principle, there is no reason why the university and higher education cannot be united with the totality of the Earth and all that is in it, on it and above it. And unless we give ourselves a licence to think and to imagine utopias of the university, we are unlikely to gain the kind of new trajectory that is absolutely necessary.

Envoi
A constitution for universities on Earth

In declaring that 'we have never been modern,' Bruno Latour's wit was running away. The reality is, unfortunately, that we have been all too modern. Not only that, but the beginning *and* the end of modernity can be identified with surprising accuracy. It has two bookends as it were. Its dawn was tacitly launched by Descartes in June 1637, in his declaration of *Cogito, ergo sum* and in the implication that he drew out that the thinking 'I' was 'entirely distinct' not only from the world but even from his own body. In these thoughts were announced the separation of humanity from the world *and* the separation of thinking from being, and it is the aftermath of such ideas that has seen emerge the state of the Earth today, with humanity separated from Nature. The end of this modernity was signalled on 18 August 2019, at a ceremony in Iceland to mark the shrinking and then the complete loss of the Okjökull glacier, generally held to be a result of climate change.

Admittedly, the upward curves of ecological crisis took some time to get going, taking off in a serious way after the Second World War and then rocketing upwards with great velocity from the 1960s. It was at that point too, through the second half of the twentieth century, that mass higher education and research took off. Correlation should never be mistaken for cause and effect, but we are here in the presence of a significant cluster of connections. The crisis cannot be solely laid at the door of universities and higher education since an even more serious, and much deeper, set of connections have been at work. In large part, the crisis is the inevitable outcome of an instrumental conception of knowledge deep within modernity – in which Nature has come to constitute a resource – and it is a conception of knowledge that is now deep, too, within universities.

We need urgently, therefore, a *Constitution for Universities-on-Earth*, both as major knowledge institutions in society and – for higher education – as important sets of educational processes. Such a constitution would posit relationships of care between universities and the wider world and would seek to institutionalise an ethic of *critical stewardship* within research and scholarly activities, in the educational practices, in the students' experiences and in universities' ways of engaging with the wider world. It would spell out responsibilities of universities to the whole Earth *and* responsibilities of the

DOI: 10.4324/9781003102939-27

world towards its universities. It would also have an eye to the challenges and opportunities that are present across the disciplines and professional fields, differing so much as they do.

These injunctions call for imaginative thinking about universities and higher education. All of their fundamental concepts – knowledge, truth, research, learning, teaching, being a student, societal engagement, academic freedom, social justice, culture and so forth – are at issue. These concepts need fundamentally to be revisited, critiqued, rethought – and, where necessary, entirely *abandoned* – so as to be adequate to the challenges in front of this Earth. This would include concerns for Nature, but the task would go *much beyond that*. Nothing short of the whole set of relationships within humanity, the world, knowledge, and sheer being as such is at stake. Horizons of particularity *and* universality should be present. The idea of *ecological justice* might just provide a foundation on which such textual crafting can build.

This, then, is the challenge in front of the philosophy of higher education. Not simply to understand or even to critique the place of the university and higher education in a troubled world but imaginatively and fearlessly to envisage new concepts, new ideas and new frames of thinking and, on that basis, to assist in drafting the Constitution. This work will not be sufficient to save the world, but it is a necessary condition, and that task – forever ongoing – has now to start, and with some urgency.

Bibliography

(Magazine articles, web-sites and reports are shown separately at the end of this listing.)

Aaen, J. H. (2019) *Student Darkness: An Inquiry into Student Being at the University*, unpublished PhD Thesis, Aarhus University, Denmark.

Abbinnett, R. (2015) 'The Politics of Spirit in Stiegler's Techno-Pharmacology', *Theory, Culture & Society*, 32 (4) 65–80.

Abbott, R. (1999) *The World as Information*. Exeter: Intellect.

Abram, D. (1997) *The Spell of the Sensuous*. New York: Vintage.

Adorno, T. W. (2008) *Lectures on Negative Dialectics: Fragments of a lecture course, 1965–1966*. Cambridge and Malden, MA: Polity.

Adorno, T. W. (2014/1966) *Negative Dialectics*. New York and London: Bloomsbury.

Adorno, T. W. (2019/1964) *Philosophical Elements of a Theory of Society*. Cambridge and Medford, MA: Polity.

Adorno, T. W., Albert, H., Dahrendorf, R., Habermas, J., Pilot, H. and Popper, K. R. (1977) *The Positivist Dispute in German Sociology*. London: Heinemann.

Adorno, T. W., and Horkheimer, M. (1989/1944) *Dialectic of Enlightenment*. London and New York: Verso.

Agamben, G. (1998) *Homo Sacer: Sovereign Power and Bare Life*. Stanford, CA: Stanford University.

Aguiar Pereira, E. M. (2019) 'The Importance of Córdoba's Reform to the Latin American Academic Context: One Hundred Years of Contribution', *Revista Internacional de Educação Superior*, 5, 1–11.

Ahenakew, C. (2016) 'Grafting Indigenous Ways of Knowing onto Non-Indigenous Ways of Being: The (Underestimated) Challenges of a Decolonial Imagination', *International Review of Qualitative Research*, 9 (3) 323–340.

Al-Samarraie, H., Shamsuddin, A. and Alzahrani, A. I. (2020) 'A Flipped Classroom Model in Higher Education: A Review of the Evidence across Disciplines', *Educational Technology Research and Development*, 68, 1017–1051.

Allen, G. (2017) 'The Conversation of a University', in A. Stoller and E. Kramer (Eds.), op. cit.

Althusser, L. (1971) 'Ideology and Ideological State Apparatuses (Notes towards an Investigation)', in his *Lenin and Philosophy and other Essays*. New York: Monthly Review Press.

Althusser, L. (2017) *Philosophy for Non-Philosophers*. London and New York: Bloomsbury.

Altorf, H. (2019) 'Dialogue and Discussion: Reflections on a Socratic Method', *Arts and Humanities in Higher Education*, 18 (1) 60–75.

Amsler, S. and Facer, K. (2017) Introduction to 'Learning the Future Otherwise: Emerging Approaches to Critical Anticipation in Education', *Futures*, 94. https://doi.org/10.1016/j.futures.2017.09.004

Aoun, J. E. (2017) *Robot-Proof: Higher Education in the Age of Artificial Intelligence*. Cambridge, MA: MIT.

Archer, M. (2007) 'Addressing the Cultural System', in M. Archer, R. Bhaskar, A. Collier, T. Lawson and A. Norrie (Eds.) *Critical Realism: Essential Readings*. London and New York: Routledge, pp. 503–543.

Archer, M. S. and Maccarini, A. M. (Eds.) (2014) *Engaging with the World: Agency, Institutions, Historical Formations*. London and New York: Routledge.

Arendt, H. (1958) *The Human Condition*. Chicago, IL and London: University of Chicago.

Argyris, C. and Schön, D. (1974) *Theory in Practice: Increasing Professional Effectiveness*. San Francisco, CA: Jossey-Bass.

Arndt, S. and Mika, C. (2018) 'Dissident Thought: A Decolonising Framework for Revolt in the University', in S. S. E. Bengtsen and R. Barnett (Eds.) *The Thinking University*. Cham: Springer, pp. 47–60.

Arnold, M. (1969/1932) *Culture and Anarchy*. London: University of Cambridge.

Arthur, J. with Bohlin, K. E. (Eds.) (2005) *Citizenship and Higher Education: The Role of Universities in Communities and Society*. London and New York: Routledge.

Arvanitakis, J. and Hornsby, D. J. (2018) 'Citizenship and the Thinking University: Towards the Citizen Scholar', in S. S. E. Bengtsen and R. Barnett (Eds.) *The Thinking University*. Cham: Springer, pp. 87–101.

Ashenden, S. and Owen, D. (Eds.) (1999) *Foucault Contra Habermas*. London and Thousand Oaks, CA: Sage.

Assié-Lumumba, T. (2018) 'The Idea of the University in the Evolving Higher Education Landscape in Africa', in R. Barnett and M. A. Peters (Eds.), op. cit.

Astley, J., Francis, L., Sullivan, J. and Walker, A. (Eds.) (2004) *The Idea of a Christian University: Essays on Theology and Higher Education*. Bletchley: Paternoster.

Auxier, R. (2017) 'The Coming Revolution in (Higher) Education: Process, Time, and Singularity', in A. Stoller and E. Kramer (Eds.), op. cit.

Azumah Dennis, C. (2018) 'Decolonising Education: A Pedagogic Intervention', in G. K. Bhambra, D. Gebrial and K. Nişancıoğlu (Eds.), op. cit.

Bachelard, G. (1994–1958) *The Poetics of Space*. Boston, MA: Beacon.

Bachelard, G. (2000–1950) *The Dialectic of Duration*. Manchester: Clinamen.

Badiou, A. and Žižek, S. (2009) *Philosophy in the Present*. Malden, MA and Cambridge: Polity.

Bahti, T. (1992) 'The Injured University', in R. Rand (Ed.), op. cit.

Bakhurst, D. (2011) *The Formation of Reason*. Malden, MA and Chichester: Blackwell.

Bandura, A. (1977). 'Self-efficacy: Toward a Unifying Theory of Behavioral Change', *Psychological Review*, 84 (2) 191–215. https://doi.org/10.1037/0033-295X.84.2.191

Baptista, B. V. and Rojas-Castro, S. (2020) 'Transdisciplinary Institutionalization in Higher Education', *Studies in Higher Education*, 45 (6) 1075–1092.

Barad, K. (2007) *Meeting the Universe Halfway: Quantum Physics and the Entanglement of Matter and Meaning*. Durham, NC and London: Duke University.

Barnett, R. (1990) *The Idea of Higher Education*. Stony Stratford: Open University Press/ Society for Research into Higher Education.

Barnett, R. (1997) *Higher Education: A Critical Business*. Buckingham: Open University & Society for Research into Higher Education.

Barnett, R. (2000) *Realizing the University in an age of supercomplexity*. Buckingham and Philadelphia, PA: Open University Press.

Barnett, R. (2007) *A Will to Learn: Being a Student in an Age of Uncertainty*. Maidenhead: McGraw-Hill/ Society for Research into Higher Education.

Barnett, R. (2011) *Being a University*. London and New York: Routledge.
Barnett, R. (Ed.) (2012) *The Future University: Ideas and Possibilities*. London and New York: Routledge.
Barnett, R. (2013) *Imagining the University*. London and New York: Routledge.
Barnett, R. (2016) *Understanding the University*. London and New York: Routledge.
Barnett, R. (2018a) *The Ecological University: A Feasible Utopia*. London and New York: Routledge.
Barnett, R. (2018b) 'The Thinking University: Two Versions, Rival and Complementary', in S. S. E. Bengtsen and R. Barnett (Eds.), op. cit.
Barnett, R. (2018c) 'Culture and the University: An Ecological Approach', in A. Stoller and E. Kramer (Eds.), op. cit.
Barnett, R. (2019a) 'Leadership and Critical Thinking: Oxymoron and a Feasible Utopia', in J. Jameson (Ed.), op. cit.
Barnett, R. (2019b) 'Re-valuing the University: An Ecological Approach', in P. Gibbs, J. Jameson and A. Elwick (Eds.), op. cit.
Barnett, R. (2020) 'Ernest Gellner (1925-1995): Nought for the University's Comfort?', in R. Barnett and A. Fulford (Eds.), op. cit.
Barnett, R. and Bengtsen, S. (2020) *Knowledge and the University: Re-claiming Life*. London and New York: Routledge.
Barnett, R. and Coate, K. (2005) *Engaging the Curriculum in Higher Education*. Maidenhead and New York: McGraw-Hill.
Barnett, R., Coate, K. and Parry, G. (2004) 'Conceptualising Curriculum Change', *Teaching in Higher Education*, 6 (4) 435–450.
Barnett, R. and Fulford, A. (Eds.) (2020) *Philosophers on the University: Reconsidering Higher Education*. Cham: Springer.
Barnett, R. and Jackson, N. (Eds.) (2020) *Ecologies for Learning and Practice: Emerging Ideas, Sightings, and Possibilities*. London and New York: Routledge.
Barnett, R. and Peters, M. A. (Eds.) (2018) *The Idea of the University: Contemporary Perspectives*. Vol. 2. New York: Peter Lang.
Bartelson, J. (2009) *Visions of World Community*. Cambridge: Cambridge University.
Bartlett, P. F. and Chase, G. W. (Eds.) (2013) *Sustainability in Higher Education: Stories and Strategies for Transformation*. Cambridge, MA and London: MIT.
Baruchello, G. (2013) 'Odd Bedfellows: Cornelius Castoriadis on Capitalism and Freedom', in I. S. Straume and G. Baruchello (Eds.), op. cit.
Batchelor, D. (2014) 'Finding a Voice as a Student', in P. Gibbs and R. Barnett (Eds.), op. cit.
Becher, T. (1989) *Academic Tribes and Territories*. Stony Stratford: Open University Press/SRHE.
Becher, T. and Trowler, P. R. (2001) *Academic Tribes and Territories: Intellectual enquiry and the culture of disciplines*. Buckingham and Philadelphia, PA: Open University Press/SRHE.
Beckett, D. and Hager, P. (2018) 'A Complexity Thinking Take on Thinking in the University', in S. S. E. Bengtsen and R. Barnett (Eds.) *The Thinking University*. Cham: Springer.
Bengtsen, S. S. E. (2014) 'Into the Heart of Things: Defrosting Educational Theory', in P. Gibbs and R. Barnett (eds.), *Thinking about Higher Education*, Cham: Springer, 175–191.
Bengtsen, S. S. E. and Barnett, R. (2017) 'Confronting the Dark Side of Higher Education', *Journal of Philosophy of Education*, 51 (1) 114–131. https://doi.org/10.1111/1467-9752.12190
Bengtsen, S. S. E. and Barnett, R. (Eds.) (2018) *The Thinking University: A Philosophical Examination of Thought and Higher Education*. Cham: Springer.
Benhabib, S. (1994) 'Models of Public Space: Hannah Arendt, the Liberal Tradition and Jürgen Habermas', in C. Calhoun (Ed.), op. cit.

Bennett, J. (2010) *Vibrant Matter: A Political Ecology of Things.* Durham and London: Duke University.
Bennett, T. (2013) *Making Culture, Changing Society.* London and New York: Routledge.
Benson, L., Harkavy, I., Puckett, J., Hartley, M., Hodges, R. Al, Johnston, F. E. and Weeks, J. (2017) *Knowledge for Social Change: Bacon, Dewey, and the Revolutionary Transformation of Research Universities in the Twenty-First Century.* Philadelphia, PA: Temple University.
Bergson, H. (1998–1911) *Creative Evolution.* Mineola, NY: Dover.
Berlin, I. (1979–1969) 'The Two Concepts of Liberty', 118–172, in his *Four Essays on Liberty.* Oxford: Oxford University.
Berlin, I. (1998) *The Proper Study of Mankind: An Anthology of Essays.* London: Pimlico.
Berlin, I. (2000) *The Power of Ideas.* Ed. Henry Hardy. London: Chatto and Windus.
Berman, M. (1995) *All That Is Solid Melts into Air: The Experience of Modernity.* London and New York: Verso.
Bernstein, B. (1996) *Pedagogy, Symbolic Control and Identity: Theory, Research, Critique.* London: Taylor and Francis.
Berquist, W. H. and Pawlak, K. (2008) *Engaging the Six Cultures of the Academy.* San Francisco, CA: Jossey-Bass.
Berry, D. M. (2015) *Critical Theory and the Digital.* London and New York: Bloomsbury.
Berubé, M. and Ruth, J. (2015) *The Humanities, Higher Education, and Academic Freedom: Three Necessary Arguments.* London and New York: Palgrave Macmillan.
Beyes, T. and Michels, C. (2014) 'Performing University Space: Multiplicity, Relationality, Affect', in P. Temple (Ed.), op. cit.
Bhambra, G. K., Gebrial, D. and Nisaancioglu, K. (Eds.) (2018) *Decolonising the University.* London: Pluto.
Bhaskar, R. (2002a) *From Science to Emancipation: Alienation and the Actuality of Enlightenment.* New Delhi and London: Sage.
Bhaskar, R. (2002b) *Reflections on Meta-Reality: Transcendence, Emancipation and Everyday Life.* New Delhi and London: Sage.
Bhaskar, R. (2008a/1975) *A Realist Theory of Science.* Verso: London and New York.
Bhaskar, R. (2008b) *Dialectic: The Pulse of Freedom.* London and New York: Routledge.
Bhaskar, R. (2010a) *From East to West: Odyssey of a Soul.* London and New York: Routledge.
Bhaskar, R. (with Hartwig, M.) (2010b) *The Formation of Critical Realism: A Personal Perspective.* Abingdon and New York: Routledge.
Bhaskar, R. (2011a/1991) *Philosophy and the Idea of Freedom.* London and New York: Routledge.
Bhaskar, R. (2011b) *Reclaiming Reality: A Critical Introduction to Contemporary Philosophy.* London and New York: Routledge.
Bhaskar, R. (2012) 'Critical Realism in Resonance with Nordic Ecophilosophy', in R. Bhaskar, et al. (Eds.), op. cit.
Bhaskar, R. (2015) *The Possibility of Naturalism: A Philosophical Critique of the Contemporary Human Sciences.* 4th Ed. London and New York: Routledge.
Bhaskar, R., Frank, C., Hoyer, K. G., Naess, P. and Parker, J. (Eds.) (2010) *Interdisciplinarity and Climate Change: Transforming Knowledge and Practice for our Global Future.* London and New York: Routledge.
Bhaskar, R., Hoyer, K. G. and Naess, P. (Eds.) (2012) *Ecophilosophy in a World of Crisis: Critical realism and the Nordic contributions.* London and New York: Routledge.
Biesta, G. (2012) 'Becoming Public: Public Pedagogy, Citizenship and the Public Sphere', *Social and Cultural Geography*, 13 (7) 683–697. https://doi.org/10.1080/14649365.2012.723736

Biesta, G. J. J. (2006) *Beyond Learning: Democratic Education for a Human Future*. London and New York: Routledge.
Biesta, G. J. J. (2016) *The Beautiful Risk of Education*. London and New York: Routledge.
Biesta, G. J. J. (2017) *The Rediscovery of Teaching*. New York and Abingdon: Routledge.
Biesta, G. J. J. (2019) 'Should Teaching Be Re(dis)covered? Introduction to a Symposium', *Studies in Philosophy and Education*, 38 (5) 549–553. https://link.springer.com/article/10.1007/s11217-019-09667-y
Bilgrami, A. and Cole, J. R. (Eds.) (2015) *Who's Afraid of Academic Freedom?* New York: Columbia University.
Blake, N., Smith, R. and Standish, P. (1998) *The Universities We Need: Higher Education after Dearing*. London: Kogan Page.
Bligh, B. (2014) 'Examining New Processes for Learning Space Design', in P. Temple (Ed.), op. cit.
Bloom, A. (1987) *The Closing of the American Mind: How Higher Education Has Failed Democracy and Impoverished the Souls of Today's Students*. London: Penguin.
Boddington, A. and Boys, J. (Eds.) (2011) *Re-Shaping Learning: A Critical Reader – The Future of Learning Spaces in Post-Compulsory Education*. London and New York: Sense.
Boehnert, J. (2018) *Design, Ecology, Politics: Towards the Ecocene*. London and New York: Bloomsbury.
Bou-Habib, P. (2010) 'Who Should Pay for Higher Education?', *Journal of Philosophy of Education*, 44 (4) 479–496.
Bourdieu, P. (1990) *Homo Academicus*. Cambridge: Polity.
Bourdieu, P. (2000a) *Practical Reason*. Cambridge: Polity.
Bourdieu, P. (2000b) *Pascalian Meditations*. Cambridge: Polity.
Bourdieu, P. and Passeron, J-C. (1990) *Reproduction in Education, Society and Culture* (2nd ed). London and Newberry Park, CA: Sage.
Bourner, T. (2018) 'The Fully Functioning University', in R. Barnett and M. A. Peters (Eds.), op. cit.
Bourner, T., Rospigliosi, A. and Heath, L. (2020) *The Fully Functioning University*. Bingley: Emerald.
Boutang, Y.-M. (2011) *Cognitive Capital*. Cambridge and Malden, MA: Polity.
Bovill, C. (2019) 'Co-creation in Learning and Teaching: The Case for a Whole-Class Approach in Higher Education', *Higher Education*, 79, 1023–1037. https://link.springer.com/article/10.1007/s10734-019-00453-w
Bowen, W. M., Schwartz, M. and Camp, L. (2014) *End of Academic Freedom: The Coming Obliteration of the Core Purpose of the University: The Coming Obliteration of the Core Purpose of the University*. Charlotte, NC: Information Age.
Boyer, E. (1990) *Scholarship Reconsidered: Priorities of the Professoriate*. Princeton, NJ: Carnegie Foundation.
Bozalek, V., Braidotti, R., Shefer, T. and Zembylas, M. (Eds.) (2020) *Socially Just Pedagogies: Posthumanist, Feminist and Materialist Perspectives in Higher Education*. London and New York: Bloomsbury.
Bradley, J. P. N. and Kennedy, D. (2019) 'On the Organology of Utopia: Stiegler's Contribution to the Philosophy of Education', *Educational Philosophy and Theory*. https://doi.org/10.1080/00131857.2019.1594779
Bradwell, P. (2009) *The Edgeless University: Why Higher Education Must Embrace Technology*. London: Demos.
Brady, M. and Pritchard, D. (Eds.) (2003) *Moral and Epistemic Virtues*. Malden, MA and Oxford: Blackwell.
Braidotti, R. (2013) *The Posthuman*. Cambridge and Malden, MA: Polity.

Braidotti, R. (2016) 'The Contested Posthumanities', in R. Braidotti and P. Gilroy (Eds.) *Conflicting Humanities*. London and New York: Bloomsbury, pp. 9–45.

Brandom, R. B. (1998) *Making It Explicit: Reasoning, Representing, and Discursive Commitment*. Cambridge, MA and London: Harvard University.

Brannmark, J. (2019) 'Contested Institutional Facts', *Erkenntnis*, 84 (5) 1047–1064.

Brennan, J. and Cochrane, A. (2019) 'Universities: In, of, and beyond Their Cities', *Oxford Review of Education*, 45 (2) 188–203. https://doi.org/10.1080/03054985.2018.1551198

Briggs, A. (1964) 'Drawing a New Map of Learning', in D. Daiches (Ed.) *The Idea of a New University: An Experiment in Sussex*. London: Deutsch, pp. 60–80.

Brighouse, H. and McPherson, M. (2015) *The Aims of Higher Education: Problems of Morality and Justice*. Chicago, IL and London: University of Chicago.

Brighouse, H. and Robeyns, I. (Eds.) (2011) *Measuring Justice: Primary Goods and Capabilities*. Cambridge: Cambridge University Press.

Brink, C. (2018) *The Soul of a University: Why excellence is not enough*. Bristol: Bristol University.'

Brooks, M. (2010) *Laws of Physics May Change across the Universe*, New Scientist, 8 September. https://www.newscientist.com/article/dn19429-laws-of-physics-may-change-across-the-universe/

Brubacher, J. S. (1977) *On the Philosophy of Higher Education*. San Francisco, CA and London: Jossey-Bass.

Buchanan, A. (2015) 'Education and Social Moral Epistemology', in H. Brighouse and M. McPherson (Eds.), op. cit.

Butler, Jane (2020) 'Learning to Lead: A Discussion of Development Programs for Academic Leadership Capability in Australian Universities', *Journal of Higher Education Policy and Management*, 42 (4) 424–437.

Butler, Judith (2015) 'Exercising Rights: Academic Freedom and Boycott Politics', in A. Bilgrami and J. R. Cole (Eds.), op. cit.

Butler, Judith (2018) *Notes towards a Performative Theory of Assembly*. Cambridge, MA and London: Harvard University.

Butler, Judith (2020) *The Force of Nonviolence: An Ethico-Political Bind*. London and New York: Verso.

Butler, J., Laclau, E. and Žižek, S. (2000) *Contingency, Hegemony, Universality: Contemporary Dialogues on the Left*. London and New York: Verso.

Calhoun, C. (Ed.) (1994a) *Habermas and the Public Sphere*. Cambridge, MA: MIT.

Calhoun, C. (1994b) 'Introduction: Habermas and the Public Sphere', in C. Calhoun (Ed.), op. cit.

Calhoun, C. (2012) 'The Public Mission of the Research University', in D. Rhoten and C. Calhoun (Eds.), op. cit.

Calhoun, C. (2017) 'Facets of the Public Sphere: Dewey, Arendt, Habermas', in F. Englestad, H. Larsen, J. Rogstad and K. Steen-Johnsen (Eds.), *Institutional Change in the Public Sphere: Views on the Nordic Model*. Berlin: De Gruyter.

Calvino, I. (1997/1974) *Invisible Cities*. London: Vintage.

Carlin, M. (2016) 'Amputating the State: Autonomy and La Universidad de la Tierra', in M. Carlin and J. Wallin (Eds.), op. cit.

Carlin, M. and Wallin, J. (Eds.) (2016) *Deleuze and Guattari, Politics and Education: For a People-Yet-to-Come*. New York and London: Bloomsbury.

Castoriadis, C. (1997/1975) *The Imaginary Institution of Society*. Cambridge: Polity.

Chamberlain, J. and Rée, J. (Eds.) (2001) *The Kierkegaard Reader*. Malden, MA and Oxford: Blackwell.

Chankseliani, M. and McCowan, T. (2021) 'Higher Education and the Sustainable Development Goals', *Higher Education*, 81, 1–8.

Clark, B. R. (1983) *The Higher Education System: Academic Organization in Cross-National Perspective*. Berkeley and London: University of California.
Charbonneau, B. (2018), *The Green Light: A Self-Critique of the Ecological Movement*. New York and London: Bloomsbury.
Cochrane, A. (2018) 'Placing the University: Thinking in and Beyond Gobalisation', in P. Meusburger, M. Heffernan and L. Suarsana (Eds.), op. cit.
Code, L. (2006) *Ecological Thinking: The Politics of Epistemic Location*. Oxford: Oxford University.
Cohen, E. (2021) *The University and its Boundaries: Thriving or Surviving in the 21st Century*. London and New York: Routledge.
Cohen, T. (2001) *Jacques Derrida and the Humanities: A Critical Reader*. Cambridge: University of Cambridge.
Collini, S. (2012) *What Are Universities for?* London and New York: Penguin.
Connell, R. (2019) *The Good University: What Universities Actually Do and Why It's Time for Radical Change*. London: Zed.
Coole, D. and Frost, S. (Eds.) (2010) *New Materialisms: Ontology, Agency, and Politics*. Durham, NC and London: Duke University.
Cowden, S. and Singh, G. (2013) *Acts of Knowing: Critical Pedagogy in, against and beyond the University*. New York and London: Bloomsbury.
Cox, A. M. (2018) 'Space and Embodiment in Informal Learning'. *Higher Education*, 75 (6) 1077–1090.
Critchley, S. (2001) *Continental Philosophy: A Very Short Introduction*. Oxford: Oxford University.
Cutright, M. (Ed.) (1999) *Chaos Theory and Higher Education: Leadership, Planning and Policy*. New York: Peter Lang.
Dall'Alba, G. (2012) 'Re-imagining the University: Developing a Capacity to Care', in R. Barnett (Ed.), op. cit.
Dall'Alba, G. and Bengtsen, S. (2019) 'Re-imagining Active Learning: Delving into Darkness', *Educational Philosophy and Theory*, 51 (14) 1477–1489. https://doi.org/10.1080/00131857.2018.1561367
Dall'Alba, G. and Sandberg, J. (2020) 'Bodily Grounds of Learning: Embodying Professional Practice in Biotechnology', *Studies in Higher Education*. January. https://doi.org/10.1080/03075079.2019.1711047
Davids, N. and Waghid, Y. (2017) *Educational Leadership in becoming: On the Potential of Leadership in Action*. London and New York: Routledge.
Davids, N. and Waghid, Y. (2019) *Universities, Pedagogical Encounters, Openness and Free Speech: Reconfiguring Democratic Education*. Lanham, MD and London: Lexington.
Davies, M. and Barnett, R. (Eds.) (2015) *The Palgrave Handbook of Critical Thinking in Higher Education*. New York: Palgrave Macmillan.
Dawson, M. C. (2020) 'Rehumanising the University for an Alternative Future: Decolonisation, Alternative Epistemologies and Cognitive Justice', *Identities*, 27 (1) 71–90. https://doi.org/10.1080/1070289X.2019.1611072
de Sousa Santos, B. (2016) *Epistemologies of the South: Justice against Epistemicide*. London and New York: Routledge.
de Sousa Santos, B. (2018) *The End of the Cognitive Empire: The Coming of Age of Epistemologies of the South*. Durham and London: Duke University.
de Sousa Santos, B and Meneses, M. P. (Eds.) (2020) *Knowledges Born in the Struggle: Constructing the Epistemologies of the Global South*. New York and London: Routledge.
Decuypere, M. and Vanden Broeck, P. (2020) 'Time and Educational (re-)forms – Inquiring the Temporal Dimension of Education', *Educational Philosophy and Theory*, 52 (6) 606–612. https://doi.org/10.1080/00131857.2020.1716449
DeLanda, M. (2013/2006) *A New Philosophy of Society: Assemblage Theory and Social Complexity*. London and New York: Bloomsbury.

DeLanda, M. and Harman, G. (2017) *The Rise of Realism*. Cambridge and Malden, MA: Polity.
Delanty, G. (2001) *Challenging Knowledge: The University in the Knowledge Society*. Buckingham: Open University Press/SRHE.
Deleuze, G. (2006/1988) *Bergsonism*. Brooklyn, NY: Zone.
Deleuze, G. (2012/1965) *Pure Immanence: Essays on a Life*. Brooklyn, NY: Zone.
Deleuze, G. and Guattari, F. (2007/1980) *A Thousand Plateaus: Capitalism and Schizophrenia*. London and New York: Continuum.
Deleuze, G. and Guattari, F. (2013) *What Is Philosophy?* London and Brooklyn, NY: Verso.
Derrida, J. (1991) *Of Spirit: Heidegger and the Question*. Chicago, IL and London: University of Chicago.
Derrida, J. (1992) 'Mochlos; or, The Conflict of the Faculties', in R. Rand (Ed.), op. cit.
Derrida, J. (2001a) 'The Future of the Profession or the University without Condition (Thanks to the Humanities, What Could Take Place Tomorrow)', in T. Cohen (Ed.), op. cit.
Derrida, J. (2001b) *Deconstruction Engaged*. (The Sydney Seminars). Sydney: University of Sydney.
Derrida, J. (2004) *Eyes of the University: Right to Philosophy 2*. Stanford, CA: University of Stanford.
Derrida, J. (2005) *The Politics of Friendship*. London and New York: Verso.
Derycke, M. (2011) 'Ignorance and Translation, "Artefacts" for Practices of Equality', in M. Simons and J. Masschelein (Eds.) Rancière, *Public Education and the Taming of Democracy*. Chichester: Wiley.
Descartes, R. (1966) *Essential Works*. New York: Bantam, pp. 43–59.
Descola, P. (2013) *The Ecology of Others*. Chicago, IL: Prickly Paradigm.
Diaz Villa, M. (2012) 'The Idea of the University in Latin America in the Twenty-First Century', in R. Barnett (Ed.), op. cit.
Doherty, T. (2015) *Universities at War*. London and Los Angeles, CA: Sage.
Doll, W. E. (1993) *A Post-Modern Perspective on Curriculum*. New York and London: Teachers College.
Eagleton, T. (2000) *The Idea of Culture*. Oxford and Malden, MA: Blackwell.
Eagleton, T. (2007) *The Meaning of Life*. Oxford: Oxford University.
Eagleton, T. (2009) *Reason, Faith and Revolution: Reflections on the God Debate*: New Haven, CT and London: Yale.
Eco, U. and Carriere, J.-C. (2012) *This Is Not the End of the Book*; London: Vintage.
Ehrlich, T. (Ed.) (2000) *Civic Responsibility and Higher Education*. Phoenix, AZ: Oryx & American Council on Education.
Ekman, R. and Quandt, R. E. (Eds.) (1999) *Technology and Scholarly Communication*. Berkeley and London: University of California.
Elliott, R. (1975) 'Education and Human Being', in S. C. Brown (Ed.) *Philosophers Discuss Education*. Basingstoke: Palgrave Macmillan, pp. 45–72.
Eliot, T. S. (1948) *Notes towards the Definition of Culture*. (1962 printing) London: Faber and Faber.
Elton, L. (2000) 'Turning Academics into Teachers: A Discourse on Love', *Teaching in Higher Education*, 5 (2) 257–260. https://doi.org/10.1080/135625100114894
Englund, T. (2008) 'The University as an Encounter for Deliberative Communication: Creating Cultural Citizenship and Professional Responsibility', *Utbildning & Demokrati*, 17 (2) 97–114.

Engwall, L. (Ed.) (2020) *Missions of the University: Past, Present, Future*. Cham: Springer.
Ennis, R. H. (1985) 'A Logical Basis for Measuring Critical Thinking Skills', *Educational Leadership*, 43 (2) 44–48.
Eraut, M. (1994) *Developing Professional Knowledge and Competence*. London: Falmer.
Erguyan, M. M., Parjanadze, N. and Hirschi, K. (2019) 'Educating for the Cooperative Society: The Role of Universities, Research and the Academic Professions in Fostering Good Citizenship', in G. Redding, A. Drew and S. Crump (Eds.), op. cit.
Faber, G. (1954) *Oxford Apostles: A Character Study of the Oxford Movement*. London: Pelican.
Facer, K. (2019a) 'The University as Engine for Anticipation: Stewardship, Modelling, Experimentation, and Critique in Public', in R. Poli (Ed.) *Handbook of Anticipation: Theoretical and Applied Aspects of the Use of Future in Decision Making*. Cham: Springer, 1439–1457. https://link.springer.com/referenceworkentry/10.1007/978-3-319-91554-8_29.
Facer, K. (2019b) 'Storytelling in Troubled Times: What is the Role for Educators in the Deep Crises of the 21st Century?', *Literacy*, 53 (1) 3–13. https://doi.org/10.1111/lit.12176
Facer, K. (2020) 'Convening Publics? Co-produced Research in the Entrepreneurial University', *Philosophy and Theory of Higher Education*, 2 (2) 19–44.
Facione, P., Facione, N. C. and Giancarlo, C. A. (2000) 'The Disposition toward Critical Thinking: Its Character, Measurement, and Relationship to Critical Thinking Skill', *Informal Logic*, 20 (1). https://doi.org/10.22329/il.v20i1.2254
Ferraris, M. (2015) *Introduction to New Realism*. London and New York: Bloomsbury.
Feyerabend, P. (1975) *Against Method*. London: Verso.
Feyerabend, P. (1977) 'Consolations for the Specialist', in I. Lakatos and A. Musgrave (Eds.) *Criticism and the Growth of Knowledge*. Cambridge: Cambridge University. 197-230
Feyerabend, P. (1978) *Science in a Free Society*. London: Verso.
Feyerabend, P. (2016) *Philosophy of Nature*. Cambridge and Malden, MA: Polity.
Filippakou, O. and Williams, G. (Eds.) (2015) *Higher Education as a Public Good: Critical Perspectives on Theory, Policy and Practice*. New York: Peter Lang.
Finnegan, R. (Ed.) (2005) *Participating in the Knowledge Society: Researchers beyond the University Walls*. Basingstoke and New York: Palgrave Macmillan.
Floridi, L. (Ed.) (2015) *The Onlife Manifesto: Being Human in a Hyperconnected Era*. Cham: Springer.
Ford, M. P. (2002) *Beyond the Modern University: Towards a Constructive Postmodern University*. Westport, CT and London: Praeger.
Foucault, M. (1977) *The Archaeology of Knowledge*. Tavistock: London.
Foucault, M. (1980) *Power/ Knowledge: Selective Interviews and other Writings 1972–1977*. London: Harvester Wheatsheaf.
Foucault, M. (1991/1975) *Discipline and Punish: The Birth of the Prison*. London: Penguin.
Fricker, M. (2010) *Epistemic Injustice: Power & the Ethics of Knowing*. Oxford: Oxford University.
Fridland, E. and Pavese, C. (Eds.) (2021) *The Routledge Handbook of Philosophy of Skill and Expertise*. London and New York: Routledge.
Fromm, E. (1960/1942) *Fear of Freedom*. London: Routledge and Kegan Paul.
Fuller, S. (2009) 'The Genealogy of Judgement: Towards a Deep History of Academic Freedom', *British Journal of Educational Studies*, 57 (2) 164–177.
Fuller, S. (2018) *Post-Truth: Knowledge as a Power Game*. London and New York: Anthem.
Gadamer, H-G. (1985/1965) *Truth and Method*. London: Sheed and Ward.
Gadamer, H-G. (2018) 'The Idea of the University: Yesterday, Today, Tomorrow', in M. A. Peters and R. Barnett (Eds.), op. cit.

Gadotti, M. (1996) *Pedagogy of Praxis: A Dialectical Philosophy of Education*. New York: University of New York.
Gallant, T. B. (Ed.) (2011) *Creating the Ethical Academy: A Systems Approach to Understanding Misconduct and Empowering Changes in Higher Education*. New York and London: Routledge.
Garry, A. and Pearsall, M. (Eds.) (1996) *Women, Knowledge and Reality: Explorations in Feminist Philosophy*. London and New York: Routledge.
Geerts, E. and Carstens, D. (2019) 'Ethico-onto-Epistemology', *Philosophy Today*, 63 (4) 915–925.
Gellner, E. (1964) 'The Crisis in the Humanities and the Mainstream of Philosophy', in J. H. Plumb (Ed.) *Crisis in the Humanities*. London: Penguin, pp. 45–81.
Gellner, E. (1969) *Thought and Change*. London: Weidenfeld and Nicolson.
Gellner, E. (1970) 'Concepts and Society', in B. R. Wilson (Ed.) *Rationality*. Oxford: Blackwell. 18-49
Gellner, E. (1974) *Legitimation of Belief*. London: Cambridge University Press.
Gellner, E. (1992) *Reason and Culture*. Oxford: Blackwell.
Gettier, E. L. (1963) 'Is Justified True Belief Knowledge?' *Analysis*, 23, 121–123.
Giannakakis, V. (2019). 'Neoliberalism and Culture in Higher Education: On the Loss of the Humanistic Character of the University and the Possibility of Its Reconstitution', *Studies in Philosophy and Education*. https://doi.org/10.1007/s11217-019-09682-z
Gibbons, M., Limoges, C., Nowotny, H., Schwartzman, S., Scott, P. and Trow, M. (1994) *The New Production of Knowledge: The Dynamics of Science and Research in Contemporary Societies*. London and Thousand Oaks, CA: Sage.
Gibbs, P. (Ed.) (2017) *Transdisciplinary Higher Education: A Theoretical Basis Revealed in Practice*. Cham: Springer.
Gibbs, P. (2019) 'Duties before Rights: A Notion of the University of the Future', in P. Gibbs, J. Jameson and A. Elwick (Eds.), op. cit.
Gibbs, P. and Barnett, R. (Eds.) (2014) *Thinking about Higher Education*. Cham: Springer.
Gibbs, P. and Beavis, A. (2020) *Contemporary Thinking on Transdisciplinary Knowledge: What Those Who Know, Know*. Cham: Springer.
Gibbs, P., Jameson, J. and Elwick, A. (Eds.) (2019) *Values of the University in a Time of Uncertainty*. Cham: Springer.
Gibbs, P., Ylijoiki, O-H., Guzmán-Valenzuela, C. and Barnett, R. (Eds.) (2015) *Universities in the Flux of Time: An Exploration of Time and Temporality in University Life*. London and New York: Routledge.
Gibbs, P. T. (2004) *Trusting in the University: The Contribution of Temporality and Trust to a Praxis of Higher Learning*. Dordrecht: Kluwer.
Gibbs, P. T. (2017) *Why Universities Should Seek Happiness and Contentment*. London and New York: Bloomsbury.
Gildersleeve, R. E. and Kleinhesselink, K. (Eds.) (2019) 'Introduction: The Anthropocene as Context and Concept for the Study of Higher Education.' Special Issue on the Anthropocene in the Study of Higher Education. *Philosophy and Theory in Higher Education*, 1 (1) 1–16.
Giroux, H. A. (1983) *Theory & Resistance in Education: A Pedagogy for the Opposition*. London: Heinemann.
Giroux, H. A. (2001) 'Vocationalising Higher Education: Schooling and the Politics of Corporate Culture', in H. A. Giroux and K. Mysiades (Eds.), op. cit.
Giroux, H. A. (2012) *On Critical Pedagogy*. New York and London: Continuum.

Giroux, H. A. and Mysiades, K. (Eds.) (2001) *Beyond the Corporate University: Culture and Pedagogy in the New Millennium.* Lanham, MD and Oxford: Rowman and Littlefield.

Glassner, A. and Back, S. (2020) *Exploring Heutagogy in Higher Education: Academia Meets the Zeitgeist.* Singapore: Springer.

Gluckler, J., Suddaby, R. and Lenz, R. (Eds.) (2018) 'On the Spatiality of Institutions and Knowledge', in their *Knowledge and Institutions.* Cham: Springer, pp. 1–14.

Goddard, J. and Valance, P. (2013) *The University and the City.* London and New York: Routledge.

Goodlad, S. (1976) *Conflict and Consensus in Higher Education.* London: Hodder and Stoughton.

Goodyear, P. and Ellis, R. A. (2020) 'Ecological Thinking about Educational Strategy in Universities', in R. Barnett and N. Jackson (Eds.), op. cit.

Gorky, M. (1992/1923) *My Universities.* London: Penguin.

Gottlieb, B. (2018) *Digital Materialism: Origins, Philosophies, Prospects.* Bingley: Emerald.

Gouldner, A. (1957) 'Cosmopolitans and Locals: Toward an Analysis of Latent Social Roles', *Administrative Science Quarterly,* 2 (3) 281–306. https://doi.org/10.2307/2391000

Gouldner, A. (1979) *The Future of Intellectuals and the Rise of the New Class: The Role of Intellectuals and Intelligentsia in the International Class Contest of the Modern Era.* Basingstoke: Macmillan.

Grabina, G. L. (undated) 'A Critical Analysis of Fricker's Testimonial Justice': https://www.academia.edu/48777217/A_Critical_Analysis_of_Frickers_Testimonial_Injustice

Gratton, P. (2014) *Speculative Realism: Problems and Prospects.* London and New York: Bloomsbury.

Grayling, A. C. (2005) *Descartes: The Life of René Descartes and Its Place in His Times.* London: Free Press, Simon and Schuster.

Greco, J. (2011) *Achieving Knowledge: A Virtue-Theoretic Account of Epistemic Normativity.* Cambridge and New York: Cambridge University.

Green, A. (1990) *Education and State Formation: The Rise of Education Systems in England, France and the USA.* Basingstoke: Macmillan.

Grosfoguel, R. (2007) The Epistemic Decolonial Turn: Beyond Political-Economy Paradigms', *Cultural Studies,* 21 (2–3) 211–233. https://doi.org/10.1080/09502380601162514

Guattari, F (2000/1989) *The Three Ecologies.* London and New York: Continuum.

Guattari, F. (2016) *Lines of Flight: For Another World of Possibilities.* London and New York: Bloomsbury.

Gutmann, A. (2015) 'What Makes a University Education Worth-While?', in H. Brighouse and M. McPherson (Eds.), op. cit.

Guzmán-Valenzuela, C. and Bernasconi, A. (2018) 'The Latin-American University: Past, Present and Future', in M. A. Peters and R. Barnett (Eds.), op, cit.

Guzmán-Valenzuela, C. and Gómez, C. (2019) 'Advancing a Knowledge Ecology: Changing Patterns of Higher Education Studies in Latin America', *Higher Education,* 77 (1) 115–133. https://doi.org/10.1007/s10734-018-0264-z

Haas, P. (2016) *Epistemic Communities, Constructivism and International Environmental Politics.* London and New York: Routledge.

Habermas, J. (1970) *Towards a Rational Society.* London: Heinemann.

Habermas, J. (1978/1968) *Knowledge and Human Interests.* London: Heinemann.

Habermas, J. (1984) *The Theory of Communicative Action, Vol. One: Reason and the Rationalization of Society.* Cambridge: Polity.

Habermas, J. (1987a) 'The Idea of the University: Learning Processes', *New German Critique*, 41, 3–22. (trans. J. R. Blazek).
Habermas, J. (1987b) *The Theory of Communicative Action. Vol. Two: The Critique of Functionalist Reason*. Cambridge: Polity.
Habermas, J. (1994) 'Further Reflections on the Public Sphere', in C. Calhoun (Ed.), op. cit.
Habermas, J. (2005/1962) *The Structural Transformation of the Public Sphere*. Cambridge: Polity.
Habermas, J. (2010a) *An Awareness of What Is Missing: Faith and Reason in a Post-Secular Age*. Cambridge: Polity.
Habermas, J. (2010b) *Between Naturalism and Religion: Philosophical Essays*. Cambridge: Polity.
Hajrasouliha, A. (2016) 'Campus Score: Measuring University Campus Qualities', *Landscape and Urban Planning*, 158, 166–176. https://doi.org/10.1016/j.landurbplan.2016.10.007
Hall, J. A. (2010) *Ernest Gellner: An Intellectual Biography*. London and New York: Verso.
Hamilton, C., Bonneuil, C. and Gemenne, F. (Eds.) (2015) *The Anthropocene and the Global Environmental Crisis: Rethinking Modernity in a New Epoch*. London and New York: Routledge.
Hampshire, S. (1970/1959) *Thought and Action*. London: Chatto and Windus.
Haraway, D. (2016a) *Staying with the Trouble: Making Kin in the Chthulucene*. Durham, NC and London: Duke University.
Haraway, D. (2016b) *Manifestly Haraway*. Minneapolis: University of Minnesota.
Hardt, M. and Negri, A. (2000) *Empire*. Cambridge, MA and London: Harvard University.
Harman, G. (2009) *Towards Speculative Realism: Essays and Lectures*. Winchester and Washington: Zero.
Harman, G. (2018) *Object-Oriented Ontology: A New Theory of Everything*. London: Pelican.
Hartwig, M. and Morgan, J. (Eds.) (2014) *Critical Realism and Spirituality*. London and New York: Routledge.
Hassan, R. (2003) *The Chronoscopic Society: Globalization, Time and Knowledge in the Network Society*. New York: Peter Lang.
Hauerwas, S. (2007) *The State of the University: Academic Knowledges and the Knowledge of God*. Malden, MA and Oxford: Blackwell.
Heap, S. (Ed.) (2017) *The Universities We Need: Theological Perspectives*. London and New York: Routledge.
Hegel, G. W. F. (1977/1952) *Phenomenology of Spirit*. Oxford: Oxford University.
Heidegger, M. (1996/1957) *The Principle of Reason*. Bloomington: Indiana University.
Heidegger, M. (1998/1962) *Being and Time*. Oxford: Blackwell.
Heidegger, M. (2004/1954) *What Is Called Thinking?* New York: Harper Collins.
Heidegger, M. (2018) 'The Self-Assertion of the German University: Address Delivered on the Solemn Assumption of the Rectorate of the University of Freiberg', reproduced in M. A. Peters and R. Barnett (Eds.), op. cit.
Henkel, M. and Little, B. (Eds.) (1999) *Changing Relationships between Higher Education and the State*. London and Philadelphia, PA: Jessica Kingsley.
Herbrachter, S. (2013) *Posthumanism: A Critical Analysis*. London and New York: Bloomsbury.
Heuser, B. L. and Drake, T. A. (2011) 'Towards Global Academic Ethics through Accountability Systems', in T. B. Gallant (Ed.), op. cit.
Higgs, J., Barnett, R., Billett, S., Hutchins, M. and Trede, F. (Eds.) (2012) *Practice-Based Education: Perspectives and Strategies*. Rotterdam: Sense.

Higgs, P. and Waghid, Y. (Eds.) (2017) *A Reader in Philosophy of Education*. Cape Town: Juta.
Higton, M. (2013) *A Theology of Higher Education*. Oxford: Oxford University.
Hill, M. A. (Ed.) (1979) *Hannah Arendt: The Recovery of the Public World*. New York: St. Martin's Press.
Hodgson, N., Vlieghe, J. and Zamojski, P. (2017) *Manifesto for a Post-Critical Pedagogy*. Earth City, MO: Punctum.
Hodgson, N., Vlieghe, J. and Zamojski, P. (Eds.) (2020) *Post-Critical Perspectives on Higher Education: Reclaiming the Educational in the University*. Cham: Springer.
Holmwood, J. (Ed.) (2011) *A Manifesto for the Public University*. London and New York: Bloomsbury.
Honneth, A. (2005/1995) *The Struggle for Recognition: The Moral Grammar of Social Conflicts*. Cambridge: Polity.
hooks, b. (1994) *Teaching to Transgress: Education as the Practice of Freedom*. New York and London: Routledge.
Horton, R. (1973) 'Lévy-Bruhl, Durkheim and the Scientific Revolution', in R. Horton and R. Finnegan (Eds.) *Modes of Thought: Essays on Thinking in Western and Non-Western Societies*. London: Faber and Faber, pp. 249–305.
Howard, C. G. (1991) *Theories of General Education*. Basingstoke: Macmillan.
Høyer, K. G. (2012) 'Ecophilosophy and the Contemporary Environmental Debate', in R. Bhaskar, et al. (Eds.), op. cit.
Hroch, P. (2016) 'Deleuze, Guattari, and Environmental Pedagogy and Politics: *Ritournelles* for a Planet Yet-to-Come', in M. Carlin and J. Wallin (Eds.), op. cit.
Humboldt, W. von (2018) 'On the Spirit and the Organisational Framework of Intellectual Institutions in Berlin', in M. A. Peters and R. Barnett (Eds.), op. cit.
Hutchins, R. M. (1936) *The Higher Learning in America*. New Haven, CT: Yale University.
Ignatieff, M. (1994) *The Needs of Strangers*. London: Vintage.
Irigaray, L. (1999) *The Forgetting of Air in Martin Heidegger*. Austin, TX: University of Austin.
Jackson, N. (Ed.) (2011) *Learning for a Complex World: A Lifewide Concept of Learning, Education and Personal Development*. Bloomington, IN: AuthorHouse.
Jameson, J. (Ed.) (2019) *International Perspectives on Leadership in Higher Education: Critical Thinking for Global Challenges*. London and New York: Routledge.
Jandric, P. and McClaren, P. (2020) 'Postdigital Cross Border Reflections on Critical Utopia', *Educational Philosophy and Theory*, 52 (14) 1470–1482. https://doi.org/10.1080/00131857.2020.1731687
Jaspers, K. (1965) *The Idea of the University*. London: Peter Owen.
Jay, M. (2005) *Songs of Experience: Modern American and European Variations on a Universal Theme*. Berkeley and London: University of California.
Jessop, B. (1990) *State Theory*. Cambridge: Polity.
Johnson, R. E., Murphy, M., Griffiths, F. (2019) 'Conveying troublesome concepts: Using an open-space learning activity to teach mixed-methods research in the health sciences', *Methodological Innovations*. https://doi.org/10.1177/2059799119863279
Johnston, B., Mitchell, R., Myles, F. and Ford, P. (2011) *Developing Student Criticality in Higher Education: Undergraduate Learning in the Arts and Social Sciences*. London and New York: Continuum.
Kagan, J. (2009) *The Three Cultures: Natural Sciences, Social Sciences and the Humanities in the 21st Century*. Cambridge: Cambridge University.
Kahn, C. H. (1987). *The Art and Thought of Heraclitus*. Cambridge: Cambridge University.

Kahn, R. (2010) *Critical Pedagogy, Ecoliteracy & Planetary Crisis: The Ecopedagogy Movement*. New York: Peter Lang.
Kant, I. (1992/1798) *The Conflict of the Faculties*. Lincoln and London: University of Nebraska.
Karlsohn, T. (Ed.) (2016) *Universitetets Idé: Sexton Nyckeltexter*. Göteborg: Daidalos.
Karlsohn, T. (2018) 'Bildung, Emotion and Thought', in S. S. E. Bengtsen and R. Barnett (Eds.) *The Thinking University*. Cham: Springer, pp. 103–118.
Karran, T., Beieter, K. and Appiagyei-Atua, K. (2017) 'Measuring Academic Freedom in Europe: A Criterion Referenced Approach', *Policy Reviews in Higher Education*, 1 (2) 209–239. https://doi.org/10.1080/23322969.2017.1307093
Keenan, W. J. (2020). 'Learning to Survive: Wicked Problem Education for the Anthropocene Age', *Journal of Global Education and Research*, 4 (1) 62–79. https://doi.org/10.5038/2577-509X.4.1.1038
Keet, A. (2018) 'The Plastic University – Knowledge, Disciplines and Decolonial "Circulations"', *Inaugural Lecture*, Nelson Mandela University, https://www.academia.edu/37278671/Draft_The_Plastic_University_Knowledge_Disciplines_and_Decolonial_Circulations
Kennedy, M. D. (2015) *Globalizing Knowledge: Intellectuals, Universities, and Publics in Transformation*. Stanford, CA: Stanford University.
Kerr, C. (1995/1963) *The Uses of the University*. Cambridge, MA and London: Harvard.
Kerr, C. (2001) *The Gold and the Blue: A Personal Memoir of the University of California 1949–1967. Vol 1: Academic Triumphs*. Berkeley and London: University of California.
Khine, M. S. (Ed.) (2008) *Knowing, Knowledge and Beliefs*. Cham: Springer.
Kidd, I. J., Medina, J. and Pohlhaus, G. (Jr.) (Eds.) (2017) *The Routledge Handbook of Epistemic Injustice*. London and New York: Routledge.
Klein, J. T. (2008) 'Evaluation of Interdisciplinary and Transdisciplinary Research: A Literature Review'. *American Journal of Preventative Medicine*, 35 (2S) 116–123.
Knorr Cetina, K. (1999) *Epistemic Cultures: How the Sciences Make Knowledge*. Cambridge, MA: Harvard.
Kogan, M. and Hanney, S. (2000) *Reforming Higher Education*. London and Philadelphia, PA: Jessica Kingsley.
Kogan, M. and Marton, S. G. (2000) 'State and Higher Education', in M. Kogan, M. Bauer, I. Bleiklie and M. Henkel (Eds.) *Transforming Higher Education: A Comparative Study*. London and Philadelphia, PA: Jessica Kingsley.
Komljenovic, J. (2020) 'The Future of Value in Digitalised Higher Education: Why Data Privacy Should Not Be Our Biggest Concern', *Higher Education*. https://doi.org/10.1007/s10734-020-00639-7
Kreber, C. (Ed.) (2009) *The University and Its Disciplines: Teaching and Learning within and beyond Disciplinary Boundaries*. New York and London: Routledge.
Kress, G. and Van Leeuwen, T. (2001) *Multimodal Discourse: The Modes and Media of Contemporary Communication*. Arnold: London.
Kuhn, T. S. (1970) *The Structure of Scientific Revolutions*. 2nd ed. Chicago, IL and London: University of Chicago.
Kuntz, A. M. (2019) 'Inquiry, Refusal, and Virtuous Resistance in the Anthropocene', *Philosophy and Theory in Higher Education*, 1 (1) 41–64.
Kupers, W. M. (2020) 'From the Anthropocene to an "Ecocene" – Eco-Phenomenological Perspectives on Embodied, Anthrodentric Transformations towards Enlivening Practices of Organising Sustainability', *Sustainability*, 12 (9) 3633. https://doi.org/10.3390/su12093633

Kurzweil, R. (2006) *The Singularity is Near: When Humans Transcend Biology.* London: Duckworth.
Laclau, E. (1999) 'Preface', in S. Žižek (Ed.), op. cit.
Lake, D., McFarland, A. and Jennrich, J. (Eds.) (2018) 'Remaking the Academy: The Potential and the Challenge of Transdisciplinary Collaborative Engagement', in A. Stoller and E. Kramer (Eds.), op. cit.
Latour, B. (1993) *We Have Never Been Modern.* Cambridge, MA: Harvester Wheatsheaf and Harvard.
Latour, B. (2004) *Politics of Nature: How to Bring the Sciences into Democracy.* Cambridge, MA and London: Harvard University.
Latour, B. (2013) *An Inquiry into Modes of Existence: An Anthropology of the Moderns.* Cambridge, MA: Harvard University.
Latour, B. (2016) *Is Geo-logy the New Umbrella for All the Sciences? Hints for a Neo-Humboldtian University.* Cornell University, 25 October. http://www.bruno-latour.fr/sites/default/files/150-CORNELL-2016-.pdf
Latour, B. (2019) *Down to Earth: Politics in the New Climatic Regime.* Cambridge and Medford, MA: Polity.
Latour, B., Harman, G. and Erdélyi, P. (2011) *The Prince and the Wolf: Latour and Harman at the LSE.* Winchester: Zero.
Leask, B. (2015) *Internationalizing the Curriculum.* London and New York: Routledge.
Leavis, F. R. (1969) *English Literature in our Time and the University.* London: Chatto and Windus.
Leavis, F. R. (1979/1943) *Education and the University.* Cambridge and New York: Cambridge University.
Lefebvre, A. and Schott, N. F. (Eds.) (2020) *Introduction in A. Lefebvre and N. F. Schott, Interpreting Bergson: Critical Essays.* Cambridge: Cambridge University.
Lefebvre, H. (2004/1992) *Rhythmanalysis: Space, Time and Everyday Life.* London and New York: Continuum.
Leibowitz, B. and Bozalek, V. (2018) 'Towards a Slow Scholarship of Teaching and Learning in the South', *Teaching in Higher Education*, 23 (8) 981–994. https://doi.org/10.1080/13562517.2018.1452730
Lesk, M. (1999) 'Digital Libraries: A Unifying or Distributing Force?', in R. Ekman and R. E. Quandt (Eds.), op. cit.
Lessem, R., Adobo, A. and Bradley, T. (2019) *The Idea of the Communiversity: Releasing the Natural, Cultural, Technological and Economic GENE-ius of Societies.* Manchester: Beacon.
Levin, M. and Greenwood, D. J. (2016) *Creating a New Public University and Reviving Democracy: Action Research in Higher Education.* New York and Oxford: Berghahn.
Levinson, M. (2017) *The Humanities and Everyday Life.* Oxford: Oxford University.
Lévy, P. (2020) 'Towards an Epistemological Mutation in the Humanities and Social Sciences', in M. A. Peters, T. Besley, P. Jandric and X. Zhu (Eds.), op. cit.
Li, J. and Eryong, X. (2020) *Innovating World-Class Technology-Oriented Higher Education in China: Ideas, Strategies and Practices,* Cham: Springer.
List, C. and Pettit, P. (2011) *Group Agency: The Possibility, Design, and Status of Corporate Agents.* Oxford and New York: Oxford University.
Locke, J. (1968/1690) *An Essay Concerning Human Understanding.* London and Glasgow: Collins.
Loftus, S. and Kinsella, E. A. (Eds) (2022) *The Embodied University.* Cham: Springer.

Longino, H. (1996) 'Can There Be a Feminist Science?', in A. Garry and M. Pearsall (Eds.), op. cit.
Løvlie, L., Mortenson, K. P. and Nordenbo, S. E. (Eds.) (2003) *Educating Humanity: Bildung in Postmodernity*. Malden, MA and Oxford: Blackwell.
Løvlie, L. and Standish, P. (2003) 'Introduction: Bildung and the Idea of a Liberal Education', in L. Løvlie, K. P. Mortenson and S. E. Nordenbo (Eds.), op. cit.
Luhmann, N. (2018) *Organization and Decision*. Cambridge and New York: Cambridge University.
Lyotard, J-F. (1984) *The Postmodern Condition: A Report on Knowledge*. Manchester: University of Manchester.
Lysgaard, J. A., Bengtssson, S. and Laugesen, M. H-L. (2019) *Dark Pedagogy: Education, Horror and the Anthropocene*. Cham: Palgrave.
Maccarini, A. M. (2014) 'A Morphogenetic-Relational Account of Social Emergence: Processes and Forms', in M. Archer and A. M. Maccarini (Eds.), op. cit.
Macfarlane, B. (2004) *Teaching with Integrity: The Ethics of Higher Education Practice*. London and New York: Routledge.
Macfarlane, B. (2007) *The Academic Citizen: The Virtue of Service in Academic Life*. London and New York: Routledge.
Macfarlane, B. (2009) *Researching with Integrity: The Ethics of Academic Inquiry*. London and New York: Routledge.
Macfarlane, B. (2017) *Freedom to Learn: The Threat to Student Academic Freedom and Why It Needs to Be Reclaimed*. London and New York: Routledge.
Macfarlane, B. (2020) 'Reclaiming Democratic Values in the Future University', *Philosophy and Theory in Higher Education*, 1 (3) 97–114.
MacIntyre, A. (1985) *After Virtue: A Study in Moral Theory*. London: Duckworth.
MacIntyre, A. (1990) *Three Rival Versions of Moral Theory*. London: Duckworth.
MacIntyre, A. (2011) *God, Philosophy, Universities: A Selective History of the Catholic Philosophical Tradition*. Lanham, MD: Rowman and Littlefield.
MacIntyre, A. (2018; orig. 2009) 'The Very Idea of a University: Aristotle, Newman and Us', in M. A. Peters and R. Barnett (Eds.), op. cit.
Magee, B. (1978) 'Marcuse and the Frankfurt School' (interview with Herbert Marcuse.), in *Men of Ideas: Some creators of contemporary philosophy*. London: BBC, pp. 60–73.
Magee, B. (1987) *The Philosophy of Schopenhauer*. Oxford: Clarendon Press.
Malpas, J. (Ed.) (2015) *The Intelligence of Place: Topographies and Poetics*. London and New York: Bloomsbury.
Manathunga, C. (2018) 'Decolonising the Curriculum: Southern Interrogations of Time, Place and Knowledge', *SOTL in the South*, 2 (1) 95–111.
Manathunga, C. (2019) '"Timescapes" in Doctoral Education: The Politics of Temporal Equity in Higher Education', *Higher Education Research and Development*, 38 (6) 1227–1239. https://doi.org/10.1080/07294360.2019.1629880
Marcus, D. M. (1997) 'On Knowing What One Knows', *Psychoanal Q*, 66 (2) 219–41.
Marginson, S. (2007) 'The New Higher Education Landscape: Public and Private Goods, in Global/ National/ Local Settings', in S. Marginson (Ed.) *Prospects of Higher Education: Globalization, Market Competition, Public Goods and the Future of the University*. Rotterdam: Sense, pp. 29–77.
Marginson, S. (2010a) 'Space, Mobility and Synchrony in the Knowledge Economy', in S. Marginson, P. Murphy and M. A. Peters (Eds.), op. cit.
Marginson, S. (2010b) 'University', (chapter 5) and 'Nation' (chapter 6) in P. Murphy, M. A. Peters and S. Marginson (Eds.) *Imagination: Three Models of Imagination in the Age of the Knowledge Economy*. New York: Peter Lang, pp. 167–223; 225–325.

Marginson, S. (2012) 'The "Public" Contribution of Universities in an Increasingly Global World', in B. Pusser, et al. (Eds.), op cit.
Marginson, S. (2020) 'The World Research System: Expansion, Diversification, Network and Hierarchy', in C. Callender, W. Locke and S. Marginson (Eds.) *Changing Higher Education for a Changing World*. London and New York: Bloomsbury, pp. 35–51.
Marginson, S., Murphy, P. and Peters, M. A. (2010) *Global Creation: Space, Mobility and Synchrony in the Age of the Knowledge Economy*. New York: Peter Lang.
Margolis, E. (2001) *The Hidden Curriculum in Higher Education*. London and New York: Routledge.
Margolis, J. and Rockmore, T. (Eds.) (2000) *The Philosophy of Interpretation*. Oxford and Malden, MA: Blackwell.
Marion, R. (1999) *The Edge of Organization: Chaos and Complexity Theories of Formal Social Systems*. Thousand Oaks, CA and London: Sage.
Masschelein, J. (2019) 'Turning a City into a Milieu of Study: University Pedagogy as "Frontline"', *Educational Theory*, 69 (2) 185–203.
Masschelein, J. and Simons, M. (2012) 'The Universities: A Public Issue', in R. Barnett (Ed.), op cit.
Masschelein, J. and Simons, M. (2018) 'The University as Public Pedagogic Form', in R. Barnett and M. A. Peters (Eds.), op. cit.
Maxwell, N. (1984) *From Knowledge to Wisdom: A Revolution in the Aims and Methods of Science*. Oxford: Blackwell.
Maxwell, N. (2012) 'Creating a Better World: Towards the University of Wisdom', in R. Barnett (Ed.), op. cit.
Maxwell, N. (2014) *How Universities Can Help Create a Wiser World: The Urgent Need for an Academic Revolution*. Exeter: Imprint Academic.
McArthur, J. (2014) *Rethinking Knowledge within Higher Education: Adorno and Social Justice*. London and New York: Bloomsbury.
McArthur, J. (2018) 'When Thought Gets Left Alone: Thinking, Recognition and Social Justice', in S. S. E. Bengtsen and R. Barnett (Eds.), op. cit.
McArthur, J. (2019) 'Towards a Moral University: Horkheimer's Commitment to the "Vicissitudes of Human Fate"', *Philosophy and Theory in Higher Education*, 1 (3) 131–152.
McClaren, P. (1995) *Critical Pedagogy and Predatory Culture: Oppositional Politics in a Postmodern Era*. London and New York: Routledge.
McClaren, P. and Jandric, P. (2020) *Postdigital Dialogues: On Critical Pedagogy, Liberation Theology and Information Technology*. London and New York: Bloomsbury.
McDowell, J. (2002/ 1994) *Mind and World*. Cambridge, MA and London: Harvard University.
McGregor, S. L. T. and Gibbs, P. (2020) 'Being in the Hidden Third: Insights into Transdisciplinary Ontology', *Transdisciplinary Journal of Engineering & Science*, 11, 142–157.
McLean, M. (2008) *Pedagogy and the University: Critical Theory and Practice*. London and New York: Bloomsbury.
McPeck, J. E. (1990) *Teaching Critical Thinking: Dialogue and Dialectic*. New York and London: Routledge.
Meillassoux, Q. (2014) *After Finitude: An Essay on the Necessity of Contingency*. London and New York: Bloomsbury.
Merleau-Ponty, M. (1994/1962) *Phenomenology of Perception*. London and New York: Routledge.
Merry, M. S. (2020) *Educational Justice: Liberal Ideals, Persistent Inequality, and the Constructive Uses of Critique*. Cham: Palgrave.

Metz, T. (2010) 'A Dilemma Regarding Academic Freedom and Public Accountability', *Journal of Philosophy of Education*, 44 (4) 529–550.

Metz, T. (2018) 'An African Theory of the Point of Higher Education: Communion as an Alternative to Autonomy, Truth and Citizenship', in A. Stoller and E. Kramer (Eds.), op. cit.

Meusburger, P. (2018) 'Knowledge Environments at Universities: Some Theoretical and Methodological Considerations', in P. Meusburger, M. Heffernan and L. Suarsana (Eds.), op. cit.

Meusburger, P., Heffernan, M. and Suarsana, L. (Eds.) (2018) *Geographies of the University*. Cham: Springer.

Meusburger, P., Welker, M. and Wunder, E. (Eds.) (2008) *Clashes of Knowledge: Orthodoxies and Heterodoxies in Science and Religion*. Cham: Springer.

Meyer, J.H.F. and Land, R. (2005) 'Threshold concepts and troublesome knowledge (2): epistemological considerations and a conceptual framework for teaching and learning', *Higher Education*, 49 (3), 373–388.

Mickey, S. (2016) *Whole Earth Thinking and Planetary Coexistence: Ecological Wisdom at the Intersection of Religion, Ecology and Philosophy*. London and New York: Routledge.

Mickey, S., Kelly, S. and Robbert, A. (Eds.) (2017) *The Variety of Integral Ecologies: Nature, Culture, and Knowledge in the Planetary Era*. New York: State University of New York.

Middlehurst, R. (2001) 'University Challenges: Borderless Higher Education, Today and Tomorrow', *Minerva*, 39 (1), 3–26. https://doi.org/10.1023/A:1010343517872

Mill, J. S. (1964) *Utilitarianism*. London: Collins & Fontana.

Mill, J. S. (1969/1859) *The Six Great Humanistic Essays of John Stuart Mill*. New York: Washington Square. Chapters: 'On Liberty', 127–242; 'Inaugural Address at St. Andrews', 311–362.

Miller, S. (2012) *The Moral Foundations of Social Institutions: A Philosophical Study*. New York and Cambridge: University of Cambridge.

Mills, J. (Ed.) (1994) *A Pedagogy of Becoming*. Amsterdam and New York: Rodopi.

Minogue, K. R. (1973) *The Concept of a University*. London: Weidenfeld and Nicolson.

Moberly, Sir W. (1949) *The Crisis in the University*. London: SCM.

Molesworth, M., Scullion, R. and Nixon, E. (Eds.) (2011) *The Marketisation of Higher Education and the Student as Consumer*. London and New York: Routledge.

Moog, S. and Stones, R. (Eds.) (2009) *Nature, Social Relations and Human Needs: Essays in Honour of Ted Benton*. Basingstoke and New York: Palgrave Macmillan.

Morgan, C. E. (1992) 'Women, work and consciousness in the mid-nineteenth English cotton industry', *Social History*, 17 (1), 23–41. https://doi.org/10.1080/03071029208567821

Morton, A. (2014) *Bounded Thinking: Intellectual Virtues for Limited Agents*. Oxford: Oxford University.

Morton, T. (2013) *Hyperobjects: Philosophy and Ecology after the End of the World*. Minneapolis and London: University of Minnesota.

Mosco, V. (2017) *Becoming Digital: Towards a Post-Internet Society*. Bingley: Emerald.

Münch, R. (2020) *Academic Capitalism: Universities in the Global Struggle for Excellence*. London: Routledge.

Murphy, P. (2018) 'The Platform University: The Destruction and Resurrection of Universities in the Auto-Industrial Age', in R. Barnett and M. A. Peters (Eds.), op. cit.

Murphy, P., Peters, M. A. and Marginson, S. (2010) *Imagination: Three Models of Imagination in the Age of the Knowledge Economy*. New York: Peter Lang.

Naess, A. (2012) 'The Deep Ecological Movement: Some Philosophical Aspects', in R. Bhaskar, et al. (Eds.), op. cit.

Nagel, J. (2014) *Knowledge: A Very Short Introduction*. Oxford: Oxford University.
Neary, M. (2014) 'The University and the City: Social Science Centre, Lincoln – Forming the Urban Revolution', in P. Temple (Ed.), op. cit.
Neave, G. (1998) 'The Evaluative State Reconsidered', *European Journal of Education*, 33 (3) 1 265–284. *JSTOR*, www.jstor.org/stable/1503583. Accessed 2 January 2021.
Nelson, E. S. (2011) 'Revisiting the Dialectic of Environment: Nature as Ideology and Ethics in Adorno and the Frankfurt School', *Telos*, 155, 105–126. https://doi.org/10.3817/011155105
Newman, J. H. (1976/1873) *The Idea of a University*. Oxford: Clarendon.
Nial, T. (2018) 'The Ontology of Motion', *Qui Parle*, 27 (1) 47–76. https://doi.org/10.1215/10418385-4382983
Nial, T. (2019) *Being and Motion*. New York: Oxford University.
Niblett, W. R. (1974) *Universities between Two Worlds*. London: University of London.
Nikolaidis, A. C. (2021) 'A Third Conception of Epistemic Justice', *Studies in Philosophy and Education*, 40, 381–398. https://doi.org/10.1007/s11217-021-09760-1
Nicolescu, B. (2014) *From Modernity to Cosmodernity: Science, Culture and Spirituality*. Albany: State University of New York.
Nicolescu, B. (2016) *The Hidden Third*. New York: Quantum Prose.
Nietzsche, F. (1968) *The Will to Power*. New York: Vintage.
Nietzsche, F. (1969) *Thus Spake Zarathustra*. London: Penguin.
Nietzsche, F. (1988) *Beyond Good and Evil*. London: Penguin.
Nietzsche, F. (2003) *Twilight of the Idols* and *The Anti-Christ*. London: Penguin.
Nietzsche, F. (2008) *The Birth of Tragedy*. Oxford and New York: Oxford University.
Nixon, J. (2008) *Towards the Virtuous University: The Moral Bases of Academic Practice*. New York and London: Routledge.
Nixon, J. (2011) *Higher Education and the Public Good: Imagining the University*. New York and London: Routledge.
Nixon, J. (2012a) *Interpretative Pedagogies for Higher Education: Arendt, Berger, Said, Nussbaum and Their Legacies*. London and New York: Routledge.
Nixon, J. (2012b) 'Universities and the Common Good', in R. Barnett (Ed.), op. cit.
Nixon, J. (2018) 'Universities as Civic Spaces: In the Footsteps of Arendt and Jaspers', in R. Barnett and M. A. Peters (Eds.), op. cit.
Nixon, J. (2019) 'Taking Responsibility: Truth, Trust, and Justice', in P. Gibbs, J. Jameson and A. Elwick (Eds.), op. cit.
Noddings, N. (2003) A Feminine Approach to Ethics and Moral Education. 2nd Ed. Berkeley and London: University of California.
Nørgård, R. and Bengtsen, S. E. (2018a) 'Academic Citizenship beyond the Campus: A Call for the Placeful University', in R. Barnett and M. A. Peters (Eds.), op. cit.
Nørgård, R. and Bengtsen, S. S. E. (2018b) 'The Worldhood University: Design Signatures & Guild Thinking', in S. S. E. Bengtsen and R. Barnett (Eds.), op. cit.
Nørgård, R. T. and Aaen, J. (2019) 'A University for the Body: On the Corporeal Being of Academic Existence', *Philosophy and Theory in Higher Education*, 1 (3) 178–199.
Nørgård, R. T., Toft-Nielsen, C. and Whitton, N. (2017) 'Playful Learning in Higher Education: Developing a Signature Pedagogy', *International Journal of Play*, 6 (3) 272–282. https://doi.org/10.1080/21594937.2017.1382997
Novikoff, A. J. (2013) *The Medieval Culture of Disputation: Pedagogy, Practice, and Performance*. Philadelphia: University of Pennsylvania.
Nowotny, H. (1996) *Time: The Modern and Postmodern Experience*. Cambridge: Polity.
Nowotny, H., Scott, P. and Gibbons, M. (2001) *Re-Thinking Science: Knowledge and the Public in an Age of Uncertainty*. Cambridge: Polity.

Nowotny, H., Scott, P. and Gibbons, M. (2003) 'Mode 2 Revisited: The New Production of Knowledge', *Minerva*, 41, 179–194.

Nussbaum, M. (1997) *Cultivating Humanity: A Classical Defense of Reform in Liberal Education*. Cambridge, MA and London: Harvard University.

Nussbaum, M. (2010) *Not for Profit: Why Democracy Needs the Humanities*. Princeton, NJ and Oxford: Princeton University.

Nussbaum, M. (2011) *Creating Capabilities: The Human Development Approach*. Cambridge, MA and London: Harvard University.

Nussbaum, M. (2018) 'Education for Citizenship in an Era of Global Communication', in A. Stoller and E. Kramer (Eds.), op. cit.

Nyawasha, T. S. (2020) '"I am of Popper", "I am of Asante": The Polemics of Scholarship in South Africa', *Studies in Philosophy and Education*, 39, 415–428. https://doi.org/10.1007/s11217-019-09688-7

Nybom, T. (2018) 'European Universities: Another Somewhat Lamenting – Yet Basically Hopeful – Account', in R. Barnett and M. A. Peters (Eds.), op. cit.

Oakeshott, M. (1989) *The Voice of Liberal Learning*. Ed. Timothy Fuller. New Haven, CT: Yale University.

O'Neill, M. (2019) 'Power, Predistribution, and Social Justice', *Philosophy*, 95 (1) 3–91. https://doi.org/10.1017/S0031819119000482

O'Neill, O. (2002) *A Question of Trust*. (The BBC Reith Lectures 2002) Cambridge: Cambridge University.

Ortega y Gasset, J. (1946) *Mission of the University*. London: Kegan Paul, Trench, Trübner.

Ossa-Richardson, A. (2014) 'The Idea of a University and Its Concrete Form', in P. Temple (Ed.), op. cit.

Östling, J. (2018) *Humboldt and the Modern German University: An Intellectual History*. Lund: Lund University.

Ovenden, R. (2020) *Burning the Books: A History of Knowledge Under Attack*. London: John Murray.

Parfit, D. (1987) *Reasons and Persons*. Oxford: Oxford University.

Passmore, J. (1980) *The Philosophy of Teaching*. London: Duckworth.

Paul, R. (1981) 'Teaching Critical Thinking in the "Strong" Sense: A Focus on Self-deception Worldviews, and a Dialectical Mode of Analysis', *Informal Logic*, 4 (2) 2–7.

Pelletier, C. (2012) 'No Time or Place for Universal Teaching: The Ignorant Schoolmaster and Contemporary Work on Pedagogy', in J.-P. Deranty and A. Ross (Eds.) *Jacques Rancière and the Contemporary Scene: The Philosophy of Radical Equality*. London and New York: Continuum, pp. 99–115.

Peters, M. A. (2011a) 'The Last Post? Post-Postmodernism and the Linguistic U-Turn in Educational Theory', in M. A. Peters (Ed.) *The Last Book of Postmodernism*. New York: Peter Lang, pp. 207–219.

Peters, M. A. (2011b) 'Algorithmic Capitalism and Educational Futures', in M. A. Peters and E. Bulut (Eds.), op. cit.

Peters, M. A. (2013) *Education, Science and Knowledge Capitalism: Creativity and the Promise of Openness*. New York: Peter Lang.

Peters, M. A. (2015) 'The University in the Epoch of Digital Reason: Fast Knowledge in the Circuits of Cybernetic Capitalism', *Analysis and Metaphysics*, 14, 35–58.

Peters, M. A. (2018) 'Renewing the Idea of the University', in R. Barnett and M. A. Peters (Eds.), op. cit.

Peters, M. A. and Barnett, R. (Eds.) (2018) *The Idea of the University: A Reader*. Vol. 1. New York: Peter Lang.

Peters, M. A., Besley, T., Jandric, P. and Zhu, X. (Eds.) (2020) *Knowledge Socialism: The Rise of Peer Production: Collegiality, Collaboration and Collective Intelligence*. Singapore: Springer.
Peters, M. A. and Bulut, E. (Eds.) (2011) *Cognitive Capitalism, Education and Digital Labour*. New York: Peter Lang.
Peters, M. A., Gietzen, G. and Ondercin, D. J. (2012a) 'Knowledge Socialism: Intellectual Commons and Openness in the University', in R. Barnett (Ed.), op. cit.
Peters, M. A. and Jandric, P. (2018a) *The Digital University: A Dialogue and a Manifesto*. New York: Peter Lang.
Peters, M. A. and Jandric, P. (2018b) Peer Production and Collective Intelligence as the Basis for the Public Digital University', *Educational Philosophy and Theory*, 50 (13) 1271–1284.
Peters, M. A. and Jandric, P. (2019) 'Posthumanism, Open Ontologies and Bio-Digital Becoming: Response to Luciano Floridi's Onlife Manifesto', *Educational Philosophy and Theory*, 51 (10) 971–980.
Peters, M. A., Liu, T-C. and Ondercin, D. J. (2012b) *The Pedagogy of the Open Society: Knowledge and the Governance of Higher Education*. Rotterdam: Sense.
Peters, R. S. (1970) *Ethics and Education*. London: George Allen & Unwin.
Philips Griffiths, A. (1965) 'A Deduction of Universities', in R. D. Archambault (Ed.) *Philosophical Analysis and Education*. London and New York: Routledge and Kegan Paul, pp. 187–207.
Piaget, J. (1972) *Psychology and Epistemology: Towards a Theory of Knowledge*. London: Penguin.
Plumb, J. H. (Ed.) (1964) *Crisis in the Humanities*. London: Penguin.
Plumwood, V. (2002) *Environmental Culture: The Ecological Crisis of Reason*. London and New York: Routledge.
Pogge, T. (2011) 'A Critique of the Capability Approach', in H. Brighouse and I. Robeyns (Eds.), op. cit.
Polanyi, M. (1966) *The Tacit Dimension*. New York: Doubleday.
Polanyi, M. (1978/1958) *Personal Knowledge: Towards a Post-Critical Philosophy*. London: Routledge and Kegan Paul.
Popper, K. (1975) *Objective Knowledge: An Evolutionary Approach*. Oxford: Clarendon Press.
Posner, R. A. (Ed.) (2003) *Public Intellectuals: A Study of Decline*. Cambridge, MA and London: Harvard University.
Pusser, B. (2012) 'Power and Authority in the Creation of a Public Sphere through Higher Education', in B. Pusser, et al. (Eds.), op. cit.
Pusser, B., Kempner, K., Marginson, S. and Ordorika, I. (Eds.) (2012) *Universities and the Public Sphere: Knowledge Creation and State Building in the Era of Globalization*. New York and London: Routledge.
Quijano, A. (2000) 'Coloniality of Power, Eurocentrism, and Latin America', *Nepantia: Views from the South*, 1 (3) 533–580.
Rancière, J. (1991) *The Ignorant Schoolmaster*. K. Ross, trans. Stanford, CA: Stanford University.
Rand, R. (Ed.) (1992) *Logomachia: The Conflict of the Faculties*. Lincoln and London: University of Nebraska.
Rawls, J. (1958) 'Justice as Fairness', *The Philosophical Review*, 67 (2) 164–194.
Rawls, J. (1989/1971) *A Theory of Justice*. Oxford: Oxford University.
Readings, B. (1997) *The University in Ruins*. Cambridge, MA and London: Harvard University.

Redding, G. (2019a) 'Criticality, Academic Autonomy, and Societal Progress', in G. Redding, A. Drew and S. Crump (Eds.), op. cit.
Redding, G. (2019b) 'Managing a University in Turbulent Times', in G. Redding, A. Drew and S. Crump (Eds.), op. cit.
Redding, G., Drew, A. and Crump, S. (Eds.) (2019) *The Oxford Handbook of Higher Education Systems and University Management.* Oxford: Oxford University Press.
Reeves, M. (1988) *The Crisis in Higher Education: Competence, Delight and the Common Good.* Stony Stratford and Philadelphia, PA: SRHE and Open University Press.
Rhode, D. L. (2006) In *Pursuit of Knowledge: Scholars, Status and Academic Culture.* Stanford, CA: Stanford University.
Rhoten, D. and Calhoun, C. (Eds.) (2011) *Knowledge Matters: The Public Mission of the Research University.* New York and Chichester: Columbia University.
Ricoeur, P. (1990) *Time and Narrative.* Volume 1. Chicago, IL and London: University of Chicago.
Rider, S. (2018) 'Truth, Democracy and the Mission of the University', in S. S. E. Bengtsen and R. Barnett (Eds.) *The Thinking University.* Cham: Springer, pp. 15–29.
Rider, S., Peters, M. A., Hyvönen, M. and Besley, T. (Eds.) (2020), *World Class Universities: A Contested Concept.* Singapore: Springer.
Ringer, F. K. (1990/1969) *The Decline of the German Mandarins: The German Academic Community, 1890–1933.* Hanover and London: University Press of New England.
Ripatti-Torniainen, L. (2018) 'Becoming (a) Public: What the Concept of Public Reveals about a Programmatic Public Pedagogy at the University', *Higher Education*, 75 (6) 1015–1029. https://doi.org/10.1007/s10734-017-0182-5
Robbins, L. (1963) *Higher Education.* (Report of a Committee of Inquiry presented to the UK Parliament.) Cmnd. 2154. London: HMSO.
Robins, K. and Webster, F. (Eds.) (2002) *The Virtual University: Knowledge, Markets, and Management.* Oxford: Oxford University.
Robinson, E. (1968) *The New Polytechnics.* London: Penguin.
Robinson, S. (2005) Values, Spirituality and Higher Education', in S. Robinson and C. Katulushi (Eds.) *Values in Higher Education.* St Bride's Major: Aureus and University of Leeds, pp. 189–215.
Robinson, S. (2019) 'University, Integrity and Responsibility', in P. Gibbs, J. Jameson and A. Elwick (Eds.), op. cit.
Rolfe, G. (2013) *The University in Dissent: Scholarship in the Corporate University.* London and New York: Routledge and the Society for Research into Higher Education.
Rorty, R. (1980) *Philosophy and the Mirror of Nature.* Oxford: Blackwell.
Rorty, R. (1999) *Philosophy and Social Hope.* London: Penguin.
Rosen, M. (1996) *On Voluntary Servitude: False Consciousness and the Theory of Ideology.* Cambridge: Polity.
Rothblatt, S. (1997) *The Modern University and its Discontents: The fate of Newman's legacy in Britain and America.* Cambridge: University of Cambridge.
Rothblatt, S. and Wittrock, B. (Eds.) (1993) *The European and American University since 1980: Historical and Sociological Essays.* Cambridge: Cambridge University.
Rouse, J. (1987) *Knowledge and Power: Towards a Political Philosophy of Science.* New York: Cornell University.
Rowland, S. (2000) *The Enquiring University Tutor.* Buckingham and Philadelphia, PA: Open University Press/ SRHE.
Rowland, S. (2006) *The Enquiring University: Compliance and Contestation in Higher Education.* Maidenhead: McGraw-Hill/ SRHE.
Russell, B. (1967/1912) *The Problems of Philosophy.* London: Oxford University Press.
Russell, C. (1993) *Academic Freedom.* London and New York: Routledge.

Ruuska, T., Heikkurinen, P. and Wilén, K. (2020) 'Domination, Power, Supremacy: Confronting Anthropolitics with Ecological Realism', *Sustainability*, 12 (7) 2617. https://doi.org/10.3390/su12072617
Ryan, A. and Cotton, D. (2013) 'Times of Change: Shifting Pedagogy and Curricula for Future Sustainability', in S. Sterling, L. Maxey and H. Luna (Eds.), op. cit.
Sahin, A. (2019) 'Islamic and Western Liberal Secular Values of Higher Education: *Convergence or Divergence?*', in P. Gibbs, J. Jameson and A. Elwick (Eds.), op. cit.
Salter, B. and Tapper, T. (1994) *The State and Higher Education*. Ilford: Woburn.
Sandel, M. (2020) *The Tyranny of Merit: What's become of the Common Good?* New York: Farrar, Straus and Giroux.
Satre, J. P. (2004/1940) *The Imaginary*. London and New York: Routledge.
Savin-Baden, M. (2003) *Facilitating Problem-Based Learning: Illuminating Perspectives*. Maidenhead: McGraw-Hill/ SRHE.
Savin-Baden, M. (2015) *Rethinking Learning in an Age of Digital Fluency: Is Being Digitally Tethered a New Learning Nexus?* London and New York: Routledge.
Schatzki, T. R. (2002) *The Site of the Social: A Philosophical Account of the Constitution of Social Like and Change*. University Park: The Pennsylvania State University.
Schatzki, T. R. (2008/1996) *Social Practices: A Wittgensteinian Approach to Human Activity and the Social*. Cambridge and New York: Cambridge University.
Schatzki, T. R. (2012) 'A Primer on Practices: Theory and Research', in J. Higgs, et al. (Eds.) *Practice-Based Education: Perspectives and Strategies*. Rotterdam: Sense, pp. 13–26.
Schatzki, T. R., Knorr Cetina, K. and von Savigny, E. (Eds.) (2001) *The Practice Turn in Contemporary Theory*. London and New York: Routledge.
Schön, D. (1987) *Educating the Reflective Practitioner*. San Francisco, CA and Oxford: Jossey-Bass.
Schopenhauer, A. (1997) *The World as Will and Idea*. London: Dent/ Everyman.
Schopenhauer, A. (2004) *Essays and Aphorisms*. London: Penguin.
Scott, D. (2019) 'Virtues and Dispositions as Learning Theory in Universities', in P. Gibbs, J. Jameson and A. Elwick (Eds.), op. cit.
Scott, P. (1984) *The Crisis in the University*. London and Sydney: Croom Helm.
Scott-Bauman, A. (2009) *Ricoeur and the Hermeneutics of Suspicion*. London and New York: Continuum.
Scruton, R. (2016/1998) *Modern Culture*. London and New York: Bloomsbury.
Searle, J. (1972) *The Campus War: A Sympathetic Look at the University in Agony*. London: Pelican.
Selingo, J. J. (2017). *The Networked University: Building Alliances for Innovation in Higher Education*. London: Pearson. https://www.pearson.com/content/dam/one-dot-com/one-dot-com/global/Files/about-pearson/innovation/the-networked-university/Pearson_The_Networked_University_v22-1_WEB.pdf
Sen, A. (2010) *The Idea of Justice*. London: Penguin.
Sen, A. (2011) 'The Place of Capability in a Theory of Justice', in H. Brighouse and I. Robeyns (Eds.), op. cit.
Sheldrake, P. (2012) *Spirituality: A Very Short Introduction*. Oxford: Oxford University.
Shipway, B. (2011) *A Critical Realist Perspective of Education*. London and New York: Routledge.
Shor, I. (1992) *Empowering Education: Critical Teaching for Social Change*. Chicago, IL: University of Chicago.
Shpeizer, R. (2018) 'Teaching Critical Thinking as a Vehicle for Personal and Social Transformation', *Research in Education*, 100 (1) 32–49. https://doi.org/10.1177/0034523718762176

Shumar, W. and Robinson, S. (2018) 'Universities as Societal Value Drivers: Entrepreneurial practices for a Better Future', in S. S. E. Bengtsen and R. Barnett (Eds.), *The Thinking University*. Cham: Springer.

Siegel, H. (1990) *Educating Reason: Rationality, Critical Thinking and Education*. New York and London: Routledge.

Siegel, H. (1997) *Rationality Redeemed: Further Dialogues on an Educational Ideal*. New York and London: Routledge.

Singh, S., Bhaskar, R. and Hartwig, M. (2020) *Reality and its Depths: A Conversation between Savita Singh and Roy Bhaskar*. Singapore: Springer.

Slaughter, S. and Rhoades, G. (2009) *Academic Capitalism and the New Economy: Markets, State, and Higher Education*. Baltimore: Johns Hopkins.

Sloterdijk, P. (2009) *God's Zeal: The Battle of the Three Monotheisms*. Cambridge: Polity.

Small, H. (Ed.) (2002) *The Public Intellectual*. Oxford: Blackwell.

Small, H. (2013) *The Value of the Humanities*. Oxford: Oxford University.

Snow, C. P. (1978/1959) *The Two Cultures and a Second Look*. Cambridge: Cambridge University.

Snowden, M. (2017) 'Heutagogy in an Emerging Curriculum', in J. P. Halsall and M. Snowden (Eds.) *The Pedagogy of the Social Sciences Curriculum*. Cham: Springer, pp. 25–38.

Solbrekke, T. D. and Sugrue, C. (Eds.) (2020) *Leading Higher Education as and for Public Good*. London and New York: Routledge.

Sporn, B. (1996) 'Managing University Culture: An Analysis of the Relationship between Institutional Culture and Management Approaches', *Higher Education*, 32, 41–61.

Staley, D. J. (2019) *Alternative Universities: Speculative Design for Innovation in Higher Education*. Baltimore, MA: Johns Hopkins University.

Standaert, N. (2012) 'Towards a Networked University', in R. Barnett (Ed.), op. cit.

Stein, S. (2018) 'Beyond Higher Education as We Know It: Gesturing towards Decolonial Horizons of Possibility', *Studies in Philosophy and Education*, 38, 143–61. https://doi.org/10.1007/s11217-018-9622-7

Stein, S. (2020) '"Truth before Reconciliation": The Difficulties of Transforming Higher Education in Settler Colonial Contexts', *Higher Education Research and Development*, 39 (1) 156–170. https://doi.org/10.1080/07294360.2019.1666255

Sterling, S., Maxey, L. and Luna, H. (Eds.) (2013) *The Sustainable University: Progress and prospects*. London and New York: Routledge.

Stiegler, B. (2014a) *The Re-Enchantment of the World: The Value of Spirit against Industrial Populism*. London and New York: Bloomsbury.

Stiegler, B. (2014b) *For a New Critique of Political Economy*. Cambridge and Malden, MA: Polity.

Stiegler, B. (2015) *States of Shock: Stupidity and Knowledge in the 21st Century*. Cambridge and Malden, MA: Polity.

Stoller, A. and Kramer, E. (Eds.) (2018) *Contemporary Philosophical Proposals for the University: Toward a Philosophy of Higher Education*. Cham: Palgrave Macmillan.

Stratford, R. (2018) 'Higher Education and the Anthropocene – Towards an ecological approach to higher education policy in New Zealand', PhD thesis, University of Waikato, New Zealand.

Stratford, R. and Wals, A. (2020) 'In Search of Healthy Policy Ecologies for Education in Relation to Sustainability: Beyond Evidence-Based Policy and Post-Truth Policies', *Policy Futures in Education*, 18 (8) 976–994. https://doi.org/10.1177/1478210320906656

Straume, I. S. and Baruchello, G. (Eds.) (2013) *Creation, Rationality and Autonomy: Essays on Cornelius Castoriadis*. Copenhagen: NSU & Nordiskt Sommaruniversitet.
Szadkowski, K. (2019) 'The Common in Higher Education: A Conceptual Approach', *Higher Education*, 78, 241–255.
Szadkowski, K. and Krzeski, J. (2020) 'Political Ontologies of the Future University: Individual, Public, Common', *Philosophy and Theory in Higher Education*, 1 (3) 29–50.
Taylor, C. (1992) *Sources of the Self: The Making of the Modern Identity*. Cambridge: University of Cambridge.
Taylor, C. (2007) *Modern Social Imaginaries*. Durham, NC and London: Duke University.
Taylor, D. (1968) *The Godless Students of Gower Street*. London: University College London Union.
Temple, P. (Ed.) (2014) *The Physical University: Contours of Space and Place in Higher Education*. London and New York: Routledge.
Temple, P. (2018) 'Space, Place and Institutional Effectiveness in Higher Education', *Policy Reviews in Higher Education*, 2 (2) 133–150.
Temple, P. (2021) 'The University Couloir: exploring physical and intellectual connectivity', *Higher Education Policy*. https://doi.org/10.1057/s41307-021-00253-x
Terashima, N. (2001) 'The Definition of Hyperreality', in J. Tiffin, J. and N. Terashima (Eds.) *Hyperreality: Paradigm for the Third Millennium*. London and New York: Routledge, pp. 4–24.
Tesar, M., Peters, M. and Jackson, L. (2021) 'The University as an Ethical Academy?', *Educational Philosophy and Theory*, 53 (5) 419–425. https://doi.org/10.1080/00131857.2021.1884977
Thrift, N. (2008) *Non-Representational Theory: Space, Politics, Affect*. London and New York: Routledge.
Toulmin, S. (2001) *Return to Reason*. Cambridge, MA and London: Harvard University.
Tribe, J. (2002) 'The Philosophic Practitioner', *Annals of Tourism Research*, 29 (2) 338–357.
Trow, M. (1970) 'Reflections on the Transition from Mass to Elite Higher Education' *Daedalus* 99 (1) 1–42.
Tuana, N. (2017) 'Feminist Epistemology: The Subject of Knowledge', in I. J. Kidd, J. Medina, and G. Pohlhaus (Jr.) (Eds.), op. cit.
Ullman-Margalit, E. (Ed.) (2000) *Reasoning Practically*. New York: Oxford University.
Ulmer, J. B. (2019) 'The Anthropocene Is a Question, Not a Strategic Plan', *Philosophy and Theory in Higher Education*, 1 (1) 65–84.
Valimaa, J. (2018) 'The Nordic Idea of University', in R. Barnett and M. A. Peters (Eds.), op. cit.
Valimaa, J. and Ylijoki, O-H (Eds.) (2008) *Cultural Perspectives on Higher Education*. Cham: Springer.
Vattimo, G. (2011) *A Farewell to Truth*. New York and Chichester: Columbia University.
Van Rooijen, M. (2019) 'Leading in Higher Education', in G. Redding, A. Drew and S. Crump (Eds.), op. cit.
van Wyk, R. and Higgs, P. (2012) 'The Future of University Research in Africa', in R. Barnett (Ed.), op. cit.
Viberg, O., Hattaka, M., Balter, O. and Mayroudi, A. (2018) 'The Current Landscape of Learning Analytics in Higher Education', *Computers in Human Behavior*, 89, 98–110.
Virilio, P. (2005) *Negative Horizon: An Essay in Dromoscopy*. London and New York: Continuum.
Virilio, P. (2010) *The University of Disaster*. Cambridge and Malden, MA: Polity.
Volkmer, I. (2014) *The Global Sphere: Public Communication in the Age of Reflective Interdependence*. Cambridge and Malden, MA: Polity.

Vostal, F. (2016) *Accelerating Academia: The Changing Structure of Academic Time*. Basingstoke: Palgrave Macmillan.

Waghid, Y. and Davids, N. (2018) 'Towards an African University in Becoming: Positive Risk, Hope and Imagination', in R. Barnett and M. A. Peters (Eds.), op. cit.

Waghid, Y. and Davids, N. (2020) *The Thinking University Expanded: On Profanation, Play and Education*. London and New York: Routledge.

Walker, M. (2006) *Higher Education Pedagogies: A Capabilities Approach*. Maidenhead: McGraw-Hill/ SRHE.

Walker, M. and Martinez-Vargas, C. (2020) 'Epistemic Governance and the Colonial Epistemic Structure: Towards Epistemic Humility and Transformed South-North Relations', *Critical Studies in Education*. DOI: 10.1080/17508487.2020.1778052

Wals, E. J. (2015) *Beyond Unreasonable Doubt: Education and Learning for Socio-Ecological Sustainability in the Anthropocene*. Inaugural address, Wageningen University, 17 December. Wageningen: Wageningen University.

Wals, E. J. (2020) 'Sustainability-Oriented Ecologies of Learning: A Response to Systemic Global Dysfunction', in R. Barnett and N. Jackson (Eds.), op. cit.

Warren, K. (2010) *Ecofeminist Philosophy: A Western Perspective on What It Is and Why It Matters*. Lanham, MD: Rowman & Littlefield.

Watson, D., Hollister, R. M., Stroud, S. E. and Babcock, E. (Eds.) (2011) *The Engaged University: International Perspectives on Civic Engagement*. New York and London: Routledge.

Western, S. and Garcia, E-J. (2018) *Global Leadership Perspectives: Insights and Analysis*. London and Los Angeles, CA: Sage.

Whitchurch, C. (2012) *Reconstructing Identities in Higher Education: The Rise of 'Third Space' Professionals*. London and New York: Routledge and Society for Research into Higher Education.

White, J. (1997) 'Philosophy and the Aims of Higher Education', *Studies in Higher Education*, 22 (1). https://doi.org/10.1080/03075079712331381101

White, M. (2017) *Towards a Political Theory of the University: Public Reason, Democracy and Higher Education*. London and New York: Routledge.

Whitley, R. (2012) 'Transforming Universities: National Conditions of Their Varied Organisational Actorhood', *Minerva*, 50 (4) 493–510.

Wiberg, M. (2019) 'The Will to Know and the Radical Commitment to Knowledge in Higher Education', *Philosophy and Theory in Higher Education*, 1 (3) 105–130.

Williams, B. (2002) *Truth and Truthfulness: An Essay in Genealogy*. Princeton, NJ and Oxford: Princeton University.

Williams, R. (2003) *Silence and Honey Cakes: The Wisdom of the Desert*. Oxford: Lion Hudson.

Willinsky, J. (2011) 'Rethinking What Is Made Public in the University's Public Mission', in D. Rhoten and C. Calhoun (Eds.), op. cit.

Wittgenstein, L. (1978) *Philosophical Investigations*. Oxford: Blackwell.

Wittgenstein, L. (2003/1969) *On Certainty*. Malden, MA and Oxford: Blackwell.

Wittrock, B. (1993) 'The Modern University: The Three Transformations', in S. Rothblatt and B. Wittrock (Eds.), op. cit.

Wolff, R. P. (1997/1969) *The Ideal of the University*. New Brunswick and London: Transaction.

Wrenn, C. (2015) *Truth*. Cambridge and Malden, MA: Polity.

Wright, A. (2014) *Christianity and Critical Realism: Ambiguity, Truth and Theological Literacy*. London and New York: Routledge.

Wright, R. G. (2007) 'The Emergence of First Amendment Academic Freedom', *Nebraska Law Review*, 85 (3) 793–829.
Wright, S. and Shore, C. (2019) *Death of the Public University? Uncertain Futures for Higher Education in the Knowledge Economy*. New York and Oxford: Berghahn.
Wyatt, J. (1990) *Commitment to Higher Education*. Buckingham: Open University Press/Society for Research into Higher Education.
Wyatt, J. (1994) 'Maps of Knowledge: Do They Form an Atlas?', in R. Barnett (Ed.) *Academic Community: Discourse or Discord?* London: Jessica Kingsley, pp. 36–51.
Young, M. (2008) *Bringing Knowledge Back In: From Social Constructivism to Social Realism in the Sociology of Education*. London and New York: Routledge.
Young, M. D. (1958) *The Rise of the Meritocracy*. London: Pelican.
Young, R. (1992) 'The Idea of a Chrestomathic University', in R. Rand (Ed.), op. cit.
Žižek, S. (1997) *Tarrying with the Negative: Kant, Hegel and the Critique of Ideology*. Durham, NC: Duke University.
Žižek, S. (1999/1989) *The Sublime Object of Ideology*. London and New York: Verso.
Žižek, S. (2001) *The Fragile Absolute – or, Why Is the Christian Legacy Worth Fighting for?* London and New York: Verso.
Žižek, S. (2003) *The Puppet and the Dwarf: The Perverse Core of Christianity*. Cambridge, MA and London: MIT.
Žižek, S. (2009) *The Parallax View*. Cambridge, MA: MIT.
Žižek, S. (2013) *Less than Nothing: Hegel and the Shadow of Dialectical Materialism*. London and New York: Verso.
Zuboff, S. (2019) *The Age of Surveillance Capitalism: The Fight for a Human Future at the New Frontier of Power*. London: Profile.
Zweig, F. (1963) *The Student in an Age of Anxiety*. Heinemann: London.

Magazine articles

Basken, P. (2019) 'No Strings Attached?', *Times Higher Education*, 3 January: 33–37.
Bothwell, E. (2020) 'Distance Shifts Perceptions of Strong Fields: At Home and Abroad, Views of Institutions' Subject Strengths Vary', *Times Higher Education*, 12 November: 12.
Chasi, S. (2020) 'Decolonisation – A Chance to Reimagine North-South Partnerships'. *University World News*, 27 August 2020. https://www.universityworldnews.com/post.php?story=20200826111105105
DeLaquil, T. (2020) 'Neo-nationalism is a Threat to Academic Cooperation', *University World News*, 4 July. https://www.universityworldnews.com/post.php?story=20200630104920899
Flier, J. (2018) 'University leaders cannot fulfil the role of public intellectual', *Times Higher Education*, 22 November, 27. https://www.timeshighereducation.com/opinion/university-leaders-cannot-be-public-intellectuals
Fredua-Kwarteng, E. (2020) 'What is China's Higher Education Agenda in Africa?', https://www.universityworldnews.com/post.php?story=20201120110117700
Galea, S. (2019) 'University leaders must be free to air challenging views', *Times Higher Education*, 6 June, 29. https://www.timeshighereducation.com/opinion/university-leaders-must-be-free-air-views-challenge-their-communities
Hommel, U. and Stévenin, B. (2020) 'Managing Risk to HE Institutions in an Uncertain World', *University World News*. https://www.universityworldnews.com/post.php?story=20200217101820203

Ignatieff, M. (2018) 'The Role of Universities in an Era of Authoritarianism'. *University World News*. https://www.universityworldnews.com/post.php?story=20180413093717351

Jump, P. (2020) 'Location, Location, Location' (the THE power of place survey), *Times Higher Education*. https://www.timeshighereducation.com/features/times-higher-educations-power-place-survey

Maslen, G. (2020) 'Murdoch University Abandons Action to Silence Academic'. *University World News*, 16 June. https://www.universityworldnews.com/post.php?story=20200616093754231

Mathews, D. (2014) 'Thomas Doherty to Face Insubordination in Tribunal'. *Times Higher Education*. https://www.timeshighereducation.com/news/thomas-docherty-to-face-insubordination-charge-in-tribunal/2014711.article

Mathews, D. (2017) 'Fuzzy Logic' (on critical thinking), *Times Higher Education*, 3 August, 33–37. https://www.timeshighereducation.com/features/do-critical-thinking-skills-give-graduates-the-edge

O'Malley, B. (2019a) 'Hyper-Authorship Skews Science Literature Impact Analysis', *University World News*, 14 December. https://www.universityworldnews.com/post.php?story=20191214075947159

O'Malley, B. (2019b) '32 Deaths in Hundreds of Violent Attacks on HE Globally', *University World News*, 22 November. https://www.universityworldnews.com/post.php?story=20191122065228133

Reisz, M. (2018) 'A Bit on the Side', *Times Higher Education*, 18 January 2018, 45–47.

Stolen, S. and Gornitzka, A. (2019) 'The Bologna Process Needs to Go Back to Basics', *University World News*, 6 July. https://www.universityworldnews.com/post.php?story=20190705111026608

Wilson, A. and Watson, C. (2017) Contribution to 'Will Learning Analytics Empower or Entrap Students and Academics?' https://www.timeshighereducation.com/features/will-learning-analytics-empower-or-entrap-students-and-academics

Young-Powell, A. (2017) 'How Serious is Essay Plagiarism?', *The Guardian*, 30 December. https://www.theguardian.com/education/2017/dec/30/is-plagiarism-really-a-growing-problem-in-universities

Žižek, S. (2020) 'Hegel on the Future, Hegel in the Future', *Philosophy Now*, 140, https://philosophynow.org/issues/140/Hegel_On_The_Future_Hegel_In_The_Future

Web-sites

Academic Freedom – University of Chicago: Report of the Committee on Freedom of Expression: https://provost.uchicago.edu/sites/default/files/documents/reports/FOECommitteeReport.pdf

Bonn declaration on Freedom of Scientific Research: https://www.bmbf.de/files/10_2_2_Bonn_Declaration_en_final.pdf

Character Development: https://www.jubileecentre.ac.uk/userfiles/jubileecentre/pdf/character-education/Character_Education_in_Universities_Final_Edit.pdf (accessed 14 August 2020)

Death of a Glacier: Jacinta Bowler. (2019) 'Iceland Just Held a Funeral for the First Glacier Killed by Climate Change', *Science Alert*. https://www.sciencealert.com/iceland-just-held-a-funeral-for-the-first-glacier-killed-by-climate-change

Free Universities – Michael Ignatieff in Conversation: https://www.bbc.co.uk/news/av/world-europe-43904662

Global Forum on Academic Freedom, Institutional Autonomy, and the Future of Democracy: https://academeblog.org/2019/07/07/declaration-of-the-global-forum-on-academic-freedom-institutional-autonomy-and-the-future-of-democracy/

Healey, M. (2013) *Linking Research and Teaching: A Selected Bibliography*. https://adminlb.imodules.com/s/1250/images/editor_documents/healey_linking_research_teaching.pdf?sessionid=8a4c2444-97ae-47a1-bfbb-61db5aef5da6&cc=1

Magna Charta Universitatum, 2020: http://www.magna-charta.org/magna-charta-universitatum/mcu-2020

Richard III – Discovery of His Bones and Demonstration of Findings: https://britishheritage.com/richard-iii/king-richard-iii-skeleton

STEM Research and China: https://www.studyinternational.com/news/china-stem-research/

The Clerk's Tale, General Prologue, Canterbury Tales: https://genius.com/Geoffrey-chaucer-the-canterbury-tales-general-prologue-annotated

The (KK) Knowing That One Knows Principle, *Internet Encyclopedia of Philosophy* (IEP): https://iep.utm.edu/kk-princ/#H1

'Theatre of Discovery', Interdisciplinary and Interactive Module, King's College London, Built around Concepts of Creativity and Complexity: https://vimeo.com/channels/kcl (accessed 30 December 2020)

Thieving Magpies (Allegedly): http://www.bbc.com/earth/story/20150408-the-truth-about-magpies

Sandel, M. (2018) The Public Philosopher: 'Should There Be Any Limits to Free Speech?': https://www.bbc.co.uk/programmes/p069dx6m

Van Driska, N. (2015) *Understanding Glaciers through Indigenous Cultures*: https://glacierhub.org/2015/11/04/cultural-significance-glaciers-ignored-modern-society/ (accessed 19 July 2020)

Women in Cotton Mills in Eighteenth Century England: https://coverstory2017.wordpress.com/2017/04/25/lancashire-cotton-mills/ (accessed 7 December 2020)

Reports

Civic Universities: *Truly Civic: Strengthening the Connection between Universities and Their Places*. Final Report of the UPP Foundation Civic University Commission. https://upp-foundation.org/wp-content/uploads/2019/02/Civic-University-Commission-Final-Report.pdf

Education in the Anthropocene: '*Learning to become with the World: Education for Future Survival*', UNESCO, 2020, Common Worlds Research Collective.

Hinchcliffe, T. (Ed.) (2020) *The Hidden Curriculum of Higher Education*. London: Advance HE.

Learning Analytics: JISC Reports: *Learning Analytics in Higher Education: A Review of UK and International Practice*. https://www.jisc.ac.uk/reports/learning-analytics-in-higher-education

Student Suicide among Higher Education Students, England and Wales: https://www.ons.gov.uk/peoplepopulationandcommunity/birthsdeathsandmarriages/deaths/articles/estimatingsuicideamonghighereducationstudentsenglandandwalesexperimentalstatistics/2018-06-25

University Engagement: Douglas, R. B., Grant, J. and Wells, J. (2020) *Advancing University Engagement: University Engagement and Global League Tables*. Nous Group: University of Chicago, King's College London, The University of Melbourne. https://www.kcl.ac.uk/policy-institute/assets/advancing-university-engagement.pdf

Index

Note: *Especially significant entries are* **emboldened**; *those associated with the work of particular scholars are placed in quotations; names are in italics, as are the few key works that are cited here.*

Aaen, J. 111, 139
Abbinnett, R. 175
Abbott, R. 195
Abelard 188
Abram, D. 97
'absence' 22, 32, 195, 202, 216, 219
academic autonomy *see* autonomy, institutional
academic freedom 1, 18, 40, **85–95**, 185
access (to higher education) 31, 225
action 139, 145, 149, 204; critical 149
admissions policy 232
Adorno, T. 6, 16, 18–19, 33, 51, 106, 186, 226
Africa 28, 98, 104
Agambem, G. 220
agency 116, 118, 135, 137, 150, 165, 178, 183; corporate 183–85, 187
Aguiar Pereira, E. M. 85–86
Ahenakew, C. 53, 229
air 175
Allen, G. 43
Al-Samarraie, H. 110
Althusser, L. 19, 221
Altorf, H. 201
Amsler, S 244
Anthropocene 234–244
anthropocentricism 98; epistemological 235
anthropology 124, 144
antinomies 33
'anything goes' 122
anxiety 113, 198
Aoun, J. E. 190, 198
archaeology 99, 215
Archer, M. 232
architecture 110, 190
Arendt, H. 56, 128, 149, 201, 203–05

Argentina 85
argument 182; truth as 57–58
Argyris, C. 180
Arndt, S. 97
Arnold, M. 77
art and design 48
Arthur, J. 207
Arvanitakis, J. 207
Ashenden, S. 236
Asia 98, 104
assemblages 5, 71, 128, 130, 149, 242
assessment, student 232
Assié-Lumumba, T. 28
Astley, J. 24, 167
astrology 56
audit 64, 103, 124, 160, 185, 192
authenticity 7, 45, 102, 143, 189, 198
authoritarian regimes 30
authority 110, 140
autonomy 18, 29, 80, 86, 111, 15; institutional 19, **86–88**, 93
autopoiesis 186
Auxier, R. 126
Azumah Dennis, C. 231

Bach, J. S. 71
Bachelard G. 41–42, 158, 188, 191, 198
Back, S. 118
Badiou, A. 9
Bahti, T. 3
Bakhurst, D. 96, 99
Bandura, A. 139
Baptista, B. V. 59
Barad, K. 50, 241
Barnett, R. 2, 4–6, 15–16, 22, 27, 29–30, 34, 36, 77, 82, 97, 105, 112–13, 117, 122,

129, 133, 143, 146, 149, 151, 162, 178, 180, 232, 237, 240, 243; *A Will to Learn* 113, 141; *The Idea of Higher Education* 2–3, 27
Bartelson, J. 221
Bartlett, P. F. 126
Basken, P. 38
Batchelor, D. 171
Beavis, A. 126, 243
Becher, T. 74, 82, 156
Beckett, D. 31
becoming 110–11, 129, 151, 179
being 111, 114, 124, **127–29**, 138, 140, 143–44, 150–51, 161, 189; *being-possible* 128; *see also* student, being a
belief, justified true 55
Bengtsen, S. E. E. 2, 16, 73, 97, 117, 139, 164
Benhabib, S. 204–05, 207
Bennett, J. 170
Bennett, T. 82
Benson, L. 63
Bergson, H. 35, 169
Berlin, I. 39, 44, 127
Berman, M. 38
Bernasconi, A. 28
Bernstein, B. 120
Berquist, W. H. 83
Berry, D. M. 198
Berubé, M. 85
Beyes, T. 182
Bhambra, G. K. 230
Bhaskar, R. 20–21, 24, 31–33, 36, 86, 91, 117–18, 126, 147, 167, 195, 219, 233, 237, 240, 243
bibliographies 102
biochemistry 190
Biesta, G. 109–10, 112, 137, 148, 204
Bildung 39, 64, 77, 80–82, 132, 135
Bilgrami, A. 85
Blake, N. 64
Bligh, B. 110
Bloom, A. 125
Boddington, A. 110
books 39, 55, 188, 198
Bou-Habib, P. 207, 225
Bourdieu, P. 66–67, 81–82, 87
Bourner, T. 215
Boutang, Y-M. 18, 31, 39, 65, 68
Bovill, C. 118
Bowen, W. M. 87
Boyer, E. 70
Boys, J. 110
Bozalek, V. 70, 232
Bradley, J. P. N. 175

Bradwell, P. 191
Brady, M. 43, 79, 137
Braidotti, R. 67, 127, 189
Brandom, R. 96–97
Brannmark, J. 180, 183
Brennan, J. 156
Briggs, A. 126
Brink, C. 162
Brubacher, J. S. 2
Buchanan, A. 45
business studies 113, 160
Butler, Jane 178
Butler, Judith 38, 88, 91, 105, 163, 221

cake 103
Calhoun, C. 63, 201, 206
Calvino, I. 155
capabilities 206
capital: cultural 83, 93; learning 112; reputational 184; *see also* epistemic
capitalism: 'academic' 68; 'algorithmic' 68; information 73; late 116, 149, 220; 'surveillance' 220; *see also* cognitive capitalism
care 41, 103, 135, 181, 217–18
Carlin, M. 87, 123
Carstens, D. 50
Castoriadis, C. 87, 148
cave 141
censorship 101–02
challengeability 134–35
Chamberlain, J. 117
Chankseliani, M. 216
character 137
Chase, G. W. 126
Chaucer, G. 69
chemistry 144
Chile 18
China 28, 49, 53, 65, 86, 229, 231, 238
Christianity 75, 167
citizenship 67, 72, 80–81, 125, 152, 203, 210; global 126, 207, 217
civic engagement 213
civic society 212
civic university 212
clarity 10
Clark, B. R. 156
closure 125
clouds 20–22, 25
Coate, K. 122, 129
Cochrane, A. 156–57
Code, L. 49, 98
'cognitive capitalism' 16, 18, 31, 33, 39, 65, 68, 151, 193, 209

Index   279

Cohen, E. 221
Cole, J. R. 85
Collini, S. 209
coloniality 16, 82, 104, 220, 229–30; epistemic 230–31
colonisation 231
commitment 140, 168
commons 210, 212
communication 42, **182–83**, 190, 206–07
community 105, 169, 183, 208, 217, 226; world 221
complexity 72, 111, 135, 141, 150, 178, 180, 217–18
computing science 236
concepts 6–8, 16, 19–20, **22**, 23–24, 29, 70, 134, 202, 216, 246
concern 73
conditions 7, 28–30, 55, 90–92
conditions of adequacy 6
conflict 34
connectivity 4, 8–9, 95, 100, 131–32, 135, 217, 237–38, 242
Connell, R. 230–31
consensus 37
constitution for universities 245–46
contestability 133–35, 139
context 89, 92, 105, **231–32**
contingency 38, 148
conversation 160
Coole, D. 167
corporate strategies 38
corruption 194
cosmopolitanism 195
Cotton, D. 127
courage 91, 103, 149, 151, 167, 196, 206
Cowden, S. 115
creativity 168, 174, 186, 196
crisis: ecological 4, 49, 98, 205, 237, 245
crisis of higher education 3–4
crisis of university 29
'criteria of adequacy' 22
critical action 143, **149**, 151
critical being 150–51
critical dialogue 40
critical intellectuals 143
critical interdisciplinarity 145
criticality 40, 116, **142–52**, **150–52**, 194, 216
critical orientation 144
critical powers 147
critical realism 20, 22, 24, 31–32, 36, 86, 117, 147, 167, 195, 237; *see also* Bhaskar
critical spirit 96
critical standards 19
critical theory 142, 228

critical thinking 21, 28, 142–52, 219
critical thought 151
critic of society 156
critique 18–19, 33, 128, 143, 145, **147–50**, 182, 220, 228; 'explanatory critique' 147; 'transformatory critique' 149
culture 39, 67, **74–84**, 104, 117, 125, 236, 242; absence of 76–77, 81; claiming 45; cognitive 237; common 75, 78; high 75; meta-culture 84; *see also* multiculturalism
culture of critical discourse 83
culture of constructive argument 83–84
cultures 49, 83, 98, 120, 132, 183; pedagogic 132; *see also* epistemic
culture wars 82, 183
curriculum 38, 55, 79–80, **120–30**, 230, 242; general 125–27; problem-based 130; modes of 124
curriculum-as-experienced 122
curriculum-as-realised 123
curriculum-as-text 122–23
Cutright, M. 178

Dall'Alba, G. 41, 52, 111, 139
danger 142, 152
darkness 112, 117, 139, 141
data 50, 195–97
Davids, N. 97, 179, 215
Davies, M. 143, 146, 149
Dawson, M. C. 229
debate 90, 205
decisionism 159
Decuypere, M. 192
Delanda, M. 20, 32, 71
Delanty, G. 195
Deleuze, G. 5, 7, 15, 35, 103, 127–28, 142, 156, 172, 179, 192, 201, 240
demarcation, axes of 51
democracy 19, 33, 185, 209–10, 239
depth 145, 147
Derrida, J. 7, 30, 67, 82, 91, 99, 114, 173, 217
Derycke, M. 112
Descartes, R. 82, 128, 156, 245
Descola, P. 222, 234
design 124, 181, 242
de Sousa Santos, B. 58, 104, **227–31**, 237, 239
'deterritorialisation' 156
dictators 30; *see also* authoritarian regimes
digital era 4, 16, 21, 48, 65, 69, 90, 100, 102, 105, 118, 156, 175, 180, 188–89, **193–98**, 203, 215, 220; *see also* internet; post-digital
Diogenes 195

disaster 197
disciplines 79, 81, 98, 103, 105, 110, 112–14, 126, 132, 136, 144, 160, 185, 226, 231, 242–43, 246
discomfort 159
disequilibrium, reasoned 131
disinterestedness 45
dispositions 91, 111, 113, **135–38**, 144, 146–47, 152, 208, 214
disputations 57, 185
dispute 57, 185
disruption 187, 193
dissent 182
Doherty, T. 3, 86
Doll, W. E. 123
Drake, T. A. 40
dystopia 244

Eagleton, T. 24, 74–75
earth 4, 34, 41, 43, 49, 53, 98, 132, 135, 170, 178, 187, 191, 196–97, 214, 221, 235, 237, 242, 244, 245–46; citizen of 207
Eco, U. 188–89, 198
Ecocene 242–44
ecological age 48, 100
ecological bearings 5
ecological feminism 239
ecological degradation 236
ecological leadership 187
ecological realm 239
ecological situation 72; *see also* crisis, ecological
ecological studies 242
ecological zones 239
ecologies 239, 241; learning 112
ecology 98, 162, 164, 186, 217, 228, 235, **237–39, 241**; deep 235; idea of 170, 237–39; study of 99; *see also* knowledge ecology
ecology of knowledges *see* knowledges, ecology of
ecology of others 222
ecology of recognition 239
ecology of spirit 175
ecology of things 234
economics 160
economy 132, 241–42; *see also* knowledge
ecophilosophy 240
ecosophy 235, 239, 243–44
ecosystems 72, 187, **239–42**
eco-world 239–40
education 96; as initiation 113; general 126–27; study of 48
educational processes 27, 30, 74, 78–79, 96, 110, 115, **119**, 121, 203, 213, 225, 245; *see also* practices, educational

Egypt 28
Eliot. T. S. 77
Elliott, R. 129
Ellis, R. A. 162
Elton, L. 110
emancipation 80
embodiment 114, 135; *see also* reason, embodied
emergence 23, 31, 38, 147, 150
emotions 99, 105
empathy 102
Empire 220–21
empiricism 105
employability 127–28
endorsement 151
energy 113–14, 167, 171–73, 176, 178, **186–87**, 195
engagement **212–222**, 245; civic 213
engineering 34, 48, 110, 122, 128–29, 160, 190, 215, 236
England 15, 28, 206; *see also* United Kingdom
Englund, T. 182, 185
Engwall, L. 32
enlightenment 81–82, 97, 112, 175, 235
enquiry 30
entanglement 194, 241
entrepreneurialism 22, 78, 86; intellectual entrepreneurialism 112
entropy 171, 186
environment 235, 239, 241
environmental sciences 242
ephemerality 156
epistemic borders 172
epistemic capital 93
epistemic communities 190, 195
epistemic cultures 31, 49, 100
epistemic hierarchies 196, 231
'epistemicide' 104, 212, 231
epistemic injustice *see* justice
epistemic landscapes 160
epistemic narrowness 127
epistemic specificity 160
epistemic plurality 56
epistemic specificity 160
epistemic violence 33, 104
epistemic virtues 43, 47, 79, 103, 132, 136–37, 149
epistemological borders 52, 243
epistemological diversity 117–18
epistemological geography 214
epistemological space 17
epistemological spread 174
epistemological state apparatus 221

epistemological wars 54
epistemologies 49, 53–54, 217
epistemology 43, 55, 58, **111–13**, 118, 133, 140, 190, 238, 244; dominant 50; trickle-down 203; Western 50, 53, 98
equality 233
Erasmus 188
Eraut, M. 52
Erguyan, M. M. 203
escalators 150–51
Escher, M. C. 150
essays 98, 117, 143, 175
ethical corruption 47
ethical evolution 47
ethical trickle-down 46
ethics 23, 42, 135, 149; *see also* virtue
ethnic minorities 39
Europe 17, 28, 38, 135, 206
Eryong, X. 28
'excellence' 122
excitation 131, 133, 135, 138, 140, 172
explicitness 130

Faber, G. 80
Facer, K. 3, 119, 207, 242, 244
Facione, P. 145
facts 54, 139, 214, 238, 242
fairness 33, 223–26, 233
faith 24
fast life 41; *see also* research
feasibility 23, 179
feminist knowledge 24, 48, 53–54, 228; *see also* ecological feminism
feminist literature 87–89
Ferraris, M. 20, 33, 132
Feyerabend, P. 53, 71, 122, 185
Fillipakou, O. 208
Finnegan, R. 203
Floridi, L. 188
forms of life 40
Foucault, M. 97, 117, 121–22, 146, 236
fourth industrial revolution (IR4) 151, 160
fragility 134
fragmentation 167
frameworks 51–52, 57
France 28, 166
Frankfurt School of Critical Theory 97
Fredua-Kwarteng, E. 229
free speech 91
freedom 86, 117, 164, 222; civic 89–90
Freire, P. 115
Fricker, M. 195, 227–29, 231
Fridland, E. 16
Frost, S. 167

Fulford, A. 2
Fuller, S. 56, 86–87

Gadamer, H-G. 51, 85
Gadotti, M. 115
Galea, S. 186
Gallant, T. B. 40
Garcia, É-J. 177, 179
Geerts, E. 50
Gellner, E. 40, 56–57, 66, 81–82, 232
'generative mechanisms' 21, 32
geology 111, 113, 117, 146–47, 160
geology of university 157–58, 161, 164, 179
geophilosophy 240
geopolitics 24, 90, 174
Germany 28, 71, 80, 86–87, 94
Gettier, E. 55
Giannnakakis, V. 78
Gibbons, M. 65, 228
Gibbs, P. 2, 48, 97, 126, 135, 160, 184, 191–92
Giroux, H. 78, 115
glaciers 4–5, 16, 57, 73, 132, 233, 239, 245
Glassner, A. 118
global citizenship *see* citizenship, global
global economy 44
Global North 22, 24, 53, 82, 104, 173, 215, 227–28, 231, 235
Global South 22, 53, 82, 104, 173, 195, 215, 219, 228, 230–32
globalisation 21, 33
Gluckler, J. 192
Goddard, J. 156
Gómez, C. 53, 229
Goodlad, S. 129, 138–40
goods 79; societal 208; *see also* moral; public
Goodyear, P. 162
Gorky, M. 79
Gornitzka, A. 87
Gottlieb, B. 189
Gouldner, A. 82–83, 195
Grabina, G. L. 228
Gratton, P. 20
Greco, J. 137
Green, A. 220
Greenwood, D. J. 201
Griffiths, F. 134
Grosfogel, R. 53, 127, 230
Guattari, F. 5, 7, 35, 103, 127–28, 142, 151, 156, 172, 179, 192, 201, 235, 239–44; *The Three Ecologies* 239
Gutman, A. 225
Guzmán-Valenzuela, C. 28, 53, 229

Habermas, J. 24, 57, 83, 87, 99, 126, 201, 203, 228–29, 236; *The Structural Transformation of the Public Sphere* 205
Habitus 128
Hager, P. 31
Hajrasouliha, A. 157
Hall, J. A. 232
Hamilton, C. 234–35
Hampshire, S. 96
Hanney, S. 220
Haraway, D. 53
Hardt, M. 220–21
Harman, G. 20, 72, 132
Hartwig, M. 24
Hassan, R. 188
Hauerwas, S. 24
Heap, S. 24
Healey, M. 114
Hegel, G. W. F. 167
Heidegger, M. 32, 67, 87, 92, 97–98, 112, 118, 128, 149, 166, 191
Henkel, M. 220
Herbrachter, S. 68, 189
Heuser, B. L. 40
Higgs, J. 111
Higgs, P. 2, 50
higher education 5–6, 20, 23, 36, 55, 74, 76–77, 81, 96, 101, 118, 131, 134, 167, 170, 223, 235, 240, 244; concept of 6, 18, **26–31**, 36, 86, 111, 122, 137, 140, 202, 225; ecosystem of 88; institutions of 121; mass 76, 113, 120, 245; systems of 162; *see also* philosophy of higher education
Higton, M. 24, 167
Hill, H. 204
Hinchcliffe, T. 120
history 144, 160
Hodgson, N. 116
Holmwood, J. 201
Hommel, U. 179
Honneth, A. 101
Horkheimer, M. 97
Hornsby, D. J. 207
Horton, R. 104
Hoyer, K. G. 243
Hroch, P. 243
hubris 10
Hutchins, R. 32, 125
human being 68, 127, 143, 242, 244
human rights 72, 181, 185
humanities 49, 52–53, **65–68**, 69, 79, 101, 104, 157, 171, 187, 203, 230, 235, 238

humanity 5, 49, 67, 126, 132, 234–35, 237, 241, 244
Hume, D. 32
hyperreality 189

Iceland 245
idea of the university *see* higher education; university
ideal speech situation 206
idealism 64
ideas 9, 32, 36, 187
ideational realm 35, 157, 220, 235
identity 171, 189; digital 194; student 27
ideologies 22–23, 24–25, 36, 48, 54, 58, 71, 170, 174, 217
ideology 73, 106, 116–17, 122, 125, 127, 142, 150, 175, 192, 238
ideology critique 143
Ignatieff, M. 94, 103
ignorance 102
imaginaries 7, 32, 39, 65, **148–49**, 161, 230
imagination 25, 34, 36, 124, 128, 148, 158, 164, 168, 184, 243; cultural 32
impairment 216
improvement 24
incommensurability 56
indeterminacy 31, 133, 150
India 28
indigenous communities 16, 22, 24, 53, 78, 99, 104, 147, 211
indigenous knowledge 48, 230
individuality 137, 168
injustice *see* justice
innovation 78
inquiry 101, 169–70
inspiration 114, 147
instability 127, 133, 135, 138, 140
instrumentalism 49, **98**, 123, 143, 196, 236, 245
integrity 40, 42, 194, 197
intelligence, artificial 160, 190
inter-connectivity *see* connectivity
interdisciplinarity 68, 126, 145; *see also* critical; transdisciplinarity
interests 49–50, 57–58, 143
internet 39, 68, 86, 90, 112, 118, 160, 207, 219; *see also* digital era
interpretation 51
Irigaray, L. 114, 173
Ivory tower 219

Jackson, N. 112, 128, 131, 197, 237
Jameson, J. 178
Jandric, P. 115–16, 118, 189–90

Japanese literature 124
Jaspers, K. 64, 166–67, 169; *The Idea of the University* 166, 168
Jay, M. 167
Jessop, B. 220
Johnson, R. E. 134
Johnston, B. 151
judgement 86, 113, 129, 140, 143, 149, 151, 180, 222
Jump, P. 157
justice 67, **223–33**; cognitive 16, 228–29, 231; ecological 39, 233, 239, 246; educational 225–26; epistemic 39, 48, 53, 58, 104, 195, **227–30**, 232; social 39–40, 45, 164, 229, 232–33

Kahn, R. 243
Kant, I. 49, 57, 76, 104, 195; *The Conflict of the Faculties* 76
Karlsohn, T. 2, 99
Karran, T. 85
Keenan, W. J. 244
Keet, A. 229
Kennedy, D. 175
Kennedy, M. D. 162
Kerr, C. 31–32
Kidd, I. J. 48
Kinsella, E. A. 52
Kierkegaard, S. 117
Khine, M. S. 53
Klein, J. T. 126, 243
Knorr-Cetina, K. 49
knowledge 17, **48–56**, 80, 112, 118, 127–28, 132, 135, 164, 167, 169, 189, 191, 235, 237–38, 242, 245; academic 49, 238; forms of 59; globalised 162; 'mode 2' 65, 228; performative 57; practical 132; professional 52; processual 57; propositional 48, 52; tacit 55, 132; Western 229, 236; *see also* epistemology; feminist; indigenous; instrumentalism; reason
knowledge ecology 58, 72, 194, 238
knowledge economy 21, 33, 38, 126, 174
'knowledge-in-action' 52
knowledge inquiry 168
knowledge police 52
knowledge-power 236
knowledge production 65
knowledge socialism 215
knowledges 24, 51, 235; *ecology of* 229, 237
Kogan, M. 220
Kramer, E. 2
Kreber, C. 82, 112

Kress, K. 189
Krzeski, J. 210
Kuhn, T. S. 194
Kuntz, A. M. 235
Kurzweil, R. 188

laboratories 64, 117, 144, 159, 171
labour market 128
Laclau, E. 16, 105
Lake, D. 126
Land, R. 134
Latin America 28, 98
Latour, B. 4, 53, 71, 127, 133, 207, 239, 245
law *see* legal studies
leadership 171, 176, **177–187**; concept of 178; ecological 187
learning 92, 109, 131–33, 135, 242, 244; digital 110; distance 31; double-loop 180; informal 131; lifelong 33, 111, 128; life-*wide* 128, 131; organisational 179; single-loop 180; *see also* capital, learning; space, learning; letting learn
learning analytics **180–81**, 189
learning environments 180
learning outcomes 122, 174
learning spaces 189
learning systems 203
Leask, B. 127
Leavis, F. R. 77, 82, 122, 124
lectures 110, 117
Lefebvre, A. 35
Lefebvre, H. 41, 159, 161
legal studies 110–11, 122, 160, 219
legitimacy 46–47, 56, 125, 205, 214
Leibowitz, B. 70
Lerhfreiheit 87, 92
Lerhnfreiheit 87, 92
Lesk, M. 189
Lessem, R. 231
letting learn 112
Levin, M. 201
Levinson, M. 67
Lévy, P. 215
Li, J. 28
liberal arts 225; *see also* humanities
liberal education 80–82, 135
liberty 223; *see also* freedom
library 111, 181, 188–90
life 4, 6, 15, 25, 44, 80, 114, 140, 169–70; academic 42, 172, 218, 227; *see also* forms of
life chances 213, 223, 231
life sciences 157
lifeworld 72, 151

light 112
List, C. 32
literacy 39, 66
Lithuania 194
Little, B. 220
Locke, J. 18
Loftus, S. 52
logic 98, 105
Longino, H. 53
Løvlie, L. 80
Luhmann, N. 186
Lyotard, J-F 30, 38, 159
Lysgaard, J. A. 112, 117

Maccarini, A. M. 72
Macfarlane, B. 38, 41, 43
MacIntyre, A. 43–44, 79, 126, 203
madness 197
Magee, B. 19, 168
Magpie tendency 193–94
Malpas, J. 191
management 176, 178–81; performance 174, 189; university 104, 122
management studies 116
managerialism 173
Manathunga, C. 229
Marcus, D. M. 55
Marcuse, H. 229
Marginson, S. 18–19, 156, 192, 207–09
Margolis, E. 120
Margolis, J. 51
Marion 178
markets 160, 206, 208
Martinez-Vargas, C. 195, 215
Marton, S. G. 220
Marxism 56
Maslen, G. 89
Masschelein, J. 122, 159, 204
mass higher education *see* higher education
materialism 31, 167
mathematics 65, 129, 160, 236
Mathews, D. 151, 178
Maxwell, N. 24, 44, 98, 127, 196
Meyer, J. H. F. 134
McArthur, J. 101, 226
McClaren, P. 78, 115–16, 118, 190
McCowan, T. 216
McDowell, J. 96
McGregor, S. L. T. 126
McPeck, J. E. 146
mechanisms, generative *see* generative mechanisms
medicine 48, 52, 72, 104, 110–11, 119, 122, 125, 128, 134–35, 144, 190, 219

Meillassoux, Q. 50, 148
Meneses, M. P. 230
Merleau-Ponty, M. 111
Metaphor 20, 150
Meusberger, P. 31, 53, 156, 161
Michels, C. 182
Mickey, S. 98, 234–35
Middle ages 6, 17, 26, 28, 39, 44, 57, 68, 86, 90–91, 155, 185, 188, 195
Middlehurst, R. 191
Mika, C. 97
Mill, J. S. 92, 140
Miller, S. 46
Mills, J. 110
mind 80–81, 150
Minogue, K. 103
mistrust 142
Moberly, Sir W. 3
modernity 53, 78, 235, 245
modern languages 113, 160
Moebius strip 34
Molesworth, M. 121
Moog, S. 53
morale 186
moral goods 41–43, 45–46, 208
Morgan, J. 24
Morton, A 137
Morton, T. 31, 164
Mosco, V. 189
motion 5–6, 31, 35–36, 37, 65, 123, 129, 132, 135, 137, 150–51, 164, 171–72, 178, 222
multiculturalism 76
multimodality 189
multiplicities 43, 172–73, 214–15
Murphy, M. 134
Murphy, P. 19, 64, 186, 196
music 160

nanotechnology 87–89, 117, 156
nationalism 117
nature 50–51, 53, 126, 148, 189, 209, 216, 235–37, 242, 245–46
Nazism 91
Neave, G. 86, 220
Negri, A. 220–21
Nelson, E. S. 236
neoliberalism 21, 33, 105, 235
networks 71, 128, 151
Newman, J. H. 15, 24, 77, 80, 122, 156; *The Idea of a University* 80
News, bad 3
Nial, T. 6
Niblett, R. 2, 7, 20
Nicolescu, B. 73

Nietzsche, F. 49, 97, 166, 171
Nikolaidis, A. C. 228
Nixon, J. 43, 46, 110–11, 155, 207–08, 219
Noddings, N. 53
no-platforming 90
Nørgård, R. 111, 117, 164, 195
Novikoff, A. J. 185
Nowotny, H. 65, 191–92, 203
nursing studies 52, 117
Nussbaum, M. 67, 81–82, 126, 195, 203, 206–07, 224
Nyawasha, T. S. 231
Nymbom, T. 29

Oakeshott, M. 17, 77, 79, 103
Objectivity 57
O'Malley, B. 65, 85
O'Neill, M. 232
O'Neill, O. 184
ontological disturbance 118
ontological realist 117
ontological stratification 31
ontology 20, 32, 34–35, **111–13**, 117–18, 127, 132–33, 136, 140, 149, 157, 190, 213–14, 220, 244
openness 80, 86–87, 90, 122, 144; *see also* pedagogical situation
Ortega y Gasset, J. 32, 131; *Mission of the University* 32
Ossa-Richardson, A. 158
Östling, J. 64, 76
otherness 67
outreach 242–43
Ovenden, R. 188
Owen, D. 236

Parfitt, D. 96
Passeron, J-C 81
Passmore, J. 110
Paul, R. 145
Pavese, C. 16
Pawlak, K. 83
peace 44, 197
pedagogical cultures 132
pedagogical openness 122, 125
pedagogical relationship 79, 132
pedagogical responsibility 124
pedagogical situation 143, 204, 213; closed 144; open 144, 146, 152
pedagogical spirit 169, 171
pedagogy 78–79, **114**, 175, 229; critical 115–16; eco 243; post-critical 116
pedagogy of 'vulnerability' 117
Pelletier, C. 112

performance indicators 186
performativity 38, 128, 159–60, 194
performing arts 48, 52, 99, 111, 113, 119, 128–29, 190
Persia 28
Peters, M. A. 2, 15, 19, 27, 30, 68, 77, 189–90, 195, 197, 215
Peters, R. S. 113
Pettit, P. 32
pharmaceutical companies 145, 196, 214
phenomenology 157–58, 174
Philips Griffiths, A. 109
philosophy 144, 170, 185; social 9, 16
philosophy of higher education 1–4, 7–9, 11, **15–25**, 27, 56, 63, 105
philosophy of science 21
physics 185, 225
Piaget, J. 129, 158
Pisa, tower of 34
place 113, **155–65**, 191–92
plagiarism 193, 196
planes 155, 179, 187, 213; *see also* three planes
Plato 141
Plumb, J. H. 49
Plumwood, V. 49, 104, 228, 235
pluralism 39, 78
poetry 22, 158
Pogge, T. 224
Polanyi, M. 55, 129
polytechnics (UK) 31
Popper, Sir K. 43, 110, 238
populism 220
positivism 51
possibilities 1, 4, 22, 35, 67, 125, 130, 145, 163–64, 178, 187, 190, 213, **215**
post-digital 156, 189–90
posthumanism 68, 127, 220
postmodernism 29, 142, 159
post-truth 46, 48, 56, 142
power 41, 71, 102, 121–22, 124, 168, 172, 175
powers 31–32, 80, 145, 147–48, 150, 157
practice 111, 130
practices of education 3, 17, 19, 26, 43, 110; *see also* educational processes
praxis 111, 115
principles, practical 3
Pritchard, D 43, 79, 137
professional life 24, 111, 118, 135, 149
professional studies 236
professors 45, 123, 143
provocation: self 148; *see also* teaching as
public engagement 203

public good, the 22, 72, 162, 201–03, 208–09
public goods 21, 41, 201–03, 208–10
public, idea of **201–11**
public intellectuals 143, 207; *see also* moral goods; space, public
public interest 210
public mission 201
public realm 202, 204–05, 208, 210, 242
publics 206–07
public sphere 152, 164, 202, 205–07, 210

qualities **135–38**, 178
quality assurance 122
quantum mechanics 124
quietness 41
Quijano, A. 230

racism 91, 185, 218
Rancière, J. 112
rankings 63, 157, 161, 163, 174, 180, 227
rationality 83, 97, 118; judgemental 118; *see also* reason
Rawls, J. 223–24
Readings, B. 3, 22, 75–76, 80–81, 83, 122, 174; *University in Ruins* 3, 22
real, the 9, 32, 35–36, 132–33, 136, 140, 157–58, 160, 187, 215, 238, 244
realism 25, 33; ecological 3
reality 99
reason 40, 45, 66, 81–82, **96–106**; critical 196; digital 190; embodied 98, 111; practical 98; Western 98, 105; *see also* instrumentalism
reasonableness 40
recognition 233
reconciliation 54
Redding, G. 87, 179
Rée, J. 117
Rees, Sir M. 197
Reeves, M. 3
reflexivity 55
Reisz, M. 88
relativism 57–58
religion 24, 235
research 5, 17, 26, **63–73**, 109, 120, 144, 156, 161, 172, 175, 202, 208–09, 227, 242–43, 245; concept of 24, 63–65, 70, 72; fast 100; pedagogical 70; relationship with teaching 114–15, 169
researchers 38, 103
resilience 149, 167
respect 45, 91
responsibilities of universities 19, 21, 35, 95, 123, 165, 211–12, 221, 245–46

responsibility 30, 110, 124, 131, 197, 207, 216, 218–19
reticence 103, 204, 210
Rhoten, D. 63
Rhinos 4, 16, 57, 73, 233, 239
Rhizome 5, 128, 194
Rhoades, G. 68
rhythm 41–42, 156, **159–60**, 172
Ricoeur, P. 142, 191
Rider, S. 56
right to think 101–02
rights *see* human
Ringer, F. K. 64, 77, 80, 94
Ripatti-Torniainen, L. 204
risk 113, 121, 146, 148, 180, 215
Robbins, Sir L. 75–76
Robins, K. 190
Robinson, S. 40, 219
Rockmore, T. 51
Rolfe, G. 66
Rorty, R. 50
Rosen, M. 142
Rothblatt, S. 29
Rouse, J. 71
Rowland, S 30, 70, 110
Royas-Castro, S. 59
Ruins, in 29; *see also* readings
Russell, B. 25
Russell, C. 86
Ruth, J. 85
Ruuska, T. 243
Ryan, A. 127
Ryle, G. 111, 156, 161

Sahin, A. 39
Salter, B. 220
Sandberg, J. 52, 111
Sandel, M. 118, 203, 226
Sartre, J. P. 149
Savin-Baden, M. 130, 189
Scandinavia 28, 77
Schatzki, T. R. 17, 43, 110
scholars 112
scholarship 30, 65–66, 69–70, 80, 103, 120, 161, 175, 198, 209, 242
Schön, D. 52, 180
Schopenhauer, A. 167
Schott, N. F. 35
science 52, 64, 66, 71, 73, 82, 99–100, 104, 144, 171, 197, 203, 236
scientism 50–51
Scott, D. 137
Scott, P. 3
Scott-Bauman, A. 142

Scruton, R. 74–75
Searle, J. 87, 89
Selingo, J. J. 191
semi-colon 188, 198
Sen, A. 224
service 215–17, 221
Sheldrake, P. 167
Shor, I. 115
Shore, C. 6, 29, 162, 201
Shpeizer, R. 149
Siegel, H. 96
Sigh 178
Simons, M. 122, 204
Singh, G. 115
Singh, S. 24
singularity, the 188
skills 16, 21, 23, 114, 124, 127–29, 145–46, 148–50, 217
Sloterdijk, P. 24
slow processes 160, 196–97
Small, H. 67
Snow, C. P. 49, 82
Snowden, M. 118
social sciences 50–51, 66, 72, 104, 203, 236
social theory 101, 116–17
social work 122
society 16, 40, 81
sociology 48, 82, 144
Solbrekke, T. D. 211
South Africa 85, 92, 194
South Korea 225
sovereignty 220
space 35, 42, 103, 110, 157, 183, 192; ethical 45; learning 33, 110; pedagogical 92; public 92, 204–06
'space of reasons' 99, 189
space of spaces 160
space-time complexes *see* time-space complexes
spaces 42, 83, **155–65**, 190–92; educational 124; public 205; unsettling 127
speed 41
spirits 25, 114, 139, **166–76**, 172–73, 179, 183, 235; *see also* critical spirit
spiritualism 167
spirituality 167, 169
Sporn, B. 74
sports science 190
squid 5
Standaert, N. 157
Standish, P. 80
State, the 15, 121, 125, 206, 220
statistics 236
Staley, D. 124, 243

steadfastness 103, 149, 206
Stein, S. 229, 231, 244–45
STEM 49, 65–66, 73, 187, 223, 226, 230–31
STEMM 221
Sterling, S. 243
Stévenin, B. 179
Stiegler, B. 102–03, 125, 166, **174–75**, 181, 186, 194, **196–97**, 218
Stolen, S. 87
Stoller, A. 2
Stones, R. 53
strangeness 138
strangers 47, 54
Stratford, R. 234, 243
structures 22, 116, 196
student 79, 84, 111, 114, 117–18, 123, 128, 138, 169, 171, 244; being a 3, 15, 79, 124, **131–141**
student experience 43, 109, 245
students 17, 33, 36, 40, 42, 45, 53, 78, 80–81, 112, 117–18, 120–21, 124–25, 160, 163, 172, 175, 181, 202, 217; international 89, 173
students' character 78–81
stupidity 102, 125, 175, 196
Sugrue, C. 211
suicide 138
supercomplexity 133–34, 138, 141, 180, 194, 217–18
surveillance 73, 84, 174, 189, 205, 220–21
sustainability 100, 126, 180, 237
systems: closed 31; open 31
Szadkowski, K. 210

Talloires network 219
Tapper, T. 220
Taylor, C. 39, 43, 149
Taylor, D. 31
teachers 79, 109, 111, 114–15, 118; as scholars 115
teaching **109–19**, 169, 171, 179, 242–44; as affirmation 113; as provocation 113, 118–19, 127, 138; *see also* learning; students
Techné 150
technology 236
Temple, P. 163, 164, 192
Terashima, N. 189
Tesar, M. 214
theology 24
theory-ladenness 51–52, 57
therapy 194
'*Third-space*' professionals 183, 218
thought 41, **96–106**, 128, 132, 139, 145, 159, 181, 192, 196; forethought 159

288 Index

thoughtlessness 102–03, 196
three planes of university 27, **34–36**, 46–47, 161, 179, 210, 220, 232, 235
Thrift, N. 192
time 35, 155–56, 162–63, 179, **192**
time-space complexes 191
tolerance 79–80
topology of university 157–58, 161, 164, 179
Toulmin, S. 96
tradition 105
transdisciplinarity 48, 54, 59, 126, 130, **159**, 235; ecological 73, 241
transgression of boundaries 16
Tribe, J. 129
troublesomeness 134–35
Trowler, P. R. 74, 82
trust 184
truth 17, 40, 44, 55, **56–58**, 59, 164, 217; truth to power 143, 149, 151
truthfulness 42, 45, 57, 219, 222
truth-telling 40
Tuana, M. 53
turbulence 4–5, 135
twenty-first century 19

Ullman-Margalit, E. 98
uncertainty 38, 133–35, 138–41; *authoritative uncertainty* 129, 138–40; committed uncertainty 141
understanding 182, 217; public 238
undermining, double 4
understanding 21, 42–43, 102, 128, 189–90
United Kingdom 49, 75, 126, 140; *see also* England
United Nations' Sustainability Development Goals 24, 38, 46, 162, 171, 212, 216, 219–20
universality 9, 15, 32, 35, 38–40, 66, **103–06**, 124, 136–37, 187, 194, 209, 221; ethic of 221
universals 35, 163–64
universe 25
universities 6, 17–19, 36, 38, 43, 48, 63, 77, 81, 97, 104, 214, 235; Berlin 64, 76; Buenos Aires 28; California 32; Cambridge 31, 69; Chicago 85, 125; European 38, 86; Johns Hopkins 157; 'free' 103; Freiburg 166; Leicester 68; Open (UK) 31; Oxford 31, 156, 161, 204, 223; Sydney 170; UNAM (Mexico city) 28; University College London 31; 'world-class' 63; *see also* constitution for; university as institution
university 5, 33, 35, 160, 162–63; being a 97, 168; borderless 191; concept of 6, 15, 18, 26, 29, 36, 162, 202, 207; death of 29; digital 188–90; debating society 44; eco 163; ecological 243–44; 'edgeless' 191; ethical 37; idea of **27–32**, 35, 85–86, 156–57, 166; networked 191; post-historical 81; public 201; sustainable 212; teaching 29; the 6, 17, 44, 46, 50, 57, 72, 77, 83, 105, 156, 163–64, 210, 235–36, 240, 244; virtual 190; 'without walls' 203; 'worldhood' 164; *see also* Middle Ages; three planes of
university as institution 17, 24, 35, 37, 57, 74, 90, 138, 157, 178
university as moral agent 40, 45
university as pedagogical form 159
university of culture 77, 80
University of disaster 197
university 'without condition' 91, 116
unpredictability 133–35, 139
unsettlement 118, 139
USA 28, 32, 115, 118, 126, 158, 194, 215
Utopias 118, 195, 244; Feasible 6

Valance, P. 156
validity claims 206
Valimaa, J. 74
value 44, 139, 207, 214, 238, 242; cultural 84
value anchoring 46
value background 40–41
value base 41, 216
value conflict 39, 44, 47
value depletion 100
value differences 40
value entrepreneur 43
value evolution 40
value frameworks 38–39
value freedom 37–38, 67, 100
value incorporation 40
value interests 39
value-ladenness 37–38, 54, 100, 122
value neutrality 43
values 24, 33, **37–47**, 54, 67, 91, 180, 186, 216; foundational 45–46; hierarchy of 45
value sets 41
value situation 37
value statements 38
value substrate 45
value structure 179
value turbulence 46
value umpire 43
Vanden Broeck, P. 192
Van Leeuwen, T. 189
Van Wyk, R. 50

Vattimo, G. 58
Verstehen 52
Viberg, O. 181
Vibrancy 5
vigilance 103
Virilio, P. 41, 69, **196–97**
virus 4, 71
vitality 32, 132, 168, 171–72, 194
virtue ethics 41, 43, 138
virtues 78, 103, 136; *see also* epistemic vitality 114, 170
voice 95, 170
Volkmer, I. 203
Vostal, F. 192
von Humboldt, W. 64, 76–77

Waghid, Y. 2, 97, 179, 216
Walker, M. 195, 215
Wallin, J. 123
Wals, E. J. 241, 243
Warren, K. 228, 239
Watson, C. 181
Watson, D. 219
webinars 117
Webster, F. 190
wellbeing 8
Western, S. 178–79
whistle-blowers 148–49
Whitchurch, C. 183
White, J. 17
Whitley, R. 184

will 111, 113, 139, 147, 167, 169, 184; *will to learn* 141
Williams, B. 57
Williams, G. 208
Williams, R. 195
Willinsky, J. 207
Wilson, A. 181
wisdom 164, 195–96, 210, 235
witchcraft 56
Wittgenstein, L. 40, 48, 232
Wittrock, B. 29
work 16, 128
world 50–51, 54, 84, 116, 126, 130, 132, 134, 138, 140, 170, 212, 214
Wrenn, C. 56, 57
Wright, A. 24
Wright, R. G. 85
Wright, S. 6, 29, 162, 201
writing 182
Wyatt, J. 76, 140

Ylijoki, O-H. 74
Yeats, W. B. 148
Young, M. 112
Young, M. D. 226
Young, R. 31
Young-Wilson, A. 193

Žižek, S. 9, 24, 33–34, 105, 151
Zweig, F. 112
Zuboff, S. 220

For Product Safety Concerns and Information please contact our EU
representative GPSR@taylorandfrancis.com
Taylor & Francis Verlag GmbH, Kaufingerstraße 24, 80331 München, Germany

www.ingramcontent.com/pod-product-compliance
Lightning Source LLC
Chambersburg PA
CBHW052014290426
44112CB00014B/2230